TRACK & FIELD ATHLETICS
ATHLETICS
THE RECORDS

Editor: Beatrice Frei
Design: David Roberts

© Peter Matthews and Guinness
Superlatives Ltd, 1986

Published in Great Britain by Guinness
Superlatives Ltd, 33 London Road, Enfield,
Middlesex

Typeset in Linotron Times and Helvetica
by Input Typesetting Ltd, London
Printed and bound in Great Britain by
Dotesios (Printers) Ltd., Bradford-on-Avon,
Wiltshire

Daley Thompson (ASP)

British Library Cataloguing in Publication Data

Matthews, Peter, *1945–*
    Track and field athletics : the records.
    1. Track-athletics—Records
    I. Title
    796.4'2'09   GV1060.67

ISBN 0−85112−463−1

TRACK & FIELD ATHLETICS

THE RECORDS

PETER MATTHEWS

GUINNESS BOOKS

Contents

In order to save space, throughout this book I have used the standard event abbreviations, well known in track and field athletics. I have also generally abbreviated countries, particularly in tables.

Events

		Miscellaneous	
CC	cross-country		
Dec	decathlon	b.	date of birth
DT	discus	d.	died
h	hurdles	dnf	did not finish
Hep	heptathlon	ft	feet
HJ	high jump	i	indoor
HT	hammer	in	inches
JT	javelin	kg	kilograms
LJ	long jump	km	kilometres
Mar	marathon	m	metres
Pen	pentathlon	min	minutes
PV	pole vault	m/s	metres per second
R	relay	M	miles
SP	shot	sec	seconds
St	steeplechase	sf	semi-final
TJ	triple jump	w	wind assisted
W	walk	y	yards
Wt	weight		

Countries

Alg	Algeria	Jap	Japan
Arg	Argentina	Ken	Kenya
Aus	Australia	Kor	Korea (South)
Aut	Austria	Lux	Luxembourg
Bah	Bahamas	Mal	Malaysia
Bel	Belgium	Mex	Mexico
Ber	Bermuda	Mor	Morocco
Bra	Brazil	NI	Northern Ireland
Bul	Bulgaria	Nig	Nigeria
Bur	Burma	NKo	North Korea
Can	Canada	Nor	Norway
Chl	Chile	NZ	New Zealand
Chn	China	Pak	Pakistan
	(People's Republic)	Pan	Panama
Col	Colombia	Per	Peru
Cs	Czechoslovakia	Phi	Philippines
Cub	Cuba	Pol	Poland
Den	Denmark	Por	Portugal
Egy	Egypt	PR	Puerto Rico
Eng	England	Rom	Romania
Eth	Ethiopia	SAf	South Africa
Fin	Finland	Sco	Scotland
Fra	France	Sen	Senegal
GDR	German	Spa	Spain
	Democratic Republic	Sud	Sudan
Ger	Germany (pre-1945)	Swe	Sweden
GFR	German	Swi	Switzerland
	Federal Republic	Tai	Taiwan
Gha	Ghana	Tan	Tanzania
Gre	Greece	Tha	Thailand
Gua	Guatemala	Tri	Trinidad & Tobago
Hol	Holland/	Tun	Tunisia
	Netherlands	Uga	Uganda
Hun	Hungary	UK	United Kingdom
Ice	Iceland		(GB & NI)
Ind	India	USA	United States
Ire	Ireland	USSR	Soviet Union
Isr	Israel	Ven	Venezuela
Ita	Italy	Wal	Wales
IvC	Ivory Coast	Yug	Yugoslavia
Jam	Jamaica		

Governing Bodies

AAA	Amateur Athletic Association (UK)
AAU	Amateur Athletic Union (USA)
IAAF	International Amateur Athletic Federation
IAC	International Athletes Club (UK)
NCAA	National Collegiate Athletic Association (USA)
TAC	The Athletics Congress (USA)
WAAA	Women's Amateur Athletic Association (UK)

Throughout this book measurements are given in the metric system. For those readers who are more familiar with imperial units this basic conversion table should assist in understanding. It specifically covers those distances achieved by top-class athletes in the field events.

metres	ft in	metres	ft in
1.70	5 7	17.50	57 5
1.75	5 8¾	18.00	59 0¾
1.80	5 10¾	18.50	60 8½
1.85	6 0¾	19.00	62 4
1.90	6 2¾	19.50	63 11¾
1.95	6 4¾	20.00	65 7½
2.00	6 6¾	20.50	67 3¼
2.05	6 8¾	21.00	68 10¾
2.10	6 10¾	21.50	70 6½
2.15	7 0½	22.00	72 2¼
2.20	7 2½	22.50	73 10
2.25	7 4½	23.00	75 5½
2.30	7 6½	50.00	164 0
2.35	7 8½	52.00	170 7
2.40	7 10½	54.00	177 2
4.60	15 1	56.00	183 9
4.80	15 9	58.00	190 3
5.00	16 4¾	60.00	196 10
5.20	17 0¾	62.00	203 5
5.40	17 8½	64.00	210 0
5.60	18 4½	66.00	216 6
5.80	19 0¼	68.00	223 1
6.00	19 8¼	70.00	229 8
6.25	20 6¼	72.00	236 3
6.50	21 4	74.00	242 9
6.75	22 1¾	76.00	249 4
7.00	22 11¾	78.00	255 11
7.25	23 9½	80.00	262 5
7.50	24 7¼	82.00	269 0
7.75	25 5¼	84.00	275 7
8.00	26 3	86.00	282 2
8.25	27 0¾	88.00	288 8
8.50	27 10¾	90.00	295 3
8.75	28 8½	92.00	301 10
9.00	29 6½	94.00	308 5
15.00	49 2½	96.00	314 11
15.50	50 10¼	98.00	321 6
16.00	52 6	100.00	328 1
16.50	54 1¾	102.00	334 8
17.00	55 9¼	104.00	341 2

yards	metres	miles	yards	metres
50	45.72	1		1609.34
54.68	50	1	427.23	2000
60	54.86	1	1520.84	3000
65.62	60	2		3218.69
100	91.44	3		4828.03
109.36	100	3	188.07	5000
218.72	200	6		9656.06
220	201.17	6	376.13	10 000
437.44	400	10		16 093.44
440	402.34	12	752.27	20 000
874.89	800	18	1128.40	30 000
880	804.67	26	385	42194.99
1000	914.40			(marathon)
1093.61	1000	31	120.66	50 000

MULTI-EVENTS

Note that in tables of Championship events decathlon and heptathlon performances have been rescored using the current (1984) tables, except where otherwise indicated.

Introduction

An athletics meeting is a multi-coloured, multi-faceted spectacle. Sitting waiting for the first event, the fan experiences that keen edge of anticipation, ready for men and women to test their skills in competition, striving to better their opponents or their own personal targets of time and distance. Often, for safety reasons, the hammer throwers are first into the arena and if they may fret against competing before the crowds arrive, at least one has the opportunity to savour fully their event, without the distraction of races around them, to witness that 16-pound ball soaring high to thump to earth far away. Then the pole vault, that blend of gymnastic ability, speed, strength and the courage needed to descend to the ground from a height of nearly 20 feet. Then the first track race, perhaps the 400 metres hurdles, another test of the maintenance of technique against speed and endurance.

There are so many dimensions to track and field athletics, variations on a theme of running, jumping and throwing. The main elements have evolved into a series of standardized events, and these are contested by men and women all over the world. The governing body of world athletics, the International Amateur Athletic Federation (IAAF) has 174 nations affiliated to it, more than any other international organization, sporting or otherwise. Formed from a meeting held in 1912, it aims to 'establish friendly and loyal co-operation between all members for the benefit of amateur athletics throughout the world'. Such universality gives extra interest to followers of the sport. Different nations or groups of people have developed particular strengths and abilities into traditions such as the Finns at javelin throwing, the East Africans at long distance running and the Caribbean islanders at sprinting. Technical expertise and application has brought great success to Soviet hammer throwers, Mexican walkers and French pole vaulters. The importance given to sport as a way of life and the resultant provision of facilities and support for athletes has brought the GDR the greatest success per capita of any nation. For all there is the fascination of trying to improve, of striving, and enjoying the competition.

In this book I have surveyed the history of the sport and summarized the deeds of the athletes who have made the greatest impact in major events or who have broken through barriers of time and distance. The contents are divided into the following main sections: (a) event by event survey, (b) milestones in the history of the sport, (c) features, (d) major championships, (e) national surveys.

In the first section world records are shown for each event at ten-yearly intervals throughout this century up to the present day, accompanied by details of barrier-breaking achievements—the first four-minute mile, seven-foot high jump, 100-metre javelin throw and so on. These lists are followed by notes on athletes who have set most records and who have achieved the most notable championships success.

Features on notable athletes are included in the middle section, followed by summaries of the major championships and games—world, international and continental. This leads into the final section, wherein national record-setting achievements are listed for the most important athletics countries.

Track and field athletics is a booming sport. Wise management by international and national governing bodies should ensure that it retains and enhances its prestige and attraction for participants and spectators all round the world.

Peter Matthews

January 1986

100 Metres

The lists of world record holders and Olympic medallists at the sprints are dominated by athletes from the USA.

Since 1976, for sprinting events up to 400m, records are recognized only if timed on fully automatic electrical devices. In the tables that follow the best known automatic timings (in hundredths) are shown as well as the hand timed world records prior to that date. Many of the best sprint times were, for one reason or another, never put forward for ratification.

Valeriy Borzov, by far the greatest ever Soviet sprinter, led the USSR to relay medals, but achieved even greater success individually. (All-Sport)

WORLD RECORD AT TEN-YEARLY INTERVALS

1905	10.8	Luther Cary (USA) 4 Jul 1891 and many others
1915	10.5	Richard Rau (Ger) Braunschweig 13 Aug 1911
1925	10.2	Charles Paddock (USA) Pasadena, Cal. 18 Jun 1921 (at 110y)
1935	10.2	Charles Paddock, Ralph Metcalfe (USA) Chicago 11 Jun 1932 (unofficial); official record 10.3 by many runners
	10.38	Eddie Tolan (USA) and Ralph Metcalfe (USA) Los Angeles 1 Aug 1932
1945	10.2	also by Jesse Owens (USA) Chicago 20 Jun 1936, Hal Davis (USA) 6 Jun 1941 (official)
1955	10.1	Lloyd La Beach (Pan) Guayaquil 7 Oct 1950
	10.33*	Barney Ewell (USA) Evanston 9 Jul 1948 (10.2 hand timing)
1965	10.0	Armin Hary (GFR) Zürich 21 Jun 1960 (10.25 auto), and others
	10.06	Bob Hayes (USA) Tokyo 15 Oct 1964
1975	9.8	Steve Williams (USA) Eugene 20 Jun 1975 (but 10.19 automatic!)
	9.95	Jim Hines (USA) Mexico City 14 Oct 1968
1985	9.93	Calvin Smith (USA) Colorado Springs 3 Jul 1983

*sound-activated (=c.10.35–10.36)

The best time at low altitude: 9.96 by Mel Lattany (USA) Athens, Georgia 5 May 1984. Colorado Springs is at 2195m and Mexico City 2240m altitude. The best ever time is 9.87 by Bill Snoddy (USA) aided by a very strong wind of 11.2m/s at Dallas on 1 Apr 1978.

THE BARRIER BREAKERS—the first to better

11 sec Luther Cary (USA). His time was recorded as 10¾ sec at Paris on 4 Jul 1891.
10 sec Bob Hayes (USA) ran the 100m in 9.9 at Walnut, Cal. on 27 Apr 1963 but aided by wind assistance of 5m/s. He ran the first automatically timed sub-10 time with 9.91 in the Olympic semi-final at Tokyo on 15 Oct 1964, but again the wind, at 5.3m/s, was well over the permitted limit. The first 'legal' 9.9 on hand timing was run by Jim Hines (USA) in the AAU semi-final at Sacramento on 20 Jun 1968 (the automatic timing showed a record 10.03). The first sub-10-sec 100m with automatic timing was 9.95 by Jim Hines to win the 1968 Olympic title in Mexico City, and the first at sea-level was 9.97 by Carl Lewis (USA) at Modesto, Cal. on 14 May 1983.

MOST OFFICIAL IAAF WORLD RECORDS

4 Steve Williams (USA), all at 9.9, in 1974, 1975 (twice) and 1976. He had an auto-timed best of 10.07 at Zürich in 1978.

THE BEST CHAMPIONSHIPS RECORDS

Valeriy Borzov (USSR) won the Olympic title at both 100m and 200m in 1972. He added an Olympic silver medal at the sprint relay in 1972 and two bronze medals, at 100m and relay, in 1976. He won three European 100m titles, 1969, 1971 and 1974, and the 200m in 1971, the 100m/200m/4×100mR treble at the 1968 European Juniors, and 13 USSR titles, seven at 100m, six at 200m. Indoors he won seven European titles at 50m/60m. His best times were 10.07 and 20.00, both at the Olympic Games in Munich in 1972. His record assures his place amongst the world's greatest runners of all time. He was the complete sprinter, strong in all aspects of the event; a fine starter, good pick-up, a smooth and relaxed style, and above all had a supreme temperament.
b. 20 Oct 1949 Sambor, Ukraine. Married to the great gymnast Lyudmila Turishcheva.

Don Quarrie (l) and Allan Wells (r). Between them they won 18 Olympic and Commonwealth medals, and both had long careers, sprinting at top level well into their thirties. (All-Sport)

Carl Lewis (USA). No man has retained an Olympic 100m title, but Lewis became the first double world champion at 100m as he preceded his Olympic victory in 1984 with the World title in 1983. On both occasions he also won gold medals at LJ and sprint relay and added the 200m in 1984. His international career had started with a Pan-American bronze medal at LJ in 1979. See feature for list of titles won and records set.
b. 1 Jul 1961 Birmingham, Alabama.

Allan Wells (UK) won Olympic gold at 100m and silver at 200m in 1980. At the Commonwealth Games he won gold medals at 100m in 1982 and 200m in 1978 and 1982, and silver at 100m in 1978. He was fourth at both 100m and 200m in the 1983 World Championships. At 100m/200m his Cup Final record was: World 1981—1/2; European 1979—3/1, 1981—1/2, 1983—2/1. He is the oldest ever Olympic 100m champion, and emerged as a world-class sprinter in 1978 at an age by which many of the great American sprinters of the past had retired. UK record holder at 10.11 and 20.21 in 1980.
b. 3 May 1952 Edinburgh.

100 Yards

This was the classic sprint distance for athletes, particularly from the USA and the British Commonwealth. Like other imperial distances, however, it was removed from the world record list in 1976.

'Even time' of 10.0 seconds was for long a target for sprinters. The first 10.0 to be recorded was by John Watkins (UK) on 14 Mar 1860, and the first sub-10-second time in a major race was 9.8 by John Owen (USA) in the AAU championships on Anastolan Island, Washington DC on 11 Oct 1890, although by then a number of other men had claimed such a time in lesser races. One has to regard timekeeping in the 19th century with care, and there were many claims for extraordinary sprint marks.

WORLD RECORD AT TEN-YEARLY INTERVALS

1905	9.6	Arthur Duffey (USA) New York 31 May 1902
1915	9.6	Arthur Duffey; Daniel Kelly (USA) Spokane 23 Jun 1906, Howard Drew (USA) Berkeley, Cal. 28 Mar 1914, and other claims
1925	9.5	Jackson Scholz (USA) Greensboro 9 May 1925 (unofficial)
1935	9.4	George Simpson (USA) Chicago 8 Jun 1929, and others
1945	9.4	as above
1955	9.3	Mel Patton (USA) Fresno 15 May 1948, Hector Hogan (Aus) Sydney 13 Mar 1954, Jim Golliday (USA) Evanston 14 May 1955
1965	9.1	Bob Hayes (USA) St Louis 21 Jun 1963 and three occasions in 1964
1975	9.0	Ivory Crockett (USA) Knoxville 11 May 1974
	9.0	Houston McTear (USA) Winter Park, Fl. 9 May 1975

Best ever on automatic timing: 9.21 Charlie Greene (USA) Provo, Utah 16 Jun 1967. Reggie Jones (USA) ran a wind assisted 9.18 at Austin on 7 Jun 1974.

MOST OFFICIAL IAAF WORLD RECORDS

6 Charles Paddock (USA) all at 9.6, four in 1921 and one each in 1924 and 1926. The last was actually 9.5, but records at the time were recognized in fifths of a second, so the time was rounded up.

Mel Patton won 1948 Olympic gold at 200m and relay, but was only fifth at the 100m. He won all five NCAA titles that he contested. (University of Southern California)

200 Metres

Until 1958 records at 200m or 220y (201.17m) could be set on any type of course. In that year the IAAF brought in separate lists of records around a full turn; until then most records at these distances were set on straightaway tracks, prevalent in the USA. The lack of a turn enabled times to be 0.3–0.4 sec faster.

Times run over the longer distance of 220y are equivalent to a 200m run in 0.1 sec less.

WORLD RECORD FOR 220y (STRAIGHT TRACK) AT TEN-YEARLY INTERVALS

1905	21.2	Bernie Wefers (USA) New York 30 May 1896
1915	20.8	Albert Robinson (USA) State College, Pa. 2 May 1913
1925	20.8	also by Charles Paddock (USA) Berkeley, Cal. 26 Mar 1921
1935	20.3	Jesse Owens (USA) Ann Arbor, Michigan 25 May 1935
1945	20.3	Jesse Owens as above
1955	20.2	Mel Patton (USA) Los Angeles 7 May 1949
1965	20.0	Dave Sime (USA) Sanger, Cal. 9 Jun 1956
	20.0	Frank Budd (USA) Villanova 12 May 1962
1975	19.5	Tommie Smith (USA) San Jose, Cal. 7 May 1966

WORLD RECORD FOR 200m AROUND A TURN AT TEN-YEARLY INTERVALS

1905	21.4	(for 220y) James Maybury (USA) Chicago 5 Jun 1897
1915	21.2	(for 220y) William Applegarth (UK) London 4 Jul 1914
1925	21.2	(for 220y) also by H. T. Evans (USA) Ann Arbor 17 May 1924
	21.2	Charles Paddock (USA) Paris 6 May 1923
1935	20.6	(for 220y) James Carlton (Aus) Sydney 18 Jun 1932 (unratified)
1945	20.6	as above
1955	20.6	(for 220y) Andy Stanfield (USA) Philadelphia 26 May 1951
	20.81	Andy Stanfield (USA) Helsinki 23 Jul 1952
1965	20.2	(for 220y) Henry Carr (USA) Tempe 4 Apr 1964
	20.36	Henry Carr Tokyo 17 Oct 1964
1975	19.83	Tommie Smith (USA) Mexico City 16 Oct 1968
1985	19.72	Pietro Mennea (Ita) Mexico City 12 Sep 1979

The best time at low altitude: 19.75 Carl Lewis (USA) 19 Jun 1983 Indianapolis

THE BARRIER BREAKERS—the first to better

20 sec Ralph Metcalfe (USA) ran 220y on a straight course in 19.8 at Toronto on 3 Sep 1932, but this was wind assisted. Tommie Smith with his 19.5 in 1966 was the first to break 20 sec under record conditions. The first man to break 20 sec around a turn and with automatic timing was John Carlos (USA) with 19.92 (19.7 hand timed) at Echo Summit, South Lake Tahoe on 12 Sep 1968, but this was disallowed as a record as Carlos wore the outlawed 'brush' spikes manufactured by Puma. Tommie Smith then ran 19.83 to win the 1968 Olympic final. The first man to better 20 sec around a turn at low altitude was Pietro Mennea with 19.92 at Barletta on 17 Aug 1980.

Harry Edward (r) wins the first of three successive AAA 100 yards titles in 1920 from defending champion William Hill (l). Next to Edward is Harold Abrahams, who went on to take the 1924 Olympic 100m title. (All-Sport)

MOST WORLD RECORDS

5 Ray Norton (USA). He first ran two unratified marks of 20.6 for 200m in 1959 and then three ratified marks in 1960: 20.6 (220y), 20.6 and 20.5. Norton also ran world records for 100y (9.3 twice) and 100m (10.1) and won the 100/200 double at the 1959 Pan-Americans and in the 1959 and 1960 AAU Championships, but, favourite for the Olympic titles, was sixth in both events in 1960.

THE BEST CHAMPIONSHIPS RECORDS

Pietro Mennea was the 1980 Olympic 200m champion, and competed in three more Olympic finals at this distance; 3rd 1972, 4th 1976, 7th 1984. Also at 200m he was European champion in 1974 and 1978, World Student Games champion in 1973, 1975 and 1979 and third in the 1983 World Championships. He won ten Italian titles at 200m as well as three at 100m, at which distance he won European gold in 1978 and silver in 1974. He was also European Indoor champion at 400m in 1978 and won an Olympic bronze medal at 4×400m relay in 1980.
In his long career from 1969 to 1984 he ran 164 200m races in under 21 sec. headed by his 1979 world record.
b. 28 Jun 1952 Barletta.

Andy Stanfield (USA) won the Olympic 200m title in 1952 and the silver medal in 1956. He was AAU champion in 1949 (also at 100y), 1952 and 1953. He set two world records at 20.6, the first at 220y in 1951 and the second at 200m in 1952.
b. 29 Dec 1927 Washington, DC; d. 15 Jun 1985.

Don Quarrie (Jam) won Olympic gold at 200m and silver at 100m in 1976 and completed his set with bronze at 200m in 1980. He added a sprint relay silver medal in 1984.
He first came to worldwide attention with sprint trebles, 100m, 200m and relay, at the 1970 Commonwealth and 1971 Pan-American Games. He had three more Commonwealth successes, at 100m and 200m in 1974 and at 100m in 1978, and set four world records: at 100m, a 9.9 at Modesto, California in 1976, and at 200m, three times of 19.8. The first, also auto-timed at 19.86, was when he won the Pan-American title at the high altitude of Cali, Columbia in 1971. Then he twice ran 19.8 at Eugene, Oregon in June 1975. The latter (20.12 auto) was when he won the third of his AAU 200m titles (he also won two at 100m), and in both those 1975 races he beat Steve Williams, whom he considered his greatest rival.
b. 25 Feb 1951 Kingston.

400 Metres

From 1976 the IAAF no longer recognized records at 440y, but in the 19th century and in the early part of this century most of the best times were recorded at this slightly longer distance (402.34m). A generally accepted conversion factor is 0.3 sec.

Wearing black power socks Lee Evans anchors the US team to victory at the 1968 Olympic Games. The world records set in the relay and by Evans in the individual event still stand. (Ed Lacey/ASP)

WORLD RECORD AT TEN-YEARLY INTERVALS
(y = 440y times)

1905	47.8y	Maxie Long (USA) New York 29 Sep 1900 Long ran 47.0y on a straight track at Guttenburg, NJ on 4 Oct 1900
1915	47.8y	Maxie Long
1925	47.4y	Ted Meredith (USA) Cambridge, Mass. 27 May 1916
	47.4y	Binga Desmond (USA) Evanston 3 Jun 1916 (unratified)
1935	46.2	(46.28 auto-timing) Bill Carr (USA) Los Angeles 5 Aug 1932
1945	46.0	Rudolf Harbig (Ger) Frankfurt/Main 12 Aug 1939
	46.0	Grover Klemmer (USA) Philadelphia 29 June 1941
1955	45.4	Lou Jones (USA) Mexico City 18 Mar 1955
1965	44.9y	Adolph Plummer (USA) Tempe 25 Mar 1963 (and other 44.9 times for 400m)
1975	43.86	Lee Evans (USA) Mexico City 18 Oct 1968
1985	43.86	Lee Evans (as above)

Low-altitude bests: 44.26 Alberto Juantorena (Cuba) Montreal 29 Jul 1976, and hand timed: 44.1 Wayne Collett (USA) Eugene 9 Jul 1972.

THE BARRIER BREAKERS—the first to better

50 sec The professional Harold Reed 48.5y London 25 Jun 1849
45 sec Otis Davis (USA) and Carl Kaufmann (GFR) 44.9 Rome 6 Sep 1960. On automatic timing, however, they recorded 45.07 and 45.08. Herb McKenley (Jam) ran 440y in 45.0 on a boardwalk straightaway with a following breeze at Long Branch, NJ on 23 Aug 1947.

MOST WORLD RECORDS

4 Herb McKenley (Jam) set 440y bests at 46.2 in 1946 and 1947 and at 46.0 in 1948. He improved the 400m record to 45.9 (46.00 auto) at Milwaukee on 2 Jul 1948. He won Olympic silver medals at 400m in 1948 and 1952, and in the latter Games ran a 44.6 relay leg, the fastest ever at the time, on Jamaica's gold medal winning run. He also won the AAU 440y in 1945, 1947 and 1948 and the NCAA 440y for Illinois in 1946 and 1947.

THE BEST CHAMPIONSHIPS RECORDS

Few athletes have had multiple success at this event, which is perhaps the greatest test of pure athleticism, demanding sustained speed.

Lee Evans won the Pan-American title in 1967 and the Olympic title in 1968, when he set the still-standing world record at 43.86. He had earlier improved the world best to 44.06, but this was disallowed as he wore illegal 'brush' spikes. He won the 1968 NCAA title, representing San Jose State and won five AAU titles, 1966–9 and 1972. He also ran a world best for 600m of 1:14.3 in 1968. He turned professional in 1972, after placing only fourth in the US Olympic Trials.
b. 25 Feb 1947 Madera, Cal.

Bert Cameron (Jam) was Commonwealth champion in 1982 and World champion in 1983. Favourite for the 1984 Olympics he had to scratch through injury from the final, but not before showing his ability. In his semi-final he pulled up with a hamstring cramp at 130m, but having lost some ten metres to his rivals set off again and blazed through to fourth place in a time of 45.10 and a place in the final. He won three NCAA titles, 1980–1 and 1983, for the University of Texas at El Paso and was also Central American champion in 1982.
b. 16 Nov 1959 Spanish Town. Best time: 44.58 in 1981.

When free of injuries Bert Cameron has been a match for any 400m runner in the 1980s. (ASP)

800 Metres

Just 18 world records have been ratified at 800m by the IAAF from Ted Meredith's 1:51.9 to Seb Coe's 1:41.73. This is fewer than for any other standard men's event.

From 1976 the IAAF no longer recognized records at 880y, but as with the 440y/400m most of the best times in the early years were recorded at this longer distance (804.68m). The conversion factor is 0.6 to 0.7 sec.

WORLD RECORD AT TEN-YEARLY INTERVALS
(y = 880y times)

1905	1:53.4y	Charles Kilpatrick (USA) New York 21 Sep 1895
1915	1:51.9	Ted Meredith (USA) Stockholm 8 Jul 1912
1925	1:52.2y	Ted Meredith (USA) Philadephia 13 May 1916
1935	1:49.8y	Ben Eastman (USA) Princeton 16 Jun 1934
	1:49.70	Tom Hampson (UK) Los Angeles 2 Aug 1932
1945	1:46.6	Rudolf Harbig (Ger) Milan 15 Jul 1939
1955	1:45.7	Roger Moens (Bel) Oslo 3 Aug 1955
1965	1:44.3	Peter Snell (NZ) Christchurch 3 Feb 1962 (in 1:45.1 880y)
1975	1:44.1y	Rick Wohlhuter (USA) Eugene 8 Jun 1974
	1:43.7	Marcello Fiasconaro (Ita) Milan 27 Jun 1973
1985	1:41.73	Sebastian Coe (UK) Florence 10 Jun 1981

THE BARRIER BREAKERS—the first to better

2 min Harold Reed (UK) 1:58y as a professional in 1854
1:55 Francis Cross (UK) 1:54.4y Oxford 9 Mar 1888
1:50 Thomas Hampson (UK) 1:49.70 Los Angeles 2 Aug 1932
1:45 Peter Snell (NZ) 1:44.3 Christchurch 3 Feb 1962.
Snell had run an 880y relay leg in 1:44.8 for the British Commonwealth v USA in London on 14 Sep 1960.

Ray Roseman (1) and John Boulter (r) admire the style of Peter Snell in the all-black of New Zealand. (Mark Shearman)

MOST WORLD RECORDS

7   Lawrence 'Lon' Myers (USA) in pre-IAAF days, all at 880y, from 1:56.2 in 1880 to 1:55.4 in 1885. The very thin Myers set world bests at all events from 100y to 880y and was undefeated at 440y and 800y. His record 15 AAU titles included three at 800y. He won AAA titles at 440y in 1881 and 1885, and at 880y in 1885, and went on to further success as a professional.

THE BEST CHAMPIONSHIPS RECORDS

Mal Whitfield (USA) was Olympic 800m champion in 1948 and 1952, won the Pan-American title in 1951 and five AAU titles. He won further Olympic medals: gold (1948) and silver (1952) at 4×400m relay and silver (1948) at 400m. From June 1948 to the end of the 1954 season he lost only three of 69 races at 800m or 880y. He set two world records at 880y, 1:49.2 in 1950 and 1:48.6 in 1953.
b. 11 Oct 1924 Bay City, Texas.
Peter Snell was a surprise winner of the Olympic 800m in 1960 and retained his title in 1964, when he also won gold at 1500m. He won the Commonwealth 880y/1 mile double in 1962 and set world records at 800m and 1 mile (twice). A very strong runner, at his best he seemed invincible.
b. 17 Dec 1938 Opunake.
Douglas Lowe (UK) was the first to retain his Olympic 800m title, as he won in 1924 and 1928. He was also AAA champion at both 440y and 880y in 1927 and 1928. His best 800m was 1:51.2 in 1928.
b. 7 Aug 1902 Manchester; d. 30 Mar 1981.

1000 Metres

WORLD RECORD AT TEN-YEARLY INTERVALS

1905	2:35.8	Henri Deloge (Fra) Paris 14 Jul 1902
1915	2:32.3	Georg Mickler (Ger) Hannover 22 Jun 1913
1925	2:28.5	Sven Lundgren (Swe) Stockholm 27 Sep 1922
1935	2:23.6	Jules Ladoumègue (Fra) Paris 19 Oct 1930
1945	2:21.5	Rudolf Harbig (Ger) Dresden 24 May 1941
1955	2:19.0	Auden Boysen (Nor) Göteborg 30 Aug 1955
	2:19.0	Istvan Rozsavolgyi (Hun) Tata 21 Sep 1955
1965	2:16.2	Jürgen May (GDR) Erfurt 20 Jul 1965
1975	2:13.9	Rick Wohlhuter (USA) Oslo 30 Jul 1974
1985	2:12.18	Sebastian Coe (UK) Oslo 11 Jul 1981

THE BARRIER BREAKERS—the first to better

2:30:   Anatole Bolin (Swe) 2:29.1 Stockholm 22 Sep 1918
2:15:   Rick Wohlhuter (USA) 2:13.9 Oslo 30 Jul 1974

MOST WORLD RECORDS

3   Auden Boysen (Nor) one each year from 1953 to 1955: 2:20.4, 2:19.5, 2:19.0. At 800 m Boysen

won the Olympic bronze medal in 1956 and at the Europeans was second in 1958 and third in 1954. He ran his best 800m, 1:45.9, when runner-up to Roger Moens in the latter's world record in 1955.

1500 Metres

The four-lap race over 1 mile or 1500 metres is for many people their favourite athletics event. It is long enough for strategies to develop and short enough to sustain the maintenance of interest. Its practitioners must balance speed and endurance with a keen sense of harnessing their abilities to particular races and tactics appropriate to them. The popularity of the event has been reflected by the intensity of competition over the years. There is such a wealth of talent at the top that even such outstanding athletes as Steve Cram and Seb Coe have Said Aouita, Steve Scott, Sydney Maree, José Luis Gonzales, José Abascal and others in keen contention for major honours. The few men that have established supremacy even for a few years therefore stand out all the more. Herb Elliott stands at the head of such a list for he was undefeated in 44 races at 1500m or 1 mile from 1954 to 1960. He smashed the world record for both distances, with 3:36.0 and 3:35.6 for 1500m and 3:54.5 for 1 mile, and won the 1958 Commonwealth and 1960 Olympic titles in commanding fashion.

Seb Coe sets his fourth world record 2:13.40 for 1000m, in Oslo. Willi Wülbeck is second. (Keystone Press)

World record at ten-yearly intervals

1905	4:05.4	James Lightbody (USA) St Louis 3 Sep 1904
1915	3:55 est	Norman Taber (USA) Cambridge, Mass. 16 Jul 1915
1925	3:52.6	Paavo Nurmi (Fin) Helsinki 19 Jun 1924
1935	3:48.8	Bill Bonthron (USA) Milwaukee 30 June 1934
1945	3:43.0	Gunder Hägg (Swe) Göteborg 7 Jul 1944
1955	3:40.8	Sandor Iharos (Hun) Helsinki 28 Jul 1955, Laszlo Tabori (Hun) and Gunnar Nielsen (Den) Oslo 6 Sep 1955
1965	3:35.6	Herb Elliott (Aus) Rome 6 Sep 1960
1975	3:32.16	Filbert Bayi (Tan) Christchurch 2 Feb 1974
1985	3:29.46	Said Aouita (Mor) W.Berlin 23 Aug 1985

The barrier breakers—the first to better

4 min Harold Wilson (UK) 3:59.8 London 30 May 1908
3:50 Jules Ladoumègue (Fra) 3:49.2 Paris 5 Oct 1930
3:40 Stanislav Jungwirth (Cs) 3:38.1 Stara Boleslav 12 Jul 1957
3:30 Steve Cram (UK) 3:29.67 Nice 16 Jul 1985

Most world records

3 Gunder Hägg (Swe): 3:47.6 in 1941, 3:45.8 in 1942 and 3:43.0 in 1944. Hägg ran 16 world records at all events in the war years 1941–5. With his great rival Arne Andersson, he was suspended from amateur competition in 1945, so did not contest the international meetings after the war. He was Swedish champion at 1500m in 1941 and at 5000m in 1944 and 1945.

3 Abel Kiviat (USA). His 3:55.8 at Cambridge, Mass. in 1912 was the first official IAAF record for the event. Earlier that year he had improved the world best to 3:59.2 and 3:56.8. Kiviat was second to Arnold Jackson (UK) in the Olympic 1500m in 1912 and was AAU 1 mile champion three times.

3 Steve Ovett (UK). His first record, 3:32.09 at Oslo on 15 Jul 1980, was actually slower than Seb Coe's 1979 mark of 3:32.03, but under the rules then in force both marks were rounded up to 3:32.1. Ovett improved the record to 3:31.36 in 1980 and 3:30.77 in 1983. He also set two 1 mile world records.

The best championships records

Sebastian Coe (UK) won the Olympic 1500m title in 1980 and 1984 as well as the silver medal at 800m in both years. He ran a world record 3:32.03 at Zürich on 15 Aug 1979, and his best ever is 3:31.95 in 1981.
b. 29 Sep 1956 Chiswick, London.
Kip Keino (Kenya) won the Olympic 1500m in 1968, and was second in 1972. He won Commonwealth titles at 1 mile in 1966 and 1500m in 1970, to which he added titles at 3000m steeplechase in 1972 and 3 miles in 1966. He was second in the 1968 Olympic 5000m and third in the 1970 Commonwealth 5000m. He was also African champion at both 1500m and 5000m in 1965. He ran world records at 3000m and 5000m in 1965,

The incomparable Herb Elliott won Olympic gold in 1960 in Rome, and went through his international career undefeated at 1500m or 1 mile. (All-Sport)

and his bests at 1500m and 1 mile were 3:34.91 in 1968 and 3:53.1 in 1967 respectively.
b. 17 Jan 1940 Kipsamo.
Steve Cram (UK) uniquely won Commonwealth (1982), European (1982), and World (1983) 1500m titles, before returning from injury to earn the 1984 Olympic silver medal. He also won three AAA 1500m titles, 1981–3, and the European Cup Final 1500m races of 1983 and 1985. He had run on the UK team that had set a world record at 4×800m relay in 1982, but first entered the world record lists as an individual in 1985, when he ran three world records in 19 days at 1500m, 1 mile and 2000 metres.
b. 14 Oct 1960 Gateshead.

1 Mile

The classic four-lap event has remained a standard event, even though other imperial distance events have disappeared. Of course, major championships are contested at the slightly shorter distance of 1500m, but the 1 mile (1609.36m) retains its attractions to middle distance runners and the general public.

World record at ten-yearly intervals

1905	4:12¾	Walter George (UK) London 23 Aug 1886 (professional)

1915	4:12.6	Norman Taber (USA) Cambridge, Mass. 16 Jul 1915
1925	4:10.4	Paavo Nurmi (Fin) Stockholm 23 Aug 1923
1935	4:06.7	Glenn Cunningham (USA) Princeton 16 Jun 1934
1945	4:01.3	Gunder Hägg (Swe) Malmo 17 Jul 1945
1955	3:57.9	John Landy (Aus) Turku 21 Jun 1954
1965	3:53.6	Michel Jazy (Fra) Rennes 9 Jun 1965
1975	3:49.4	John Walker (NZ) Göteborg 12 Aug 1975
1985	3:46.32	Steve Cram (UK) Oslo 27 Jul 1985

BARRIER BREAKERS—the first to better

4:20 William Lang and William Richards (UK) 4:17¼ Manchester 19 Aug 1865 (professionals)
4:10 Jules Ladoumègue (Fra) 4:09.2 Paris 4 Oct 1931
4:00 Roger Bannister (UK) 3:59.4 Oxford 6 May 1954
3:50 John Walker (NZ) 3:49.4 Göteborg 12 Aug 1975

MOST WORLD RECORDS

3 Gunder Hägg (Swe): 4:06.1 and 4:04.6 in 1942, and 4:01.3 in 1945. In the first and third of these records Arne Andersson was runner-up in 4:06.4 and 4:02.2 respectively.
3 Arne Andersson (Swe): 4:06.2 in 1942, 4:02.6 in 1943 and 4:01.6 in 1944. Andersson was beaten 15–8 by Hägg at all distances, including 11–5 at 1500m and 1 mile. At 1500m he set a world record at 3:44.9 in 1943 and had a best time of 3:44.0 behind Hägg in 1944. He was Swedish 1500m champion in 1943 and 1944.
3 Sebastian Coe (UK) improved his personal best by a remarkable 8.72 sec when he set his first mile world record at 3:48.95 at Oslo in the 1979 Golden Mile. He improved to 3:48.53 at Zürich and to 3:47.33 at Brussels in 1981.

Defending champion Murray Halberg leads in 1964 Olympic 5000m heat with silver medallist Harald Norpoth behind him. (ASP)

2000 Metres

Although this distance is most infrequently run, there have nonetheless been some highly meritorious performances at it, not least John Walker's world record of 4:51.4 (4:51.52 auto) in 1976, when he ran successive 400m laps in 60.1, 58.5, 57.7, 57.9 and 57.2. This lasted for nine years, before Steve Cram trimmed the time.

WORLD RECORD AT TEN-YEARLY INTERVALS

1905	5:37.0*	Alfred Shrubb (UK) Glasgow 11 Jun 1904
1915	5:37.0*	Alfred Shrubb (UK) as above
1925	5:25.9	Edvin Wide (Swe) Stockholm 11 Jun 1925
1935	5:21.8	Jules Ladoumègue (Fra) Paris 2 Jul 1931
1945	5:11.8	Gunder Hägg (Swe) Ostersund 23 Aug 1942
1955	5:02.2	Istvan Rozsavolgyi (Hun) Budapest 2 Oct 1955
1965	5:01.2	Josef Odlozil (Cs) Stara Boleslav 8 Sep 1955
1975	4:56.2	Michel Jazy (Fra) Saint Maur 12 Oct 1966
1985	4:51.39	Steve Cram (UK) Budapest 4 Aug 1985

*time at 1¼ mile (2011.68m)

THE BARRIER BREAKERS—the first to better

5:30 Paavo Nurmi (Fin) 5:26.4 Tampere 4 Sep 1922
5:00 Harald Norpoth (GFR) 4:57.8 Hagen 10 Sep 1966

MOST WORLD RECORDS

2 Paavo Nurmi (Fin): 5:26.4 in 1922 and 5:24.6 in 1922
2 Gunder Hägg (Swe): 5:16.4 and 5:11.8 in 1942
2 Michel Jazy (Fra): 5:01.6 in 1962 and 4:56.2 in 1966

3000 Metres

Although not on the Olympic programme, this event, as a stepping stone between 1500m and 5000m, is a popular one at major invitational meetings.

WORLD RECORD AT TEN-YEARLY INTERVALS

1905	9:02.4	Louis de Flemrac (Fra) Paris 19 Jun 1904
1915	8:36.9	Hannes Kolehmainen (Fin) Stockholm 12 Jul 1912
1925	8:27.5	Edvin Wide (Swe) Halmstad 7 Jun 1925
1935	8:18.3	Henry Nielsen (Den) Stockholm 24 Jul 1934
1945	8:01.2	Gunder Hägg (Swe) Stockholm 28 Aug 1942
1955	7:55.6	Sandor·Iharos (Hun) Budapest 14 May 1955
1965	7:39.5	Kipchoge Keino (Ken) Halsingborg 27 Aug 1965
1975	7:35.2	Brendan Foster (UK) Gateshead 3 Aug 1974
1985	7:32.1	Henry Rono (Ken) Oslo 27 Jun 1978

THE BARRIER BREAKERS—the first to better

8:30 Paavo Nurmi (Fin) 8:28.6 Turku 27 Aug 1922
8:00 Gaston Reiff (Bel) 7:58.7 Gävle, Swe 12 Aug 1949

Most world records:

4   Paavo Nurmi (Fin), three official: 8:28.6 in 1922, 8:25.4 and 8:20.4 in 1926 and an unrecognised 8:27.8 in 1923.

2 Miles

Dropped from IAAF record schedules in 1976, when the 'final' world record was 8:13.68 by Brendan Foster (UK) in London on 27 Aug 1973. The best ever mark: 8:13.2 (indoors) Emiel Puttemans (Bel) West Berlin 18 Feb 1973.

THE BARRIER BREAKERS—the first to better

9:30   Jack White (UK) 9:20 Manchester 1861
         (professional)
9:00   Paavo Nurmi (Fin) 8:59.5 Helsinki 24 Jul 1931
8:30   Jim Beatty (USA) 8:29.8 Los Angeles 8 Jun 1962

MOST WORLD RECORDS

3   Gunder Hägg (Swe): 8:47.8 in 1942, 8:46.4 and 8:42.8
     in 1944.

Henry Rono set world records at 3000m, 5000m, 10,000m and steeplechase in 1978. (ASP)

(above) Vladimir Kuts was the top distance runner of the mid-1950s. A decade later Ron Clarke, here leading Lajos Mecser in the 1967 AAA 3 miles, smashed his times. (Ed Lacey/Spor⌐ & General).

3 Miles

Dropped from the IAAF record schedules in 1976, when the 'final' record was 12:47.8 by Emiel Puttemans (Bel) at Brussels on 20 Sep 1972.

THE BARRIER BREAKERS--the first to better

15 min Jack White (UK) 14:36 Hackney, London 11 May 1863 (professional)
14 min Lauri Lehtinen (Fin) 13:50.6 Helsinki 19 Jun 1932 (In 14:16.9 5000m)
13 min Ron Clarke (Aus) 12:52.4 London 10 Jul 1965 (12:52.26 auto)

MOST WORLD RECORDS

4   Vladimir Kuts (USSR), an unratified 13:31.4 in 1953 and three marks in 1954, headed by 13:26.4 at Prague on 23 October, en route to 13:51.2 for 5000m.
4   Ron Clarke (Aus): 13:07.6 in 1964, 13:00.4 and his epic 12:52.4 at the AAA Championships in 1965, and 12:50.4 at Stockholm on 5 July 1966 en route to 13:16.6 for 5000m.

5000 Metres

WORLD RECORD AT TEN-YEARLY INTERVALS

1905	15:20.0	Charles Bennett (UK) Paris 22 Jul 1900
1915	14:36.6	Hannes Kolehmainen (Fin) Stockholm 10 Jul 1912
1925	14:28.2	Paavo Nurmi (Fin) Helsinki 19 Jun 1924
1935	14:16.9	Lauri Lehtinen (Fin) Helsinki 19 Jun 1932
1945	13:58.1	Gunder Hägg (Swe) Göteborg 20 Sep 1942
1955	13:40.6	Sandor Iharos (Hun) Budapest 23 Oct 1955
1965	13:24.2	Kipchoge Keino (Ken) Auckland 30 Nov 1965
1975	13:13.0	Emiel Puttemans (Bel) Brussels 20 Sep 1972
1985	13:00.40	Said Aouita (Mor) Oslo 27 Jul 1985

Kip Keino was the greatest miler never to set world records at 1500m or 1 mile, but he did at 3000m and 5000m. (ASP)

THE BARRIER BREAKERS—the first to better

15 min Hannes Kolehmainen (Fin) 14:36.6 Stockholm 10 Jul 1912
14 min Gunder Hägg (Swe) 13:58.1 Göteborg 20 Sep 1942

MOST WORLD RECORDS

4   Vladimir Kuts (USSR) succeeded Emil Zatopek as record holder at this distance when he won the 1954 European title in 13:56.6. He lost the record to other athletes, but regained it three times: 13:51.2 in 1954, 13:46.8 in 1955 and 13:35.0 at Rome on 13 Oct 1957.
4   Ron Clarke (Aus) broke Kuts's record with 13:34.4 in 1965, improved it twice that year, 13:33.6 and 13:25.7, and, after Keino had taken that record, ran 13:16.6 at Stockholm on 5 Jul 1966.

THE BEST CHAMPIONSHIPS RECORDS

Lasse Viren (Fin) won the Olympic double of 5000m and 10 000m in both 1972 and 1976. This great runner showed above all the ability to peak when it really mattered, with devastating sustained pace over the later stages of a race. After his Olympic triumphs his form in lesser events was often indifferent; in European Championships he was seventh and third at 5000m and seventeenth and seventh at 10 000m in 1971 and 1974 respectively. He was also fifth in the Olympic marathon in 1976 and at 10 000m in 1980. His tenacity and quick thinking was shown when he fell in his first Olympic final, at 10 000m in 1972, yet got up to win in a world record of 27:38.35. His best 5000m was a world-record 13:16.4 in 1972.
b. 22 Jul 1949 Myrskyla.
Murray Halberg (NZ) overcame the handicap of a withered left arm to be Olympic 5000m champion in 1960 and win the Commonwealth 3 miles in 1958 and 1962. His international career had started with fifth at 1 mile in the 1954 Commonwealth Games. He set world records at 2 miles (8:30.0) and 3 miles (13:10.0) in 1961 and had a 5000m best of 13:35.2 in 1961.
b. 7 Jul 1933 Eketahuna.
Vladimir Kuts (USSR) won the 1954 European and 1956 Olympic 5000m titles. In 1956 he also set a world 10 000m record of 28:30.4 in Moscow and went on to complete the Olympic distance double. He was Soviet champion five times at 5000m and four times at 10 000m.
b. 7 Feb 1927 Aleksino, Ukraine; d. 16 Aug 1975.
Paavo Nurmi (Fin) won three Olympic medals at 5000m: gold in 1924 and silver in 1920 and 1924 and two golds at 10,000m (1920 and 1928). See the Olympic section for full details of his nine Olympic gold medals at all events. He dominated the world of distance running in the 1920s, revolutionising the sport with his hard training methods. Two of his many world records were at 5000m: 14:35.3 in 1922 and then his 14:28.2 which

was run just an hour after his 3:52.6 world record at 1500m. Between 1920 and 1933 he won 20 Finnish titles at distances from 800m to 10 000m and cross-country. His statue stands outside the Olympic stadium in Helsinki, where he carried the Olympic flame at the opening ceremony in 1952.

b. 13 Jun 1897 Turku; d. 2 Oct 1973.

For Emil Zatopek see 10 000 metres.

6 Miles

Dropped from IAAF record schedules in 1976, when the 'final' world record was 26:47.0 by Ron Clarke (Aus) at Oslo on 14 Jul 1965 en route to 27:39.4 for 10 000m.

THE BARRIER BREAKERS—the first to better

30 min UK professionals Jack White, 29:50.0 and William Lang, 29:50.2 at Hackney, London on 11 May 1863.

MOST WORLD RECORDS

2 by Viljo Heino (Fin): 28:38.6 in 1944 and 28:30.8 in 1949; and by Emil Zatopek (Cs): 28:08.4 in 1953 and 27:59.2 in 1954.

10 000 Metres

WORLD RECORD AT TEN-YEARLY INTERVALS

1905	31:02.4	Alfred Shrubb (UK) Glasgow 5 Nov 1904
1915	30:58.8	Jean Bouin (Fra) Colombes, Paris 16 Nov 1911
1925	30:06.1	Paavo Nurmi (Fin) Kuopio 31 Aug 1924
1935	30:06.1	Paavo Nurmi as above
1945	29:35.4	Viljo Heino (Fin) Helsinki 25 Aug 1944
1955	28:54.2	Emil Zatopek (Cs) Brussels 1 Jun 1954
1965	27:39.4	Ron Clarke (Aus) Oslo 14 Jul 1965
1975	27:30.80	David Bedford (UK) London 13 Jul 1973
1985	27:13.81	Fernando Mamede (Por) Stockholm 2 Jul 1984

THE BARRIER BREAKERS—the first to better

30 min Taisto Mäki (Fin) 29:52.6 Helsinki 17 Sep 1939
27:30 Henry Rono (Ken) 27:22.47 Vienna 11 Jun 1978

MOST WORLD RECORDS

5 Emil Zatopek (Cs) from 29:28.2 in 1949 to 28:54.2 in 1954, the latter just one day after he had run a world record 13:57.2 for 5000m. At that time he held world records at all nine recognized distances from 5000m to 30 000m.

THE BEST CHAMPIONSHIPS RECORDS

Emil Zatopek (Cs) was double Olympic (1948 and 1952) and European (1950 and 1954) champion at 10 000m. In his first Olympic year he added a

Multiple Olympic champions: (above) Lasse Viren acknowledges the tributes for his first gold medal, as Emiel Puttemans is second, in the 1972 Olympic 10 000 metres. (below) Emil Zatopek leads Gordon Pirie in the 1955 London v Prague match at the White City. (ASP, H. W. Neale)

silver at 5000m and in 1952 completed his unique triple with wins also at 5000m and the marathon in his first attempt at the distance. He won his first 38 races at 10 000m from 1948 to 1954, and in his career at all distances won 261 of 334 races. At his peak supremacy, the three years 1949–51, he won all 69 races at various distances. He was national champion eight times at 5000m and twice at 10 000m.
b. 19 Sep 1922 Koprivnice. His wife Dana, 1952 Olympic javelin champion, was born on the same day.
Alberto Cova (Ita) completed a major championships treble with the 1984 Olympic title, having earlier won the 1982 European and 1983 World titles. In all these races he displayed a devastating finishing kick off a much faster second half. After a third and a second in 1983, he scored a double win at 5000m and 10 000m in the 1985 European Cup Final. His best time to date is 27:37.59 in 1983.
b. 1 Dec 1958 Inverigo, Como.
Ilmari Salminen (Fin) was Olympic champion in 1936 and European champion in 1934 and 1938.

He broke Nurmi's 13-year-old world record with 30:05.5 in 1937 and won four Finnish titles at 10 000m as well as one at 5000m.
b. 21 Sep 1902 Elimäki; d. 6 Jan 1986.

For Lasse Viren and Paavo Nurmi see 5000m.

Long distances

The IAAF now recognizes just four events longer than 10 000m: 20km, 25km, 30km and 1 hour. Records at 10 and 15 miles were recognized up to 1976 and in the early days many more distances were included on the record lists.
The most world records at these distances is ten in four races by Emil Zatopek, two each at 20km, 25km, 1 hour and 15 miles and one each at 30km and 10 miles. He twice set three records in a race at Stara Boleslav: 10 miles, 20km and 1 hour on 29 Sep 1951 and 15 miles, 25km and 30km on 26 Oct 1952.

WORLD RECORDS and BESTS—LONG DISTANCE TRACK EVENTS

	hr:min:sec			
15km	42:54.8	Jos Hermens (Hol)	Papendal	14 Sep 1975
10 miles	45:57.6	Jos Hermens (Hol)	Papendal	14 Sep 1975
20km	57:24.2	Jos Hermens (Hol)	Papendal	1 May 1976
15 miles	1:11:43.1	Bill Rodgers (USA)	Saratoga, Cal.	21 Feb 1979
25km	1:13:55.8	Toshihiko Seko (Jap)	Christchurch	22 Mar 1981
30km	1:29:18.8	Toshihiko Seko (Jap)	Christchurch	22 Mar 1981
20 miles	1:39:14.4	Jack Foster (NZ)	Hamilton	15 Aug 1971
30 miles	2:42:00	Jeff Norman (UK)	Timperley	7 Jun 1980
50km	2:48:06	Jeff Norman (UK)	Timperley	7 Jun 1980
40 miles	3:48:35	Don Ritchie (UK)	Hendon, London	16 Oct 1982
50 miles	4:51:49	Don Ritchie (UK)	Hendon, London	12 Mar 1983
100km	6:10:20	Don Ritchie (UK)	Crystal Palace	28 Oct 1978
100 miles	11:30:51	Don Ritchie (UK)	Crystal Palace	15 Oct 1977
200km	15:11:10	Yiannis Kouros (Gre)	Montauban, Fra	15–16 Mar 1985
200 miles	27:48:35	Yiannis Kouros (Gre)	Montauban, Fra	15–16 Mar 1985
500km	60:23:00	Yiannis Kouros (Gre)	Colac, Aus.	26–30 Nov 1984
500 miles	105:42:09	Yiannis Kouros (Gre)	Colac, Aus.	26–30 Nov 1984
1000km	136:17:00	Yiannis Kouros (Gre)	Colac, Aus.	26–30 Nov 1984
	kilometres			
1h	20.944	Jos Hermens (Hol)	Papendal	1 May 1976
2h	37.994	Jim Alder (UK)	Walton-on-Thames	17 Oct 1964
24hr	283.600	Yiannis Kouros (Gre)	Montauban, Fra	15–16 Mar 1985
48hr	452.270	Yiannis Kouros (Gre)	Montauban, Fra	15–17 Mar 1985
6 days	1023.2	Yiannis Kouros (Gre)	Colac, Aus.	26 Nov–1 Dec 1984

LONG DISTANCE ROAD BESTS

Where superior to track bests and run on properly measured road courses.

	hr:min:sec			
15km	42:27.6	Mike Musyoki (Ken)	Portland	26 Jun 1983
10 miles	45:13	Ian Stewart (UK)	Stoke-on-Trent	8 May 1977
half marathon	1:00:55	Mark Curp (USA)	Philadelphia	15 Sep 1985
30km	1:29:04	Bill Rodgers (USA)	Albany, NY	28 Mar 1976
20 miles	1:36:28	Ron Hill (UK)	Huyton	25 May 1968
40 miles	3:46:31	Barney Klecker (USA)	Chicago	5 Oct 1980
50 miles	4:50:21	Bruce Fordyce (SAf)	London-Brighton	25 Sep 1983
1000 miles	12 days 12:36:20	Siegfried Bauer (NZ)	Melbourne-Colac	15–28 Nov 1983
	kilometres			
24 hours	286.463	Yiannis Kouros (Gre)	New York	28–29 Sep 1985

It should be noted that road times must be assessed with care as course conditions can vary considerably.

10 miles
50 min—Walter George (UK) was reputed to have run a time trial in 49:29 as a professional in 1886. The first recognized sub-50 time was run by Viljo Heino (Fin), 49:41.6 at Turku on 30 Sep 1945.

20 kilometres
1 hour—Emil Zatopek (Cs) 59:51.6 Stara Boleslav 29 Sep 1951

1 hour
12 miles—Viljo Heino (Fin) 19 339m (12M 29y) Turku 30 Sep 1945; 20km—Emil Zatopek (Cs) 20 052m Stara Boleslav 29 Sep 1951

30 kilometres
1 hr 30 min—Toshihiko Seko (Jap) Christchurch, NZ 22 Mar 1981

Carlos Lopes, at the age of 37 the oldest Olympic marathon victor. (Mark Shearman)

Marathon

The marathon is run over a distance of 26 miles 385 yards (42.195km). This distance was that used for the race at the 1908 Olympic Games, run from Windsor to the White City stadium, and which became standard from 1924.

The marathon introduced to the 1896 Olympic Games was held that year at 40km and was so named to commemorate the legendary run of Pheidippides (or Philippides) from the battlefield of Marathon to Athens, a distance of about 40km, in 490 BC. He was supposed to have conveyed the news of the victory of the Greeks over the Persians and then collapsed and died. Better substantiated is his feat of running from Athens to Sparta, some 219km (136 miles). The 1896 Olympic marathon was preceded by trial races that year.

The first marathon held outside Greece was run from Paris to Conflans, France on 19 Jul 1896. The first Boston marathon, the world's longest lasting major marathon, was held on 19 Apr 1897 at 39km (24 miles 1232 yards) and the first national marathon championship was that of Greece on 10 Mar 1896, followed by Norway in 1897.

WORLD BEST AT TEN-YEARLY INTERVALS

1915	2:36:06.6	Alexis Ahlgren (Swe) Windsor to Stamford Bridge 31 May 1913
1925	2:29:01.8	Al Michelsen (USA) Port Chester 12 Oct 1925
1935	2:26:42	Sohn Kee Chung (Kor)* Tokyo 3 Nov 1935
1945	2:26:42	as above
1955	2:17:39.4	Jim Peters (UK) Windsor to Stamford Bridge 26 Jun 1954
1965	2:12:00	Morio Shigematsu (Jap) Windsor to Stamford Bridge 12 Jun 1965
1975	2:08:33.6	Derek Clayton (Aus) Antwerp 30 May 1969
1985	2:07:11.6	Carlos Lopes (Por) Rotterdam 20 Apr 1985

*Known as Kitei Son in Japan, which at the time incorporated Korea.

THE BARRIER BREAKERS—the first to better

3hr	Johnny Hayes (USA) 2:55:18.4 Windsor to White City 24 Jul 1908
2:50	James Clark (USA) 2:46:52.6 New York 12 Feb 1909
2:40	Harry Green (UK) 2:38:16.2 Stamford Bridge 12 May 1913 (on a track)
2:30	Al Michelsen (USA) 2:29:01.8 Port Chester 12 Oct 1925
2:20	Jim Peters (UK) 2:18:40.2 Windsor to Chiswick 13 Jun 1953
2:10	Derek Clayton (Aus) 2:09:36.4 Fukuoka 3 Dec 1967

It should be noted that times for the marathon, as for all road races, should be regarded with care, due to the fact that the conditions of terrain can vary considerably from one course to another. A number of major courses have subsequently been found to be short, such as that of Boston in the 1950s and New York in the early 1980s. On the latter Alberto Salazar (USA) set what was regarded as a world best of 2:08:12.7 in 1981. In 1984 the course was remeasured and found to be 170y (150m) short, equivalent to about 30 seconds at marathon running pace.

THE MOST WORLD BESTS

4   Jim Peters (UK) ran a world's best each year from 1952 to 1954 on the Polytechnic marathon course from Windsor to Chiswick: 2:20:42.2, 2:18:40.2 and 2:17:39.4 respectively. He also ran a record 2:18:34.8 at Turku in 1953. He failed to finish in his two major international championships races, at the 1952 Olympics and at the 1954 Empire Games at Vancouver, when his collapse due to dehydration, yards from the finish, and some 20 minutes ahead of the next man, caught the horrified imagination of millions.

THE BEST CHAMPIONSHIPS RECORDS

Abebe Bikila (Eth) surprised the world when he won the 1960 Olympic title as a complete outsider. That was his third marathon and his first outside his hometown of Addis Ababa. In 1964 he became the first man ever to retain an Olympic

A very special quality is needed to retain an Olympic marathon title. Waldemar Cierpinski had that quality. Mark Shearman

marathon title when he won in Tokyo in the world best 2:12:11.2. He had had an operation for appendicitis only six weeks earlier! In his career he won 12 of his 15 marathons, his last being when a recurrence of an injury caused him to drop out of the 1968 Olympic marathon.
b. 7 Aug 1932 Mout. He suffered severe injuries, including a broken neck, in a car accident in 1969. Paralysed, he died on 25 Oct 1973.
Waldemar Cierpinski (GDR) emulated Bikila in winning two Olympic marathons, 1976 and 1980. A man for the big occasion, he also placed third at the 1983 World Championships. He did less well in the Europeans: fourth in 1978 and sixth in 1982, but he won the European Cup race in 1983 and was second in 1981. His best time was 2:09:55 in his first Olympic win.
b. 3 Aug 1950 Neugattersleben.
Frank Shorter (USA) won the 1972 Olympic title in his sixth marathon, four of which he had won, including the 1971 Pan-American. After another six wins in eight marathons, he was second at the 1976 Olympics. A talented track runner, he won the US 3 miles title in 1970 and five titles at 6 miles or 10 000m. At 10 000m he was also Pan-American champion in 1971 and third in 1979.
b. 31 Oct 1947 Munich.

A hoaxer led him into the stadium, but Frank Shorter won the gold medal at Munich in 1972. (Mark Shearman)

3000 Metres Steeplechase

World records for the steeplechase were first recognized and rules standardized by the IAAF in 1954, although the steeplechase had been an Olympic event at various distances since 1900, and at 3000m since 1920. The race comprises 28 hurdles and seven water jumps, all the obstacles 3ft (91.4cm) high. The water jump is 12ft (3.66m) long and the water is 2ft 4in (70cm) deep immediately in front of the barrier, sloping up to ground level.

WORLD RECORD AT TEN-YEARLY INTERVALS

1945	8:59.6	Erik Elmsäter (Swe) Stockholm 4 Aug 1944
1955	8:40.2	Jerzy Chromik (Pol) Budapest 11 Sep 1955
1965	8:26.4	Gaston Roelants (Bel) Brussels 7 Aug 1965
1975	8:09.70	Anders Gärderud (Swe) Stockholm 1 Jul 1975
1985	8:05.4	Henry Rono (Ken) Seattle 13 May 1978

THE BARRIER BREAKERS—the first to better

9 min Erik Elmsäter (Swe) 8:59.6 Stockholm 4 Aug 1944
8:30 Gaston Roelants (Bel) 8:29.6 Louvain 7 Sep 1963

MOST WORLD RECORDS

4 Anders Gärderud from 8:20.7 in 1972 to 8:08.02 to win the 1976 Olympic title. The latter was his first major title, since he won the 1964 European Junior 1500m steeplechase. Despite immense talent, and fast flat times as well as steeplechase records, he had gone out in the heats of the Olympics in 1968 and 1972 and the Europeans in 1966. In European finals he was only tenth in 1971 but was second in 1974 before finally triumphing in perfect style in 1976.

THE BEST CHAMPIONSHIPS RECORDS

Volmari Iso-Hollo (Fin) won the Olympic titles of 1932 and 1936. On the former occasion he won easily, but a judging error meant that the runners ran an extra lap; on the latter he ran a world best 9:03.8. He also won Olympic medals at 10 000m: silver in 1932, bronze in 1936.
b. 1 May 1907 Ylöjärvi; d. 23 Jun 1969.
Gaston Roelants was the world's best steeplechaser in the early 1960s, winning Olympic (1964) and European (1962) titles as well as setting two world records. After a bronze at the 1966 Europeans, he turned with great success to longer distances, setting world records at 20km and 1 hour in 1972 and winning a silver (1969) and a bronze (1974) in European marathon races. He also won four International Cross-Country titles. His career continued into his 40s: he won five world titles in his first year in veteran's ranks.

b. 5 Feb 1937 Opvelp.
Bronislaw Malinowski (Pol), a determined front runner, was European champion in 1974 and 1978 and Olympic champion in 1980, after fourth in 1972 and second in 1976, when he ran his best time of 8:09.11. His major championships career had started with the European Junior title in 1970.
b. 4 Jun 1951 Nowe; killed in a car crash on 26 Sep 1981.
Patriz Ilg (GFR) has yet to set a national record, and his best time is only 8:15.06 in 1983. However, he has proved a master at winning big races—1982 European (after a silver in 1978), 1983 World and 1985 European Cup Final. He was also European indoor champion at the flat 3000m in 1982.
b. 5 Dec 1957 Aalen-Oberalfingen.

110 Metres Hurdles

Hurdling was first practised over sheep hurdles about 3ft 6in (1.067m) in height. It was at this height that the sprint hurdles for men over ten flights was standardized. The modern hurdle was invented by Harry Hillman (USA), who won three Olympic gold medals in 1904. He introduced a hurdle with an L-type base with weighted feet on the approach side, presenting a toppling moment of 3.6kg. The imperial distance of 120y is 109.73m. so, to convert 120y times to 110m times, one just adds 0.03 sec. Thus, while times were recorded to tenths of a second, results at either distance could be regarded as comparable.

The 1972 Olympic steeplechase final: although stumbling here, Kip Keino won the gold medal, Ben Jipcho (574) was second and Tapio Kantanen (207) third. (ASP)

Dips for the finish by three of the greatest high hurdlers of all time. Rod Milburn won the 1972 Olympic title, with Guy Drut (l) second. Defending champion Willie Davenport (r) was fourth. (ASP)

Times at the slightly shorter 120y could not be recognized as world records at 110m, although naturally the reverse could happen. In the following summary times at 120yh are indicated by y.

The lists of world record holders and Olympic medallists at the hurdles are dominated by athletes from the USA even more than those of the flat sprints. Since 1976 records have been recognized only if timed on fully automatic electrical devices.

WORLD RECORD AT TEN-YEARLY
INTERVALS—110mh or 120yh(y)

1905	15.2y	Alvin Kraenzlein (USA) Chicago 18 Jun 1898
	15.2y	George Smith (NZ) Auckland 8 May 1902
1915	15.0	Forrest Smithson (USA) London 25 Jul 1908, and others
1925	14.4y	Earl Thomson (USA) Philadelphia 20 May 1920
1935	14.1y	George Saling (USA) Chicago 11 Jun 1932 (unratified)
	14.1y	Jack Keller (USA) Evanston 20 May 1933 (unratified)
1945	13.7	Forrest Towns (USA) Oslo 27 Aug 1936
	13.7	Fred Wolcott (USA) Philadelphia 29 Jun 1941
1955	13.5y	Dick Attlesey (USA) Fresno 13 May 1950
	13.5	Dick Attlesey (USA) Helsinki 10 Jul 1950
1965	13.2	Martin Lauer (GFR) Zürich 7 Jul 1959 (only 13.56 auto)
	13.2	Lee Calhoun (USA) Bern 21 Aug 1960
1975	13.0y	Rod Milburn (USA) Eugene 20 Jun 1971 (and twice more)
	13.0	Guy Drut (Fra) Berlin 22 Aug 1975
	13.24	Rod Milburn (USA) Munich 7 Sep 1972 (auto record)
1985	12.93	Renaldo Nehemiah (USA) Zürich 19 Aug 1981

The best ever hand-timed 110mh is 12.8 by Renaldo Nehemiah at Kingston, Jamaica on 11 May 1979.
The best ever auto-time irrespective of wind is 12.91 by Nehemiah at Champaign on 1 Jun 1979, with a following wind of 3.5m/s.

THE BARRIER BREAKERS—the first to better

15 sec Earl Thomson (USA) 14.8y Columbia 27 May 1916
14 sec Forrest Towns (USA) 13.7 Oslo 27 Aug 1936
13 sec Renaldo Nehemiah (USA) 12.8 Kingston 11 May 1979 (hand)
Renaldo Nehemiah 12.91w and 12.93 as above (auto)

MOST OFFICIAL IAAF WORLD RECORDS

6 Rod Milburn (USA)—four at 110mh, three hand-timed and one auto, and two at 120yh. In a great season in 1971, when he won all his 28 races, he ran the first ever 13–flat times for 120yh; first wind-aided on 4 June at Billings, Montana and then with a 'legal' wind of 1.95m/s three weeks later. He ran a further 13.0y in 1973 and (unratified) in 1975 as a professional. He set two world records at 13.1 for 110mh in 1973 and the first accepted auto-time of 13.24 to win the 1972 Olympic title. He was reinstated for amateur competition in 1980.

THE BEST CHAMPIONSHIPS RECORDS

Lee Calhoun (USA) won the Olympic title in both

Glenn Davis retains his Olympic 400mh title in 1960 and leads a US 1–2–3: Cliff Cushman second and Dick Howard third. Helmut Janz (GFR) was fourth. (Keystone Press)

1956 and 1960, on both occasions by narrow margins. He was second in the 1959 Pan-American Games and was AAU champion three times and NCAA champion twice for North Carolina Central. He set a world record 13.2 in 1960.
b. 23 Feb 1933 Laurel, Mississippi.

Guy Drut (Fra) was Olympic champion in 1976 and second in 1972, and was European champion in 1974. He also won the European indoor 50mh title in 1972. He ran three world records in 1975, headed by his hand-timed 13.0 at Berlin. His auto-timed best was 13.28, also in 1975. A talented all-rounder, he had a pole vault best of 5.20m.
b. 6 Dec 1950 Oignies.

Thomas Munkelt (GDR) was Olympic champion in 1980 and European champion in 1978 and 1982. He was also four times European indoor champion at 60mh and nine times GDR 110mh champion. His best time was 13.37 in 1977.
b. 3 Aug 1952 Zedlitz.

Harrison Dillard (USA) was hot favourite for the 1948 Olympic title, but sensationally failed to qualify for the US team when he hit three hurdles at the Olympic Trials. Nonetheless, such was his ability that he made the team at the flat 100m and won the Olympic title. Four years later he duly won the 110mh title to seal a great hurdling career. In his collegiate career at Baldwin-Wallace College he won 201 of 207 sprint and hurdles finals and compiled a win streak of 82 consecutive sprints and hurdles races indoors and out from 31 May 1947 to 26 Jun 1948. He was AAU sprint hurdles champion three times outdoors and eight times indoors and NCAA

champion twice. He ran a world record 13.6y in 1948.
b. 8 Jul 1923 Cleveland.

400 Metres Hurdles

The 400 metres hurdles has been entitled the 'mankiller' event, for it demands a combination of speed, stamina and a finely honed technique. Athletes clear ten flights of hurdles, 91.4cm (3ft) high, spaced 35m apart, with 45m from the start to the first hurdle and a run-in of 40m.

The event was first held at the Olympic Games in 1900, but was a comparatively late addition to national championship programmes—UK, USA and Sweden 1914 and Germany 1922, although French titles have been contested since 1893.

From 1976 the IAAF no longer recognized records at 440y (402.34m) hurdles; a generally accepted conversion factor is 0.3 sec.

WORLD RECORD AT TEN-YEARLY INTERVALS
(y= 440y times)

1915	54.6y	William Meanix (USA) Cambridge, Mass.
		16 Jul 1915

1925	52.1	Ivan Riley (USA) Ann Arbor, Michigan 31 May 1924 (unofficial)
1935	50.6	Glenn Hardin (USA) Stockholm 26 Jul 1934
1945	50.6	Glenn Hardin as above
1955	50.4	Yuriy Lituyev (USSR) Budapest 20 Sep 1953
1965	49.1	Rex Cawley (USA) Los Angeles 13 Sep 1964
	49.3y	Gert Potgieter (SAf) Bloemfontein 16 Apr 1960
1975	47.82	John Akii-Bua (Uga) Munich 2 Sep 1972
1985	47.02	Edwin Moses (USA) Koblenz 31 Aug 1983

THE BARRIER BREAKERS—the first to better

60 sec Samuel Morris (UK) 59.8y 5 Jul 1886
55 sec William Meanix (USA) 54.6y Cambridge, Mass. 16 Jul 1915
50 sec Glenn Davis (USA) 49.5 Los Angeles 29 Jun 1956

MOST WORLD RECORDS

4 Edwin Moses (USA): 47.63 at the 1976 Olympic Games, 47.45 in 1977, 47.13 in 1980 and 47.02 in 1983.
3 Glenn Hardin (USA). His first of 51.9 was actually run in second place at the 1932 Olympic Games, as the 51.7 by winner Bob Tisdall (Ire) was not accepted due to Tisdall knocking over a hurdle. Hardin improved in 1934 to 51.8 and then to 50.6, with the biggest ever improvement in the record, and a time which was not broken until 1953. He won the 1936 Olympic title and was three times AAU champion.

THE BEST CHAMPIONSHIPS RECORDS

Edwin Moses is supreme in every aspect of this event. He was Olympic champion in 1976 and 1984, having to miss Moscow in 1980 due to the US boycott. He was world champion in 1983, won the World Cup races of 1977, 1979 and 1981, was US champion in 1977, 1979, 1981 and 1983 and AAA champion in 1979.
b. 31 Aug 1955 Dayton, Ohio.
Glenn Davis (USA) won the 1956 Olympic title in his first year of intermediate hurdling, having earlier run the first sub-50-sec time ever in only his ninth race at the event. He improved the world record to 49.2 in 1958 and won further Olympic gold medals in 1960 at 400mh and the 4×400m relay. In this period he won four AAU hurdles titles. He was also a world-class runner at the flat quarter-mile and in 1958 was NCAA

champion and set two world records (45.8 and 45.7) at 440y.
b. 12 Sep 1934 Wellsburg, West Virginia.
Harald Schmid (GFR) has had to yield to Ed Moses at major championships, but has nonetheless compiled a formidable record: second 1983 World, third 1984 Olympics, first 1978 and 1982 European. He also has three firsts and two seconds at 400mh in European Cup finals (and a win at 400m in 1979) and has won eight GFR 400mh titles. Of course, he is also the last man to beat Moses—at Berlin on 26 Aug 1977. His fastest time is the European record of 47.48 that he recorded in winning the 1982 European title.
b. 29 Sep 1957 Hanau.

Relays

The IAAF currently ratify records at five men's relay events. Up to 1976 records were also recognized at the five equivalent imperial distances. The first relay race is thought to have been staged at Berkeley, Cal. on 17 Nov 1883, a four-man, two mile inter-class race at the University of California. The first relay race using a baton was held in 1893 at the University of Pennsylvania, where the famous Penn Relays were first held in 1895.

4 × 100 Metres Relay

The sprint relay has been included on the Olympic programme since 1912, and world records have been set at 12 of the 16 Games from then. The final record at the imperial equivalent of 4×110y was 38.6 by the University of Southern California team of Earl McCullouch, Fred Kuller, O. J. Simpson and Lennox Miller in 1967. That time was also a record for the shorter distance of 4×100m.

WORLD RECORD AT TEN-YEARLY INTERVALS

1915	42.3	Germany (Otto Röhr, Max Herrman, Erwin Kern, Richard Rau) Stockholm 8 Jul 1912
1925	41.0	USA (Frank Hussey, Louis Clarke, Loren Murchison, Alfred Leconey) Paris (Colombes) 12 Jul 1924
1935	40.0	USA (Robert Kiesel, Emmett Toppino, Hector Dyer, Frank Wykoff) Los Angeles 7 Aug 1932

MEN'S WORLD BESTS—NON-STANDARD EVENTS OUTDOORS

	min:sec			
150m	14.8	Pietro Mennea (Ita)	Cassino	22 May 1983
300m	31.70	Kirk Baptiste (USA)	London (Crystal Palace)	18 Aug 1984
500m	1:00.35	Hartmut Weber (GFR)	Nussdorf	8 May 1983
600m	1:14.16	Johnny Gray (USA)	Sacramento	21 Jul 1985
2000m Steeple	5:20.00	Krzysztof Wesolowski (Pol)	Oslo	28 Jun 1984
200mh	22.5	Martin Lauer (GFR)	Zürich	7 Jul 1959
(auto)	22.69	Glenn Davis (USA)	Berne	20 Aug 1960
220yh (Straight)	21.9	Don Styron (USA)	Baton Rouge	2 Apr 1960
300mh	34.6	David Hemery (UK)	London (Crystal Palace)	15 Sep 1972
Pentathlon	4282 points	Bill Toomey (USA)	London (Crystal Palace)	16 Aug 1969
(1984 tables)				

1945	39.8	USA (Jesse Owens, Ralph Metcalfe, Foy Draper, Frank Wykoff) Berlin 9 Aug 1936
1955	39.8	as above
1965	39.06	USA (Paul Drayton, Gerald Ashworth, Dick Stebbins, Bob Hayes) Tokyo 21 Oct 1964
1975	38.19	USA (Larry Black, Robert Taylor, Gerald Tinker, Eddie Hart) Munich 10 Sep 1972
1985	37.83	USA (Sam Graddy, Ron Brown, Calvin Smith, Carl Lewis) Los Angeles 11 Aug 1984

THE MOST OFFICIAL WORLD RECORDS BY AN INDIVIDUAL

3 Frank Wykoff who ran records on three US gold medal-winning Olympic teams—first leg in 1928 (41.0), anchor in 1932 (40.0) and in 1936 (39.8). He was AAU 100y/100m champion in 1928 and 1931, and NCAA 100y champion in 1930 and 1931 for Southern California. He anchored his college team to a further world record at 4×110y of 40.8 in 1931. In 1930 he ran the first officially accepted 100y in 9.4.

3 Martin Lauer ran in German teams which three times equalled the world record of 39.5 in 1958–60. He excelled at 100m hurdles, at which he set a world record of 13.2 in 1959, and was European champion in 1958 as well as fourth at the Olympics in 1956 and 1960.

4 × 400 Metres Relay

With the sprint relay this event was added to the Olympic programme in 1912. Eight of the 12 official world records have been set in Olympic competition.

WORLD RECORD AT TEN-YEARLY INTERVALS

1915	3:16.6	USA (Melvin Sheppard, Charles Reidpath, Ted Meredith, Edward Lindberg) Stockholm 15 Jul 1912
1925	3:16.0	USA (Commodore Cochran, William Stevenson, Oliver Macdonald, Alan Helffrich) Paris (Colombes) 13 Jul 1924
1935	3:08.2	USA (Ivan Fuqua, Edgar Ablowich, Karl Warner, Bill Carr) Los Angeles 7 Aug 1932
1945	3:08.2	as above

In an era of great US sprinters, Frank Wykoff made three Olympic relay teams. He came from that great nursery – the University of Southern California.

Black power and gold medals for the US 4 × 400m relay team at the 1968 Games. From left: Lee Evans, Ron Freeman, Larry James and Vince Matthews. (Ed Lacey/ASP)

1955	3:03.9	Jamaica (Arthur Wint, Leslie Laing, Herb McKenley, George Rhoden) Helsinki 27 Jul 1952 (3:04.04 on auto-timing)
1965	3:00.7	USA (Ollan Cassell, Mike Larrabee, Ulis Williams, Henry Carr) Tokyo 21 Oct 1964
1975	2:56.16	USA (Vince Matthews, Ron Freeman II, Larry James, Lee Evans) Mexico City 20 Oct 1968
1985	2:56.16	as above

The fastest ever 400m relay leg is 43.2 by Ron Freeman II on the 1968 US Olympic team. An intrinsically faster time of 43.4 for 440y was run by Maurice Peoples for Arizona State University at the 1973 NCAA Championships at Baton Rouge, Louisiana.

The first sub 3-minute time was run by Bob Frey, Lee Evans, Tommie Smith and Theron Lewis with 2:59.6 for the USA against the British Commonwealth at Los Angeles on 24 July 1966.

World Records and Bests—Other Relays

4 × 200m 1:20.23 The Tobias Striders (Guy Abrahams (Pan), Mike Simmons (USA), Don Quarrie (Jam), James Gilkes (Guy)) Tempe 27 May 1978. Not ratified as this team, all graduates of USC, were of various nationalities. 1:20.26 University of Southern California (USA) (Joel Andrews, James Sanford, Billy Mullins, Clancy Edwards) Tempe 27 May 1978
4 × 800m 7:03.89 UK (Peter Elliott 1:49.14, Garry Cook 1:46.20, Steve Cram 1:44.54, Sebastian Coe 1:44.01) London 30 Aug 1982
4 × 1500m 14:38.8 GFR (Thomas Wessinghage 3:38.8,

Harold Hudak 3:39.1, Michael Lederer 3:43.0, Karl Fleschen 3:36.3) Köln 17 Aug 1977
4 × 1 mile 15:49.08 Ireland (Eamonn Coghlan 4:00.2, Marcus O'Sullivan 3:55.3, Frank O'Mara 3:56.6, Ray Flynn 3:56.9) Dublin 17 Aug 1985

High Jump

Nowadays the vast majority of top-class high jumpers employ the flop technique which was pioneered by Dick Fosbury (USA), the 1968 Olympic champion. The first world record with this style was 2.30m by Dwight Stones in 1973. The flop technique seems easier to master than the straddle, which was introduced in the 1930s, and last employed to set a world best by Vladimir Yashchenko at 2.35m indoors in 1978. Earlier techniques included the 'Eastern cut-off' and the 'Western roll', for which the first world record holders were Michael Sweeney and George Horine respectively.

WORLD HIGH JUMP RECORD AT TEN-YEARLY INTERVALS

1905	1.97m	Michael Sweeney (USA) New York 21 Sep 1895
1915	2.01m	Edward Beeson (USA) Berkeley, Cal. 2 May 1914
1925	2.03m	Harold Osborn (USA) Urbana 27 May 1924
1935	2.07m	Walter Marty (USA) Fresno 7 Apr 1934
1945	2.11m	Lester Steers (USA) Los Angeles 17 Jun 1941
1955	2.12m	Walt Davis (USA) Dayton, Ohio 27 Jun 1953
1965	2.28m	Valeriy Brumel (USSR) Moscow 21 Jul 1963
1975	2.30m	Dwight Stones (USA) Munich, GFR 11 Jul 1973
1985	2.41m	Igor Paklin (USSR) Kobe 4 Sep 1985

In 1941 Les Steers set the five best ever high jump marks. His third world record, 2.11m (6ft 11in), was not improved for twelve years. (Central Press)

THE BARRIER BREAKERS—the first to clear

6 ft	Marshall Brooks (UK) 1.83m Oxford 17 Mar 1876
2.00m	George Horine (USA) 6ft 7in/2.00 m Palo Alto 18 May 1912
2.10m	Lester Steers (USA) 2.10m Seattle 26 Apr 1941
7ft	Charles Dumas (USA) 2.15m Los Angeles 29 Jun 1956
2.20m	John Thomas (USA) 2.22m Palo Alto 1 Jul 1960
2.30m	Dwight Stones (USA) 2.30m Munich 11 Jul 1973
2.40m	Rudolf Povarnitsin (USSR) Donetsk 11 Aug 1985

MOST WORLD RECORDS—outdoors

6 Valeriy Brumel (USSR), who took the record by a centimetre at a time from 2.23m to 2.28m in the three years 1961 to 1963. His great rival, the American John Thomas, set the previous record at 2.22m in 1960. Brumel first exceeded this indoors with 2.25m at Leningrad on 29 Jan 1961, before embarking on his record-breaking outdoors. No other jumper exceeded his 2.28m until 1970, but Brumel's career was cut short by a serious motorcycle accident on 7 Oct 1965, when he suffered multiple fractures in his right leg.

4 John Thomas (USA), who in a marvellous year in 1960, when he had his 19th birthday on 3 March, first set four indoor bests (2.17, 2.17, 2.18, 2.19) and then four world records outdoors (2.17, 2.17, 2.18, 2.22). Unbeaten for two years he was surprisingly beaten in the Olympic Games that year by the Soviet pair of Robert Shavlakadze and Valeriy Brumel.

INDOOR BESTS

John Thomas, Valeriy Brumel and Vladimir Yashchenko all set indoor bests above the outdoor world record (see above).
Most indoor bests:
11 John Thomas—from 2.10 at the age of 17 at Cambridge, Mass. on 10 Jan 1959 to 2.19 at Chicago on 11 Mar 1960.
7 Dwight Stones (USA)—five in 1975 (2.26 to 2.28) and two in 1976 (2.29 and 2.30). The ebullient Stones also set outdoor records at 2.30 in 1973, and at 2.31 and 2.32 in 1976. He improved with a US outdoor record of 2.34 in 1984, and has had the longest career at world class of any of the top high jumpers, with Olympic bronze medals in 1972 and 1976, and fourth place in 1984.

THE BEST CHAMPIONSHIPS RECORDS

Valeriy Brumel started his international career at the age of 18 in 1960, when he won the Olympic silver medal at 2.16m, the same height as the winner, Shavlakadze. From then until injuries suffered in a motorcycling accident in 1965 forced him out of the sport, he was supreme in world high jumping, winning the European title in 1962

Conversions 6ft = 1.83m. 6ft 3in = 1.90m. 6ft 6in = 1.98m. 6ft 9in = 2.05m. 7ft = 2.13m. 7ft 3in = 2.21m. 7ft 6in = 2.28m. 7ft 9in = 2.36m. 8ft = 2.44m.

and the Olympics in 1964, although on the latter occasion he only won on the count-back from John Thomas, who cleared the same height of 2.18m. He was Soviet champion four times, 1960–3.
b.Tolbuzino, Siberia 14 Apr 1942; 1.85m tall.
Dietmar Mögenburg is the tallest (with Povarnitsin) of world high jump record holders. Such height is an obvious advantage, but more than that the West German has displayed great competitive ability in major events. He has won the following titles: European Junior 1979, European 1982, Olympics 1984, European Indoor 1980, 1982 and 1984. He was also fourth equal in the 1983 World Championships, won a silver in the 1981 European indoors, and had started his international career with a win at the age of 17 in the 1979 European Cup Final. He was GFR champion each year from 1980 to 1984. He equalled the world record with 2.35m in 1980 and set a world indoor best of 2.39m at Köln in 1985.
b.Leverkusen 15 Aug 1961; 2.01m tall.

Pole Vault

Pole vaulting, originally for distance, dates back at least to the 16th century. In the 19th century heavy wooden poles, usually of ash or hickory, with iron spikes on the end were used by vaulters around Ulverston in the English Lake District. The technique used was a 'climbing' one whereby the vaulters moved their hands up the pole when it was vertical. The greatest exponent of this art was Thomas Ray (UK), who raised the best height cleared nine times, from 3.42m in 1879 to 3.57m in 1888. The 'climbing' technique was banned in the USA in 1889 but not until 1919 by the AAA.
Bamboo poles were widely used in the early part of this century, but were generally superseded by light, durable steel poles in the late 1940s and 1950s. Until 1936 the IAAF rules specified that poles be made of wood or bamboo, but from that time there have been no restrictions on the material used or on the length and diameter of poles.
Early experiments with glass-fibre poles had been conducted in the USA in the late 1940s, and these much more flexible poles began to come into use by leading vaulters in the mid 1950s. The first world record made with such a pole was on 2 May 1961, when George Davies (USA) cleared 4.83m at Boulder, Colorado. That presaged a big jump in vaulting standards as these new poles and safe landing areas became universal.

Up to the heights – John Pennel played a major part in improving world standards in the mid-1960s. He made two Olympic appearances, but had a best placing of fifth in 1968. (Keystone Press)

WORLD POLE VAULT RECORD AT TEN-YEARLY INTERVALS

1905	3.74m	Fernand Gonder (Fra) Bordeaux 6 Aug 1905
1915	4.02m	Marcus Wright (USA) Cambridge, Mass. 8 Jun 1912
1925	4.25m	Charles Hoff (Nor) Turku, Finland 27 Sep 1925
1935	4.39m	Keith Brown (USA) Cambridge, Mass. 1 Jun 1935
1945	4.77m	Cornelius Warmerdam (USA) Modesto, Cal. 23 May 1942 (and 4.78 m indoors Chicago 20 Mar 1943)
1955	4.77m	Cornelius Warmerdam (4.78 m (i)) (as above)
1965	5.28m	Fred Hanson (USA) Los Angeles 25 Jul 1964
1975	5.65m	Dave Roberts (USA) Gainesville 28 Mar 1975
1985	6.00m	Sergey Bubka (USSR) Paris 13 Jul 1985

THE BARRIER BREAKERS—the first to clear

12ft	Norman Dole (USA) 3.69m Oakland, Cal. 23 Apr 1904
13ft	Robert Gardner (USA) 3.99m Philadelphia 1 Jun 1912
4m	Marcus Wright (USA) 4.02m Cambridge, Mass. 8 Jun 1912
14ft	Sabin Carr (USA) 4.26m Philadelphia 27 May 1927

15ft	Cornelius Warmerdam (USA) 4.57m Compton, Cal. 6 Jun 1941
16ft	John Uelses (USA) 4.88m (i) New York 2 Feb 1962
5m	Pentti Nikula (Fin) 5.10m (i) Pajulahti 2 Feb 1963
17ft	John Pennel (USA) 5.20m Coral Gables, Fl. 24 Aug 1963
18ft	Christos Papanikolaou (Gre) 5.49m Athens 24 Oct 1970
19ft	Thierry Vigneron (Fra) 5.80m Macon 20 Jun 1981
6m	Sergey Bubka (USSR) 6.00m Paris 13 Jul 1985

MOST WORLD RECORDS—OUTDOORS

9 John Pennel (USA)—from 4.95m at Memphis on 23 Mar 1963 to 5.44m at Sacramento on 21 Jun 1969. Pennel had only four world records officially accepted, as such was the rate of progress of the world standard, especially in 1963 when the record was broken or equalled ten times in all, that recognition of several of his efforts was not applied for.

7 Cornelius 'Dutch' Warmerdam—The first 15ft vaulter dominated his contemporaries more than any other vaulter in history. His career best of 4.78m indoors was not bettered until Robert Gutowski (USA) cleared 4.82m at Austin on 15 Jun 1957, 14 years 87 days later. Warmerdam cleared 15ft (4.57m) or higher in 43 competitions between 1940 and 1944, and no other vaulter cleared 15ft until Robert Richards (USA) succeeded at 15ft 1in (4.59m) indoors in New York on 27 Jan 1951.

6 Bob Seagren (USA)—from 5.32m at Fresno on 14 May 1966 to 5.63m at Eugene on 2 Jul 1972.

INDOOR BESTS

On several occasions vaulters have set indoor bests above the world outdoor record. Sabin Carr (USA) was the first to do so when he vaulted 4.29m in New York on 25 Feb 1928, 'Dutch' Warmerdam did so as referred to above, and most recently Thierry Vigneron (Fra) won the 1984 European Indoor title with 5.85m, 2cm above the outdoor record.

Most indoor bests:

12 Charles Hoff (Nor) all on a barnstorming tour of the USA in 1926. He started with 13ft 1in (3.99m) in New York on 4 Feb and inched the record up to 13ft 8.25in (4.17m) in Chicago on 9 Apr. Later in the year he was barred by the AAU on a charge of professionalism and his records removed from the books.

10 Billy Olson (USA) from 5.71m at Toronto on 29 Jan 1982 by a centimetre at a time, until a 4cm leap to 5.80m in 1983, then 5.86m in 1985 and 5.88m and 5.89m in January 1986.

8 Bob Seagren with successive improvements from 5.18m, the first indoor 17ft clearance, at Albuquerque on 5 Mar 1966 to 5.33m (17ft 6in) at Los Angeles on 8 Feb 1969.

Conversions 13ft = 3.96m. 14ft = 4.26m. 15ft = 4.57m. 16ft = 4.87m. 17ft = 5.18m. 18ft = 5.48m. 19ft = 5.79m. 20ft = 6.09m.

THE BEST CHAMPIONSHIPS RECORDS

Robert Richards (USA) is the only double Olympic gold medallist with wins in 1952 and 1956, and a bronze medal in 1948. He won the Pan-American title in 1951 and 1955 and a record nine AAU titles outdoors and eight indoors. A fine all-rounder, he also won three AAU decathlon titles. As the Reverend Bob Richards he was known as 'The Vaulting Vicar', and although he never bettered 'Dutch' Warmerdam's world record, cleared 15ft or higher in 126 competitions between 1951 and 1957. His best mark was 4.72m indoors in 1957.
b.20 Feb 1926 Champaign, Illinois.

Wolfgang Nordwig (GDR) won a record three European titles, 1966, 1969 and 1971 and a record four European indoor titles 1968–9 and 1971–2. He was Olympic champion in 1972 and won the bronze medal in 1968. He also won the World Student Games title in 1970 and was GDR champion for eight successive years from 1965 to 1972. He set two world records—5.45m and 5.46m in 1970 and had a best of 5.50m in 1972.
b. 27 Aug 1943 Siegmar, Chemnitz.

Bob Seagren (USA) followed his Olympic win in 1968 with the silver medal in 1972. He won the Pan-American title in 1967, was AAU champion three times indoors and three times outdoors, and won the NCAA title for the University of Southern California in 1967 and 1969.
b. 17 Oct 1946 Pomona, Cal.

Long Jump

Two of the greatest feats in the history of athletics dominate the story of the long jump world record. Jesse Owens jumped 26ft 8¼in (8.13m) on his great record breaking day at Ann Arbor in 1935 and Bob Beamon fully utilized all the conditions in his favour at Mexico City in 1968 to annihilate the record with his 8.90m (29ft 2½in).

Jesse Owens jumped 26ft (7.92m) or better 15 times in 1935–6, but it was 12 years before anyone else exceeded that distance more than once. His record remained unbroken for 25 years 79 days, the longest duration for any standard Olympic event. If any record is to better that longevity then Beamon's must be the prime candidate. Beamon, whose previous best in 1968 was 8.33m (and 8.39m wind assisted), exceeded both 28ft and 29ft barriers in one leap, but it was not until 1980 that any other athlete surpassed 28ft, when Lutz Dombrowski (GDR) won the Olympic title at 8.54m (28ft 0¼in). Beamon himself, having achieved everything in just a few seconds' activity, never again jumped over even 27ft, falling an inch short in 1969. But at Mexico City with the stimulus of Olympic competition, the maximum permissible wind speed of 2.0m/s (curiously the same as several other readings that day) and most importantly the thin air of Mexico City's

2214m altitude, he had produced the perfect jump on his first of the competition. However, since then Carl Lewis (USA) has amassed easily the greatest collection of great long jumps, with 28 of the 35 28ft jumps ever made to the end of 1985. His best to date is 8.79m, to win the TAC title at Indianapolis in 1983 and again, indoors at the Millrose Games in New York in 1984.

WORLD LONG JUMP RECORD AT TEN-YEARLY INTERVALS

1905	7.61m	Peter O'Connor (Ire) Dublin 5 Aug 1901
1915	7.61m	Peter O'Connor as above
1925	7.89m	William DeHart Hubbard (USA) Chicago 13 Jun 1925
1935	8.13m	Jesse Owens (USA) Ann Arbor, Michigan 25 May 1935
1945	8.13m	Jesse Owens as above
1955	8.13m	Jesse Owens as above
1965	8.35m	Ralph Boston (USA) Modesto, Cal. 29 May 1965
1975	8.90m	Bob Beamon (USA) Mexico City 18 Oct 1968
1985	8.90m	Bob Beamon as above

THE BARRIER BREAKERS—the first to jump

24ft	William Newburn (Ire) 7.33m Dublin 16 Jul 1898
7.50m	Myer Prinstein (USA) 7.50m Philadelphia 28 Apr 1900
25ft	Edwin Gourdin (USA) 7.69m Cambridge, Mass. 23 Jul 1921
26ft	Silvio Cator (Haiti) 7.93m Paris 9 Sep 1928
8.00m	Jesse Owens (USA) 8.13m Ann Arbor, Michigan 25 May 1935
27ft	Ralph Boston (USA) 8.24m Modesto 27 May 1961
28ft	Bob Beamon (USA) 8.90m Mexico City 18 Oct 1968
8.50m	Bob Beamon as above
29ft	Bob Beamon as above

THE MOST WORLD RECORDS

6 Ralph Boston (USA), who was the first to surpass Owens, when he jumped 8.21m at Walnut on 12 Aug 1960 and took the record to its pre-Beamon 8.35m, which he achieved at Modesto on 29 May 1965. He recorded an even better jump of 8.49m at the US Olympic Trials in Los Angeles on 12 Sep 1964, but this had wind assistance over the permissible limit at 2.6m/s.

THE BEST CHAMPIONSHIPS RECORDS

Ralph Boston won a complete set of Olympic medals: gold in 1960, silver in 1964 and bronze in 1968. He also won the Pan-American title in 1963 and 1967 and AAU titles outdoors six times from 1961 to 1966 as well as indoors in 1961. While at Tennessee State University he won the NCAA title in 1960. He was a talented all-rounder, with bests of 2.05m for high jump, 15.89m triple jump, 9.6 for 100y and 13.7 for 120y hurdles.
b. 9 May 1939 Laurel, Mississippi
Igor Ter-Ovanesyan (USSR) achieved greatest success in the European Championships, with three gold and two silver medals between 1958 and 1971. He also won European Indoor titles in 1966 and 1968 and a silver medal in 1971; the

The most famous long jump performance – and picture – Ed Lacey captures the moment that Bob Beamon leapt 8.90m in Mexico City in 1968. (ASP)

European indoor best of 8.23m that he set to win the first of those titles was not equalled until 1985. Outdoors he set six European records from 8.01m in 1959 to 8.31m in 1962 and 8.35m in 1967, the latter two also world records.
At the Olympic Games he won bronze medals in 1960 and 1964 and placed fourth in 1968. He also won five World Student Games and a record 12 Soviet titles. Amazingly he was second in the long jump in all nine USSR v USA matches from 1958 to 1971.
b. 19 May 1938 Kiev. His father Aram set two USSR discus records in 1933.
Lynn Davies (UK) simultaneously held Olympic (1964), European (1966) and Commonwealth (1966 and 1970) long jump titles. At the European Championships he was also second in 1969, fourth in 1971 and twelfth in 1962 outdoors, and was first in 1967 and second in 1969 indoors. Competing at two further Olympics he was ninth in 1968, his inspiration drained by Beamon's epic jump, and did not qualify for the final in 1972. He was AAA champion five times outdoors and

---

Conversions 24ft = 7.31m. 25ft = 7.62m. 26ft = 7.92m. 27ft = 8.23m. 28ft = 8.53m. 29ft = 8.84m.

Both Olympic champions, Lynn Davies (l) and Ralph Boston (r) had many great duels. Boston won this one easily, at the 1965 Welsh Games in Cardiff. (Ed Lacey/ASP)

three times indoors. His eight UK records were headed by his best jump of exactly 27ft (8.23m) at Bern on 30 Jun 1968.
b. 20 May 1942 Nantymoel.

Carl Lewis has been unbeaten in long jump competition from 1981, winning 44 successive competitions to September 1985. He won the World title in 1983 and the Olympic in 1984, linked of course with his sprinting triumphs. He also won TAC titles outdoors 1981–3 and indoors 1982–4, and NCAA titles both indoors and out in 1980–1 while at Houston University.
b. 1 Jul 1961 Birmingham, Alabama.

Triple Jump

The first IAAF record for the triple jump was 15.52m by Daniel Ahearne, an Irish emigrant to the USA, in 1911. By then the event had been standardized as the hop, step and jump, although early practitioners in Ireland had used two hops and a jump, Ahearne himself achieving the best distance for the old technique with 15.72m at New York on 3 Jul 1910.

Conversions 47ft 6in = 14.48m. 50ft = 15.24m. 52ft 6in = 16.00m. 55ft = 16.76m. 57ft 6in = 17.52m. 60ft = 18.29m.

THE BARRIER BREAKERS—the first to jump

15m/50ft Daniel Ahearne (USA) 15.39m Boston 31 Jul 1909. (With two hops and a jump: Daniel Shanahan (Ire) 15.57m Newcastle West 8 Sep 1886)
16m Naoto Tajima (Jap) 16.00m Berlin 6 Aug 1936
55ft/17m Jozef Schmidt (Pol) 17.03m Olsztyn 5 Aug 1960

MOST WORLD RECORDS

5 Adhemar Ferreira da Silva, the first Brazilian world record holder at any event. His first record was when he equalled Tajima's 14-year-old record with 16.00m at Sao Paulo on 3 Dec 1950. He improved to 16.01m in 1951, twice in the 1952 Olympic final: 16.12m and 16.22m, and finally to 16.56m to win the 1955 Pan American title at altitude in Mexico City in 1955.

The **most world records in one competition** came at the 1968 Olympic Games in Mexico City. In the qualifying round Giuseppe Gentile (Ita) added 7cm to the record with 17.10m, then in the final, records were set by Gentile 17.22m, Viktor Saneyev (USSR) 17.23m, Nelson Prudencio (Bra) 17.27m and finally Saneyev again to win with 17.39m.

THE BEST CHAMPIONSHIPS RECORDS

Viktor Saneyev won three successive Olympic titles, 1968, 1972 and 1976 and added a silver medal in 1980. He was European champion in 1969 and 1974, and won the silver medal in 1971 and 1978. He also won six European Indoor titles (and one silver medal), the World Student Games title of 1970 (second 1973) and eight USSR championships. At the 1964 European Junior Championships he won silver medals at both long and triple jumps, and he won the European Cup Final TJ in 1967, 1973 and 1975. He set three world records, the two at the 1968 Olympics and his best of 17.44m in his hometown of Sukhumi on 17 Oct 1972.
b. 3 Oct 1945 Sukhumi, Georgia.

Jozef Schmidt was Olympic champion in 1960 and 1964 (7th, 1968) and European champion in 1958 and 1962 (5th, 1966). As shown above he was the first 17m triple jumper.
b. 28 Mar 1935 Miechowice.

Adhemar Ferreira da Silva dominated triple jumping in the early 1950s, winning 60 successive competitions 1950–6. He was Olympic champion in 1952 and 1956, Pan-American champion 1951, 1955 and 1959, and South American champion in 1952, 1954 and 1958.

b. 29 Sep 1927 Sao Paulo.

Shot

Throwing an object has, from the earliest times, been one of man's basic elements of play and indeed hunting. The modern shot put, using a solid metal ball weighing 16lb (7.26kg), has evolved from stone throwing, but a really heavy stone cannot be thrown, but must be pushed or 'put' forwards from the shoulder. Putting the stone was an event established in classical times, and was for hundreds of years a popular event in the rural sports of the British Isles. Such British practice no doubt determined its imperial measures of 16lb weight and 7ft (2.135m) throwing circle. Shot putting techniques have, as for all athletics events, developed considerably over the years. Particularly significant was the pioneering by Parry O'Brien of the method of starting the throw from a backward pointing position and making a 180-degree turn before releasing the shot in order to make the most of the dimensions of the circle in gaining momentum. More recently several leading putters, including Aleksandr Baryshnikov (USSR) and Brian Oldfield (USA) have used a rotational technique.

WORLD SHOT RECORD AT TEN-YEARLY INTERVALS

1905	15.09m	Wesley Coe (USA) Portland, Oregon 5 Aug 1905
1915	15.54m	Ralph Rose (USA) San Francisco 21 Aug 1909
1925	15.54m	Ralph Rose as above
1935	17.40m	Jack Torrance (USA) Oslo 5 Aug 1934
1945	17.40m	Jack Torrance as above
1955	18.54m	Parry O'Brien (USA) Los Angeles 11 Jun 1954
1965	21.52m	Randy Matson (USA) College Station, Texas 8 May 1965
1975	22.86m	Brian Oldfield (USA) El Paso 10 May 1975 (professional)
	22.02m	George Woods (USA) Inglewood 8 Feb 1974 (indoors)
	21.82m	Al Feuerbach (USA) San José 5 May 1973
1985	22.86m	Brian Oldfield as above
	22.62m	Ulf Timmermann (GDR) East Berlin 22 Sep 1985

THE BARRIER BREAKERS—the first to exceed

15m	Wesley Coe (USA) 15.09m Portland 5 Aug 1905
50ft	Ralph Rose (USA) 15.39m Seattle 14 Aug 1909
60ft	Parry O'Brien (USA) 18.42m Los Angeles 8 May 1954
20m	Bill Nieder (USA) 20.06m Walnut, Cal. 12 Aug 1960
70ft	Randy Matson (USA) 21.52m College Station, Texas 8 May 1965

MOST WORLD RECORDS

14 Parry O'Brien (USA). Of these improvements on the world record, ten performances

Conversions 50ft = 15.24m. 55ft = 16.76m. 60ft = 18.29m. 65ft = 19.81m. 70ft = 21.33m. 75ft = 22.86m.

were ratified by the IAAF, from 18.00m at Fresno on 9 May 1953 to 19.30m at Albuquerque on 1 Aug 1959. Although he was then surpassed by younger throwers, O'Brien continued to improve and recorded a best of 19.69m in 1966.

9 Dallas Long, including seven official records. Long, who qualified as a dentist, was the first man to better O'Brien, with 19.25m at Santa Barbara on 28 Mar 1959. His best year was 1964, when he won the Olympic title and set his last world record of 20.68m for USA v USSR at Los Angeles on 25 Jul.

7 Ralph Rose (USA), all in pre-IAAF days. A huge man at 1.98m and 130kg, Rose took the world best from 14.81m in 1904 to 15.54m in 1909. The latter stood for a record duration of 18 years 241 days. His most remarkable achieve-

Dallas Long puts the shot for USC, for whom he won NCAA shot titles in 1960–2. He now practises a gentler pursuit, dentistry. (University of Southern California)

In 1972 Brian Oldfield qualified for the Olympic Games, at which he placed sixth, by keeping world record holder Randy Matson off the team. He later achieved sensational performances as a professional. (ASP)

ment, however, came in an unsanctioned meet at Healdsburg, Cal. on 26 June 1909, when he put the shot 16.56m, a mark unsurpassed by anyone until Jack Torrance in 1934, and also passed the world hammer best with 54.38m.

The most world bests in one competition came from Brian Oldfield in his well-nigh incredible day at El Paso on 10 May 1975. In an ITA professional meeting he took just three throws, each an outdoor world best: 21.94m, 22.25 m and 22.86m, the last exactly 75ft. He had earlier put 22.11m indoors. While many people have remained sceptical about these performances which were not subject to the checking procedures needed for world record breaking, Oldfield backed them up with further puts at 22.28m at Edinburgh in 1975 and 22.45m at El Paso in 1976. As a reinstated amateur he improved the US record to 22.02m in 1981 and again to 22.19m in 1984 at the age of 39.

THE BEST CHAMPIONSHIPS RECORDS

Parry O'Brien was Olympic champion in 1952 and 1956, won the silver medal in 1960, and was fourth in 1964. He was Pan-American champion in 1955 and 1959 and won AAU titles indoors nine times and outdoors eight times. While at the University of Southern California he was NCAA champion in 1952 and 1953. The complete master of his event, he set the record win streak by a male athlete with 116 consecutive victories between July 1952 and June 1956. He also won the AAU discus title in 1955.
b. 28 Jan 1932 Santa Monica, Cal.
Ralph Rose was Olympic champion in 1904 and 1908 and was second in 1912. He won a third gold medal at the two-handed shot in 1912 and won silver and bronze medals at discus and hammer in 1904. He won four AAU shot titles, 1907–10.
b. 17 Mar 1885 Louisville; d. 16 Oct 1913 San Francisco.
Udo Beyer has been the outstanding shot putter of the late 1970s and 1980s. *Track & Field News* ranked him first in the world each year from 1977 to 1984, except 1983, when, as in 1976, he was second. At Olympic Games he won in 1976 and was third in 1980. He won European titles in

1978 and 1982, World Student Games in 1979, European Junior in 1973, nine successive GDR titles 1977–85, and won both European and World Cup Finals in 1977, 1979 and 1981. He set world records at 22.15m in 1978 and 22.22m in 1983.
b. 9 Aug 1955 Eisenhüttenstadt.

Discus

Diskos was a Greek word meaning 'thing for throwing'. Metal or stone *discoi*, probably heavier than the modern discus, were used for what became a standard event at the ancient Olympic Games. The Greek standing throw method has, of course, long since been superseded by the turning throw, applying principles of rotation and weight transfer. The throwing circle was standardized at 2.50m (8ft 2in) in 1912; previously 7ft (2.13m) circles or squares or a larger circle of

Ludvik Danek was for long Europe's most consistent discus thrower. Over a four-year period in the mid-1960s he had 118 wins to just three losses. (Ed Lacey/ASP)

2.70m (8ft 10in) had been used in various parts of the world. The discus weighs 2kg (4.4lb).

<u>WORLD RECORD AT TEN-YEARLY INTERVALS</u>

1905	43.66m	Martin Sheridan (USA) New York 10 Sep 1905 (7ft circle)
1915	48.27m	unofficial—Armas Taipale (Fin) Copenhagen 14 Aug 1913 (and 48.90m exhibition in 1914)
	47.58m	official—James Duncan (USA) New York 27 May 1912
1925	47.89m	official—Glenn Hartranft (USA) Cambridge, Mass. 31 May 1924
1935	53.79m	unofficial—Gordon Dunn (USA) Eureka 24 May 1935
	53.10m	official—Wilhelm Schröder (GFR) Magdeburg 28 Apr 1935
1945	53.34m	official—Adolfo Consolini (Ita) Milan 26 Oct 1941
1955	59.28m	Fortune Gordien (USA) Pasadena, Cal. 22 Aug 1953
1965	65.22m	Ludvik Danek (Cs) Sokolov 12 Oct 1965
1975	69.08m	John Powell (USA) Long Beach 4 May 1975
1985	71.86m	Yuriy Dumchev (USSR) Moscow 29 May 1983

Ben Plucknett (USA) has the greatest recorded distance as he threw 72.34m at Stockholm on 7 Jul 1981. However, this was not ratified as a world record because Plucknett failed a dope test from the Pacific Conference Games earlier in that year.

<u>THE BARRIER BREAKERS</u>—the first to exceed

40m	Martin Sheridan (USA) 40.72m New York 2 Nov 1902. Werner Järvinen (Fin) threw 44.00m at Reipas in August 1901 from the 2.70m circle used in Scandinavia.
150ft	James Duncan (USA) 47.58m New York 27 May 1912
50m	Eric Krenz (USA) 51.03m Palo Alto 17 May 1930
60m	Jay Silvester (USA) 60.56m Frankfurt/Main 11 Aug 1961
200ft	Al Oerter (USA) 61.10m Los Angeles 18 May 1962. Oerter had thrown 61.73m at Fayetteville, Arkansas on 5 Apr 1958, but this was disallowed due to a 2.5% downhill slope.
70m	Jay Silvester (USA) 70.38m Lancaster 16 May 1971. Due to lack of sufficient graded officials, this throw in highly favourable conditions (70km/hr quartering winds) in Antelope Valley, Cal. was not ratified.

<u>THE MOST WORLD RECORDS</u>

Before the standardization of the discus circle, Martin Sheridan made five improvements on the best from a 2.50m circle. Since then:

6 Jay Silvester (USA), of which four were ratified, from 60.56m in 1961 to 70.38m in 1971 (above). He competed at four Olympic Games (1964–76), but only won one medal, a silver in 1972.

4 Fortune Gordien (USA) from 56.46 m at Lisbon in 1949 to 59.28m at Pasadena, Cal. in 1953. By the end of 1954 Gordien had 12 of the best 13 marks ever, all at the John Muir College in Pasadena. At Olympic Games from 1948 he was successively third, fourth and second.

4 Al Oerter (USA) from 61.10m in 1962 to 62.94m in 1964. After winning his fourth Olympic gold medal with a personal best 64.78m in 1968, he retired from competition for eleven years. In an awe-inspiring comeback he improved to 69.46m at the age of 43 in 1980. Even in 1985, at the age of 49, he had a season's best of 64.38m.

4 Mac Wilkins (USA). His first was 69.18m at Walnut in 1976, then a week later, at San José on 1 May, he set the most world records in one competition. On his first three throws he set records at 69.80m, 70.24m and 70.86m, for the first 70m throws in official competition. He sealed a great year with Olympic victory, to which he added a silver medal in 1984.

<u>THE BEST CHAMPIONSHIPS RECORDS</u>

Al Oerter (USA) stands supreme with four Olympic victories, each year from 1956 to 1968. He also won the Pan-American title in 1959, the AAU six times between 1959 and 1966 and the NCAA for Kansas in 1957 and 1958. He retired to concentrate on his career as a systems analyst and computer engineer in 1969. On his comeback he placed fourth in the 1980 US Olympic Trials, but by then the US Government had determined to boycott the Games in Moscow. If that competition had been 'for real' who can say but that his tremendous competitive spirit might not once again have returned him to the Olympic arena. b. 19 Sep 1936 Astoria, New York.

Martin Sheridan (USA) won Olympic titles in 1904, 1908 and at the Intercalated Games of 1906. He won further gold medals with the Greek style discus in 1908 and the shot in 1906. He won four AAU titles at discus, one at shot and three All-Around championships. b. 28 Mar 1881 Bohola, Co. Mayo, Ireland; d. 27 Mar 1918 New York, of pneumonia.

Adolfo Consolini (Ita) won three European titles (1946, 1950 and 1954) in five championships. At the Olympics his record was: 1948 1st, 1952 2nd, 1956 6th, 1960 17th. He won 15 Italian titles between 1939 and 1960 and also set three world records, all in Milan from 53.34m in 1941 to 55.33m in 1948. His best mark was a European record 56.98m in 1955. b. 5 Jan 1917 Costermano; d. 20 Dec 1969.

Ludvik Danek (Cs) won a complete set of Olympic medals, gold 1972, silver 1964 and bronze 1968. At European Championships he won in 1971 and was second in 1974 in five appearances. He won 13 Czechoslovak titles 1963–69, 1971–6, and the 1965 AAU. He set three world records in 1964–6 and had a best of 67.18m in 1974. b. 6 Jan 1937 Horice.

Conversions
Discus, 150 ft = 45.72 m.
160 ft = 48.78 m. 170 ft = 51.82 m. 180 ft = 54.86 m.
190 ft = 57.92 m. 200 ft = 60.96 m. 210 ft = 64.02 m.
220 ft = 67.06 m. 230 ft = 70.10 m. 240 ft = 73.16 m.

Hammer

Romuald Klim, the third of nine USSR throwers to have set world hammer records. (ASP)

The greatest hammer exponents in the early days, from the 1880s, were the Irish-Americans, such as John Flanagan, Pat Ryan and Matt McGrath. In recent years the event has been dominated by throwers from the Eastern bloc, especially the USSR.

WORLD RECORD AT TEN-YEARLY INTERVALS

1905	52.71m	John Flanagan (USA) New York 31 Jul 1904
1915	57.77m	Pat Ryan (USA) New York 17 Aug 1913
1925	57.77m	Pat Ryan (record lasted for 25 years)
1935	57.77m	Pat Ryan
1945	59.00m	Erwin Blask (Ger) Stockholm 27 Aug 1938
	59.55m	unratified—Pat O'Callaghan (Ire) Fermoy 22 Aug 1937
1955	64.52m	Mikhail Krivonosov (USSR) Belgrade 19 Jul 1955
1965	73.74m	Gyula Zsivotzky (Hun) Debrecen 4 Sep 1965
1975	79.30m	Walter Schmidt (GFR) Frankfurt/Main 14 Aug 1975
1985	86.34m	Yuriy Sedykh (USSR) Cork 3 Jul 1984

THE BARRIER BREAKERS—the first to exceed

150ft	John Flanagan (USA) 45.94m Bayonne, NJ 31 May 1897
50m	John Flanagan 50.01m Boston 22 Jul 1899
60m	Jozsef Csermak (Hun) 60.34m Helsinki 24 Jul 1952
200ft	Sverre Strandli (Nor) 61.25m Oslo 14 Sep 1952
70m	Hal Connolly (USA) 70.33m Walnut, Cal. 12 Aug 1960
250ft	Walter Schmidt (GFR) 76.40m Lahr 4 Sep 1971
80m	Boris Zaichuk (USSR) 80.14m Moscow 9 Jul 1978

THE MOST WORLD RECORDS

14 John Flanagan (USA) in pre-IAAF days, from 44.46m at Clonmel, Ireland on 9 Sep 1895 to 56.19m at New Haven, USA on 24 Jul 1909. He emigrated from his native Ireland to the USA in the autumn of 1896 and dominated the event for the next decade. He returned to Ireland in 1911 and in his final international appearance won the hammer for Ireland against Scotland.

7 Hal Connolly (USA). His first record was an unratified 66.71m at Boston on 3 Oct 1956. He set six official records from 68.54m in 1958 to 71.26m in 1956, and competed at four Olympics, winning at his first attempt in 1956.

7 Mikhail Krivonosov (USSR), including one unratified mark, from 63.34m in 1954 to win the European title to 67.32m in 1956, just prior to his Olympic silver medal behind Connolly.

7 James Mitchell (USA), the first of the great Irish-Americans, took the best mark from 36.40m at Limerick in 1886 to 44.21m at New York in 1892.

The greatest display of world record annihilation came from Karl-Hans Riehm (GFR) at Rehlingen on 19 May 1975, when all six of his throws—76.70, 77.56, 77.10, 78.50, 77.16, 77.28—exceeded the previous world record of 76.66m by Aleksey Spiridonov (USSR). Riehm set a further record of 80.32m in 1980, and, after Sergey Litvinov (USSR) had improved the world

The origins of modern hammer throwing date back to throwing the sledge-hammer in England and Scotland in the 15th and 16th centuries, if not earlier. The sledge-head was replaced by a 16lb round iron ball around 1865, although a stiff wooden shaft was still used. The AAA permitted a metal handle from 1896, when piano-wire handles were already in use in the USA. Originally an unlimited run-up was allowed, but in 1878 a 7ft (2.13m) circle was introduced, although for a while this was expanded to 9ft (2.74m) by the AAA.

record to 81.66m, set a personal best of 80.80m the day before the 1984 Olympic final, which his country boycotted that year.

THE BEST CHAMPIONSHIPS RECORDS

Yuriy Sedykh won two Olympic (1976 and 1980), two European (1978 and 1982), a European Junior (1973) and three USSR titles. He also won the World Cup and European Cup Final hammer events in 1981. He won the silver medal at the 1983 World Championships, before regaining his world supremacy in 1984 (see feature).
b. 11 Jun 1955 Novocherkassk.
John Flanagan won the Olympic titles of 1900, 1904 and 1908. He won the AAA title in 1896 and in 1900 and seven AAU titles at the hammer as well as six with the 56lb weight.
b. 9 Jan 1873 Kilbreedy, Co. Limerick, Ireland; d. 4 Jun 1938 Ireland.
Gyula Zsivotzky (Hun) was a highly consistent thrower throughout the 1960s. His championships record: Olympics: 1960 2nd, 1964 2nd, 1968 1st, 1972 5th; European: 1958 3rd, 1962 1st, 1966 2nd, 1969 4th, 1971 11th; World Student Games: 1963 2nd, 1965 1st. He was Hungarian champion each year from 1958 to 1970 and AAA champion in 1965 and 1966. He set two world records, in 1965 and 1968, the latter his best mark of 73.76m.
b. 25 Feb 1937 Budapest.
Romuald Klim (USSR) won gold, then silver at Olympics (1964 and 1968) and Europeans (1966 and 1969 respectively). He also won four USSR titles and the European Cup Finals of 1965 and 1967. His best mark was a world record 74.52m in 1969.
b. 25 May 1933 Khvoyevo.
Dr Pat O'Callaghan (Ire) won the Olympic titles of 1928 and 1932, but was not allowed to compete in 1936 because he was a member of the National Athletic and Cycling Federation of Ireland, which body was not affiliated to the IAAF. For that reason, too, his best mark of 59.55m in 1937 could not be recognized as a world record. He won the AAU title in 1933 and the AAA in 1934.
b. 15 Sep 1905 Kanturk, Co. Cork, Ireland.
Matt McGrath (USA) was Olympic champion in 1912 and won silver medals in 1908 and 1924 at the age of 45. He won seven AAU titles between 1908 and 1926 and set a world record of 57.10m in 1911.
b. 18 Dec 1878 Nenagh, Co. Tipperary, Ireland; d. 29 Jan 1941.

Conversions
Discus, Hammer and Javelin 150 ft = 45.72 m.
160 ft = 48.78 m. 170 ft = 51.82 m. 180 ft = 54.86 m.
190 ft = 57.92 m. 200 ft = 60.96 m. 210 ft = 64.02 m.
220 ft = 67.06 m. 230 ft = 70.10 m. 240 ft = 73.16 m.
250 ft = 76.20 m. 260 ft = 79.26 m. 270 ft = 82.30 m.
280 ft = 85.34 m. 290 ft = 88.40 m. 300 ft = 91.44 m.
310 ft = 94.50 m. 320 ft = 97.54 m. 330 ft = 100.58 m.
340 ft = 103.64 m.

Javelin

Spear throwing was an important hunting technique for prehistoric man, so javelin throwing is one of the most natural of all athletic events. Like the discus, it was included in the ancient Olympic pentathlon, the Greeks using a thong looped over a finger of the throwing hand. This increased the radius of the throwing arm and the resultant spin helped steady the javelin.

The man with the greatest championships record in javelin throwing: Janis Lusis. (Ed Lacey/ASP)

The modern men's javelin weighs 800gm (1.76lb) and is 2.6–2.7m (8.5–8.8ft) in length. The IAAF announced in 1984 that the specification of the men's javelin would change in 1986. The weight would remain the same, but the regulations regarding centre of gravity would alter so as to change the flight characteristics of the javelin and considerably reduce the distances thrown.

The age of the 100-metre throw ushered in by Uwe Hohn means that there are problems in catering for the event within the restricted areas inside stadiums. However, much concern has been expressed by leading javelin throwers about the change, which will dramatically alter the nature of the event. The fact that the javelin would not 'fly' as before would not only be less aesthetically satisfying, but would make the event much more a test of strength rather than skill.

By far the greatest contribution to the event has come from the nations surrounding the Baltic Sea, especially the Finns. At the Olympic Games, Finnish throwers have won six gold, six silver and four bronze medals, with Sweden's tally four, two and three respectively. Many of the top USSR throwers have also come from the Baltic republics, for instance Olympic champions Janis Lusis and Dainis Kula from Latvia.

WORLD RECORD AT TEN-YEARLY INTERVALS

1905	53.79m	Eric Lemming (Swe) Stockholm 31 May 1903
1915	65.81m	Jonni Myyrä (Fin) Lappeenranta 18 Jul 1915
1925	68.55m	Jonni Myyrä (Fin) Richmond, Cal. 27 Sep 1925
1935	76.66m	Matti Järvinen (Fin) Turin 7 Sep 1934
1945	78.70m	Yrjö Nikkanen (Fin) Kotka 11 Oct 1938
1955	81.75m	Franklin 'Bud' Held (USA) Modesto 21 May 1955
1965	91.72m	Terje Pedersen (Nor) Oslo 2 Sep 1964
1975	94.08m	Klaus Wolfermann (GFR) Leverkusen 5 May 1973
1985	104.80m	Uwe Hohn (GDR) East Berlin 20 Jul 1984

THE BARRIER BREAKERS—the first to exceed

50m	Eric Leeming (Swe) 50.44m Jönköping 1902
60m	Mor Koczan (Hun) 60.64m Budapest 26 Oct 1911 (with freestyle grip)
200ft	Julius Saaristo (Fin) 61.45m Helsinki 25 May 1912
70m	Erik Lundqvist (Swe) 71.01m Stockholm 15 Aug 1928
250ft	Matti Järvinen (Fin) 76.66m Turkin 7 Sep 1934
80m	Franklin 'Bud' Held (USA) 80.41m Pasadena 8 Aug 1953
90m/ 300ft	Terje Pedersen (Nor) 91.72m Oslo 2 Sep 1964 (4.60m improvement)
100m	Uwe Hohn (GDR) 104.80m East Berlin 20 Jul 1984 (5.08m improvement)

MOST WORLD RECORDS

10 Matti Järvinen (Fin), from 71.57m at Viipuri on 8 Aug 1930 to 77.23m at Helsinki on 18 Jun 1936. He had 20 competitions over 75m from 1933 to 1940, compared with six for his nearest rival Yrjö Nikkanen.

9 Eric Lemming (Swe). This great pioneer set his first world best of 49.32m at Göteborg on 18 Jun 1899 and, with others also setting world bests during this period, took the record up to 62.32m at Stockholm on 29 Jun 1912. This was the first mark ratified by the IAAF. He was Olympic champion in 1908 and 1912 and won 25 Swedish titles at all events, including ten at javelin.

5 Jonni Myrrä (Fin), from 63.29m in 1914 to 68.56m in 1925, but only one of these, 66.10m in 1919, was recognized by the IAAF. He was Olympic champion in 1920 and 1924 and Finnish champion in 1917 and 1918.

The only occasion on which the world javelin record has twice been improved in one competition was at Modesto on 21 May 1955 when 'Bud' Held threw his personally designed aerodynamic javelin first to 81.29m to equal the old record and then to 81.75m.

THE BEST CHAMPIONSHIPS RECORDS

Janis Lusis (USSR) won four European titles between 1962 and 1971 and won a complete set of Olympic medals—gold 1968, silver 1972, bronze 1964. He won 12 USSR titles between 1962 and 1976, the World Student Games title of 1963, and in four European Cup Finals was first twice and second twice, for an outstandingly consistent record in a notoriously inconsistent event. A fine all-rounder, who was also a world ranked decathlete, he married the 1960 Olympic javelin champion, Elvira Ozolina.
b. 19 May 1939 Jelgava, Latvia.

Matti Järvinen (Fin) won the European title in 1934 and 1938 and the Olympics in 1932, but back injury restricted him to fifth place in 1936. He won eight Finnish titles between 1929 and 1942. His father won Finland's first Olympic gold medal, at Greek style discus in 1906, and his brother Akilles won two Olympic medals and set three world records at the decathlon.
b. 18 Feb 1909 Tampere; d. 22 Jul 1985.

Janusz Sidlo (Pol) competed in five Olympic Games, but only once gained a medal, silver in 1956. He fared better in European Championships, winning in 1954 and 1958 and getting the bronze in 1969. He won 14 Polish titles between 1951 and 1969 and set a world record at 83.66m in 1956, but his best came 14 years later at 86.22m.
b. 19 Jun 1933 Skopienice.

Decathlon

Combined events competitions date back to the pentathlon, comprising wrestling, sprinting (the 192m stade distance), long jump, discus and javelin, held in the Greek Olympic Games from 708 BC. The first combined events competition of the modern era was the AAU all-round championship in the USA, which was first held in 1884 with the following events: 100y, SP, HJ, 880y walk, HT, PV, 120yh, 56lb weight, LJ and 1 mile (completed in a day!). Such an event was included in the 1904 Olympic Games. The intercalated Games of 1906 included a pentathlon of the classical events, but from 1912 the decathlon has been the standard event, although a pentathlon of LJ, JT, 200m, DT and 1500m was also included in the three Olympic Games from 1912 to 1924.

The ten events of the decathlon are 100m, long jump, shot, high jump and 400m on the first day and 110m hurdles, discus, pole vault, javelin and 1500m on the second day.

Decathlons are scored on tables approved by the IAAF. New tables have been issued in 1912, 1920, 1934, 1950 (modified in 1952), 1962 and 1984 to take account of changing standards. The latest tables also have a slightly different basis in that separate tables are given for hand and automatic timing, reflecting the IAAF approved differentials between these systems of 0.24sec for 100m, 200m and 110mh and 0.14sec for 400m.

The discus was one of the best events for Bob Mathias, here throwing at Wembley in 1948, when he won his first Olympic title. (OPA)

WORLD RECORD PROGRESSION AT TEN-YEARLY INTERVALS

Showing performances scored on three tables

	1952T	1962T	1984T	
1915	6267	6756	6564	Jim Thorpe (USA) Stockholm 13–15 July 1912*
1925				Jim Thorpe as above. Ratified record:
	6163	6668	6476	Harold Osborn (USA) Paris 11–12 Jul 1924†
1935	7135	7292	7147	Hans-Heinrich Sievert (Ger) Hamburg 7–8 Jul 1934†
1945	7310	7421	7254	Glenn Morris (USA) Berlin 7–8 Aug 1936**
1955	7985	7758	7608	Rafer Johnson (USA) Kingsburg 10–11 Jun 1955
1965	9121	8089	8009	Yang Chuang-Kwang (Tai) Walnut, Cal. 27–28 Apr 1963
	8709	8155	8049	Phil Mulkey (USA) Memphis 16–17 Jun 1961
1975		8524	8420	Bruce Jenner (USA) Eugene 9–10 Aug 1975
1985		8797	8846	Daley Thompson (UK) Los Angeles 8–9 Aug 1984
		8798	8832	Jürgen Hingsen (GFR) Mannheim 9 Jun 1984

*Originally 8412.955 points on the 1912 Tables. Thorpe's record was not ratified as he was disqualified for minor payments received for playing baseball. He was reinstated as Olympic champion in 1984.
†Original scores on the 1920 Tables: Osborn 7710.775, Sievert 8790.460.
**Original score on the 1934 Tables: 7900.

MOST WORLD RECORDS

Except where otherwise stated all scores are on the 1984 Tables.

4 Paavo Yrjölä (Fin), three recognized by the IAAF: 6460 in 1926, 6566 in 1927 and 6587 in 1928, and an unrecognized 6700 in 1930. His second record, at 8018.99, was the first to exceed 8000 on the 1920 Tables. His third record was when he won the 1928 Olympic title with 8053.20 points. The score by the runner-up on that occasion, Akilles Järvinen (Fin), at 7931.500 is higher than Yrjölä's on the three subsequent scoring systems (6645 on the 1984 Tables). Exactly the same thing happened to Järvinen in 1932, when second to Jim Bausch (USA), 8462.230 to 8292.480 then, but 6735 to 6879 on the 1984 Tables.

4 Daley Thompson (UK) with 8648 in 1980, 8730 and 8774 in 1982, 8846 in 1984. The last record was when he won the Olympic title in Los Angeles. His final score was computed as 8797 points (on the 1962 Tables), which was just one point behind the world record set by Jürgen Hingsen (GFR) two months earlier. However, on the 1984 Tables, Thompson's score is 8846 and Hingsen's 8832.

THE BEST CHAMPIONSHIPS RECORDS

Daley Thompson has the unique record of being Olympic (1980 and 1984), World (1983), European (1982) and Commonwealth (1978 and 1982) champion. He was also European Junior champion in 1977 and second in the 1978 European championships. He won 16 of the 25 decathlons he contested 1975–1984, and apart from two in which he did not finish, was undefeated at nine in succession since 1978, demonstrating a supreme competitive ability in major events.
b. 30 Jul 1958 Notting Hill, London.

Bob Mathias (USA) won the 1948 Olympic title at the age of 17, still the youngest ever male Olympic medallist at any event. He set three world records, 7287 in 1950, 7543 and 7592 in 1952, the latter when retaining his Olympic title. He won four AAU titles, 1948–50 and 1952 and won all eleven decathlons that he contested, but has later regretted retiring before he might have reached his peak. He starred in a film version of

PERSONAL BESTS OF FAMOUS DECATHLETES

Event	THOMPSON	HINGSEN	JENNER	TOOMEY	JOHNSON	MATHIAS	YRJÖLA
100m	10.36	10.74	10.7	10.3	10.3	10.8	11.6
LJ	8.01	8.04	7.32	7.87	7.76	7.15	6.76
SP	16.10	16.42	15.35	14.38	16.75	16.05	14.72
HJ	2.14i	2.18	2.03	2.00	1.91	1.90	1.87
400m	46.86	47.65	47.51	45.6	47.9	50.2	51.7
110mh	14.26	14.07	14.3	14.3	13.8	13.8	15.5
DT	48.62	50.82	53.30	47.00	52.50	52.83	43.34
PV	5.20	5.10	4.87	4.27	4.10	4.00	3.30
JT	65.38	67.42	69.48	68.78	76.75	62.21	62.15
1500m	4:20.3	4:12.3	4:12.6	4:12.7	4:49.7	4:50.8	4:34.8

Of those not detailed above, Bruce Jenner set three world records, capped by 8634 to win the 1976 Olympic title, Bill Toomey set two world records (best 8309 in 1969) and was the 1968 Olympic champion. Jürgen Hingsen finished runner-up to Thompson at the 1982 European, 1983 World and 1984 Olympics, and set three world records to 8832 in 1984.

his life in 1954 and was elected a US Congressman in 1966.
b. 17 Nov 1930 Tulare, Cal.
Rafer Johnson (USA) won nine of the eleven decathlons he contested including the 1960 Olympics, 1955 Pan-American and three AAU titles. He set three world records: 7608 in 1955, 7789 in 1958 and 7981 in 1960. He subsequently became a film star.
b. 18 Aug 1934 Hillsboro, Texas.

After silver at the 1956 Olympics, Rafer Johnson won the decathlon gold in Rome. (All-Sport)

35lb Weight

The 35lb (15.88kg) weight has been contested at the US indoor championships since 1932. Thrown like the hammer, the event provides useful winter competition for throwers. It is only occasionally contested outside the USA.

WORLD BEST AT TEN-YEARLY INTERVALS
(i=indoors)

1915	19.00m	Pat Ryan (USA) New York 5 Jul 1915
1925	19.33m	Pat McDonald (USA) New York 30 May 1918 (record until 1954)
1955	19.33m	Pat McDonald, and Bob Backus (USA) New York (i) 20 Feb 1954
1965	21.70m	Hal Connolly (USA) New York (i) 20 Feb 1960
1975	22.34m	George Frenn (USA) Boston (i) 1 Feb 1969
1985	23.94m	Tore Johnsen (Nor) Air Academy, Col. (i) 25 Feb 1984

THE BARRIER BREAKERS—the first to exceed

15m/50ft Matt McGrath (USA) 16.43m New York 28 May 1911
20m Hal Connolly (USA) 20.33m Medford, Mass. 31 Dec 1956

Three world bests in one competition were achieved by Pat Ryan: 18.46m, 18.93m and 19.00m at New York on 5 Jul 1915, and by Yuriy Sedykh (USSR): 23.00m, 23.35m and 23.46m at Montreal (i) on 10 Mar 1979.

Walking Events

The IAAF currently ratify records at just four track walking events—at 20, 30 and 50 kilometres and at 2 hours. At one time their list embraced a large number of distances, but the shorter distance records were dropped due in particular to difficulties in judging whether walkers were maintaining the strict disciplines of the event. The standard road walking events have become established at 20 and 50 kilometres.

THE BARRIER BREAKERS FOR THE MOST IMPORTANT DISTANCES—the first to better: (R—road walk, t—track walk)

20 KILOMETRES

1hr 30min: Konstantin Kudrov (USSR) 1:29:11.8t Minsk 10 May 1955 (unratified); Leonid Spirin (USSR) 1:28:45.2t Kiev 13 Jun 1956

50 KILOMETRES

4hr: Gennadiy Agapov (USSR) 3:55:36R Alma-Ata 17 Oct 1965

The most official world track records at the four IAAF events is **5** by **Peter Frenkel** (GDR): 2 at 20kmW (1:25:50.0 in 1979 and 1:25:19.4 in 1972), 1 at 30kmW (2:14:21.2 in 1974), 2 at 2 hours (26 658m in 1971 and 26 930m in 1974).

THE BEST CHAMPIONSHIPS RECORDS

Vladimir Golubnichiy (USSR) competed in five Olympic 20km walks, winning in 1960 and 1964, 2nd in 1972, 3rd in 1964 and 7th in 1976. He also won a complete set of European 20kmW medals: 1st 1974, 2nd 1966 and 3rd 1962, and was Lugano Trophy runner-up in 1967 and 1970. He set his first world record, 1:30:35.2 for 20km at the age of 19 in 1955, and his best ever 20km time was 1:23:55 (road) 21 years later.
b. 2 Jun 1936 Sumy, Ukraine.
Abdon Pamich (Ita) excelled at 50km at which he was Olympic champion in 1964 (3rd 1960, 4th 1956) and European champion in 1962 and 1966 (2nd 1958). He also amassed 40 Italian titles at various distances. He set a world track record at 4:14:02.4 in 1961 and walked a road 50km best of 4:03:02 in 1960.
b. 3 Oct 1933 Fiume.
Christoph Höhne (GDR) won the Olympic 50kmW in 1968 and the European 50kmW in 1969 and 1974 (2nd 1971). He also won three Lugano Trophy 50km finals. He set two world records for 50km—4:10:51.8 in 1965 and 4:08:05.0 in 1969 and had a road best of 3:52:53 in 1974.
b. 12 Feb 1941 Borsdorf.
Venyamin Soldatenko (USSR) won the inaugural world 50km walk in 1976, when the event was temporarily dropped from the Olympics, at which he had won the silver medal in 1972. He also won a complete set of European 50kmW medals: 1st 1971, 2nd 1978, 3rd 1969. He set a world track record of 4:03:42.6 in 1972 and had a road best of 3:53:24 in 1978.
b. 4 Jan 1939 Alma-Ata.

Two 20km walk champions: (top right) **Vladimir Golubnichiy** after winning the 1974 European title, 14 years after his first Olympic victory; (bottom right) **Ernesto Canto** maintained a great tradition by winning the 1984 Olympic title. Mexico has won five Olympic athletics medals, all by walkers since 1968. (Keystone Press, Mark Shearman)

Abdon Pamich secured a great record at the 50km walk, and here seems fresh after a race almost twice as far, having won the 1965 London to Brighton walk. (Keystone Press)

WORLD RECORDS AND BESTS—TRACK WALKS

		hr:min:sec			
1500m	5:20.32	Martin Toporek (Aut)	Vienna	11 Sep 1982
1 mile	5:45.15	Martin Toporek (Aut)	Vienna	11 Sep 1982
3000m	10:54.6	Carlo Mattioli (Ita)	Milan	6 Feb 1980
5000m	18:51.2	Jozef Pribilinec (Cs)	Banska Bystrica	5 May 1981
10km	38:02.60	Jozef Pribilinec (Cs)	Banska Bystrica	31 Aug 1985
15km	59:30.0	Valdas Kaslauskas (USSR)	Moscow	16 Sep 1983
10 miles	1:05:07.6	Domingo Colin (Mex)	Fana	26 May 1979
20km	1:18:40.0	Ernesto Canto (Mex)	Fana	5 May 1984
15 miles	1:42:18.0	Reima Salonen (Fin)	Raisio	1 Sep 1979
25km	1:44:54.0	Maurizio Damilano (Ita)	San Donato Milanese	5 May 1985
30km	2:06:07.3	Maurizio Damilano (Ita)	San Donato Milanese	5 May 1985
20 miles	2:22:09.9	Raul Gonzales (Mex)	Förde	19 May 1978
30 miles	3:34:16.3	Raul Gonzales (Mex)	Fana	25 May 1979
50km	3:41:38.4	Raul Gonzales (Mex)	Fana	25 May 1979
100km	9:23:58.6	Roger Quemener (Fra)	Saint Maur	28 Mar 1976
	kilometres			
1hr	15.253	Ernesto Canto (Mex)	Fana	5 May 1984
2hrs	28.565	Maurizio Damilano (Ita)	San Donato Milanese	5 May 1985

WORLD BESTS—ROAD WALKS

Where superior to track bests and walked on
properly measured road courses.

		hr:min:sec			
25km	1:45:52	Hartwig Gauder (GDR)	Grasleben	20 Jul 1980
30km	2:03:06	Daniel Bautista (Mex)	Cherkassy	27 Apr 1980
50km	3:38:32	Ronald Weigel (GDR)	East Berlin	20 Jul 1984
100km	8:58:12	Gérard Lelièvre (Fra)	Laval	7 Oct 1984
	kilometres			
24 hours	228.930	Jesse Casteneda (USA)	Albuquerque	18–19 Sep 1976

It should be noted that road times must be assessed with care as course conditions can vary considerably.

The first official list of women's world records was issued by the Fédération Sportive Féminine Internationale (FSFI) in 1927. The IAAF have ratified women's records since 1935.

100 Metres

From 1976, as for all sprint events, records have been recognized only if timed on fully automatic electrical devices. In these tables the best known automatic timings (in hundredths) are shown as well as the hand-timed records prior to that date.

WORLD RECORD AT TEN-YEARLY INTERVALS
(unratified times prior to 1945)

1925	12.2	Helene Junker (Ger) Wiesbaden 13 Sep 1925
1935	11.6	Helen Stephens (USA) Kansas City 8 Jun 1935 and Cleveland 14 Sep 1935
1945	11.5	Helen Stephens (USA) Memphis 15 May 1936 and Dresden 10 Aug 1936
	11.5	Fanny Blankers-Koen (Hol) Amsterdam 5 Sep 1943
1955	11.3	Shirley Strickland (Aus) Warsaw 4 Aug 1955
1965	11.1	Irena Kirszenstein (Pol) Prague 9 Jul 1965
	11.1	Wyomia Tyus (USA) Kiev 31 Jul 1965
1975	10.8	(11.07 auto) Renate Stecher (GDR) Dresden 20 Jul 1973
	11.07	Renate Stecher Munich 2 Sep 1972
1985	10.76	Evelyn Ashford (USA) Zürich 22 Aug 1984

THE BARRIER BREAKERS—the first to better

13 sec Maria Kiessling (Ger) 12.9 Munich 29 Aug 1920
12 sec Tollien Schuurman (Hol) 11.9 Haarlem 5 Jun 1932
11 sec Renate Stecher (GDR) 10.9 Ostrava 7 Jun 1973 (auto-timing): Marlies Oelsner (GDR) 10.88 Dresden 1 Jul 1977

MOST WORLD RECORDS

10 Stanislawa Walasiewicz (Pol), known in the USA as Stella Walsh. Many of her best times were not put forward for official ratification, but at 100m she had four times recognized by the FSFI and two by the IAAF, from 11.9 in 1932 to 11.6 in 1937. She was reported to have run an extraordinary 11.2 at Cleveland in 1945. At 200m she recorded five improvements on the world record. She won the Olympic 100m in 1932 and was second in 1936, won the 100m/200m double at the 1938 Europeans (as well as silver at long jump) and a total of 40 AAU titles in the USA between 1930 and 1954 at a wide variety of events. However, her femininity has been questioned, particularly when a post-mortem following her murder in 1980 revealed that 'she' had male sex organs but no female ones.

9 Renate Stecher (née Meissner) (GDR) equalled or bettered the hand timed world record in 1970–3 on eight occasions, of which five were ratified, at 11.0, 10.9 and 10.8. On automatic timing she twice ran a record 11.07, one of which was her hand-timed 10.8.

THE BEST CHAMPIONSHIPS RECORDS

Marlies Göhr (GDR) excelled at 100m, at which she won European titles in 1978 and 1982 and was World champion in 1983. She started her international career with the silver medal (and relay gold) in the 1975 European Juniors. The following year she was eighth at her first Olympics and was surprisingly only second in 1980 to Lyudmila Kondratyeva (USSR). She won the 100m at five successive European Cup Finals, the World Cup of 1981 and 1985, and won nine successive GDR 100m titles from 1977 to 1985. At 200m she won the 1978 European silver medal and three GDR titles, and at 50/60m she won five European indoor titles. In addition, on the GDR sprint relay team she won two Olympic, one World and one European gold medal. She set three world records at 100m, nine at 4×100m relay and one at 4×200m relay.
b. 21 Mar 1958 Gera.

Wyomia Tyus (USA), 1964 and 1968, is the only double Olympic 100m gold medallist. She won three US championships at 100y/100m and two at 200m/220y. At the longer distance she was also Pan-American champion in 1967 and sixth in the 1968 Olympics. Her best 100m time was 11.08, ratified as a world record at 11.0, to win the 1968 Olympic title, and she also set two world records for 100y at 10.3 in 1965 and 1968.
b. 29 Aug 1945 Griffin, Georgia.

Renate Stecher's record was Olympics: 100m 1st 1972, 2nd 1976; 200m 1st 1972, 3rd 1976; Europeans: 100m 1st 1971, 2nd 1974; 200m 1st 1971, 2nd 1969 and 1974. She also won four European indoor sprint titles, the World Student Games 100m/200m double in 1970 and nine GDR titles,

Renate Stecher (l) set a world record of 22.40 when she just beat Raelene Boyle, 22.45, in the 1972 Olympic 200 metres. (Ed Lacey)

Marlies Göhr, ranked in the world's top two for 100m each year from 1977 to 1985. (Mark Shearman)

five at 100m, four at 200m. Add to that five individual victories in European Cup Finals for supremacy for this powerfully built sprinter at the start of the seventies. In addition to her 100m world records she set three at 200m, with a best of 22.38 (22.1 hand) in 1973.
b. 12 May 1950 Suptitz.

Marjorie Jackson (later Nelson) (Aus), known as the 'Lithgow Flash', was undefeated in major competition, with the 100m/200m double at the 1952 Olympics and the 100y/220y double at the 1950 and 1954 Commonwealth Games.
b. 13 Sep 1931 Coffs Harbour, New South Wales.

100 Yards

The event was, with other imperial distances, deleted from the official IAAF lists in 1976.

WORLD RECORD AT TEN-YEARLY INTERVALS

1925	11.0	Rosa Grosse (Can) Toronto 2 Jun 1925
	11.0	Fanny Rosenfeld (Can) Toronto 19 Sep 1925
1935	10.4	Helen Stephens (USA) in handicap race Toronto 2 Sep 1935
	11.0	official record
1945	10.4	Helen Stephens as above
	10.8	Fanny Blankers-Koen (Hol) Amsterdam 18 May 1944 (official)
1955	10.4	Marjorie Jackson (Aus) Sydney 8 Mar 1952
1965	10.3	Marlene Mathews/Willard (Aus) Sydney 20 Mar 1958
	10.3	Wyomia Tyus (USA) Kingston, Jamaica 17 Jul 1965
1975	10.0	Chi Cheng (Tai) Portland 13 Jun 1970

THE BARRIER BREAKERS—the first to better

12 sec Mary Lines (UK) 11.8 Paris 30 Oct 1921

11 sec Stanislawa Walasiewicz* (Pol) 10.8 Philadelphia 30 May 1930, Myrtle Cook (Can) Cornwall 4 Aug 1930
(*doubtful gender—see 100 metres)

MOST WORLD RECORDS

4 Marjorie Jackson (Aus) set the most officially ratified records, 10.8 (twice) and 10.7 in 1950 and 10.4 in 1952. She ran a wind assisted 10.3 in 1953. She also ran world records: at 100 m—11.5 and 11.4; at 200m—23.6 and 23.4, all in 1952; and two more at 220y in 1950 and 1954.

200 Metres

WORLD RECORD AT TEN-YEARLY INTERVALS

1925	26.0	(for 220 yards) Fanny Rosenfeld (Can) Toronto 22 Aug 1925
1935	23.6	by Stanislawa Walasiewicz* (Pol) Warsaw 15 Aug 1935 accepted as a world record, but track found to be 12cm short.
	24.4	Helen Stephens (USA) St Louis 1 Jun 1935
1945	23.6	Walasiewicz* as above, then:
	24.1	Helen Stephens (USA) Wuppertal 19 Aug 1936
1955	23.4	(23.59 auto) Marjorie Jackson (Aus) Helsinki 25 Jul 1952
1965	22.7	Irena Kirszenstein (Pol) Warsaw 8 Aug 1965
1975	22.21	Irena Szewinska (née Kirszenstein) Potsdam 13 Jun 1974
1985	21.71	Marita Koch (GDR) Karl-Marx-Stadt 10 Jun 1979 and Potsdam 21 Jul 1984

THE BARRIER BREAKERS—the first to better

26 sec Eileen Edwards (UK) 25.8 (for 220y) Romford 18 Sep 1926
25 sec Kinue Hitomi (Jap) 24.7 Miyoshino 19 May 1929, (straight track) Tollien Schuurman (Hol) 24.6 Scharebeek 13 Aug 1933
24 sec Stanislawa Walasiewicz* (Pol) 23.8w Osaka 14 Oct 1934 (straight), 23.6 (12cm short) Warsaw 15 Aug 1935, 23.8 Vienna 18 Sep 1938 Helen Stephens (USA) 23.9 for 220y Toronto 31 Aug 1935 (straight) Marjorie Jackson (Aus) 23.6 Helsinki 25 Jul 1952
23 sec Wilma Rudolph (USA) 22.9 Corpus Christi 9 Jul 1960
22 sec Marita Koch (GDR) 21.71 Karl-Marx-Stadt 10 Jun 1979
*Doubtful gender (see above), but many of her performances were accepted as world records.

MOST WORLD RECORDS

4 Irena Szewinska (née Kirszenstein) (Pol) set her first world record at the age of 19 with 22.7 in 1965. After equalling that in 1967 she ran 22.58 to win the 1968 Olympic title in 1968 and finally improved to 22.21 in 1974. She also set two world records at 100m and three at 400m.
4 Marita Koch (GDR) from 22.06 in 1978 to 21.71 in 1984—see feature.
4 Eileen Edwards (UK) 26.2 twice at 220y in 1924, 25.8y in 1926 and 25.3 at Berlin in 1927. She won the 1926 World Games 250m title and WAAA 100y/220y titles in 1924 and 1927.

THE BEST CHAMPIONSHIPS RECORDS

Irena Szewinska had on her retirement an undoubted claim to the title of the greatest woman athlete of all time. Perhaps her successor Marita Koch can now challenge that claim, but even she has yet to match Szewinska's tally of medals or placings at major meetings at track events from 60m to 400m and the long jump:

	Individual			Relay		
	1st	2nd	3rd	1st	2nd	3rd
Olympics	2	2	2	1	–	–
Europeans	4	1	2	1	–	2
European Junior	1	1	–			
European Indoor	2	1	2			
World Cup	2	–	1	–	1	–
European Cup	4	2	3	1	–	1
World Student Games	2	–	–	–	–	–

She won the Olympic title with a world record at 200m in 1968 and repeated the feat at 400m in 1976. Yet over and above her sheer competitive brilliance she was truly the 'Queen of the sport', setting the highest standards of graciousness and ability. She set 38 Polish records at all events and won 19 Polish titles at four individual events.
b. 24 May 1946 Leningrad. She married her coach Janusz Szewinski on 25 Dec 1967 and gave birth to a son Andrzej in 1970.
Bärbel Wöckel (née Eckert) (GDR) won Olympic titles at 200m (and sprint relay) in 1976 and 1980 and the European 200m title in 1982. She had started her international career with European Junior titles at 200m and 100mh in 1973. At 100m she won the European silver medal in 1982. Her best times: 100m 10.95 in 1982, 200m 21.85 in 1984, 400m 49.56 in 1982, and she ran on four GDR world record relay teams, three at 4×100m and one at 4×200m.
b. 21 Mar 1955 Leipzig.
Raelene Boyle (Aus) won the Commonwealth 100m/200m/sprint relay treble in 1970 and 1974, added a silver at 200m in 1978 and moved up to win a gold at 400m in 1982. She won three Olympic silver medals: at 200m in 1968 and 1972 and at 100m in 1972. Her best 200m was 22.45 in the 1972 Olympic final.
b. 24 Jun 1951 Victoria.

400 Metres

The event was added to the official IAAF lists in 1957. It became a European championship event in 1958 and an Olympic one in 1964. The USSR included a 400m in their inaugural championships in 1922, and again in 1928, but the event was not run regularly even there until the 1930s.

WORLD RECORD AT TEN-YEARLY INTERVALS

1925	60.8	(440y) Eileen Edwards (UK) London 11 Jul 1924
1935	56.8	(440y) Nellie Halstead (UK) London 9 Jul 1932
1945	56.8	(440y) Nellie Halstead as above
1955	53.9	Maria Itkina (USSR) Bucharest 1 Oct 1955
1965	51.2	Shin Keum Dan (NKo) Pyongyang 21 Oct 1964
1975	49.9	Irena Szewinska (Pol) Warsaw 22 Jun 1974
	50.14	Riitta Salin (Fin) Rome 4 Sep 1974 (best auto)
1985	47.60	Marita Koch (GDR) Canberra 6 Oct 1985

THE BARRIER BREAKERS—the first to better

70 sec	Lidia Charushnikova (USSR) 65.0 Viatka 12 Jul 1921
65 sec	Mary Lines (UK) 64.4 for 440y London 18 Jul 1922
60 sec	Kinue Hitomi (Jap) 59.0 Myashino 5 May 1928
55 sec	Zinaida Safronova (USSR) 54.8 Leningrad 21 Jul 1955
50 sec	Irena Szewinska (Pol) 49.9 Warsaw 22 Jun 1974 Christine Brehmer (GDR) 49.77 Dresden 9 May 1976 (first auto)

MOST WORLD RECORDS

7 Marita Koch (GDR) was the third woman to run 400m in under 50 sec, and took the record from 49.19 in 1978 to 48.16 to win the 1982 European title. After losing the record to Jarmila Kratochvilova's 47.99 in 1983, she regained it at the 1985 World Cup (see feature for full list).
5 Shin Keum Dan (NKo) from 53.0 in 1962 to 51.2 in 1964. Only one of these records, and none of those she set at 800m, were recognized by the IAAF as North Korea was suspended from membership of the IAAF due to its participation in the unsanctioned GANEFO (Games of the New Emerging Forces) meeting in Djakarta in 1963. She had a great margin of superiority over the rest of the world—when she ran 400m in 51.4 in 1963 it was 1.7 sec faster than the world's second best and her 1:58.0 for 800m in 1964 was 3.1 sec better than the official world record set by Ann Packer (UK).

THE BEST CHAMPIONSHIPS RECORDS

Marita Koch (GDR)—see feature.
Jarmila Kratochvilova (Cs) was runner-up to Marita Koch at the 1980 Olympics and 1982 Europeans, but beat her in the 1981 World Cup 400m, and while Koch concentrated on the sprints, won an unprecedented double at 400m (world record 47.99) and 800m at the 1983 World Championships. She followed that with an even more unusual double, 200m and 800m in the 1983 European Cup final. In 1985 she again won the European Cup Final 800m. In successive years from 1981 she was European Indoor champion three times at 400m and once at 200m.
b. 26 Jan 1951 Golcuv Jenikov.
Maria Itkina (USSR) won the first two European 400m titles, in 1958 and 1962, following her 200m victory in 1954. She went on to place fifth in the 1964 Olympic 400m. She won 14 Soviet titles, four each at 100m and 400m, six at 200m. She ran a world best 53.9 in 1955, and then, after the IAAF accepted the event, ran four official records from 54.0 in 1957 to 53.4 in 1962. Her best ever 400m was 52.9 in 1965.
b. 3 Feb 1932 Smolensk.

800 Metres

The 800 metres was one of the inaugural women's events at the 1928 Olympics, but it was not included again until 1960. It was held as an American championship event in 1927 and 1928, but not again until 1958. It was, however, a WAAA event from 1923 and included in most major European national championships.

Lillian Board (98) is poised to strike for home and win the 1969 European 800m title. Vera Nikolic (313) took the bronze. (All-Sport)

WORLD RECORD AT TEN-YEARLY INTERVALS

1925	2:24.0	(880y) Edith Trickey (UK) London 1 Aug 1925
1935	2:15.6	Nellie Halstead (UK) London 10 Aug 1935
1945	2:12.0	Yekdokiya Vasilyeva (USSR) Moscow 5 Aug 1943
1955	2:05.0	Nina Otkalenko (USSR) Zagreb 24 Sep 1955
1965	1:58.0	Shin Keum Dan (NKo) Pyongyang 5 Sep 1964
1975	1:57.48	Svetla Zlateva (Bul) Athens 24 Aug 1973
1985	1:53.28	Jarmila Kratochvilova (Cs) Munich 26 Jul 1983

THE BARRIER BREAKERS—the first to better

2:30	Mary Lines (UK) 2:26.6 for 880y London 30 Sep 1922
2:20	Inge Gentzel (Swe) 2:19.2 Amsterdam 1 Jul 1928
2:10	Nina Pletnyova (later Otkalenko) (USSR) 2:08.5 Kiev 15 Jun 1952
2:00	Shim Keum Dan (NKo) 1:59.1 Djakarta 12 Nov 1963

MOST WORLD RECORDS

Nina Otkalenko (née Pletnyova) (USSR) ran seven world records, of which five were ratified, from 2:12.0 in 1951 to 2:05.0 in 1955. She was European champion in 1954 and won four Soviet titles, 1951–54.

The women's 800m was first included in the European Championships in 1954. Nina Otkalenko won in 2:08.8 from Diane Leather 2:09.8. (ASP)

THE BEST CHAMPIONSHIPS RECORDS

Vera Nikolic (Yug) won the European titles of 1966 and 1971, and was third in 1969. She was fifth at the 1972 Olympics, and won the 1966 European Junior title. She was the first Yugoslav athlete ever to set a world record when she ran 2:00.5 to win the 1968 WAAA title from her great rival Lillian Board. Her best ever time was 1:59.62 in 1972. Firm favourite for the 1968 Olympic title, she dropped out in her semi-final, overcome by nerves.
b. 23 Sep 1948 Ouprija.

1000 Metres

This event was added to the world record lists by the IAAF in 1984. The best ever performance is 2:30.6 by Tatyana Providokhina (USSR) at Podolsk on 20 Aug 1978.
The first sub-3 minute time was run by Yevdokiya Vasilyeva (USSR) 2:58.4 Moscow 23 Aug 1936.

1500 Metres

The first record accepted by the IAAF was 4:17.3 by Anne Smith (UK) en route to her mile record on 3 Jun 1967.
The 1500m was first run in a major championship at the 1969 Europeans, when it was won by Jaroslava Jehlickova (Cs) in a world record 4:10.7, and it was first run at the Olympics in 1972. The first national championship at 1500m was that of the USSR in 1922.

WORLD RECORD AT TEN-YEARLY INTERVALS

1935	5:07.0	Anna Mushkina (USSR) Alma-Ata 16 Sep 1934
1945	4:38.0	Yevdokiya Vasilyeva (USSR) Moscow 17 Aug 1944
1955	4:25.0	Diane Leather (UK) London 21 Sep 1955 (unofficial time in 1 mile race)
1965	4:19.0	Marise Chamberlain (NZ) Perth 8 Dec 1962
1975	4:01.38	Lyudmila Bragina (USSR) Munich 9 Sep 1972
1985	3:52.47	Tatyana Kazankina (USSR) Zürich 13 Aug 1980

THE BARRIER BREAKERS—the first to better

5:00 Yevdokiya Vasilyeva (USSR) 4:47.2 Moscow 30 Jul 1936
4:30 Diane Leather (UK) 4:25.0 London 21 Sep 1955
4:00 Tatyana Kazankina (USSR) 3:56.0 Podolsk 28 Jun 1976

Mary Decker (492) leads the 1500m field at the 1983 World Championships. Others include (l–r) Yekaterina Podkopayeva (463 – 3rd), Gabriella Dorio (267 – 7th), Zamira Zaytseva (476 – 2nd). (ASP)

MOST WORLD RECORDS

4   Lyudmila Bragina (USSR), including three, in heat, semi-final and final of the 1972 Olympic Games in Munich. She had run her first record, 4:06.9, in Moscow in July 1972, before the Olympics, at which she ran 4:06.47, 4:05.07 and 4:01.38 to usher in a new era in women's distance running. She won six USSR titles between 1968 and 1974, and returned to the Olympics for fifth place in 1976.

THE BEST CHAMPIONSHIPS RECORDS

Tatyana Kazankina (USSR) achieved the unique Olympic double of 800m and 1500m in 1976, and retained her 1500m title in 1980. She had started her major championships career with fourth in the 1974 European 800m and later moved up to 3000m, at which in 1983 she was third in the World Championships and won at the European Cup Final. She set three world records at 1500m, and one each at 2000m, 3000m and 4×800m relay. She was the first sub-4 minute women's

1500m runner and her 3:52.47 at Zürich in 1980 remains unapproached. In 1984 she was suspended when her team manager refused to allow her to take a drugs test following a race in Paris.

b. 17 Dec 1951 Petrovsk. She had babies in 1978 and 1982.

Gunhild Hoffmeister (GDR) at 1500m won Olympic silver medals in 1972 and 1976, European gold in 1974 and silver in 1971. At 800m she won European silver in 1974 and Olympic bronze in 1972. She won 14 GDR titles, eight at 1500m and six at 800m between 1968 and 1976. Her best 1500m was 4:01.4 in 1976.

b. 6 Jul 1944 Forst. She has been a member of the GDR parliament.

1 Mile

The first women's mile record recognized by the IAAF was 4:37.0 by Anne Smith (UK) at Chiswick, London on 3 Jun 1967.

WORLD RECORD AT TEN-YEARLY INTERVALS

1945	5:15.3	Evelyne Forster (UK) London 22 Jul 1939
1955	4:45.0	Diane Leather (UK) London 21 Sep 1955
1965	4:41.4	Marise Chamberlain (NZ) Perth 8 Dec 1962
1975	4:28.5	Francie Larrieu (USA) indoors Richmond, Va. 3 Mar 1975
	4:29.5	Paola Pigni (Ita) Viareggio 8 Aug 1973
1985	4:15.8	Natalya Artyemova (USSR) Leningrad 5 Aug 1984 (unratified)
	4:16.71	Mary Slaney (USA) Zürich 21 Aug 1985

BARRIER BREAKERS—the first to better

5:30	Gladys Lunn (UK) 5:23.0 London 18 Jul 1936
5:00	Diane Leather (UK) 4:59.6 Birmingham 29 May 1954
4:30	Francie Larrieu (USA) 4:28.5 indoors at Richmond, Va. on 3 Mar 1975, although Adrienne Beames (Aus) had run an unconfirmed 4:28.8 at Narrabeen on 7 Jan 1972.

MOST WORLD RECORDS

5 Diane Leather (later Mrs Charles), before records for the event were recognized by the IAAF, from 5:07.6 in 1953 to 4:45.0 in 1955.

2000 Metres

This event was added to the world record lists by the IAAF in 1984. In that year Zola Budd, Mary Decker and Tatyana Kazankina successively improved the best ever time, the latter running 5:28.72 at Moscow on 5 August.

3000 Metres

The event was added to the international programme in 1974, when the first IAAF record was set at 8:52.74 by Lyudmila Bragina (USSR) and the European title was won by Nina Holmen (Fin) with 8:55.10.

The first national championship at this distance was the 1968 WAAA race won by Carol Firth in 10:06.4.

WORLD RECORD AT TEN-YEARLY INTERVALS

1975	8:46.6	Grete Waitz (Nor) Oslo 21 Jun 1976
1985	8:22.62	Tatyana Kazankina (USSR) Leningrad 26 Aug 1984

THE BARRIER BREAKERS—the first to better

10:00	Hannelore Suppe (GDR) 9:50.0 in 1966
9:30	Paola Pigni (Ita) 9:22.0 Milan 9 Sep 1969
9:00	Lyudmila Bragina (USSR) 8:53.0 Moscow 12 Aug 1972
8:30	Lyudmila Bragina 8:27.12 College Park, Md. 7 Aug 1976

MOST WORLD RECORDS

4 Paola Cacchi (née Pigni) (Ita) all prior to IAAF ratification of records for this event. In 1969 she ran times of 9:42.8, 9:38.0 and 9:22.0 and in 1972 improved to 9:09.4. Her best ever was 8:56.6 in 1973. Probably best suited to longer distances, she nonetheless won bronze medals in the 1969 European 1500m and 1972 Olympic 800m. She won 13 Italian titles at distances from 400m to 3000m.

3 Lyudmila Bragina (USSR), who improved her first IAAF record to 8:52.74 in 1974 and then took an astonishing 18.28 secs off Grete Waitz's record, when she ran 8:27.12 to win for the USSR against the USA in 1976.

THE BEST CHAMPIONSHIPS RECORDS

Svyetlana Ulmasova (USSR) won European titles in 1978 and 1982, and the 1979 World Cup 3000m and was fourth in the 1983 World Championships. She set a world record of 8:26.78 in 1982.

b. 4 Feb 1953 Novo-Balakly, Bashkir ASSR.

Maricica Puica (Rom) won the 1984 Olympic title, in that epic race when Mary Decker tripped over Zola Budd. At European Championships she had placed fourth in 1978 and second in 1982. She was world cross-country champion in 1982 and 1984, and had the added distinction of being the first woman ever to beat Grete Waitz in a road race. Her best 3000m is 8:27.83 in 1985.

b. 29 Jul 1950 Bucharest. Née Luca, married to her trainer Ion Puica.

5000 Metres

The first record accepted by the IAAF was 15:14.51 by Paula Fudge (UK) at Knarvik on 13 Sep 1981. A better time, 15:08.8, had been run by Loa Olafsson (Den) in a mixed race in 1978.

WORLD RECORD AT TEN-YEARLY INTERVALS

1975	15:48.5	Adrienne Beames (Aus) Narrabeen 5 Jan 1972
1985	14:48.07	Zola Budd (UK) Crystal Palace, London 26 Aug 1985

THE BARRIER BREAKERS—the first to better

16 min   Paola Pigni (Ita) 15:53.6 Milan 2 Sep 1969
15 min   Ingrid Kristiansen (Nor) 14:58.89 Oslo 28 Jun 1984

10 000 Metres

The first record accepted by the IAAF was 32:17.19 by Yelena Sipatova (USSR) in Moscow on 19 Sep 1981. Loa Olafsson (Den) had run the distance in 31:45.35 in a mixed race in 1978. The event now has full championship status, was included in the 1985 European and World Cup and is on the schedule for Commonwealth and Olympic Games and European and World Championships.

WORLD RECORD AT TEN-YEARLY INTERVALS

1975   34:01.4   Christa Vahlensieck (GFR) Wolfsburg
                 20 Aug 1975
1985   30:59.42 Ingrid Kristiansen (Nor) Oslo 27 Jul 1985

THE BARRIER BREAKERS—the first to better

35 min   Adrienne Beames (Aus) 34:08.0 Adelaide 28 Jan
             1974
31 min   Ingrid Kristiansen (Nor) 30:59.42 Oslo 27 Jul 1985

Crystal Palace 26 August 1985. Zola Budd has taken more than ten seconds off the world record for 5000m. She had set an unofficial world best of 15:01.83 as a 17-year-old in South Africa in January 1984. (ASP)

WORLD RECORDS and BESTS—LONG DISTANCE TRACK EVENTS

	hr:min:sec			
15km	49:44.0	Silvana Cruciata (Ita)	Rome	4 May 1981
20km	1:06:55.5	Rosa Mota (Por)	Lisbon	14 May 1983
25km	1:31:04.3	Chantal Langlacé (Fra)	Amiens	3 Sep 1983
30km	1:49:55.7	Chantal Langlacé (Fra)	Amiens	3 Sep 1983
20 miles	1:59:09*	Chantal Langlacé (Fra)	Amiens	3 Sep 1983
30 miles	3:35:42	Eleanor Adams (UK)	Bingham	20 Nov 1982
50km	3:44:08	Eleanor Adams (UK)	Bingham	20 Nov 1982
40 miles	4:55:17	Eleanor Adams (UK)	Bingham	20 Nov 1982
50 miles	6:17:30*	Monika Kuno (GFR)	Vogt	8–9 Jul 1983
100km	8:01.01	Monika Kuno (GFR)	Vogt	8–9 Jul 1983
100 miles	15:44:21	Lynn Fitzgerald (UK)	Nottingham	31 Jul–1 Aug 1983
200km	20:48:36*	Eleanor Adams (UK)	Nottingham	4–5 Aug 1985
200 miles	44:44:08	Eleanor Adams (UK)	Montauban, Fra	15–17 Mar 1985
500km	88:48:00	Eleanor Adams (UK)	Colac, Aus	26–30 Nov 1984
500 miles	143:49:00	Eleanor Adams (UK)	Colac, Aus	26 Nov–1 Dec 1984
	kilometres			
1h	18.084	Silvana Cruciata (Ita)	Rome	4 May 1981
2hrs	32.652	Chantal Langlacé (Fra)	Amiens	3 Sep 1983
24hrs	222.8	Eleanor Adams (UK)	Nottingham	4–5 Aug 1985
48hrs	334.038	Eleanor Adams (UK)	Montauban, Fra	15–17 Mar 1985
6 days	806.0	Eleanor Adams (UK)	Colac, Aus	26 Nov–1 Dec 1984

* Timed on one running watch only.

LONG DISTANCE ROAD BESTS

Where superior to track bests and run on properly measured road courses.

	hr:min:sec			
15km	47:52	Grete Waitz (Nor)	Tampa	11 Feb 1984
10 miles	53:17	Joyce Smith (UK)	Walton-on-Thames	12 Oct 1980
20km	1:05:38	Rosa Mota (Por)	New Haven	2 Sep 1985
Half-marathon	1:07:50*	Grete Waitz (Nor)	Oslo	4 Jul 1982
25km	1:22:55	Ingrid Kristiansen (Nor)	London	21 Apr 1985
30km	1:39:18	Ingrid Kristiansen (Nor)	London	21 Apr 1985
20 miles	1:46:40	Ingrid Kristiansen (Nor)	London	21 Apr 1985
50km	3:13:51	Janis Klecker (USA)	Tallahassee	17 Dec 1983
40 miles	4:43:22	Marcy Schwam (USA)	Chicago	3 Oct 1982
50 miles	5:59:26	Marcy Schwam (USA)	Chicago	3 Oct 1982
100km	7:26:01	Chantal Langlacé (Fra)	Migennes	17 Jun 1984
100 miles	15:07:45	Christine Barrett (UK)	Forthampton	14 Apr 1984
500km	82:10†	Annie van der Meer (Hol)	Paris-Colmar	8–11 Jun 1983

† for 518km
* course measurement uncertain
It should be noted that road times must be assessed with care as course conditions can vary considerably.

Marathon

The greatest women marathon runners of our time. In Los Angeles in 1984 even Grete Waitz (left) had no answer to the blitzkrieg tactics of Joan Benoit (top). (ASP)

It is only in the past decade that marathon running by women has become widespread, following the pioneering efforts, particularly in the USA, of some determined ladies who had quite a struggle to overcome prejudices against their participation.

The first championship marathon for women was organised by the Road Runners Club of America and won by Sara Berman (USA) in 3:07:10 on 27 Sep 1970. Women were officially accepted to run at the Boston marathon in 1972, and the first international race solely for women was held at Waldniel, GFR on 22 Sep 1974, won by Liane Winter (GFR) in a European record 2:50:31.4. The first national championship was that of the GFR held on 11 Oct 1975 and won by Christa Vahlensieck in 2:45:43. She set two world records: 2:40:15.8 in 1975 and 2:34:47.5 in 1977, ushering in the age of Grete Waitz and Joan Benoit.

WORLD BEST AT TEN-YEARLY INTERVALS

1935–55	3:40:22	Violet Piercy (UK) Windsor to Stamford Bridge 3 Oct 1926
1965	3:19:33	Mildred Sampson (NZ) Auckland 21 Jul 1964
1975	2:38:19	Jackie Hansen (USA) Culver City 1 Dec 1974
1985	2:21:06	Ingrid Kristiansen (Nor) London 21 Apr 1985

THE BARRIER BREAKERS—the first to better

3 hr Adrienne Beames (Aus) 2:46:30 Werribee 31 Aug 1971
2:45 Jackie Hansen (USA) 2:43:54.5 Eugene 12 Oct 1975
2:30 Grete Waitz (Nor) 2:27:32.6 New York 21 Oct 1979

THE MOST WORLD BESTS AND BEST CHAMPIONSHIPS RECORDS

4 Grete Waitz (Nor) ran three world bests in her first three marathons to win at New York each year from 1978 to 1980; her times were 2:32:29.8, 2:27:32.6 and 2:25:41. She improved further to 2:25:28.7 at London on 17 Apr 1983. She won nine of her twelve marathons from 1978 to 1985, including seven at New York and the inaugural World Championship in 1983. She was runner-up to Joan Benoit (USA) in the first women's Olympic marathon in 1984.
b. 1 Oct 1953 Oslo. Née Andersen she married Jack Nilsen, who is now her coach, and together they took the name of Waitz.

Joan Benoit (USA) ran the first sub-2:25 marathon with a stunning 2:22:43 at Boston in 1983. The following year she ran away from the field in the first Olympic marathon at Los Angeles to win in 2:24:52. That victory was all the more remarkable for the fact that she qualified by winning the US Trials race only seventeen days after undergoing arthroscopic surgery on her right knee. She won eight of her thirteen marathons from 1979 to 1985, when she improved further to win at Chicago in 2:21:21.
b. 16 May 1957 Cape Elizabeth, Maine. Married Scott Samuelson on 29 Sep 1984.

Ingrid Kristiansen (Nor) is the only athlete to set world records at 5000m (1981 and 1984), 10000m (1985) and marathon (1985). She has won eight of her 17 marathons, was third in the 1982 Europeans and fourth in the 1984 Olympics. Formerly a cross-country skier, at which she was 15th in the 1978 world championships.
b. 21 Mar 1956 Trondheim. Née Christensen, with a son, Gaute, born in 1983.

80 Metres Hurdles

The standard women's hurdles distance was 80 metres, over seven flights of 2ft 6in (76cm) hurdles, from 1927 until replaced by the 100m over eight flights of 2ft 9in (84cm) hurdles in 1969.

WORLD RECORD AT TEN-YEARLY INTERVALS

1935	11.6	Simone Schaller (USA) San Francisco 14 Aug 1932
		Ruth Engelhard (Ger) London 11 Aug 1934
1945	11.3	Claudia Testoni (Ita) Garmisch Partenkirchen 23 Jul 1939 and Dresden 13 Aug 1939; Fanny Blankers-Koen (Hol) Amsterdam 20 Sep 1942

1955	10.8	Galina Yermolenko (USSR) Leningrad 5 Jul 1955
1965	10.3	Irina Press (USSR) Tbilisi 24 Oct 1965
1975	10.2	Vera Korsakova (USSR) Riga 16 Jun 1968
	10.39	Maureen Caird (Aus) Mexico City 18 Oct 1968 (best auto)

THE BARRIER BREAKERS—the first to better

12 sec Marjorie Clark (SAf) 11.8 Pietermaritzburg 2 May 1931
11 sec Shirley Strickland (Aus) 10.9 Helsinki 24 Jul 1952

THE MOST WORLD RECORDS

6 Irina Press (USSR) from 10.6 in 1960 to 10.3 in 1965. She won the 1960 Olympic title.

100 Metres Hurdles

The first records ratified for this event were 13.3 sec by Karin Balzer (GDR) and Teresa Sukniewicz (Pol) at Warsaw on 20 Jun 1969.

WORLD RECORD AT TEN-YEARLY INTERVALS

1975	12.3	Annelie Ehrhardt (GDR) Dresden 22 Jul 1973 (12.68 auto)
	12.59	Annelie Ehrhardt Munich 8 Sep 1972 (auto)
1985	12.36	Grazyna Rabsztyn (Pol) Warsaw 13 Jun 1980

THE BARRIER BREAKERS—the first to better

13 sec Karin Balzer (GDR) Berlin 5 Sep 1969

THE MOST WORLD RECORDS

6 Karin Balzer from 13.3 in 1969 to 12.6 in 1971.

THE BEST CHAMPIONSHIPS RECORDS at 80mh and 100mh

Fanny Blankers-Koen (Hol), who set her first national record at 800m in 1935, was Olympic champion in 1948 and European champion in 1946 and 1950 at 80mh, as well as winning Olympic and European titles at both 100m and 200m. Between 1938 and 1951 she set official world records at seven individual and two relay events. She won the extraordinary total of 58 Dutch individual titles.
b. 26 Apr 1918 Amsterdam as Fanny Koen, she married Jan Blankers, who won the AAA triple jump in 1931 and 1933.
Karin Balzer (GDR) was Olympic champion in 1964 and bronze medallist in 1968, and won European titles in 1966, 1969 and 1971. She won seven 80mh/100mh GDR titles as well as two at pentathlon and one each at 200m and long jump. She also won five European indoor sprint hurdles titles. In addition to her world records at 100mh she set one at 80mh: 10.5 in 1964.
b. 5 Jun 1938 Magdeburg.
Shirley Strickland (later De la Hunty) (Aus) was

Karin Balzer became, in 1964, the first Olympic athletics champion from the GDR. Their athletes have won a further 32 titles since then. (All-Sport)

twice Olympic champion, 1952 and 1956, and bronze medallist in 1948. She also won two Olympic 100m bronze medals. Her two Commonwealth medals included the 80mh title of 1950. She set world records at 11.0 and 10.9 for 80mh at the 1952 Olympics and at 11.3 for 100m in 1955. She also emphasized her versatility by winning three Australian titles at 440y.
b. 18 Jul 1925 Guildford, W. Australia.

200 Metres Hurdles

Run over ten 2ft 6in (76cm) flights of hurdles, records at 200m were accepted only from 1969 to 1974, when the event was replaced by the 400mh.

WORLD RECORD AT TEN-YEARLY INTERVALS

| 1965 | 27.5 | Jennifer Wingerson (Can) Toronto 3 Jul 1965 |
| 1975 | 25.7 | Pamela Ryan (née Kilborn) (Aus) Melbourne 25 Nov 1971 |

THE MOST WORLD RECORDS

4 Pam Kilborn/Ryan (Aus) set four ratified and one unratified records at 200mh from 26.4 in 1969 to the 'final' record of 25.7. She won four Commonwealth titles, three at 80mh: 1962, 1966 and 1970 and long jump in 1962, and Olympic silver and bronze medals at 80mh.

400 Metres Hurdles

The first officially accepted record at this event was 56.51 by Krystyna Kacperczyk (Pol) run in 1974.

WORLD RECORD AT TEN-YEARLY INTERVALS

| 1975 | 56.51 | Krystyna Kacperczyk (Pol) Augsburg 13 Jul 1974 |

WOMEN'S WORLD BESTS—NON STANDARD EVENTS
OUTDOORS

300m	34.1	Marita Koch (GDR)	Canberra (in 400m)	6 Oct 1985
500m	1:09.9	Colette Besson (Fra)	Font Romeu	16 Aug 1970
600m	1:23.9	Anita Weiss (GDR)	Montreal (in 800m)	24 Jul 1976
Pole vault	3.59m	Jana Edwards (USA)	Fort Wayne	23 Jul 1983
Hammer (4kg)	57.50m	Carol Cady (USA)	Berkeley, Cal.	5 May 1984

1985   53.55   Sabine Busch (GDR) East Berlin 22 Sep 1985

THE BARRIER BREAKERS—the first to better

55 sec   Tatyana Zelentsova (USSR) Prague 2 Sep 1978

THE MOST WORLD RECORDS

2   Krystyna Kacperczyk ran 55.44 in 1978 in addition to her inaugural record.
2   Tatyana Zelentsova ran 55.31 and 54.89 in 1978, the latter when winning the European title.
2   Karin Rossley (GDR) ran her first world record of 55.63 to win the 1977 European Cup Final and returned to the lists with 54.28 at Jena in 1980.

Relays

The IAAF currently ratify records at four women's relay events. Up to 1976 records were also recognized at the equivalent imperial distances.

4 × 100 Metres Relay

The sprint relay has been included on the Olympic programme since 1928, and world records have been set at 11 of the 13 Games from then.

WORLD RECORD AT TEN-YEARLY INTERVALS

1925	50.2y	Canada (Myrtle Cook, Rosa Grosse, Josephine Dyment, Fanny Rosenfeld) Toronto 19 Sep 1925 (at 4x110y)
1935	47.0	USA (Mary Carew, Evelyn Furtsch, Annette Rogers, Wilhelmina von Bremen) and Canada (Mildred Frizzell, Lilian Palmer, Mary Frizzell, Hilda Strike) Los Angeles 7 Aug 1932
1945	46.4	Germany (Emmi Albus, Käthe Krauss, Marie Dollinger, Ilse Dörffeldt) Berlin 8 Aug 1936
1955	45.6	USSR (Vyera Kalashnikova, Zinaida Safronova, Irina Turova, Nadezhda Dvalishvili) Budapest 20 Sep 1953 and USSR (Lidia Polinichenko, Galina Vinogradova, Zinaida Safronova, Maria Itkina) Moscow 11 Sep 1955
1965	43.92	USA (Willye White, Wyomia Tyus, Marilyn White, Edith McGuire) Tokyo 21 Oct 1964
1975	42.51	GDR (Doris Maletzki, Renate Stecher, Christine Heinich, Bärbel Eckert) 8 Sep 1974
1985	41.37	GDR (Silke Gladisch, Sabine Rieger, Ingrid Auerswald, Marlies Göhr) Canberra 6 Oct 1985

THE MOST WORLD RECORDS BY AN INDIVIDUAL

9   Marlies Göhr (née Oelsner) on successive records by GDR teams from 42.50 in 1976 to the present. She ran the first leg in 1976 and the anchor leg on the last eight. Ingrid Auerswald ran the third leg on the last seven 1979–85. The identical team of Romy Müller, Bärbel Wöckel, Auerswald and Göhr set three records in 1980.

4 × 400 Metres Relay

This event was added to the record lists in 1969, when it was run for the first time in a major event, at the European Championships. It was added to the Olympic programme in 1972. The GDR have set the last seven records, 1971–84.

WORLD RECORD AT TEN-YEARLY INTERVALS

1965	3:49.9y	UK (Pam Piercy, Joy Jordan, Diane Leather, Shirley Pirie) London 14 Jun 1958 (for 4 × 440y)
1975	3:22.95	GDR (Dagmar Käsling, Rita Kühne, Helga Seidler, Monika Zehrt) Munich 10 Sep 1972
1985	3:15.92	GDR (Gesine Walther, Sabine Busch, Dagmar Rübsam, Marita Koch) Erfurt 3 Jun 1984

The fastest ever 400m relay leg is 47.6 by Jarmila Kratochvilova on the third leg for Czechoslovakia, second in the 1982 European Championships. Marita Koch ran 47.70 on the 1984 GDR world record team.

THE MOST OFFICIAL WORLD RECORDS BY AN INDIVIDUAL

4   Helga Seidler and **Monika Zehrt** for GDR from their 3:29.28 to win the 1971 European title to 3:22.95 to win the 1972 Olympic title. At the individual 400m Seidler was first and fourth respectively at these events. Zehrt won the 1972 Olympic and 1970 European Junior titles and set a world record of 51.08 in 1972.

World Records—other Relays

4×200m	1:28.15	GDR (Marlies Göhr, Romy Müller, Bärbel Wöckel, Marita Koch) Jena 9 Aug 1980
4×800m	7:50.17	USSR (Nadezhda Olizarenko, Lyubov Gurina, Lyudmila Borisova, Irina Podyalovskaya) Moscow 5 Aug 1984

High Jump

WORLD RECORD AT TEN-YEARLY INTERVALS

1905	1.37m	Helen Aldrich (USA) Washington 26 May 1905
	1.37m	Helen Schutte (USA) St Paul 24 Aug 1905
1915	1.445m	Isabelle Swain and Miriam Heermans (USA) New Milford 16 May 1911; Dorothy Hover (USA) Burlington 1915
	1.47m	Margaret Belasco (UK) Chatham 6 Jun 1914 (schools meeting)
1925	1.625m	Joan Belasco (UK) Ramsgate 27 May 1920 (schools meeting)
	1.525m	Phyllis Green (UK) London 11 Jul 1925 (official record)
1935	1.65m	Jean Shiley and Mildred Didrikson (USA) Los Angeles 7 Aug 1932 (and 1.67m in jump-off)
1945	1.71m	Fanny Blankers-Koen (Hol) Amsterdam 30 May 1943
1955	1.73m	Aleksandra Chudina (USSR) Kiev 22 May 1954
1965	1.91m	Iolanda Balas (Rom) Sofia 16 Jul 1961
1975	1.95m	Rosemarie Witschas (GDR) Rome 8 Sep 1974
1985	2.07m	Lyudmila Andonova (Bul) West Berlin 20 Jul 1984

THE BARRIER BREAKERS—the first to clear

5ft	Joan Belasco (UK) 1.575m Ramsgate May 1918 (schools meeting)
	Phyllis Green (UK) 1.525m London 11 Jul 1925
1.60m	Joan Belasco (UK) 1.625m Ramsgate 27 May 1920 (schools meeting)
	Marjorie Clark (SAf) 1.60m London 23 Jun 1928 (in exhibition)
	Ethel Catherwood (Can) 1.60m Halifax 2 Jul 1928
1.70m	Fanny Blankers-Koen (Hol) 1.71m Amsterdam 30 May 1943
1.80m	Iolanda Balas (Rom) 1.80m Cluj 22 Jun 1958
6ft	Iolanda Balas 1.83m Bucharest 18 Oct 1958
1.90m	Iolanda Balas 1.90m Budapest 8 Jul 1961
2.00m	Rosemarie Ackermann (GDR) 2.00m West Berlin 26 Aug 1977

High jump world record holders: Lyudmila Andonova (right) and Ulrike Meyfarth (below). (T. Kirkova, Associated Sports Photography)

THE MOST WORLD RECORDS

14 Iolanda Balas (Rom) from 1.75m in Bucharest on 14 Jul 1956 to 1.91m at Sofia on 16 Jul 1961. By the end of 1963 she had jumped 1.80 m or higher in 72 competitions, yet it was not until 27 Sep 1964 that another woman, Michele Brown (Aus) jumped as high. By the end of her career she had 93 competitions at 1.80 m or higher compared with five by the rest of the world!

7 Rosemarie Ackermann (née Witschas) (GDR) from 1.94m in 1974, to equal the record that Yordanka Blagoyeva (Bul) had set in 1972, to the first two-metre clearance in 1977.

THE BEST CHAMPIONSHIPS RECORDS

Iolanda Balas achieved the greatest domination over an event ever seen in the history of athletics. From her fifth place at the Olympic Games on 1 Dec 1956 she was unbeaten at high jump until she lost to Dagmar Melzer (GDR) on 11 Jun 1967, winning 140 consecutive competitions. She was Olympic champion in 1960 and 1964, European champion in 1958 and 1962 (and silver medallist in 1954), won the first European Indoor Games title in 1966 and won a record eight World Student titles between 1954 and 1961. She was Romania's first European and Olympic medallist in athletics, and won 16 successive national titles from 1951, at the age of 14, to 1966. At the end of 1967 she married her coach Ion Söter, who set the Romanian men's record at 2.05m in 1956. Her style was described as a cross between a scissors and the Eastern cut-off.

YEARLY PROGRESS—BEST MARK, POSITION IN WORLD LIST (COMPETITIONS OVER 1.80M)

1950	1.40	1959	1.84, 1 (12)
1951	1.51	1960	1.86, 1 (3)
1952	1.53	1961	1.91, 1 (17)
1953	1.60, 10=	1962	1.87, 1 (16)
1954	1.65, 5=	1963	1.88, 1 (8)
1955	1.70, 2	1964	1.90, 1 (9)
1956	1.75, 2	1965	1.86, 1 (9)
1957	1.76, 2	1966	1.84, 1 (4)
1958	1.83, 1 (5)	1967	1.68, 57=

b. 12 Dec 1936 Timisoara; 1.85m tall.

Sara Simeoni (Ita) won three Olympic medals, gold in 1980 and silver in 1976 and 1984, and was also sixth in 1972. She was European champion in 1978, bronze medallist in 1974 and 1982 and placed ninth in 1971. She won four European Indoor and two World Student Games titles, and was Italian champion 13 times. She twice cleared a world record 2.01m in August 1978, first at Brescia and then at Prague to win the European Championship.
b. 19 Apr 1953 Verona; 1.78m tall.

Rosemarie Ackermann was Olympic champion in 1976 and European champion in 1974. At the Olympics she was also fourth in 1980 and seventh in 1972 and at the European she was second in 1978. She was European Indoor champion three times, 1974–6, GDR champion six times and was the winner at the European Cup Final three times and the World Cup once. She had many classic competitions with Sara Simeoni and in all had an 8–5 record over her.
b. 4 Apr 1952 Lohsa; 1.76m tall; née Witschas.

Ulrike Meyfarth (GFR) was the youngest ever individual Olympic champion when she set a world record 1.92m to win at Munich in 1972. Although remaining a fine jumper, she failed to qualify for the Olympic final in 1976, and was seventh and fifth in the European championships of 1974 and 1978. However, she returned to the top when she won the 1981 World Cup high jump and she regained the world record by jumping 2.02m to win the 1982 European title. In 1983, after a silver medal in the World Championships, she set another record, with Tamara Bykova (USSR), at 2.03m in the European Cup Final. Finally she sealed her career by regaining her Olympic title in 1984. She was also European Indoor champion in 1982 and 1984, and GFR champion seven times outdoors and six indoors.
b. 4 May 1956 Frankfurt; 1.88m tall.

Long Jump

WORLD RECORD AT TEN-YEARLY INTERVALS

1915	5.00m	Ellen Hayes (USA) Sweetbriar 1914
1925	5.54m	Maria Kiessling (Ger) Munich 29 May 1921
1935	6.02m	Stanislawa Walasiewicz* (Pol) Cleveland 10 Jul 1930
	5.98m	Kinue Hitomi (Jap) Osaka 20 May 1928 (official)
1945	6.25m	Fanny Blankers-Koen (Hol) Leiden 19 Sep 1943
1955	6.31m	Galina Vinogradova (USSR) Tbilisi 18 Nov 1955
1965	6.76m	Mary Rand (UK) Tokyo 14 Oct 1964
1975	6.84m	Heide Rosendahl (GFR) Turin 3 Sep 1970
1985	7.44m	Heike Drechsler (GDR) East Berlin 22 Sep 1985

THE BARRIER BREAKERS—the first to jump

5.50m/18ft	Marie Kiessling (Ger) 5.54m Munich 29 May 1921
6m/20ft	Kinue Hitomi (Jap) 6.075m (w) Seoul 17 Oct 1929
	Stanislawa Walasiewicz* (Pol) 6.02m Cleveland 10 Jul 1930 (not ratified)
	Erika Junghanns (Ger) 6.07m Weissenfels 2 Oct 1938
6.50m	Tatyana Shchelkanova (USSR) 6.50m (w) Berlin 23 Jun 1961, and 6.53m Leipzig 10 Jun 1962
7.00m	Vilma Bardauskiene (USSR) 7.07m (twice) Kishinyov 18 Aug 1978

(w) wind assisted   *doubtful gender (see 100 metres)

Conversions 5ft 6in = 1.67m. 5ft 9in = 1.75m. 6ft = 1.83m. 6ft 3in = 1.90m. 6ft 6in = 1.98m. 6ft 9in = 2.05m.

Conversions 19ft = 5.79m. 20ft = 6.09m. 21ft = 6.40m. 22ft = 6.70m. 23ft = 7.01m. 24ft = 7.31m. 25ft = 7.62m.

MOST WORLD RECORDS

4 Tatyana Shchelkanova (USSR), from 6.48m in 1962 to 6.70m in 1964. Her absolute best was a wind assisted 6.96m in the 1966 Soviet Championships. She was European champion in 1962 and third in the 1964 Olympics.

4 Anisoara Cusmir (later married to Paul Stanciu) (Rom) set her first world record at 7.15m in 1982. In 1983 she improved to 7.21, 7.27 and 7.43, the last two in the same competition on 4 Jun at Bucharest.

THE BEST CHAMPIONSHIPS RECORDS

Anisoara Stanciu became Olympic long jump champion 1984 after gaining silver medals in the 1982 European and 1983 World Championships. She was also World Student champion in 1983 after second in 1981.
b. 28 Jun 1962 Bralia; née Cusmir.

Elzbieta Krzesinsksa (Pol) was a double medallist both at Olympics—1st 1956, 2nd 1960, and at Europeans—2nd 1962 and 3rd 1954. She twice set a world record at 6.35m in 1956.
b. 11 Nov 1934 Warsaw; neé Dunsksa.

Tatyana Shchelkanova jumps at Tokyo in 1964. She also set an indoor world best for 60m at 7.1 and ranked as the world's best pentathlete in 1963. (Keystone Press)

Anisoara Cusmir smashed the world record in 1983, but had to yield to Heike Daute at the World Championships. (ASP)

Triple Jump

The triple jump for women was first contested on a regular basis in the USA in 1984, when it was added to the NCAA championships schedule. The first champion was Terri Turner with a best on record of 13.52m (wind assisted).

The world best at the end of 1985 was 13.51m (indoors) by Esmeralda Garcia (Bra) at Syracuse on 9 Mar 1985.

Shot

The women's event is contested using a 4kg (8.82lb) shot.

WORLD RECORD AT TEN-YEARLY INTERVALS

1925   10.68m   Violette Morris (Fra) Colombes 12 Jul 1925

1935	14.38m	Gisela Mauermayer (Ger) Warsaw 15 Jul 1934
1945	14.89m	Tatyana Sevryukova (USSR) Frunze 14 Oct 1945
1955	16.67m	Galina Zybina (USSR) Tbilisi 15 Nov 1955
1965	18.59m	Tamara Press (USSR) Kassel 19 Sep 1965
1975	21.60m	Marianne Adam (GDR) East Berlin 6 Aug 1975
1985	22.53m	Natalya Lisovskaya (USSR) Sochi 27 May 1984

THE BARRIER BREAKERS—the first to exceed

12m/40ft	Auguste Hermann (Ger) 12.26m Köln 28 Jul 1928
15m	Anna Andreyeva (USSR) 15.02m Ploesti 9 Nov 1950
50ft	Galina Zybina (USSR) 15.28m Helsinki 26 Jul 1952
60ft	Tamara Press (USSR) 18.55m Leipzig 10 Jun 1962
20m	Nadezhda Chizhova (USSR) 20.09m Chorzow 13 Jul 1969
70ft	Nadezhda Chizhova (USSR) 21.45m Varna 29 Sep 1973

The mighty Nadezhda Chizhova at Munich in 1972 when she won the Olympic title and set her eighth world record at 21.03m. (ASP)

THE MOST WORLD RECORDS

15 Galina Zybina (USSR), including one indoors, in succession from 15.19m at Viborg on 30 Jun 1952 to 16.76m at Tashkent on 13 Oct 1956. Of these improvements eight were ratified by the IAAF. Her all-time best was 17.50m in 1964, by which time the record had been raised to 18.55m by Tamara Press. Her championships shot career: Olympics: 1952 1st, 1956 2nd, 1960 7th; European: 1950 4th, 1954 1st, 1962 3rd, 1966 4th. She won European bronze medals at javelin in 1950 and discus in 1954, and also won four Soviet shot and two javelin titles.
b. 22 Jan 1931 Leningrad.
10 Nadezhda Chizhova (USSR) from 18.67m at Sochi on 28 Apr 1968 to 21.45m at Varna on 29 Sep 1973; all but the last were ratified.
9 Grete Heublein (Ger) from 10.86m in 1927 to 13.70m in 1931. She won the World Games shot in 1930.
6 Tamara Press (USSR) from 17.25m in 1959 to 18.59m in 1965. Her 77cm improvement to 18.55m at Leipzig on 10 Jun 1962 was the biggest ever for a world shot record.

THE BEST CHAMPIONSHIPS RECORDS

Tamara Press was Olympic champion at shot in 1960 and 1964 and at discus in 1964 (silver in 1960). She won the European double in 1962 after winning the shot and placing third at discus in 1958. In the Soviet Championships she won nine shot and seven discus titles. Her younger sister Irina was Olympic champion at 80mh in 1960 and pentathlon in 1964. Both retired from the sport when sex testing was introduced in 1965; their exact status had previously been questioned by athletics followers.
b. 10 Mar 1939 Kharkov.
Nadezhda Chizhova achieved the unprecedented feat of four successive European titles between 1966 and 1974. She also won a set of Olympic medals: gold 1972, silver 1976, bronze 1968; won five European indoor titles, and won the European Junior shot/discus double in 1964. She also won six Soviet titles and scored three European Cup victories.
b. 29 Sep 1945 Usolye-Sibirskoye, Siberia.
Ilona Briesenick (GDR) started her career with the European Junior title in 1973 (and was second at discus). She was fifth in the 1976 Olympics, but was disqualified for drug abuse after winning the shot at the 1977 European Cup Final. Just one year and 16 days later she returned to win the 1978 European title, and she went on to further wins: Olympics 1980, European 1982, European Indoor 1979 and 1981. Seven times GDR champion she also won the 1983 World bronze medal. She set world records at 22.26m and 22.45m in 1980.
b. 24 Sep 1956 Demmin. Formerly Slupianek, née Schoknecht. She married Hartmut Briesenick, European shot champion of 1971 and 1974.

Discus

The women's event is contested using a 1kg (2lb 3oz) discus.

WORLD RECORD AT TEN-YEARLY INTERVALS

1925	33.40m	Halina Konopacka (Pol) Warsaw 21 Jun 1925
1935	47.12m	Gisela Mauermayer (Ger) Dresden 25 Aug 1935
1945	49.88m	Nina Dumbadze (USSR) Moscow 14 Aug 1944
1955	57.04m	Nina Dumbadze (USSR) Tbilisi 18 Oct 1952
1965	59.70m	Tamara Press (USSR) Moscow 11 Aug 1965
1975	70.20m	Faina Melnik (USSR) Zürich 20 Aug 1975
1985	74.56m	Zdenka Silhava (Cs) Nitra 26 Aug 1984

THE BARRIER BREAKERS—the first to exceed

30m	Violette Morris (Fra) 30.10m London 4 Aug 1924
100ft	Helina Konopacka (Pol) 31.24m Warsaw 10 May 1925
40m	Jadwiga Wajsowna (Pol) 40.34m Pabianice 15 May 1932
50m	Nina Dumbadze (USSR) 50.50m Sarpsborg 29 Aug 1946
60m/200ft	Liesel Westermann (GFR) 61.26m Sao Paulo 5 Nov 1967
70m	Faina Melnik (USSR) 70.20m Zürich 20 Aug 1975

THE MOST WORLD RECORDS

11 Faina Melnik (USSR), from 64.22m at Helsinki on 12 Aug 1971 to 70.50m at Sochi, USSR on 24 Apr 1976.

9 Jadwiga Wajsowna (Pol), later Marcinkiewicz, was the first 40m-plus thrower in 1932. Her final record (all in pre-IAAF ratification days) was 44.19m in 1934. She won Olympic silver in 1936 and bronse in 1932 and the World Games gold in 1934.

9 Gisela Mauermayer (Ger), six in 1935 starting with 44.34m and three in 1936 culminating in 48.31m. She won the 1936 Olympic and 1938 European titles, and also set three world records at the pentathlon.

7 Nina Dumbadze (USSR). Her first four improvements on the record, from 49.11m in 1939 to 50.50m in 1946 were not put forward for ratification, but she continued to revolutionize women's discus throwing as the USSR entered international competition, and the IAAF recognized her 53.25m in 1948 and 53.37m in 1951. After Nina Romashkova had thrown 53.61m in 1952, Dumbadze achieved the greatest ever improvement by adding 3.43m to that with her final record of 57.04m. This remained unsurpassed for eight years. Eight times Soviet champion, she won the European title in 1946 and 1950 and was third in her first Olympics, in 1952 at the age of 33.
b. 23 Jan 1919 Tbilisi.

6 Halina Konopacka (Pol) from 31.24m in 1925

to the 39.62m with which she won the 1928 Olympic title.

6 Tamara Press (USSR) from 57.15m in 1960 to 59.70m in 1965.

THE BEST CHAMPIONSHIPS RECORDS

Nina Ponomaryeva (née Romashkova) (USSR) won the Olympic title in 1952 and 1960 and was third in 1956. She was European champion in 1954 and won eight Soviet titles between 1951 and 1959. She set a world record at 53.61m in 1952 and her best ever was 56.62m in 1955. She achieved notoriety for allegedly shoplifting some hats from C & A Modes in Oxford Street, London, as a result of which the UK v USSR match in 1956 was cancelled.
b. 27 Apr 1929 Sverdlovsk.

Evelin Jahl (née Schlaak) (GDR) won the Olympic title in 1976 and 1980 and the European title in 1978. She started her international career by winning the European Juniors in 1973, and won six GDR titles as well as victories at one European Cup and two World Cup finals. She succeeded Melnik as world record holder with 70.72m in 1978 and 71.50m in 1980.
b. 28 Mar 1956 Annaberg.

Faina Melnik was twice European champion (1971 and 1974), and once Olympic (1972). She won 52 successive discus competitions between 1973 and 1976, so it was a major shock when she placed only fourth in the Olympics that year.

Faina Melnik bestrode the discus circle throughout the seventies. (All-Sport)

Conversions 150ft = 45.72m. 175ft = 53.34m.
200ft = 60.96m. 225ft = 68.58m.

Suddenly her all-conquering years of success were over, for she was fifth in the 1978 Europeans and failed to qualify for the 1980 Olympic final. She won nine USSR discus titles between 1970 and 1981.
b. 9 Jun 1945 Bakota, Ukraine. She was for a time married to Bulgarian discus thrower Velko Velev and competed as Veleva in 1977–9.
Tamara Press—see Shot section.

Javelin

The women's event is contested using a 600 gram (1lb 5.25oz) javelin.

WORLD RECORD AT TEN-YEARLY INTERVALS

1935	46.74m	Nan Gindele (USA) Chicago 18 Jun 1932
1945	48.39m	Lyudmila Anokina (USSR) Kiev 15 Sep 1945
1955	55.48m	Nadezhda Konyayeva (USSR) Kiev 6 Aug 1954
1965	62.40m	Yelena Gorchakova (USSR) Tokyo 16 Oct 1964
1975	67.22m	Ruth Fuchs (GDR) Rome 3 Sep 1974
1985	75.40m	Petra Felke (GDR) Schwerin 4 Jun 1985

THE BARRIER BREAKERS—the first to exceed

40m	Mildred Didrikson (USA) 40.62m Dallas 4 Jul 1930
50m	Klavdiya Mayuchaya (USSR) 50.32m Moscow 23 Sep 1947
60m/200ft	Elvira Ozolina (USSR) 61.38m Kiev 27 Aug 1964
70m	Tatyana Biryulina (USSR) 70.08m Moscow 12 Jul 1980

MOST WORLD RECORDS

6   Ruth Fuchs (GDR) added 2.36m to the record with 65.06m at Potsdam in 1972, and improved five more times to 69.96m in 1980.
4   Elvira Ozolina (USSR) from 57.92m in 1960 to 61.38m in 1964, although the latter was not ratified by the IAAF.

THE BEST CHAMPIONSHIPS RECORDS

Ruth Fuchs won 113 of 129 javelin competitions from 1970 to 1980, amazing consistency for such an unpredictable event over such a span of time. These included two Olympic (1972 and 1976) and two European (1974 and 1978) titles as well as four European Cup Final and two World Cup victories. She won eleven GDR titles from her first in 1967.
b. 11 Dec 1946 Egeln.
Dana Zatopkova (Cs), wife of the great Emil Zatopek, was a major star in her own right. She competed in four Olympics, winning in 1952 and second in 1960, and won the European titles of 1954 and 1958. She also won thirteen national titles between 1946 and 1960. Her personal best was 56.67m, having achieved a world record of 55.73m earlier that year.
b. 19 Sep 1922 Tryskat; née Ingrova.
Elvira Ozolina (USSR) was Olympic champion in 1960 and European in 1962. After such a magnificent start to her career she faded somewhat in relative standings and was fifth in the 1964 Olympics and 1966 Europeans, but added a fifth Soviet title in 1973 to those won between 1961 and 1966. Her best throw was 63.96 m in 1973, nine years after her final world record.
b. 8 Oct 1939 Leningrad. She married the great javelin thrower Janis Lusis.

Pentathlon and Heptathlon

The heptathlon has been the standard women's multi-event competition since 1981. It comprises seven events, contested in order: 100m hurdles, high jump, shot and 200m on the first day; long jump, javelin and 800m on the second day. Prior to 1984 the shot preceded the high jump.

In 1977 Kathy Schmidt threw the javelin 69.32m to become the first US woman to set a throws world record for 45 years. (ASP)

The first women's multi-events competition at a major championships was a triathlon (100m, high jump, javelin) at the 1930 World Games, but until 1980 the pentathlon was the standard competition. The events changed several times, as can be seen from the summary tables below.

Multi-events competitions are scored on tables approved by the IAAF. New tables have been issued in 1954, 1971 and 1984 to take account of changing standards. The latest set also have a slightly different basis in that separate tables are given for hand and automatic timing, reflecting the IAAF approved differentials between these systems of 0.24 sec for 200m and 100mh events.

Aleksandra Chudria was a world class javelin thrower as well as a world record holder for the pentathlon, although the javelin was not then included in multi-events competition. (United Press)

WORLD RECORD PROGRESSION AT TEN-YEARLY INTERVALS

Showing performances scored on the three tables (1954T, 1971T, 1984T).

Note that it is not entirely possible to rescore pentathlons including 100m and 80mh events on the 1984 tables, as 100m and 80mh are not included, but for comparison purposes the 1971 tables have been used for these events with 0.24 sec added to the hand times.

1928–48 PENTATHLON Day 1: SP, LJ; Day 2: 100 m, HJ, JT

As at	1954T	1971T	1984T	
1935	4155	3573	3266	Gisela Mauermayer (GFR) London 9, 11 Aug 1934
1945	4391	3899	3504	Gisela Mauermayer (GFR) Stuttgart 16–17 Jul 1938
Last	4507	4015	3660	Lena Stumpf (GFR) Frankfurt 23–24 Jul 1949

1948–61 PENTATHLON Day 1: SP, HJ, 200m; Day 2: 80mh, LJ

As at	1954T	1971T	1984T	
1955	4750	4232	4024	Aleksandra Chudina (USSR) Moscow 6–7 Sep 1955
Last	5020	4486	4298	Irina Press (USSR) Leningrad 16–17 Aug 1961

1961–8 PENTATHLON Day 1: 80 mh, SP, HJ; Day 2: LJ, 200 m

As at	1954T	1971T	1984T	
1965	4692*	5246	4602	Irina Press (USSR) Tokyo 16–17 Oct 1964

(* originally 4702, but rescored using automatic timings)

1969–76 PENTATHLON Day 1: 100mh, SP, HJ; Day 2: LJ, 200m

As at	1954T	1971T	1984T	
1975	5569	4932	5005	Burglinde Pollak (GDR) Bonn 22 Sep 1973

1977–81 PENTATHLON Day 1: 100mh, SP, HJ, LJ, 800m

As at	1971T	1984T	
Last	5083	5213	Nadezhda Tkachenko (USSR) Moscow 24 Jul 1980

1981–date HEPTATHLON

As at	1971T	1984T	
1980	6144	6095	Yekaterina Gordienko (USSR) Odessa 13–14 Sep 1980
1985	6867	6946	Sabine Paetz (GDR) Potsdam 5–6 May 1984

The composition of Paetz's current world record:
100mh: 12.64, HJ: 1.80, SP: 15.37, 200m: 23.37, LJ: 6.86, JT: 44.62, 800m: 2:08.93.

Irina Press (right) attacks the hurdles. She was Olympic champion at 80mh in 1960 and pentathlon in 1964. (Central Press)

THE MOST WORLD RECORDS

8 Irina Press (USSR) from 1959 to 1964. Her fifth record, in 1961, was the first pentathlon score to exceed 5000 points on the 1954 Tables. She was Olympic champion in 1964.

5 Aleksandra Chudina (USSR) from 1947 to 1955. She was European pentathlon champion in 1954 and won three Olympic medals in 1952: silver at LJ and JT, bronze at HJ. The pentathlon was not an Olympic event until 1964. She won ten World Student Games titles at five events, and 31 outdoor Soviet titles. She also set world records at 4×200m relay and high jump.

4 Ramona Neubert (GDR) at heptathlon (on the 1984 Tables): 6670 and 6788 in 1981, 6845 in 1982 and 6935 in 1983.

(above) Ramona Neubert at her best event, the long jump, at which she ranked second in the world in 1981. (All-Sport)

(right) Mary Peters on her way to a world pentathlon record and gold medal triumph in the Munich Olympic stadium 1972. (ASP)

THE BEST CHAMPIONSHIPS RECORDS

Nadezhda Tkachenko (USSR) was, at pentathlon, Olympic champion in 1980, having placed ninth and fifth in 1972 and 1976 respectively, World Student Games champion in 1973, European champion in 1974, and four times Soviet champion. She also 'won' the 1978 European title but was disqualified for failing the doping test. At the 1980 Olympics she became the first woman to exceed 5000 on the 1971 Tables.
b. 19 Sep 1947 Krementshuk.
Ramona Neubert (GDR) won the European

PERSONAL BESTS OF FAMOUS PENTATHLETES AND HEPTATHLETES

Event	PAETZ	NEUBERT	TKACHENKO	ROSENDAHL	PETERS	PRESS	CHUDINA
200m	23.37	23.14	24.20	22.96	24.08	24.2	25.5
800m	2:07.03	2:04.73	2:05.2				
80mh				10.7	11.0	10.3	11.3
100mh	12.54	13.13	13.24	13.28	13.29		
HJ	1.83	1.86	1.84	1.70	1.82	1.67	1.73
LJ	7.12	6.90	6.73	6.84	6.04	6.24	6.24
SP	16.16	15.44	16.86	14.28	16.40i	17.21	14.33
JT	44.62	49.94		48.16			52.75

(1982) and World (1983) heptathlon titles. She also won the 1981 and 1983 European Cup finals. At pentathlon she was fourth in the 1980 Olympics and eighth in the 1978 Europeans.
b. 26 Jul 1958 Pima; née Göhler.

Heide Rosendahl (GFR) won the 1971 European pentathlon title, was second in 1966, and won the Olympic silver medal in 1972. She won Olympic gold medals at sprint relay and long jump in 1972 and at the long jump also won a European outdoor bronze and indoor gold in 1971. She won GFR titles: five each at pentathlon and long jump, one at 100mh. She set four world records at pentathlon 1969–1972 and one at long jump in 1970.
b. 14 Feb 1947 Huckeswagen, now Ecker. Her father Heinz Rosendahl was GFR discus champion in 1951 and 1953.

Mary Peters (UK) won the 1972 Olympic title in a world record 4801 points (4841 on the 1984 Tables) on her third attempt after placing fourth in 1964 and ninth in 1968. She was Commonwealth pentathlon champion in 1970 and 1974 and also won the shot in 1970. She won eight pentathlon and two shot WAAA titles.
b. 6 Jul 1939 Halewood, Lancashire.

Heide Rosendahl ran a brilliant 22.96 for 200m and broke the world record for the pentathlon in 1972, but Mary Peters came in 1.12 seconds later to take both crowns. (ASP)

Walking Events

The IAAF have ratified records for women's track walking at 5km and 10km since 1981.
Women's walking is now an officially recognized championship event. A 5km event was included at the 1985 European Junior Championships and, with the 10km walk, the event makes its debut at a senior championships at the 1986 Europeans.

THE BARRIER BREAKERS FOR TRACK WALKING DISTANCES

3 kilometres
15min: Mary Nilsson (Swe) 14:52.6 Copenhagen 2 May 1965
14min: Anne Pembroke (Aus) 13:49.6 Sydney 15 Jan 1975
13min: Sue Cook (Aus) 12:56.5 Canberra 29 May 1982

5 kilometres
25min: May Bengtsson (Swe) 24:57.4 Varberg 11 Jul 1943
23min: Sue Cook (Aus) 22:53.20 Adelaide 21 Mar 1981
22min: Giuliana Salce (Ita) 21:51.85 L'Aquila 1 Oct 1983

10 kilometres
50min: Siw Gustavsson (Swe) 49:46.8 Örnsköldsvik 1 Aug 1976
48min: Ann Jansson (Swe) 47:58.2 Falkenberg 17 Oct 1981
46min: Sue Cook (Aus) 45:47.0 Leicester 14 Sep 1983

WORLD RECORDS and BESTS—TRACK WALK
(i=indoors)

	hr:min:sec			
1500m	6:19.0	Sue Cook (Aus)	Doncaster	8 Nov 1980
1 mile	6:28.46	Giuliana Salce (Ita)	Genoa	16 Feb 1985
3km	12:31.57	Giuliana Salce (Ita)	Florence	6 Feb 1985
	12:42.33	Giuliana Salce (Ita)	Ancona	17 Jul 1984
5km	21:36.2	Olga Krishtop (USSR)	Penza	3 Aug 1984
10km	45:39.5	Yan Hong (Chn)	Copenhagen	13 May 1984
15km	1:19:49.8	Sue Liers (USA)	Kings Point	20 Mar 1977
20km	1:48:18.6	Sue Liers (USA)	Kings Point	20 Mar 1977
	kilometres			
1 hour	12.036	Sue Cook (Aus)	Canberra	31 Jul 1984
2 hours	20.934	Lucyna Rokitowska (Pol)	Zabrze	9 Oct 1983

WORLD BESTS—ROAD WALKS

	hr:min:sec			
3km	12:32	Natalya Serbinenko (USSR)	Softeland	6 May 1984
5km	21:34	Vera Osipova (USSR)	Russe	21 Apr 1985
10 km	44:43	Yan Hong (Chn)	Shanghai	17 Mar 1985
15km	1:12:10	Sue Cook (Aus)	Melbourne	19 Oct 1982
20km	1:36:36	Sue Cook (Aus)	Melbourne	19 Oct 1982
25km	2:12:38	Sue Cook (Aus)	Canberra	20 Jun 1981
30km	2:45:52	Sue Cook (Aus)	Melbourne	5 Sep 1982
50km	5:01:52	Lilian Millen (UK)	York	16 Apr 1983
100km	11:40.07	Aaf de Rijk (Hol)	Hamm	17 Oct 1981
	kilometres			
24 hours	202.230	Annie van den Meer (Hol)	Rouen	30 Apr–1 May 1984

It should be noted that road times must be assessed with care as course conditions (and accuracy of measurement) can vary considerably.

Jesse Owens &

Four Olympic gold medals—both sprints, the long jump and the relay. To win them all at one Games is a staggering achievement, all the more so for being expected, for the mounting pressure must be extraordinary. Jesse Owens at Berlin in 1936 and Carl Lewis at Los Angeles in 1984 surmounted such pressure, both capping three individual titles with a world record on the US sprint relay team.

Jesse Owens went to the Olympics already a multi-world record holder, for he had had the greatest day in the history of the sport a year earlier. Lewis had no individual world records, although he had run and jumped faster and further than anyone else at sea-level. Up against Bob Beamon's fantastic world long jump record and the 100m and 200m records of Calvin Smith and Pietro Mennea, all set at over 2000m or 7000ft, Lewis has refused to compete at altitude because he wants to get the records without the help of the thin air of such sites as Mexico City or Colorado Springs.

J. C. Owens was born in Danville, Alabama on 12 September 1913, one of eight children of a cotton-picker. His family moved to Ohio, where he set national high school records at Cleveland East Tech in 1932–3 at 100y, 100m, 220y and long jump. In 1933 his 7.60m long jump was the world best for that year and stood as a high school record for 21 years, and his 9.4 for 100y was his first world record; he also won his first senior AAU title at long jump.

He was blessed with wonderful natural speed and co-ordination but his sprinting and jumping were further improved by Larry Snyder, track coach at Ohio State University. He set several world bests indoors and out, but his greatest day came at the Western Athletic Conference Championships, popularly known as the Big Ten, at Ann Arbor, Michigan on 25 May 1935. His afternoon's programme was as follows:

Jesse Owens beats his great rival Ralph Metcalfe in the Olympic 100m. The black-shorted Martinus Osendarp (Hol) just pips Frank Wykoff for third. (All-Sport)

Carl Lewis

3.15 p.m. 100y in 9.4 seconds to equal the world record. The time had first been run by George Simpson (USA) at Chicago on 8 June 1929, although this was not ratified as a record due to the fact that Simpson used starting blocks, which were not recognized by the IAAF until 1938. Owens himself had run 9.4 while still at high school and again at Evanston just 11 days prior to the Big Ten meeting.

3.25 p.m. Long jump of 26ft 8¼in (8.13m). On this, his one jump of the competition in a pit which had been specially dug in front of the stands for the meeting, Owens hit the board perfectly. Second was Willis Ward with 25ft 1½in (7.66m). The previous world record was 7.98m by Chuhei Nambu (Jap) in 1931. Owens himself had a previous best of 7.97m, set at the Drake Relays on 26 April 1935.

3.45 p.m. 220y in 20.3 seconds. This straight-course time was also a world record for the shorter distance of 200m. Owens again won clearly, with Andy Dooley second in 20.7. The previous record was 20.6 by Roland Locke in 1926 and Owens had run 20.7 in the Evanston meeting 11 days earlier.

4.00 p.m. 220y hurdles in 22.6, again also a record at 200m. Phil Doherty was second in 23.2. The officially ratified world record had been set 11 years previously by Charles Brookins at 23.0 in 1924, and equalled by Norman Paul in 1933. However, Glenn Hardin had run an unratified 22.7 in 1934 and Owens himself had run 22.9 at Evanston.

This series of magnificent performances was all the more amazing for the fact that Owens had a sore back, injured while rolling down stairs, which meant that he had had to be helped into Larry Snyder's car to take him to the track. The pain apparently left him at 3.15 p.m. and returned after his epic deeds.

The long jump alone must rate as one of the greatest performances in track and field history. His 15cm addition to the previous world record was the greatest ever to that date, although of course that was dwarfed when Bob Beamon added a record 55cm to the world record with his prodigious leap in Mexico City in 1968. But what set Owens's performance apart was the fact that it was to remain the world record for 25 years 79 days until Ralph Boston improved it in 1960. This duration is the longest for any world record at a standard Olympic event.

At the long jump Owens had won US titles both indoors and out in 1934 and led the world rankings that year with 7.81m. In 1935 he retained his AAU title with an indoor best of 7.85m, and this too was not bettered indoors for 25 years. Outdoors at the Drake Relays he became the third 26-footer in history. In 1935 and 1936 Owens bettered 26ft (7.92m) in 15 competitions, but it was 12 years before any other man exceeded that distance more than once. There was no shortage of great sprinters and jumpers in the 1930s. His greatest rivals were Ralph Metcalfe, who lost only eight outdoor sprints in five years of top-class competition, and whom Owens did not beat until 1936, and Eulace Peacock. Peacock beat both Metcalfe and Owens in the 1935 AAU 100m in a wind assisted 10.2 and beat Owens again in the long jump, 8.00m to 7.98m. He handed Owens four more sprint defeats the following year, but then pulled a muscle and had to miss the Olympics.

Owens went on to a triumphant season in 1936, winning all 46 competitions at sprints, hurdles and long jump that he contested in the outdoor season prior to the Olympic Games in Berlin. There he was supreme, with Olympic records and wins at 100m, 200m and long jump in 10.3, 20.7 and 8.06m respectively before his final gold in the relay. He lost at a couple of post-Olympic meetings, a 100m to Metcalfe in

After his 100m victory, Owens is congratulated by sixth-placed Lennart Strandberg (Swe), but the broadcasters as ever want their interviews. (Keystone Press)

Owens was, and at 174lb (79kg), 14lb heavier (6kg). His family, too, had moved northwards and he attended high schools in New Jersey, where he set national records in the long jump at 8.08m and 8.13m. He went to University at Houston in 1980 and speedily established himself as a major force, being world ranked that year at both 100m and long jump, the first athlete to achieve such a feat since Andy Stanfield (USA) in 1951. He has a strong family background in track and field, for his mother, as Evelyn Lawler, had been US champion and record holder at 80m hurdles, and his younger sister Carol has set two US long jump records and joined Carl on the US Olympic teams of 1980 (boycott year) and 1984.

Throughout the 1980s Lewis, despite his injury-marred season in 1985, has dominated sprints and long jump, unbeaten at the latter event in 44 successive competitions since his second place to Larry Myricks at the 1981 TAC Indoor Championships. He has recorded 28 of the 35 long jumps in history over 28ft (8.53m). The table summarises his titles and records.

Carl Lewis—titles won

Olympic Games 1984: 100m, 200m, LJ, 4×100m R
World Championships 1983: 100m, LJ, 4×100m R
World Cup 1981: LJ
TAC outdoor: 100m and LJ 1981–3; 200m 1983
TAC indoor: LJ 1982–4, 60y 1983
NCAA outdoor: LJ 1980–1, 100m 1981
NCAA indoor: LJ 1980–1, 60y 1981

Carl Lewis—records

World: 4×100m R on US team 37.86 1983, 37.83 1984
USA: as world, and 200m: 19.75 1983
World low-altitude bests: 100m: 10.00 1981 and 1982, 9.97 1983;
200m: 19.75 1983; LJ: 8.62m 1981, 8.76 m 1982, 8.79m 1983
World indoor: 60y 6.02 1983; LJ 8.49m 1981, 8.56m 1982, 8.79m 1984
Olympic: 200m 19.86 1984, 4×100m R 37.83 1984

Analysis of performances shows clearly just how good Owens was and Lewis is against the standards of brilliant contemporaries, but above all these black athletes demonstrated the true beauty of their sprinting and jumping form backed by fierce competitiveness, to triumph when it really mattered, at the pinnacle of competition in the Olympic Games.

Cologne and a long jump to Wilhelm Leichum (Ger) at Bochum, and ran his last race in a relay at the White City Stadium, London on 15 August 1936. Before his 23rd birthday he was lost to amateur athletics. By then, however, he had achieved the lot, national and Olympic titles and world records. The world was left with the memory of the greatest sprinter/jumper ever seen.

Now Carl Lewis has emulated Owens. Frederick Carleton Lewis was also born in Alabama, at Birmingham on 1 July 1961, so he was but a few months older than Owens had been when winning his gold medals. At 6ft 2in (1.88m) he is 4in (10cm) taller than

ALL-SPORT PHOTOGRAPHIC

LEFT: The first five finishers in this first round heat of the 1972 Olympic 1500m ran faster than the world record at the start of that year! Lyudmila Bragina (right— 335) set a world record, which in a unique feat, she improved further in both semi-final and final. Others prominent in the group are: (l-r) Joan Allison (UK-94), Ilja Keizer (Hol-189), Christa Merten (GFR), Jenny Orr (Aus-7), Glenda Reiser (Can), Jaroslava Jehlickova (Cs-326).

BELOW: Olympic champion Maricica Puica (left) lost only four races outdoors in 1985, but that was each time that she met Mary Decker-Slaney (right), who went through the year undefeated.

ABOVE: The world record sprint relay team from the GDR at the 1985 World Cup: (l-r) Silke Gladisch, Sabine Rieger, Ingrid Auerswald and Marlies Göhr. BELOW: Igor Paklin could manage only fourth in the 1985 World Cup, but earlier he had moved the world high jump record to just an inch off eight feet.

ABOVE: **Ralph Boston, Olympic champion in 1960, ranked number one in the world each year from 1960 to 1967.**
BELOW: **The first six-metre pole vaulter, Sergey Bubka.**
RIGHT: **The greatest woman athlete of all-time?—Marita Koch sets her sixteenth world record in winning the 1985 World Cup 400 metres.**

Marita Koch

Marita Koch has had a career of unparalleled brilliance, and must rate as a prime contender for the athlete of the past decade. She succeeded another beautiful runner, Irena Szewinska, as the world's best, and is now well on her way to emulating the latter's tremendous tally of medals and records.

Koch, a student of pediatric medicine and member of the Sports Club Empor Rostock, was unbeaten at 400m from her loss to Szewinska at the 1977 World Cup until challenged by Jarmila Kratochvilova, who beat her once in 1981. She has been brilliant also at shorter distances, the world's best at 200m, challenging her great team-mate Marlies Göhr at 100m, and even the fastest ever at 60m indoors. She has set 16 world records and the table of her records and championships shows just how impressive are her achievements and how consistent her ability to run fast and rise to the big occasion.

Marita aimed her 1985 season at the World Cup in Canberra in October. Earlier she ran brilliantly both indoors and out at the sprints, setting a couple of world indoor bests and winning the European Cup Final 200m. However, she did not attempt the 400m until the GDR warm-up meeting in East Berlin in September. She showed that she was ready with an untroubled 48.97. In Canberra she was supreme. On the first day she easily won the 200m and then took off on the final leg of the 4×400m relay with a strong challenge from the Soviet runner, Olga Vladykina, who had been unbeaten all year at 400m. Koch, however, ran a 47.9 leg and swept past, irrestistably coming off the final bend to bring her team home to victory. Then her triumphant career was topped on the final day by a wonderful run in the individual 400m. She passed 200m in an amazing 22.4 and continued to drive for home, leaving Jarmila Kratochvilova wallowing some 35 metres behind, and even Vladykina, who ran the third fastest ever at 48.27, could not get close to her as Koch regained the world record, which Kratochvilova had set at 47.99 two years earlier, and reduced it to a stunning 47.60. That time matched the time that *Chariots of Fire* man Eric Liddell had run in setting a men's world record at the Paris Olympics of 1924.

She was born on 18 February 1957 at Wismar, GDR.

Between them 29 world records outdoors and 23 world bests indoors to the end of 1985 – the brilliant GDR sprinters Marita Koch (l) and Marlies Göhr (r). (ASP)

Marita Koch world records and major championships appearances — outdoors
(R = relay legs, all for GDR national team; WR = World record; WB = World best)

Date	Venue and event		Place	Time	
23 Aug 75	Athens — European Junior	400m	2	51.60	(1. Brehmer)
24 Aug 75	Athens — European Junior	4×400m R	1	3:33.7	
28 Jul 76	Montreal — Olympics	400m	–	scratched from semis	
2 Jul 77	Dresden — GDR Ch.	400m	1	51.47	
13 Aug 77	Helsinki — European Cup	400m	1	49.53	
14 Aug 77	Helsinki — European Cup	4×400m R	1	3:23.70	
2 Sep 77	Düsseldorf — World Cup	4×400m R	1	3:24.04	
	Düsseldorf — World Cup	400m	2	49.76	(1. Szewinska)
28 May 78	Erfurt	200m	1	22.06	WR
2 Jul 78	Leipzig — GDR Ch.	400m	1	49.19	WR
19 Aug 78	Potsdam	400m	1	49.03	WR
31 Aug 78	Prague — European Ch.	400m	1	48.94	WR
3 Sep 78	Prague — European Ch.	4×400m R	1	3:21.20	
3 Jun 79	Leipzig	200m	1	22.02	WR
10 Jun 79	Karl-Marx-Stadt	200m	1	21.71	WR
	Karl-Marx-Stadt	4×100m R	1	42.10	WR
29 Jul 79	Potsdam	400m	1	48.89	WR
4 Aug 79	Turin — European Cup	400m	1	48.60	WR
5 Aug 79	Turin — European Cup	4×400m R	1	3:19.62	
11 Aug 79	Karl-Marx-Stadt — GDR Ch.	200m	1	22.05	
24 Aug 79	Montreal — World Cup	200m	2	22.02	(1. Ashford)
24 Aug 79	Montreal — World Cup	4×400m R	1	3:20.37	
26 Aug 79	Montreal — World Cup	400m	1	48.97	
12 Sep 79	Mexico C. — World Student G.	200m	1	21.91	
17 Jul 80	Cottbus — GDR Ch.	400m	1	49.55	
28 Jul 80	Moscow — Olympics	400m	1	48.88	
1 Aug 80	Moscow — Olympics	4×400m R	2	3:20.35	(1. USSR)
9 Aug 80	Jena	4×200m R	1	1:28.15	WR
8 Aug 81	Jena — GDR Ch.	400m	1	49.64	
15 Aug 81	Zagreb — European Cup	400m	1	49.43	
16 Aug 81	Zagreb — European Cup	4×400m R	1	3:19.83	
4 Sep 81	Rome — World Cup	4×400m R	1	3:20.62	
	Rome — World Cup	400m	2	49.27	(1. Kratochvilova)
1 Jul 82	Dresden — GDR Ch.	100m	3	11.01	
3 Jul 82	Dresden — GDR Ch.	200m	1	21.76	
8 Sep 82	Athens — European Ch.	400m	1	48.16	WR
11 Sep 82	Athens — European Ch.	4×400m R	1	3:19.04	WR
31 Jul 83	Berlin	4×100m R	1	41.53	WR
16 Jun 83	Karl-Marx-Stadt — GDR Ch.	100m	2	10.99	
18 Jun 83	Karl-Marx-Stadt — GDR Ch.	200m	1	21.82	
8 Aug 83	Helsinki — World Ch.	100m	2	11.02	
10 Aug 83	Helsinki — World Ch.	4×100m R	1	41.76	
14 Aug 83	Helsinki — World Ch.	200m	1	22.13	
14 Aug 83	Helsinki — World Ch.	4×400m R	1	3:19.73	
20 Aug 83	London — European Cup	4×100m R	1	42.63	
21 Aug 83	London — European Cup	200m R	2	22.40	(1. Kratochvilova)
2 Jun 84	Erfurt — GDR Ch.	400m	1	48.86	
3 Jun 84	Erfurt	4×400m R	1	3:15.92	WR
21 Jul 84	Potsdam	200m	1	21.71	WR (=)
16 Aug 84	Prague — Friendship Games	400m	1	48.16	GDR record (=)
9 Aug 85	Leipzig — GDR Ch.	100m	2	10.97	
11 Aug 85	Leipzig — GDR Ch.	200m	1	21.78	
17 Aug 85	Moscow — European Cup	4×100m R	1	41.65	
18 Aug 85	Moscow — European Cup	200m	1	22.02	
4 Oct 85	Canberra — World Cup	200m	1	21.90	
4 Oct 85	Canberra — World Cup	4×400m R	1	3:18.49	
6 Oct 85	Canberra — World Cup	400m	1	47.60	WR

Marita Koch indoor world bests and major championships

Date	Venue		Place	Time	
24 Feb 77	Milan	400m	1ht	51.80	WB
24 Feb 77	Milan	400m	1	51.57	WB
13 Mar 77	San Sebastian — European Ch.	400m	1	51.14	WB
10 Feb 78	Senftenberg	100y	1	10.47	WB
18 Feb 79	Senftenberg	100y	1	10.33	WB
25 Feb 79	Vienna — European Ch.	60m	2	7.19	(1. Göhr)
12 Jan 80	Berlin	100m	1	11.15	WB
2 Feb 80	Grenoble	50m	1	6.16	WB
2 Feb 80	Grenoble	50m	1	6.11	WB
14 Feb 81	Senftenberg	60m	1	7.10	WB (=)
22 Feb 81	Grenoble — European Ch.	50m	3	6.19	(1. Popova)
29 Jan 83	Senftenberg	60m	1	7.08	WB
29 Jan 83	Senftenberg	200m	1	22.63	WB
3 Mar 83	Budapest — European Ch.	200m	1	22.39	WB
18 Jan 85	Paris — World Indoor G.	200m	1	23.09	
16 Feb 85	Senftenberg	60m	1	7.04	WB
16 Feb 85	Senftenberg	100y	1	10.25	WB
3 Mar 85	Athens — European Ch.	200m	1	22.82	

Yuriy Sedykh

Even before the 1984 season started there could be little doubt as to Yuriy Sedykh's status as the greatest hammer thrower of all time. Despite not being able to win his third Olympic gold medal, as he surely would have but for the Soviet boycott, his performances that year reached new heights, allied to amazing consistency. One should also bear in mind that in 1983 he had been overtaken by his teammate Sergey Litvinov, who had beaten him at the World Championships and improved the world record to 84.14. Sedykh beat that 13 times in his final six competitions of 1984, in which his series of throws were:

Date	Venue	Mark	Series					
3 Jul	Cork	86.34	(86.34,	86.00,	85.20,	81.66,	82.60,	81.80)
13 Jul	London	85.60	(85.04,	85.60,	85.52,	N,	N,	82.96)
17 Aug	Moscow — Druzhba	85.60	(84.44,	83.10,	83.38,	85.60,	83.88,	84.84)
20 Aug	Budapest GP	85.02	(N,	83.06,	83.86,	83.52,	82.96,	85.02)
31 Aug	Rome — Golden Gala	83.90	(83.90,	83.90,	83.82,	83.20,	83.44,	83.50)
14 Sep	Tokyo — 8 Nations	84.60	(84.58,	84.48,	84.60,	N,	N,	81.72)

(N = no throw)

Both Sedykh's Olympic golds were at the head of Soviet 1–2–3s. His first came at the age of 21 in 1976, with Aleksey Spiridonov second and the defending champion, his coach Anatoliy Bondarchuk third. While others have threatened his position, he has consistently come through to win the major titles, the European in 1978 and 1982 and the Olympics in 1980. The latter best demonstrated his ability. He started the year with two world records, but his 80.64m was passed by Litvinov a week later with 81.66m. Juri Tamm was also over 80 metres, but Sedykh as always rose to the occasion and with the very first throw of the Olympic final sent his hammer out to a new record of 81.80m, a mark his rivals were unable to match.

In 1985 he had a relatively quiet season, leaving Juri Tamm firmly at the head of the world rankings, but with the challenge of major championships he will no doubt continue to be the man to beat in future.

Sedykh has been a great innovator in hammer throwing. His hallmark has been a finely grooved technique accentuated by great speed in the circle. His post-graduate dissertation was on 'The effectiveness of powerbuilding means in hammer throw training', and he certainly seems to have found the secret.

Annual progress:

1971 **57.02**. 1972 **62.96**. 1973 **69.04**. 1974 **70.86**.
1975 **75.00**. 1976 **78.86**. 1977 **76.60**. 1978 **79.76**.
1979 **77.58**. 1980 **81.80**. 1981 **80.18**.1982 **81.66**.
1983 **80.94**. 1984 **86.34**. 1985 **82.70**.

(ASP)

Edwin Moses

(ASP)

Ed Moses has dominated his event for longer than any athlete in the history of athletics. One has to go back to Emil Zatopek at 10 000m in the early 1950s or 'Dutch' Warmerdam at pole vault in the early 1940s to find anything remotely comparable, but even they did not sustain their superiority for so long.

He came into athletics comparatively late. Having achieved nothing of note at high school, he blossomed when he enrolled as an engineering student at Morehouse College in Georgia. In his first year, 1975, he ran one race at 440y hurdles, running the event in 52.0. The next year, however, he was sensational. He ran 50.1 in his first race at 400mh and stormed on to win the US Olympic Trials and then the Olympic title in his first world record of 47.63. He lost only three finals that year and had compiled a sequence of 18 successive victories up to his last competition of 1977. That race, at the ISTAF meeting in Berlin, goes down in history, for Harald Schmid won, 49.07 to 49.29. Since then Moses has compiled his fabulous win streak. To the end of 1984 he had won 94 successive competitions, 109 if we include heats, and why should we not since he always runs to win?

No track athlete in the history of the sport has got anywhere near this figure. He took one year off from competition, 1982, in which year he married Myrella, but returned to improve his world record to 47.02 in 1983. A particular feature of his running is his ability to use just 13 strides between the hurdles all the way, whereas others are forced to change down to 14 or 15 strides during the race.

Injury prevented him from running the hurdles in 1985, but several men, notably Andre Phillips and Danny Harris showed that they will be ready for him when he returns. But then Moses has always stayed ahead.

The enormous respect in which Edwin Moses is held in the world of athletics was shown when he was chosen at the end of 1984 as one of the three representatives of the USA to the IAAF. He thus became the first active athlete to take on this responsibility. He was chosen to take the Olympic oath on behalf of the competitors at the opening ceremony in Los Angeles, and the fact that he fluffed his words might even have enhanced his reputation, for it seemed that he was human after all.

(John Burles)

Edwin Moses — Career summary at 400m hurdles

Year	Best	No. of races	No. of wins	sub-48	48.00–48.49	48.50–48.99	49.00–49.49	49.50–49.99
1975	52.0y	1	–	–	–	–	–	–
1976	47.64	20	16	1	2	5	3	4
1977	47.45	19	18	2	–	8	4	4
1978	47.94	14	14	1	2	7	1	1
1979	47.53	25	25	4	3	8	5	4
1980	47.13	21	21	4	2	9	3	2
1981	47.14	14	14	6	2	3	2	–
1983	47.02	18	18	7	4	2	3	2
1984	47.32	13	13	5	3	3	1	1
no races in 1982 and 1985 (injured)								
Totals		**145**	**139**	**30**	**18**	**45**	**22**	**18**

The total of 30 sub-48 second times by Moses compared to just five for the rest of the world to the end of 1984: Harald Schmid (GFR) 3, Andre Phillips (USA) 1, John Akii-Bua (Uga) 1.
In 1985 Phillips ran 3, Schmid, Danny Harris (USA) and Aleksandr Vasilyev (USSR) 1 each.

(ASP)

From 'Little Mary'

Mary first caught the attention of the athletics world in 1973, when at 14 years 224 days, she became the youngest ever US international. She was third at 1 mile indoors at Richmond, Virginia against the USSR in a race won by the Olympic champion Lyudmila Bragina.

US outdoor records set by Mary Decker-Slaney

800m	1:57.60	31 Jul	1983
	1:56.90	16 Aug	1985
1000m	2:34.8	4 Jul	1985
1500m	4:01.17	12 Jul	1980
	4:00.04	17 Jul	1980
	3:59.43	13 Aug	1980
	3:57.12	26 Jul	1983
1 mile	4:23.49	30 Jun	1979
	4:21.68 WR	26 Jan	1980
	4:21.46	26 Jun	1982
	4:18.08 WR	9 Jul	1982
	4:16.71 WR	21 Aug	1985
2000m	5:38.9	7 Jul	1982
	5:32.7 WR	3 Aug	1984
3000m	8:38.73	15 Jul	1980
	8:29.71	7 Jul	1982
	8:29.69	25 Aug	1985
	8:25.83	7 Sep	1985
5000m	15:08.26 WR	5 Jun	1982
	15:06.53	1 Jun	1985
10 000m	31:35.3 WR	16 Jul	1982

WR = world record

World indoor bests set by Mary Decker-Slaney

800m	2:01.8	17 Feb	1974
880y	2:06.7	8 Feb	1974
	2:02.3	17 Feb	1974
	1:59.7	22 Feb	1980
1000y	2:26.7	19 Jan	1974
	2:23.8	3 Feb	1978
1500m	4:00.8	8 Feb	1980
	4:00.2*	16 Feb	1980
1 mile	4:24.6	22 Jan	1982
	4:21.47	12 Feb	1982
	4:20.5	19 Feb	1982
	4:17.55*	16 Feb	1980
2000m	5.49.1	5 Feb	1982
	5:34.52	18 Jan	1985
3000m	8:47.3	5 Feb	1982
2 miles	9:31.7	21 Jan	1982

* Track over 200m in circumference

The story of Mary Decker has all the ingredients of a best-selling novel—from a teenage prodigy whose career was blighted by injury to the world champion whose Olympic aspirations were dashed to the Los Angeles track. She is a beautifully smooth runner whose front-running tactics have brought her enormous success and a host of records from the indoor tracks of the USA, on which she has been undefeated since 1976, to the stadiums of the European tour.

to Superstar

Later that year, still before her 15th birthday, 5ft tall (1.52m) and weighing just 80lb (36kg), she won at 800m first the Pacific Conference title and then against the USSR in Minsk.

In 1974 Mary, who had by then grown to 5ft 3in (1.60m), set her first world indoor record, at 880y, and won again against the USSR both indoors and out. On the former occasion in Moscow she gave vent to her anger when brushed past by her opponent, Sarmite Shtula, in a 4×800m relay. Mary stumbled and then threw her baton at her opponent. She picked it up and threw it again at the end of the race. Both teams were disqualified.

Mary had achieved prodigious success but her growing body could not take the strain of a hard racing and training schedule. Over the next few years she suffered a series of leg injuries, but it is remarkable testimony to her determination that she overcame them to return an even better athlete. Crucial to her recovery were operations in 1977 and 1978 to her calves to relieve compartment syndrome, wherein the growing muscles have insufficient room within their sheaths of tissue. Dick Quax, the New Zealand runner, who later became her coach, showed her how his problems had been overcome by this treatment.

She won the 1979 Pan-American 1500m title and had a magnificent year in 1980, although the US boycott meant that she had to miss the Olympics, as she had through injury four years earlier. Further injuries to her legs meant that she had to miss the 1981 season, but in September of that year she married marathon runner Ron Tabb. Sadly that partnership was short-lived, but she was remarried on 1 January 1985 to British discus thrower Richard Slaney.

Over the past four years Mary Decker-Slaney

has repeatedly demonstrated her superb abilities, capped by her double triumph at 1500m and 3000m at the 1983 World Championships. Her long-held aspirations for Olympic success were shattered when she tumbled to the infield in the 3000m, after tripping over Zola Budd. We will never know whether she might have beaten Maricica Puica that day, but it should be noted that she had shown rather below-par form in the weeks leading up to the Games, being beaten by Ruth Wysocki in the US 1500m Trials, her first loss to a US athlete for four years. However, in 1985 she put aside her severe disappointment and had a triumphant undefeated year, including important wins over Puica and Budd.

Married in 1985, Mary and Richard Slaney. (ASP)

British years of

For the best part of a decade, starting in 1977, British athletes have been supreme at 1500m and 1 mile, winning all the major championship races. Steve Ovett, Seb Coe and Steve Cram have taken it in turns to head the world rankings and to rewrite the record books. Just to complete the picture, when neither Coe nor Ovett contested the 1978 Commonwealth Games, another British runner, Dave Moorcroft, won the 1500m gold medal. He too became a world record holder, at the longer distance of 5000m, in his *annus mirabilis* of 1982.

During the war years of 1940–45 Swedish middle distance runners, headed by Gunder Hägg and Arne Andersson, exercised similar domination to that enjoyed by Britain in the 1970s and 1980s, and set numerous records. Hägg had a glorious sequence of races in 1942, when he set ten world records in nine races in just 81 days: (In the first six of these races Arne Andersson finished runner-up. A galling record!)

1 July	1 mile	4:06.2
3 July	2 miles	8:47.8
17 July	1500m	3:45.8
21 July	2000m	5:16.4
23 August	2000m	5:11.8
28 August	3000m	8:01.2
4 September	1 mile	4:04.6
11 September	3 miles	13:35.4
20 September	3 miles	13:32.4
(same race)	5000m	13.58.6

Hägg had another spell of three world records in 40 days in 1944: 2 miles in 8:46.4 on 25

Seb Coe – No. 1 Olympic 1500m 1984. (below left) Steve Cram beats Steve Ovett at the 1983 IAC mile. (ASP)

miling glory — Ovett, Coe and Cram

Ron Pickering interviews the golden trio for BBC TV prior to the Olympics in 1984. (ASP)

June, 1500m in 3:43.0 on 7 July, 2 miles in 8:42.8 on 4 August. He also bettered the 1 mile record during this period, when he ran 4:02.0 on 18 July, but on this occasion he suffered a rare defeat by Andersson who took the record with 4:01.6.

In those years, however, few nations were able to take part in sport normally, so the run of success over the past decade by the British runners is surely without parallel.

Coe, Ovett, and later Cram had many highly talented runners to contend with, but as racers both against their rivals and against the clock they have stood supreme. Choosing their races carefully, they avoided falling prey to the trap of over-racing. That, however, combined with injuries and illness, meant that they clashed rarely. Indeed, the three raced together only twice—at 1500m in the 1980 and 1984 Olympic Games; on both occasions Coe was the winner. In 1980 he overcame the shock of losing to Ovett at 800m. when he had run a tactically inept race at a distance at which he was considered nonpareil, to triumph at 1500m with Ovett third behind Jürgen Straub (GDR) and the 20-year-old Cram eighth. In 1984 we so nearly had the thrilling sight of a British 1–2–3, but sadly Ovett was overcome by a viral infection that affected his breathing, and had to step off the track when looking challenging on the last lap. That he had even qualified for the final after collapsing following the 800m was tribute to his immense ability and character. Cram too had had his preparations for the Games severely interrupted by injuries and lacked a little of his sharpness of the two previous years, but Coe was back, after serious illness, to his glorious best as he showed, just as he had in 1981, when he set four world records, that unmatched ability to kick again off an already fast pace.

Ovett, strong and famed for his devastating kick from 200 metres out, so dominated his opponents that they were overwhelmed not just by his speed but seemingly by his presence so that they frequently played right into his hands with tactics that enabled him to use his strengths as and when he wished. But then he was such a consummate runner that he could and did win in any type of race.

20 years old, the bearded Steve Ovett beats the established 1500m men Dave Moorcroft (13) and Frank Clement (3) at the 1976 UK Olympic Trials. (ASP)

Coe, at first sight frail at 1.77m and 54kg, against the big men like John Walker or indeed Ovett and Cram, lost some big 800m races, which he should, given perfect health, have won comfortably. At his brilliant best, however, he has been one of the most beautifully balanced of all runners and above all he has showed that ability to inject yet more pace in the finishing straight, so that even the finest men have just had to watch him flow away while they fought agonizingly towards the finish.

Cram, able to hold a long, sustained drive for the line, staggered the athletics world with his prodigious feats as a teenager. He surged on, and with European, Commonwealth and World titles already to his credit, finally surpassed his rivals with a series of magnificent world records in the summer of 1985. Temperamentally so mature, physically so gifted, his feats opening up lifelong prospects, yet remaining wonderfully relaxed and approachable, he has taken over the mantle of the king of the milers.

What a trio, all British, and all in one generation! We have been fortunate indeed to see them and share in their successes. Magnificent ambassadors for the sport, they have contributed enormously to the growth in its popularity, and have set wondrous examples to all aspiring athletes.

Championships records of Coe, Cram and Ovett

Olympic Games
OVETT	1976 5th 800m, semis 1500m; 1980 1st 800m, 3rd 1500m; 1984 8th 800m, dnf 1500m
COE	1980 1st 1500m, 2nd 800m; 1984 1st 1500m, 2nd 800m
CRAM	1980 8th 1500m; 1984 2nd 1500m

European Championships
OVETT	1974 2nd 800m; 1978 2nd 800m, 1st 1500m
COE	1978 3rd 800m; 1982 2nd 800m
CRAM	1982 1st 1500m

World Championships
OVETT	1983 4th 1500m
CRAM	1983 1st 1500m

European Junior Championships
OVETT	1973 1st 800m
COE	1975 3rd 1500m
CRAM	1979 1st 3000m

European Indoor Championships
COE	1977 1st 800m

Commonwealth Games
CRAM	1978 heats 1500m; 1982 1st 1500m

World Cup
OVETT	1977 1st 1500m; 1981 1st 1500m
COE	1981 1st 800m

European Cup Final
OVETT	1975 1st 800m; 1977 1st 1500m
COE	1977 4th 800m; 1979 1st 800m; 1981 1st 800m
CRAM	1981 3rd 1500m; 1983 1st 1500m; 1985 1st 1500m

AAA Championships won:
OVETT	Youth 400m 1971–2; Senior 800m 1974–6, 1500m 1979–80
COE	Youth 1500m 1973; Junior 1500m 1975; Senior 800m 1981

CRAM   Youth 1500m 1977; Junior 3000m 1979;
                Senior 1500m 1981–3, 800m 1984

UK Championships won:
OVETT   1500m 1977, 1981
COE   800m 1978

<u>Records set by Coe, Cram and Ovett</u>
(W World, E European, UK UK national, EJ European junior, NJ UK national junior)

Steve Ovett

800m	EJ	4 Sep 1974	1:45.76	Rome
	UK	31 Aug 1978	1:44.09	Prague
1000m	NJ	17 Aug 1973	2:20.0	Crystal Palace
	UK	6 Sep 1979	2:15.91	Koblenz
1500m	NJ	25 Jul 1973	3:44.8	Motspur Park
	UK	3 Sep 1977	3:34.45	Düsseldorf
	W	15 Jul 1980	3:32.09	Oslo
	W	27 Aug 1980	3:31.36	Koblenz
	W	4 Sep 1983	3:30.77	Rieti
1 mile	NJ	25 Jul 1973	4:00.0	Motspur Park
	NJ	17 Jul 1974	3:59.4	Haringey
	UK	26 Jun 1977	3:54.69	Crystal Palace
	UK	20 Sep 1978	3:52.8	Oslo
	W	1 Jul 1980	3:48.8	Oslo
	W	26 Aug 1981	3:48.40	Koblenz
2000m	UK	3 Jun 1978	4:57.82	Crystal Palace
	UK	7 Jul 1982	4:57.71	Oslo
2 miles	W	15 Sep 1978	8:13.51	Crystal Palace

Seb Coe

800m	UK	9 Sep 1977	1:44.95	Crystal Palace
	UK	18 Aug 1978	1:44.25	Brussels
	UK	15 Sep 1978	1:43.97	Crystal Palace
	W	5 Jul 1979	1:42.33	Oslo
	W	10 Jun 1981	1:41.73	Florence
1000m	W	1 Jul 1980	2:13.40	Oslo
	W	11 Jul 1981	2:12.18	Oslo
1500m	E	17 Jul 1979	3:32.8	Oslo
	W	15 Jul 1979	3:32.03	Zürich
1 mile	W	17 Jul 1979	3:48.95	Oslo
	W	19 Aug 1981	3:48.53	Zürich
	W	28 Aug 1981	3:47.33	Brussels
4×800m	W	30 Aug 1982	7:03.89	Crystal Palace (1:44.01 leg)
		also Indoor bests:			
800m	UK	19 Feb 1977	1:47.6	Dortmund
	UK	26 Feb 1977	1:47.5	Cosford
	UK	13 Mar 1977	1:46.54	San Sebastian
	W	11 Feb 1981	1:46.0	Cosford
	W	12 Mar 1983	1:44.91	Cosford
1000m	W	19 Mar 1983	2:18.58	Oslo

Steve Cram

4×800m	W	30 Aug 1982	7:03.89	Crystal Palace (1:44.54 leg)
1500m	W	16 Jul 1985	3:29.67	Nice
1 mile	W	27 Jul 1985	3:46.32	Oslo
2000m	W	4 Aug 1985	4:51.39	Budapest

<u>Personal best performances</u>

COE
400m	46.87	1979
600m	1:15.0	1981
800m	1:41.73	1981
1000m	2:12.18	1981
1500m	3:31.95	1981
1 mile	3:47.33	1981
2000m	4:58.84	1982
3000m	7:55.2i	1981
5000m	14:06.2	1980

CRAM
400m	49.1	1982
600m	1:16.79	1983
800m	1:42.88	1985
1000m	2:12.85	1985
1500m	3:29.67	1985
1 mile	3:46.32	1985
2000m	4:51.39	1985
3000m	7:43.1	1983
2 miles	8:14.93	1983

5000m	13:48.0	1984

OVETT
400m	47.5	1974
600m	1:16.0	1979
800m	1:44.09	1978
1000m	2:15.91	1979
1500m	3:30.77	1983
1 mile	3:48.40	1981
2000m	4:57.71	1982
3000m	7:41.3	1977
2 miles	8:13.51	1978
5000m	13:25.0	1977

Miling superstars of two generations: Sir Roger Bannister and Seb Coe. (ASP)

<u>Yearly progress at 800m, 1500m and 1 mile</u>
(Shown in brackets are positions in the yearly world top 100 lists)

SEBASTIAN COE born 29 Sep 1956 Chiswick, London

	800m		1500m		1 mile	
1970			4:31.8			
1971	2:08.4		4:18.0			
1972	1:59.9		4:05.9			
1973	1:56.0		3:55.0			
1974	did not compete due to injury					
1975	1:53.8		3:45.2			
1976	1:47.7	(73)	3:42.67		3:58.35	(28)
1977	1:44.95	(4)			3:57.67	(24)
1978	1:43.97	(2)			4:02.17	
1979	1:42.33	(1)	3:32.03	(1)	3:48.95	(1)
1980	1:44.7	(2)	3:32.19	(4)		
1981	1:41.73	(1)	3:31.95	(2)	3:47.33	(1)
1982	1:44.48	(2)	3:39.1	(58)	3:59.5	
1983	1:43.80	(3)	3:35.17	(19)	3:52.93	(22)
1984	1:43.64	(5)	3:32.39	(2)	3:54.6	(20)
1985	1:43.07	(4)	3:32.13	(8)	3:49.22	(4)

STEVE CRAM born 14 Oct 1960 Gateshead

	800m		1500m		1 mile	
1973			4:31.5			
1974	2:11.0		4:22.3			
1975	2:07.1		4:13.9			
1976	1:59.7		4:07.1			
1977	1:56.3		3:47.7			
1978	1:53.5		3:40.09	(69)	3:57.43	(18)
1979	1:48.5		3:42.5		3:57.03	(27)
1980	1:48.41		3:34.74	(11)	3:53.8	(6)
1981	1:46.29	(30)	3:34.81	(9)	3:49.95	(7)
1982	1:44.45	(1)	3:33.66	(6)	3:49.90	(6)
1983	1:43.61	(1)	3:31.66	(3)	3:52.56	(18)
1984	1:46.0	(47)	3:33.13	(3)	3:49.65	(2)
1985	1:42.88	(3)	3:29.67	(2)	3:46.32	(1)

STEVE OVETT born 9 Oct 1955 Brighton

	800m		1500m		1 mile	
1970	2:00.0		4:10.7			
1971	1:55.3					
1972	1:52.5		4:01.5			
1973	1:47.34	(52)	3:44.8		4:00.0	(40)
1974	1:45.76	(10)	3:46.2		3:59.4	(38)
1975	1:46.09	(15)	3:39.5	(33)	3:57.00	(16)
1976	1:45.44	(9)	3:37.89	(25)		
1977	1:48.31		3:34.45	(2)	3:54.69	(5)
1978	1:44.09	(3)	3:35.59	(2)	3:52.8	(3)
1979	1:44.91	(7)	3:32.11	(2)	3:49.57	(2)
1980	1:45.40	(6)	3:31.36	(1)	3:48.8	(1)
1981	1:46.40	(31)	3:31.57	(1)	3:48.40	(2)
1982	1:46.08	(34)	3:38.48	(41)		
1983	1:45.25	(24)	3:30.77	(1)	3:50.49	(5)
1984	1:44.81	(20)	3:34.50	(13)		
1985			3:37.74	(41)	3:55.01	(17)

Sergey Bubka

World records have been set in the pole vault more frequently than in any other event. This is perhaps not surprising when one considers the nature of the activity. From the first world record to be set with a fibre-glass pole, 4.83m (15ft 10¼in) by George Davies in 1962, there were, to the end of the 1983 season, 47 performances from 20 men in the lists of pole vault world records broken or equalled. In 1984 Sergey Bubka became the 21st as he added four more records to that list. He had also set three world indoor bests. Then in 1985 he sealed his position in the history books with the world's first 6-metre vault.

Bubka had a disappointing start to his international career with seventh place in the 1981 European Indoor Championships, but his talent was well regarded in the Soviet Union. Nonetheless, his selection for the 1983 World Championships was a surprise, but one that was amply rewarded when he won the gold medal. Towards the end of the 1984 season he lost a couple of times to his main Soviet rivals, but by then he had compiled a formidable record. Under the guidance of his coach, Nikanorov Petrov, he contested a limited number of competitions with the aim of reaching his peak in early August to coincide with the Olympics. Of course he was denied that opportunity, but showed just what form he was in with a world record each month from May to August. His peak came in an epic duel with Thierry Vigneron in Rome, when, emulating Bob Seagren and Kjell Isaksson in 1972 and Bill Sefton and Earle Meadows in 1937, two men set world records in one competition. Vigneron set his fifth world record in five years at 5.91m only for Bubka to display his great competitive ability less than ten minutes later in clearing 5.94m.

He started 1985 in low key, but after a couple of meetings at which he jumped 5.80m, showed that he remained supreme with a wondrous clearance of six metres in Paris. In that competition he entered with a first-time clearance of 5.70m, before immediately setting the bar at this world record. He went on to show his competitive ability four days later in Nice, when after Olympic champion Pierre Quinon had succeeded at 5.90m, he went beautifully over 5.95m. He maintained fine form to win the European Cup final, the Grand Prix and the World Cup for the vault. His elder brother Vasiliy also improved in 1985 to a best of 5.85m.

Bubka's technique has greatly impressed his rivals. He is very fast and very strong and above all his shown that he can control the pole from a remarkably high grip. Using a 5.10m pole his top hand is very near the top, at about 5.03m. This ability has given him the opportunity to jump higher than his rivals as he led the way towards the six-metre vault.

Indoor world bests:

15 Jan 1984 Vilnius	5.81m
1 Feb 1984 Milan	5.82m
10 Feb 1984 Inglewood	5.83m
15 Jan 1986 Osaka	5.88m

Outdoor world records:

26 May 1984 Bratislava	5.85m
2 Jun 1984 St Denis	5.88m
13 Jul 1984 London	5.90m
31 Aug 1984 Rome	5.94m
13 Jul 1985 Paris	6.00m

Willie Banks

The preparation is total, the technique honed over the years, the enjoyment vast. Willie Banks puts himself into the mood by tuning in on his stereo headset to his favourite music—for the world record in Indianapolis in 1985, it was soul singer Whitney Houston. Then he steps on to the runway and he smiles as the crowd begin the rhythmic clapping that accelerates in tempo as he runs down for the triple phase that sends him way out into the pit. He leaps out and waves his thanks to the audience.

(ASP)

Willie Banks has elevated the triple jump to a star attraction in arenas all over the world by the force of his own exuberance. There can thus have been no more warmly received news by athletics fans than that in the 1985 TAC Championships he had smashed Joao Carlos de Oliveira's ten-year-old world record.

Willie Banks had first emerged as a top-class jumper at Westwood, Los Angeles on 3 May 1975, when as a freshman at UCLA he competed for them in their annual classic against cross-town rivals USC. First he improved his long jump best from 24ft 6in (7.47m) to a wind-assisted 26ft 2¼in (7.98m) and then, urged on by a vastly enthusiastic home crowd, produced an American junior triple jump record of 55ft 1in (16.79m), an improvement of nearly 2ft on his previous best of 53ft 2in (16.20m). Surprisingly, while at UCLA, he never won the NCAA title, placing successively 10–4–2–2 in 1975–8. He jumped consistently amongst the best in the USA, but just missed out in the big events; in 1976 he was fourth in the Olympic Trials, so failed to make the Games, and his best AAU placing was third in 1976.

Banks was carried off the field at the 1978 AAU Championships due to lower back trouble, and this determined him to retire from the sport. However, he then realised just how much he missed track and field. Over the next two years he worked much harder than before, concentrating on improving his physical fitness and technical aspects of the triple jump. This perseverance was rewarded by a breakthrough to the top. In 1979 he achieved second places at the AAU, with 17.43wm, and at the Pan-American Games behind de Oliveira. He capped a fine year, during which he was working on a Master's degree in Public Administration, with his first major title, at the World Student Games. He then enrolled at UCLA's law school, and swept to wins at both TAC and Olympic Trials in 1980, but sadly had to miss the Games due to the US boycott.

His attention to and eulogy by the European crowds started on a two-month tour in 1981. Recognizing his need to 'jump on adrenalin', at the DN Galen in Stockholm he put on his Sony Walkman, and clapped his hands to the music. The crowd saw and joined in. This interest provided just the spur that he needed and he improved throughout the competition to end with 17.55m, just a centimetre off the US record (and world low-altitude best) that he had set when winning the TAC title earlier in the year. He had been told by promoters that the triple jump was often not included at their big invitational meetings due to lack of interest. No more!

In college days Banks was involved in student administration and has often said that he would eventually want to be involved with government. It was certainly appropriate that he was one of the leaders of a move during the 1985 season to form an association of the world's top athletes. Now a veteran of the European tour, he points out the need to make track and field a viable alternative for athletes willing to attempt to make a living at the sport.

He had an epic duel with Zdzislaw Hoffmann at the 1983 World Championships, which Hoffmann won 17.42m to 17.18m, but, favoured to win a gold medal at the 1984 Olympics in his hometown of Los Angeles, Banks managed only sixth place. Bitterly disappointed, he put the tears behind him to concentrate on the world record. Working hard with Los Angeles Track Club coach Chuck DeBus he improved his runway speed and his timing to succeed gloriously on the superb facility at Indianapolis the following June in a wonderful competition. Al Joyner led the first round with 17.38m. Then Banks exploded in the second round to 17.97m (58ft 11½in). Mike Conley responded with 17.71m and with Charlie Simpkins third at 17.52m and Al Joyner fourth at 17.46m, there were in all 16 jumps in excess of Joyner's winning Olympic distance of 17.26m. Thence to Europe, Japan and Australia and another barnstorming tour culminating in a victory in the World Cup. Throughout, Banks delighted athletics fans everywhere with his skill, his ebullient personality and his infectious enthusiasm and sportsmanship.

Willie Banks was born on 11 March 1956 at the Travis Air Force Base, California.

Annual progression:
1973—15.02, 1974—15.62, 1975—16.79, 1976—16.66/16.88w, 1977—16.88, 1978—17.05, 1979—17.23/17.43w, 1980—17.13/17.36w, 1981—17.56, 1982—17.41i, 1983—17.26/17.32w, 1984—17.39, 1985—17.97.

The world's best triple jumpers of all time

17.97	Willie Banks (USA)	1985
17.89	Joao Carlos de Olivera (Bra)	1975
17.86	Charlie Simpkins (USA)	1985
17.77	Khristo Markov (Bul)	1985
17.71	Mike Conley (USA)	1985
17.69	Oleg Protsenko (USSR)	1985
17.60	Vladimir Plekhanov (USSR)	1985
17.57	Keith Connor (UK)	1982
17.57	Lazaro Betancourt (Cub)	1985
17.55	Vasiliy Grishchenkov (USSR)	1983
17.53	Aleksandr Beskrovniy (USSR)	1983
17.53	Zdzislaw Hoffmann (Pol)	1985

Ron Clarke

Despite his lack of gold medals Ron Clarke continues to be remembered as one of the greatest runners of all time. Emil Zatopek, Paavo Nurmi and Lasse Viren won the titles, but Clarke is held in such esteem by distance running enthusiasts that they would certainly rate him with such men.

Anyone who saw, as I did, his 10 000m run at Crystal Palace on 7 September 1968 could not believe that there was a runner in the world who could live with such pace. He missed his own world record by ten seconds, but the conditions, with a strong wind, made records impossible. The display of running was awe-inspiring, yet just six weeks later he came but sixth in the Olympic final at 10 000m and fifth at 5000m. Those Games were of course held at the high altitude of Mexico City, where Ron Clarke ran himself to collapse and had to be administered oxygen after the race. Who can say what might have been, but I will always believe that Clarke would have been a gold medallist but for that decision to hold the Games where the thin air destroyed the chances of many great athletes.

Ron Clarke first came to the attention of the world when he carried the Olympic flame into the stadium at the opening ceremony of the 1956 Olympic Games in Melbourne. As an 18-year-old in February that year he had set a world junior record for the 1 mile at 4:06.8. During the next few years he concentrated on his studies, qualifying as an accountant, and did not make a serious comeback until 1961. He caused a big surprise with a silver medal at 3 miles behind Murray Halberg in the 1962 Commonwealth Games. From 1963 to 1968 distance running records were revolutionised by Clarke. In all he set 18 world records, of which one was not ratified, and this included ten in 1965, equalling the IAAF record for one year set by Gunder Hägg in 1942.

Clarke did not just whittle away at the records, he smashed them, leading runners into totally new understanding of what was possible. He was not alone, particularly at 5000 metres, for in 1965, when records were being broken with such frequency, Michel Jazy of France and Kip Keino of Kenya shared in the pioneering work, and held the athletics public enthralled with great racing. In 40 days that year Clarke ran four world records, the latter two, in particular, amongst the greatest in athletics history. At the White City Stadium, London he won the first of three successive AAA 3 miles titles in 12:52.4 (shown later on automatic timing to be 12:52.26), for the first sub-

13 minute time ever, displaying as always wondrous front-running ability at a hitherto unknown pace. Just four days later he took over 30 seconds off the 10 000m record, equivalent to half a lap faster than ever before.

Sadly gold medals did not come Clarke's way. He won the Olympic 10 000m bronze in 1964; added two more Commonwealth silver medals in 1966, when beaten by the Kenyans Kip Keino and Naftali Temu at 3 and 6 miles respectively in Kingston, Jamaica; and another in his last season of 1970, second to Lachie Stewart at 10 000m in Edinburgh, before placing fifth at 5000m, when he and indeed Kip Keino could not match the devastating finish of the Scottish Ians, Stewart and McCafferty.

Soon after he retired from competition Clarke discovered that he had a heart problem. Eventually this became so serious that he had to undergo open-heart surgery in 1981 to replace a faulty valve. The operation was successful and since 1983 he has been living in London, managing sports and health clubs.

Ron Clarke was a winner and a great racer even without those elusive gold medals. He never ducked races, inevitably losing a few on his hectic European tours but on a win–loss basis he comes out ahead of most of his rivals. Jazy beat him 4–1 and with Keino he comes out level at 9–9 in races from 3000m to 10 000m, but the rest of the world had to give best to this extraordinary gentleman.

World records set by Ron Clarke

2 miles	8:19.8	Västeras	27 Jun 1967
	8:19.6	London	24 Aug 1968
3 miles	13:07.6	Melbourne	3 Dec 1964
	13:00.4	Los Angeles	4 Jun 1965
	12:52.26	London	10 Jul 1965
	12:50.4	Stockholm	5 Jul 1966
5000m	13:34.8	Hobart	16 Jan 1965
	13:33.6	Auckland	1 Feb 1965
	13:25.8	Los Angeles	4 Jun 1965
	13:16.6	Stockholm	5 Jul 1966
6 miles	27:17.8	Melbourne	18 Dec 1963
	26:47.0	Oslo	14 Jul 1965
10 000m	28:15.6	Melbourne	18 Dec 1963
	28:14.0	Turku	16 Jun 1965
	27:39.89	Oslo	14 Jul 1965
10 miles	47:12.8	Melbourne	3 Mar 1965
20 000m	59:22.8	Geelong	27 Oct 1965
1 hour	20 232m	Geelong	27 Oct 1965

ABOVE: Ron Clarke (1) tucks in behind John Freeman (6) on his way to his third successive AAA 3 miles title. He won in 12:59.6 from Lajos Mecser (hidden) and Ian McCafferty (17). No. 9 is Derek Graham and 3 Henk Altmann.

Petra Felke twice improved the world record for the javelin on one day in 1985, when she threw over 71 metres in eleven competitions. However here at Canberra she suffered her first loss in 26 meetings since May 1984.

ABOVE: The two fastest 800 runners of all time: Joaquim
Cruz leads Sebastian Coe at Köln in 1985. He won with
1:42.54 to Coe's 1:43.07. BELOW: Said Aouita on his way to
the world 5000m record at Oslo in 1985. Alberto Cova (62)
set an Italian record in third place, but ten seconds behind
the brilliant Moroccan. RIGHT: Valerie Brisco-Hooks struck
gold three times in Los Angeles.

Joan Benoit (top left) stole away from the field to win the 1984 Olympic marathon in triumphant style. TOP RIGHT: Steve Jones used the same blitz tactics in the 1985 Chicago marathon, but earlier in the year at London he (2) had company from Christoph Herle (13) and Charlie Spedding (1).

BELOW: Home ground celebrations: (left) for Ingrid Kristiansen, with a world record for 10000m in Oslo, and BELOW for John Walker at Auckland, after twelve years of top-class miling, with his 100th sub-four.

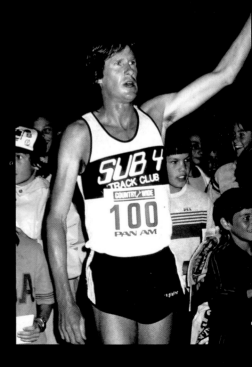

Daley Thompson

Decathletes surely deserve our respect as the supreme athletes, for not only must they master a wide range of disciplines, but they must put together their best efforts at ten very disparate events in a two-day period, when one error can mar the whole performance. Daley Thompson is the greatest of all decathletes. He has already won by far the biggest collection of major titles of any decathlete in the history of the sport and is still hungry for more success, spurred on not just by the possibilities of fame and even wealth but by the burning desire to be the best and to realize his own athletic potential.

Daley's competitive brilliance was shown in its quintessence at the 1984 Olympic Games in Los Angeles. He has always beaten Jürgen Hingsen (GFR) in head-to-head competition, but Hingsen had improved the world record exactly two months before the Olympic decathlon. Thompson had a magnificent first day, building a record half-way score to lead Hingsen by 114 points. The West German had gained a mere six points in the opening event of the second day, the 110m hurdles, but was quite capable of overtaking Thompson for he still had good events to come. The discus gave Hingsen his big chance and he proved his worth with fine throws of 49.80m and a personal best 50.82m. Thompson responded with a terrible 37.90m and a mediocre 41.24m, for a score 176 points worse than Hingsen's, who did not improve with his third effort. So when he stepped into the discus circle for his final throw Daley Thompson had lost the overall lead. He then showed just why he has compiled such a tremendous record in this most taxing of all events, for, concentrating hard, he threw 46.56m and the crisis was over. He retained the lead even if only by 32 points. Stomach trouble hindered Hingsen in the pole

vault as he could clear only 4.50m, but when Thompson vaulted 4.90 on his third attempt he knew that the competition was all but won and celebrated with a magnificent back somersault off the landing area. From then on he savoured every minute of this, his greatest day, taking part at the apex of competition at the event for which he lives.

Yet again he had won a major title and held off the challenge of Hingsen. Since his silver medal in the 1978 European Championships Daley Thompson has won every major decathlon title open to him and is now looking to repeat his victory cycle leading up to the next Olympic Games. His gold medal haul to date reads two Olympic, two Commonwealth, and one each at World, European and European Junior Championships.

Born Francis Morgan Thompson in North Kensington, London on 30 July 1958, he showed phenomenal talent from an early age. He won a Sussex Schools title at 200m in 1974 while at boarding school there, but first tried the decathlon at the age of 16 in June 1975 when he won the Welsh Open event at Cwmbran. He enjoyed this all-round test and that year went on to win the AAA Junior title and place second for Britain's senior team in an international against France. Already the best in Britain, he gained valuable experience by competing at the 1976 Olympic Games against such men as world record holders Bruce Jenner, Guido Kratschmer and Nikolay Avilov, whom he regarded with awe. Still a junior he swept all before him in 1977, and last

Daley Thompson at two of the ten decathlon events: pole vault TOP and hurdling, against his arch-rival Jürgen Hingsen, whom he has beaten in all seven decathlons at which they have met.

(right) Daley throws the discus at the 1978 Europeans, the last decathlon he lost. (below right) Gateshead 1984, Daley prepares to run for England in the sprint relay. (All-Sport, ASP)

lost a decathlon, apart from a couple of minor competitions in which he did not finish the event, at the 1978 Europeans to Aleksandr Grebenyuk, due mainly to a poor effort in the pole vault.

Daley Thompson is a highly competent performer at many disciplines: for several years he has been Britain's best long jumper, and ranked in the national top ten at sprints, hurdles and pole vault. He competes regularly for his club, Newham and Essex Beagles, in league fixtures at a variety of events and scores handfuls of points, yet at these fixtures his relaxed attitude is so very different from that which he brings to his carefully chosen decathlon efforts. Before a decathlon he is unapproachable, as his usual happy-go-lucky nature is cast aside by a fierce determination and concentration on every move. The result is a record that compares more than favourably with any decathlete in history. He goes on in search of that dream of getting everything right in one two-day competition.

Daley Thompson's decathlons
— all rescored on the 1984 Tables

1975

Cwmbran	Welsh Open	1st	6523	
Cwmbran	AAA Junior		6845	
Cwmbran	UK v France	2nd	6941	UKJR

1976

Cwmbran	AAA	1st	7517	UKJR
Copenhagen	UK international	10th	6649	
Montreal	Olympic Games	18th	7330	
Talence		4th	7748	UKR, UKJR

1977

Götzis		3rd	7865	UKR, UKJR
Madrid	UK international	1st	8056	UKR, WJR
Sittard	European Cup semi final	1st	8082	UKR, WJR
Donetsk	European Junior	1st	7568	

1978

Götzis		2nd	8226	UKR
Edmonton	Commonwealth Games	1st	8470w	
Prague	European	2nd	8258	UKR

1979

Flein		dnf	6949	

1980

Götzis		1st	8648	WR
Moscow	Olympic Games	1st	8522	

1981

Saskatoon	UK v Canada	1st	7797	

1982

Götzis		1st	8730	WR
Athens	European	1st	8774	WR
Brisbane	Commonwealth Games	1st	8424	

1983

Etobicoke		1st	8529w	
Helsinki	World Championships	1st	8714	

1984

Los Angeles		dnf	7806	
Los Angeles	Olympic Games	1st	8846	WR

WR — world (and UK) record, WJR — world (and UK) junior record, UKR — UK record, UKJR — UK junior record, w — with excess wind assistance

Milestones in Athletics History

(l–r) Chris Brasher, Roger Bannister, Franz Stampfl and Chris Chataway. Oxford 1954 and the first sub-four minute mile.

3800 Earliest evidence of organized running in Egypt at Memphis. Ritual races around the walls of the town may even have pre-dated 4100 BC. Races were held between two pillars c.800m apart and were normally of four lengths.

3300 Form of high jumping practised, with children jumping over linked arms of other children.

2650 Earliest representation of a runner, a stone relief in the pyramid temple at Saqqara, of King Djoser of Egypt running a race.

c.1600 Evidence of running in Crete.

c.1250 Vase in Cyprus depicts athletic sports.

c.800 Homer's funeral games.

776 First known Olympic champion—Coroibos.

c.500 Tailtean Games originated in Ireland.

490 Battle of Marathon and subsequent run to Athens by Pheidippides.

c.324 First indoor athletics—in a large marquee erected in India by two generals of Alexander the Great.

c.50 First known association of professional athletes in Greece was formed.

AD

3rd Century High jumping tests for military in Ireland.

393 Olympic Games abolished by decree of the Roman Emperor Theodosius.

5th Century Athletic tests celebrated in Germanic literature (Brunhilde).

7th Century St Cuthbert noted for running and leaping.

1035–1040 Harold I, King of England, known as 'Harefoot', due to his speed.

1180 William FitzSteven describes sporting events at Smithfield (Smooth Field), London.

c.1275 Poem 'Havelock the Dane' includes the earliest reference to putting the weight in England.

13th/14th Century Earliest Highland Games in Scotland.

1530 International match held between England and Scotland.

1584 First evidence of running footmen.

1589 Sir Robert Carey walked from London to Berwick (c.340 miles/550km) for a bet.

c.1604 Robert Dover starts Cotswold 'Olympic Games'. These rural sports held annually except during Civil War (1642–60) until 1852.

1630 Regular running matches in Hyde Park, London.

1664 Running matches at Newmarket regularized.

1680 First athletics 'calendar' produced at Newmarket, giving results of leading races.

1750s Artillery Ground, London is the first enclosed ground to be used for foot races, at which an entrance fee is charged.

1766 Site of ancient Olympic Games rediscovered at Olympia by Richard Chandler.

1773 Foster Powell ran from London to York and back, 402 miles in 5 days 18 hours. Twenty years later, at the age of 59, he did it in 5 days 15¼ hours.

1793 JTF Guts Muths published *Gymnastik für die Jügend*, hints on athletics techniques, from the founder of German gymnastics.

1809 Captain Barclay's 1000 miles in 1000 hours.

1813 William Thom's *Pedestrianism* published — an account of the performances of celebrated pedestrians.

1820s Athletics at Shrewsbury School.

1834 Donald Walker's *Manly Exercises* published.

1837 Crick Run first held at Rugby School; originally c.12½ miles, later c.11 miles/18km. Interclass athletics first held at Eton College. First track to be laid specifically for athletics; at Lord's Cricket Ground, London. This was a 5ft wide gravel path all round the ground, already well established as a venue for foot running matches. Earlier paths had been set aside for races, but these can hardly qualify as tracks in the modern sense.

1839 First athletics meeting in North America, at Caer Howell grounds near Toronto.

1842 Olympic Club of Montreal formed.

1845 First amateur hurdles race, at Eton.

1849 Royal Military Academy, Sandhurst stages its first athletics meeting.

1850 Exeter College, Oxford, athletics club formed; the oldest surviving one. Dr Penny Brookes inaugurates the Much Wenlock Olympic Games, to encourage outdoor recreation, and based on Greek ideals. Included were five athletics events (high jump, long jump and three races).

1854 Professional jumper John Howard jumps 9.01m/29ft 7in using weights.

1857 First sports meetings held at Cambridge University and at Trinity College, Dublin.

1860 First Oxford University Sports held.

1862 Chronograph patented by Adolphe Nicole (Swi).

1863 Founding of Mincing Lane AC (London AC from 1866). First amateur indoor meeting at Ashburnham Hall. Olympic festival at Mount Vernon Parade Ground, Liverpool, the most popular of a series of such festivals in the 1860s; a crowd of 12 000 to 15 000 attended.

1864 First Oxford v Cambridge athletics match held at Oxford. First Civil Service Sports held. First artificial steeplechase course (as opposed to cross-country) at RMA Woolwich.

1866 First national championships—English, organized by the Amateur Athletic Club at Beaufort House, Welham Green, London. National Olympian Society held its first Games at Crystal Palace, London.

1868 First indoor meeting in the USA organized by New York AC.

1874 Madison Square Garden, New York, first used for athletics. First US university competition at Saratoga. Edward Weston becomes the first man to walk 500 miles in 6 days, at Newark, New Jersey, USA.

1875 ICAAAA formed in the USA.

1876 Starting gun first used; previously races started with a drum, or 'Go' or a white handkerchief. First American championships held in New York. London AC (actually an England team) visits Ireland. First English cross-country championship.

1877 Stamford Bridge Stadium opened, home of British athletics for first 30 years of the 20th century.

1879 Northern Counties AAA formed by nine clubs in Southport.

1880 AAA founded in Oxford, first championships held.

1886 Straight-leg hurdle style pioneered by Arthur Croome of Oxford.

1888 AAU formed and first championships held in the USA.

1891 First use of 'electric' timing; at AAU Championships. Astley Cooper suggests an Empire athletic gathering.

1893 Batons first used in relay races.

1894 Baron Pierre de Coubertin organizes international conference at the Sorbonne, Paris; re-establishment of Olympic Games agreed. First international universities match: Oxford (UK) beat Yale (USA) at Queen's Club, Kensington, London.

1895 New York AC beat London AC. First women's meeting at Vassar College, New York.

1896 Olympic Games revived in Athens; athletes from ten nations compete.

1898 England beat France in first international cross-country race at Ville-d'Avray.

1900 Olympic Games in Paris; grass track used.

1903 International Cross-Country Championship inaugurated.

1904 Olympic Games held in conjunction with the World Exhibition in St. Louis.

1906 Intercollegiate AA (NCAA from 1910) formed in the USA.

1908 Olympic Games at newly opened White City Stadium, London.

1911 Inter-Empire Championships held at Crystal Palace, London. Belgium beat Holland at Rotterdam in first inter-nation match.

1912 Olympic Games in Stockholm; lanes first marked by chalk. IAAF formed with 17 nations represented.

1913 Inaugural IAAF meeting, in Berlin; 34 founding members. First Far Eastern Games held in Manila.

1914 Third IAAF Congress receives first set of technical rules for international competitions and list of world records; 96 men's events in all: 53 runs and hurdles, 30 walks, 12 field including decathlon.

1917 France forms first governing body for women's athletics.

1919 First official South American Championships held in Montevideo, Uruguay.

1920 Olympic Games in Antwerp. First USA v British Empire Relays meeting in London, forerunner of series held after each Olympics until 1960.

1921 Fédération Sportive Féminine Internationale (FSFI) formed. First women's international match, France beat Belgium in Brussels, and first multi-national women's meeting: the Monte Carlo Games. First NCAA Championships held.

1922 WAAA founded and first championships staged.

1924 Olympic Games at Colombes, Paris. IAAF proposed reduction of Olympic programme by seven events, four removed but triple jump, steeplechase and decathlon reprieved. First International Universities Games, in Warsaw.

1925 English Schools Athletic Association formed.

1926 IAAF membership now 39, women's committee formed. Exchange zones introduced for relay races. Central American and Caribbean Championships first held.

1927 First official list of women's world records issued by FSFI. Starting blocks invented in the USA by George Bresnahan (not authorized by IAAF until 1938).

1928 Olympic Games in Amsterdam; firsts: women's events, slow-motion apparatus for judging close finishes. First World Workers Spartakiade held in USSR.

1930 First British Empire Games held at Hamilton, Canada.

1931 First women's international cross-country race at Douai, France. First AAA junior championships.

1932 Olympic Games in Los Angeles; firsts: use of photo-timer, film taken and made available to Jury of Appeal, Olympic village, entries limited to three per country.

1934 First European Championships held for men in Turin.

1935 First AAA and WAAA indoor championships at Wembley, London.

1936 Olympic Games in Berlin; firsts: torch relay, televised coverage, official film. FSFI merged with IAAF. IAAF congress receives report on wind speed, later to result in 2m/s limit.

1938 First European women's championships. US men's team defeats Germany in Berlin in its first full-scale international meeting.

1940 First televised athletics in the USA: ICAAAA championships at Madison Square Garden, New York.

1948 Olympic Games at Wembley, London; starting blocks allowed for first time in Olympic competition.

1950 Association of Track and Field Statisticians (ATFS) founded at 1950 European Championships in Brussels.

1951 First stagings of Pan-American, Asian and Mediterranean Games.

1952 Olympic Games in Helsinki. Road Runners Club (RRC) formed.

1954 Roger Bannister runs first sub-four minute mile.

1956 Olympic Games held for first time in southern hemisphere, at Melbourne.

1958 Built-up high jump shoes banned. First USA v USSR international match, in Moscow. National Union of Track Statisticians (NUTS) formed.

1960 Olympic Games in Rome; electronic results boards introduced for field events.

1961 Inaugural IAAF walking team competition (later for the Lugano Trophy).

1962 First indoor international match: UK v GFR at Wembley; UK won men's match and GFR women's.

1963 British Milers Club formed.

1964 Olympic Games in Tokyo; first official use of automatic timing. European Junior Games staged (official championships from 1970). National Sports Centre, including track, opened at Crystal Palace, London.

1965 First staging of European Cup and African Games.

1966 First European Indoor Games (official championships from 1970). Sex testing introduced for women athletes at major championships.

1967 First full-scale British junior international match. At the European Cup Final Ewa Klobukowska (Pol) becomes first to fail sex test.

1968 Olympic Games in Mexico City; first use of all-weather 'Tartan' track. BAAB Junior Commission formed. Byers Committee reports on athletics in the UK.

1969 Rule changes include reduction of discus and hammer circles from 60° to 45°, neck no longer considered as part of torso, and pole allowed to pass under pole vault bar. Women's sprint hurdles changed from 80m to 100m, and women's 1500m first run at major championships (European). Eduard de Noorlander, sixth European decathlon, first athlete to be disqualified for use of drugs. National (later British) Athletics League introduced.

1970 Meadowbank Sports Centre, Edinburgh

opened for Commonwealth Games.

1972 Olympic Games at Munich; introduction of trigonometric measurement of throws; first drug testing at Games; record 1599 competitors from 122 nations.

1973 IAAF take over control of International Cross-Country Championships. European Combined Events Cup introduced. First women's national marathon championship held in GFR. ITA professional series starts.

1974 Women's 3000 metres introduced to international programme, at European Championships in Rome and 400m hurdles records accepted. Young Athletes League introduced in Britain.

1975 IAAF introduced automatic suspensions for athletes proved to have taken anabolic steroids. First World Masters (later Veterans) Championships.

1976 Olympic Games in Montreal: boycotted by 18 nations, principally from Africa in protest against New Zealand's continuing rugby links with South Africa. Separate world championship held at 50km walk, which was temporarily dropped from Olympic programme. South Africa expelled from IAAF. ITA (International Track Association) folds.

1977 First World Cup competition staged in Düsseldorf. World records at distances up to 400m accepted only if timed fully automatically. Imperial distance events, except for 1 mile, dropped.

1979 The Athletics Congress (TAC) replaces the AAU as the national governing body of the USA.

1980 Olympic Games in Moscow; boycotted by USA and about 50 other nations due to Soviet invasion of Afghanistan. Separate world championships held at women's 3000m and 400m hurdles. First TAC Grand Prix road races, with prize money paid to athletes' clubs.

1981 European Marathon Cup held for first time. Heptathlon replaces pentathlon as women's multi-event competition. First NCAA women's championship, at cross-country.

1982 IAAF introduced rules for Athletes' Funds.

1983 First World Championships held in Helsinki. IAAF women's world road race championship first held, over 10km at San Diego, California. Major meetings around the world given status as IAAF permit meetings.

1984 Olympic Games in Los Angeles; boycotted by Eastern bloc nations; women's 3000m and marathon held for first time.

1985 IAAF/Mobil Grand Prix inaugurated with programme of 15 major meetings leading to final in Rome. Women's 10 000m introduced to major events, first at the European Cup. First World Indoor Games held in Paris and first World Marathon Cup staged at Hiroshima, Japan. IAAF membership reaches 174.

1986 First World Junior Championships at Athens. New specification for men's javelin.

World Record Pace

World record attempts are a major feature at many of the major international athletics meetings. In such attempts it is fascinating to compare the pace against those of world record runs. So these tables show how a selection of middle and long distance records (some historically important ones, and the most recent) have been run. Where possible the times given are those for the record breaker, even if not leading at the time.

MEN

800 METRES

				400m	600m	800m	
8 Jul	1912	Stockholm	Ted Meredith	52.5		1:51.9	
2 Aug	1932	Los Angeles	Tom Hampson	54.8	1:22.4	1:49.70	
15 Jul	1939	Milan	Rudolf Harbig	52.5	1:19.6	1:46.6	
3 Aug	1955	Oslo	Roger Moens	52.0	1:18.8	1:45.7	
3 Feb	1962	Christchurch	Peter Snell	50.7	1:16.4	1:44.3	
25 Jul	1976	Montreal	Alberto Juantorena	50.8	1:17.0	1:43.50	
21 Aug	1977	Sofia	Alberto Juantorena	51.4	1:17.4	1:43.44	
5 Jul	1979	Oslo	Sebastian Coe	50.6	1:15.4	1:42.33	
10 Jun	1981	Florence	Sebastian Coe	49.9	1:15.0	1:41.73	

1000 METRES

				400m	600m	800m	1000m
24 May	1941	Dresden	Rudolf Harbig	56.0		1:53.0	2:21.5
14 Jul	1960	Potsdam	Siegfried Valentin	54.2		1:48.8	2:16.7
11 Jul	1981	Oslo	Sebastian Coe	51.3	1:18.4	1:44.56	2:12.18

1500 METRES

					400m	800m	1200m	1500m
19 Jun	1924	Helsinki	Paavo Nurmi		57.3	2:01.0	3:06.0	3:52.6
6 Aug	1936	Berlin	Jack Lovelock		61.5	2:05.0	3:05.0	3:47.8
7 Jul	1944	Göteborg	Gunder Hägg		56.7	1:56.5	2:58.0	3:43.0
6 Sep	1960	Rome	Herb Elliott		58.2	1:58.0	2:54.0	3:35.6
15 Aug	1979	Zürich	Sebastian Coe		54.3	1:53.2	2:49.5	3:32.03
27 Aug	1980	Koblenz	Steve Ovett		55.5	1:53.0	2:50.7	3:31.36
28 Aug	1983	Köln	Sydney Maree		54.7	1:52.8	2:49.4	3:31.24
4 Sep	1983	Rieti	Steve Ovett		54.2	1:51.9	2:49.14	3:30.77
16 Jul	1985	Nice	Steve Cram		55.5	1:53.7	2:49.66	3:29.67
23 Aug	1985	West Berlin	Said Aouita		57.0	1:53.7	2:49.4	3:29.46

An instance in which the leader has run faster than the times shown above was in Cram's run in Nice. At 400m Boubakar Niang led in 54.36, while Cram was some way back.

1 MILE

					440y	880y	1320y	mile
23 Aug	1886	London	Walter George		58.2	2:01.8	3:07.8	4:12.8
4 Oct	1931	Paris	Jules Ladoumègue		60.8	2:04.2	3:08.0	4:09.2
28 Aug	1937	Motspur Park	Sydney Wooderson		58.6	2:02.6	3:07.2	4:06.4
17 Jul	1945	Malmo	Gunder Hägg		56.6	1:58.5	2:59.7	4:01.3
6 May	1954	Oxford	Roger Bannister		57.5	1:58.2	3:00.5	3:59.4
6 Aug	1958	Dublin	Herb Elliott		56.4	1:58.2	2:59.2	3:54.5
23 Jun	1967	Kingston	Jim Ryun		59.0	1:58.9	2:58.6	3:51.1
12 Aug	1975	Göteborg	John Walker		56.3	1:55.5	2:53.5	3:49.4
19 Aug	1981	Zürich	Sebastian Coe		56.2	1:53.6	2:51.68	3:48.53
26 Aug	1981	Koblenz	Steve Ovett		56.6	1:54.5	2:51.5	3:48.40
28 Aug	1981	Brussels	Sebastian Coe		55.23	1:53.22	2:51.90	3:47.33
27 Jul	1985	Oslo	Steve Cram		57.5	1:54.9	2:53.3	3:46.32

2000 METRES

				400m	800m	1200m	1600m	2000m
10 Sep	1966	Hagen	Harald Norpoth	58.7	1:59.7	3:02.7	4:02.2	4:57.8
12 Oct	1966	St Maur	Michel Jazy	58.4	1:58.7	2:59.6	3:58.6	4:56.2
30 Jun	1976	Oslo	John Walker	60.0	1:58.6	2:56.3	3:54.2	4:51.52
4 Aug	1985	Budapest	Steve Cram	59.0	1:56.1	2:54.58	3:53.92	4:51.39

3000 METRES

				1000m	2000m	3000m
12 Aug	1949	Gävle	Gaston Reiff	2:35.0	5:19.6	7:58.8
4 Sep	1956	Malmo	Gordon Pirie	2:35.8	5:19.5	7:52.8
3 Aug	1974	Gateshead	Brendan Foster	2:31.6	5:04.0	7:35.1
27 Jun	1978	Oslo	Henry Rono	2:34.5	5:04.5	7:32.1

2 MILES

				880y	1M	1.5M	2M
8 Jun	1962	Los Angeles	Jim Beatty	2:06.1	4:15.4	6:25.8	8:29.8
27 Jun	1967	Västeras	Ron Clarke	2:06.7	4:11.5	6:17.1	8:19.8
27 Aug	1973	London	Brendan Foster	2:01.4	4:05.4	6:10.8	8:13.68
15 Sep	1978	London	Steve Ovett	2:02.9	4:09.1	6:14.4	8:13.51

5000 METRES

				1000m	2000m	3000m	4000m	5000m
20 Sep	1942	Göteborg	Gunder Hägg	2:40.0	5:27.0	8:17.5	11:09.0	13:58.1
13 Oct	1954	London	Chris Chataway	2:41.6	5:31.7	8:16.8	11:10.0	13:51.6
13 Oct	1957	Rome	Vladimir Kuts	2:37.8	5:24.3	8:08.7	10:52.9	13:35.0
5 Jul	1966	Stockholm	Ron Clarke	2:40.2	5:16.4	7:57.4	10:39.0	13:16.6
8 Apr	1978	Berkeley	Henry Rono	2:42.0	5:18.0	7:55.2	10:34.5	13:08.4
13 Sep	1981	Knarvik	Henry Rono	2:38.5	5:17.0	7:55.0	10:33.0	13:06.20
7 Jul	1982	Oslo	David Moorcroft	2:37.4	5:12.6	7:50.0	10:28.7	13:00.41
27 Jul	1985	Oslo	Said Aouita	2:35.2	5:13.9	7:51.0	10:32.2	13:00.40

10 000 METRES

				2000m	4000m	6000m	8000m	10 000m
17 Sep	1939	Helsinki	Taisto Mäki	5:56.8	12:00.6	18:00.0	23:58.0	29:52.6
1 Jun	1954	Brussels	Emil Zatopek	5:44.2	11:34.0	17:23.0	23:11.6	28:54.2
15 Oct	1960	Kiev	Pyotr Bolotnikov	5:31.0	11:13.0	16:57.0	22:42.0	28:18.8
14 Jul	1965	Oslo	Ron Clarke	5:25.0	10:58.0	16:33.0	22:13.0	27:39.89
3 Sep	1972	Munich	Lasse Viren	5:18.8	10:55.5	16:35.7	22:17.6	27:38.35
13 Jul	1973	London	Dave Bedford	5:23.2	10:54.6	16:26.2	22:02.0	27:30.80
11 Jun	1978	Vienna	Henry Rono	5:30.2	11:04.6	16:35.7	22:02.1	27:22.47
2 Jul	1985	Stockholm	Fernando Mamede	5:34.6	11:00.5	16:30.2	21:58.4	27:13.81

3000 METRES STEEPLECHASE

					1000m	2000m	3000m
14 Aug	1956	Moscow	Semyon Rzhischin	2:54.5	5:46.5	8:39.8	
7 Aug	1965	Brussels	Gaston Roelants	2:47.4	5:38.8	8:26.4	
27 Jun	1973	Helsinki	Ben Jipcho	2:52.2	5:33.0	8:13.91	
28 Jul	1976	Montreal	Anders Gärderud	2:43.6	5:29.0	8:08.02	
13 May	1978	Seattle	Henry Rono	2:43.0	5:24.8	8:05.4	

WOMEN

800 METRES

				400m	600m	800m
20 Jul	1968	London	Vera Nikolic	60.5	1:30.6	2:00.5
11 Jul	1971	Stuttgart	Hildegard Falck	58.4	1:28.5	1:58.45
26 Jul	1976	Montreal	Tatyana Kazankina	55.1	1:25.0	1:54.95
12 Jun	1980	Moscow	Nadezhda Olizarenko	..		1:54.85
27 Jul	1980	Moscow	Nadezhda Olizarenko	56.41		1:53.42
26 Jul	1983	Munich	Jarmila Kratochvilova	56.28		1:53.28

1500 METRES

				400m	800m	1200m	1500m
20 Sep	1969	Athens	Jaroslava Jehlickova	62.0	2:13.0	3:23.0	4:10.7
9 Sep	1972	Munich	Lyudmila Bragina	62.5	2:10.0	3:14.6	4:01.38
6 Jul	1980	Moscow	Tatyana Kazankina	60.0	2:07.0	3:08.2	3:55.0
13 Aug	1980	Zürich	Tatyana Kazankina	58.6	2:04.7	3:07.1	3:52.47

1 MILE

				440y	880y	1320y	mile
3 Jun	1967	Chiswick	Anne Smith	1:08.0	2:17.8	3:28.0	4:37.0
9 Jul	1982	Paris	Mary Decker	1:02.9	2:08.7	3:15.6	4:18.08
16 Sep	1982	Rieti	Maricica Puica	1:04.1	2:08.9	3:12.4	4:17.44
21 Aug	1985	Zürich	Mary Slaney	1:03.8	2:09.4	3:14.8	4:16.71

3000 METRES

				1000m	2000m	3000m
7 Aug	1976	College Park	Lyudmila Bragina		5:40.0	8:27.12
25 Jul	1982	Kiev	Svyetlana Ulmasova	2:48.0	5:40.5	8:26.78
26 Aug	1984	Leningrad	Tatyana Kazankina	2:47.5	5:36.5	8:22.62

5000 METRES

				1000m	2000m	3000m	4000m	5000m
5 Jun	1982	Eugene	Mary Decker	3:02.4	6:04.5	9:10.5	12:16.5	15:08.26
28 Jun	1984	Oslo	Ingrid Kristiansen	3:02.0	5:59.6	8:59.8	12:00.8	14:58.89
26 Aug	1985	London	Zola Budd	2:53.7	5:49.0	8:50.5	11:52.2	14:48.07

10 000 METRES

				2000m	4000m	6000m	8000m	10 000m
16 Jul	1982	Eugene	Mary Decker	6:22.0	12:48.0	19:11.0	25:33.0	31:35.3
24 Jun	1984	Kiev	Olga Bondarenko					31:13.78
27 Jul	1985	Oslo	Ingrid Kristiansen	6:18.4	12:27.5	18:41.6	24:45.1	30:59.42

Altitude

There are many factors which affect levels of athletic performance. Apart from those under the control of the athlete, such as equipment and racing tactics, meteorological conditions such as temperature, humidity and wind can have a major effect. Perhaps the most significant factor, however, is altitude.

The highest venue for an Olympic Games has been Mexico City. Its altitude provides an atmosphere where the air is 23 per cent thinner than at sea-level. This shortage of oxygen adversely affects the distance runners, whose times are significantly slower, while those taking part in explosive events show performance gains. Statisticians have established 'high altitude' at the convenient cut-off point of 1000m, but to a smaller extent sprinters can benefit even by running at the 400–700m level, at such venues as Zürich, Canberra or Edmonton.

Notable venues at altitudes of 300m or more:

2240m	Mexico City	820	Sao Paulo
1823	Colorado Springs	667	Edmonton
1753	Johannesburg	640	Madrid
1675	Nairobi	581	Canberra
1655	Boulder	564	Sofia
1507	Albuquerque	520	Munich
1426	Bloemfontein	440	Sindelfingen
1387	Provo, Utah	410	Zürich
1361	Pocatello, Idaho	402	Rieti
1338	Salt Lake City	361	Prague
1136	El Paso, Texas	354	Tempe
1046	Cali, Colombia	332	Phoenix, Arizona
1045	Calgary	309	Karl-Marx-Stadt
847	Alma Ata, USSR		

Indoor Athletics

The first indoor athletics meeting ever held was at the Ashburnam Hall in London on 7 Nov 1863, with a programme of four running events and a triple jump. The first in the USA was organized by the New York Athletic Club on 11 Nov 1868. Indoor athletics became of major importance in the USA and indeed for much of this century has attracted larger audiences, particularly on the East Coast, than outdoor track and field. It was slower to develop in Europe, although there were a fair number of meetings, particularly in Germany, in pre-World War II days. In recent years, and given a big impetus by the inauguration of European Indoor Championships, indoor athletics has become widespread in Europe and North America. Final recognition of the importance of this aspect of the sport has come with the advent of the World Indoor Championships.

WORLD INDOOR GAMES

These Games were staged at Bercy, Paris, France on 19–20 Jan 1985. From 1987, when they will be held in Indianapolis, USA, they will have full IAAF World Championship status.

In 1985 they were contested by representatives of 70 nations, each of whom had been allocated by the IAAF a number of places based on their athletics strengths. While many top athletes took part, the overall standard in depth was rather disappointing. The Games were held at the start of the indoor season and clashed with events in North America. One world indoor best was achieved, by Thomas Schönlebe in the 400 metres.

Winners

Men

60m	Ben Johnson (Can)	6.62
200m	Aleksandr Yevgenyev (USSR)	20.95
400m	Thomas Schönlebe (GDR)	45.60
800m	Coloman Trabado (Spa)	1:47.42
1500m	Mike Hillardt (Aus)	3:40.27
3000m	Joao Campos (Por)	7:57.63
60mh	Stéphane Caristan (Fra)	7.67
HJ	Patrik Sjöberg (Swe)	2.32
PV	Sergey Bubka (USSR)	5.75
LJ	Jan Leitner (Cs)	7.96
TJ	Khristo Markov (Bul)	17.22
SP	Remigius Machura (Cs)	21.22
50 kmW	Gérard Lelièvre (Fra)	19:06.22

WOMEN

60m	Silke Gladisch (GDR)	7.20
200m	Marita Koch (GDR)	23.09
400m	Diane Dixon (USA)	53.35
800m	Cristina Cojocaru (Rom)	2:04.22
1500m	Elly Van Hulst (Hol)	4:11.41
3000m	Debbie Scott (Can)	9:04.99
60mh	Xenia Siska (Hun)	8.03
HJ	Stefka Kostadinova (Bul)	1.97
LJ	Helga Radtke (GDR)	6.86
SP	Natalya Lisovskaya (USSR)	20.07
3kmW	Giuliana Salce (Ita)	12:53.42

WORLD INDOOR RECORDS

World records are not (yet) recognized by the IAAF if set indoors, although US indoor records have been ratified for many years. Marks given in the lists that follow are those accepted by leading authorities. Shown for each event is the record as at 1 February 1986, together with athletes who have set the most records at each event, subject to a minimum of three records. The standard size for indoor tracks is now 200 metres, although there are many long-established tracks in the USA with a smaller circumference, for example Madison Square Garden, New York, which is of 160y (146m). As there may be some advantage in shorter distance events in running around less severe bends, marks made on tracks of greater than 200m circumference are shown separately as 'oversized track'.

MEN'S RECORDS

50 yards *5.22* Stanley Floyd (USA) Los Angeles 22 Jan 1982. *5.0* (hand timing) by four men
most 6 Herb Washington (USA) two at 5.1 1968, four at 5.0 1972–3

50 metres *5.61* Manfred Kokot (GDR) East Berlin 4 Feb 1973 and James Sanford (USA) San Diego 20 Feb 1981
5.4 (hand timing) Bill Gaines (USA) Moscow 17 Feb 1968 and Manfred Kokot (GDR) East Berlin 31 Jan 1971

60 yards *6.02* Carl Lewis (USA) Dallas 5 Feb 1983
5.8 (hand timing) Herb Washington (USA) East Lansing, Michigan 12 Feb 1972 and Mel Pender (USA-pro) Salt Lake City 25 May 1973
most 6 Bob Hayes (USA) 6.0–5.9 1964
   5 Herb Carper (USA) all 6.0 1959–63

60 metres *6.54* Houston McTear (USA) Long Beach 7 Jan 1978
6.3 (hand timing) Andrey Prokofyev (USSR) Chelyabinsk 5 Feb 1982
most 12 Helmut Körnig (Ger) 6.7–6.6 1927–32
   6 Aleksandr Kornelyuk (USSR) all 6.4 1972–4

100 yards *9.50* Thomas Schröder (GDR) Senftenberg 7 Jan 1984 and 22 Jan 1984
9.3 (hand timing) Don Quarrie (Jam) Pocatello, Idaho 16 Jan 1971 and 15 Jan 1972, Cliff Branch (USA) Houston 12 Feb 1972, Cliff 'Greg' Simons (Ber) Moscow 3 Mar 1979

100 metres *10.16* Eugen Ray (GDR) East Berlin 25 Jan 1976

200 metres *20.52* Stefano Tilli (Ita) Turin 21 Feb 1985
most 4 Ralf Lübke (GFR) 20.98 1983 to 20.57 1984

300 yards *29.27* Terron Wright (USA) Bloomington, Ind. 7 Feb 1981; *29.16* (oversized track) Dwayne Evans (USA) Flagstaff, Ariz. (352y) 7 Feb 1981

300 metres *32.84* Pietro Mennea (Ita) Milan 4 Mar 1978
32.54 (oversized track) Willie Jones (USA) Flagstaff, Ariz. (352y) 11 Feb 1984

400 metres *45.56* Todd Bennett (UK) Athens 3 Mar 1985
45.45y (oversized track) Antonio McKay (USA) Johnson City, TN (293y) 18 Jan 1986

500 yards *53.9* Larry James (USA-pro) Salt Lake City 25 May 1973

500 metres *1:01.18* Roddie Haley (USA) Fayetteville, Ariz. 25 Jan 1986

600 yards *1:07.6* Martin McGrady (USA) New York 27 Feb 1970
most 3 Martin McGrady 1:09.0 1966 to 1:07.6 1970

600 metres *1:15.77* Donato Sabia (Ita) Genoa 4 Feb 1984

800 metres *1:44.91* Sebastian Coe (UK) Cosford 12 Mar 1983

1000 yards *2:04.7* Don Paige (USA) Inglewood, Cal. 5 Feb 1982

1000 metres *2:18.58* Sebastian Coe (UK) Oslo 19 Mar 1983

1500 metres *3:35.6* Eamonn Coghlan (Ire) San Diego 20 Feb 1981
most 3 Glenn Cunningham (USA) 3:52.2 1934 to 3:48.4 1938

1 mile *3:49.78* Eamonn Coghlan (Ire) East Rutherford 27 Feb 1983
most 3 Glenn Cunningham (USA) 4:09.8 1933 to 4:07.4 1938 (and 4:04.4 on oversized track 1938)
3 Gil Dodds (USA) 4:07.3 1944 to 4:05.3 1948
3 Ron Delany (Ire) 4:03.4 1958 to 4:01.4 1959
3 Eamonn Coghlan 3:52.6 1979 to 3:49.78 1983

2000 metres *4:58.6* Steve Scott (USA) Louisville, Ky 7 Feb 1981

3000 metres *7:39.2* Emiel Puttemans (Bel) Berlin 18 Feb 1973
most 4 Siegfried Herrmann (GDR) 7:58.8 1959 to 7:49.0 1966

2 miles *8:13.2* Emiel Puttemans (Bel) Berlin 18 Feb 1973
most 4 Greg Rice (USA) 8:56.2 1940 to 8:51.0 1943

3 miles *12:54.6* Emiel Puttemans (Bel) Paris 10 Jan 1976
most 4 Ville Ritola (Fin) 14:15.8 1923 to 13:56.2 1925

5000 metres *13:13.3* Hansjörg Kunze (GDR) Senftenberg 20 Feb 1983 (oversized track)
most 3 Emiel Puttemans (Bel) 13:30.8 1974 to 13:20.8 1976

10 000 metres *28:12.4* Emiel Puttemans (Bel) Pantin, Paris 21 Feb 1975

50 yards hurdles *5.88* Greg Foster (USA) Los Angeles 17 Jan 1986
most 4 Renaldo Nehemiah 6.04 1979 to 5.92 1982
5.8 (hand timing) by five men

50 metres hurdles *6.35* Greg Foster (USA) Rosemont, Ind. 27 Jan 1985
most 3 Guy Drut (Fra) 6.53 to 6.51 1972
6.2 (hand timing) Günter Nickel (GFR) Leverkusen 26 Feb 1970.
most 4 Günter Nickel 6.4 to 6.2 1970

60 yards hurdles *6.82* Renaldo Nehemiah (USA) Dallas 30 Jan 1982
most 5 Renaldo Nehemiah 7.07 1978 to 6.82 1982
6.7 (hand timing) Rod Milburn (USA) New York 8 Feb 1974 and Atlanta 31 May 1975
most 13 Harrison Dillard (USA) at 7.2 and 7.1 1947–56
8 Hayes Jones (USA) at 7.0 to 6.8 1958–64
5 Rod Milburn three at 6.8 1973–4, two at 6.7 1974–5

60 metres hurdles *7.48* Thomas Munkelt (GDR) Budapest 6 Mar 1983
most 3 Thomas Munkelt 7.62 1977 to 7.48 1983
7.3 (hand timing) Tom Hill (USA) Moscow 2 Mar 1974
most 6 Klaus Nüske (GFR) 8.0 1961 to 7.8 1963
6 Marcel Duriez (Fra) 7.9 1962 to 7.8 1966

110 metres hurdles *13.51* Rod Milburn (USA-pro) Houston 10 Feb 1973
13.3y (hand timing) Rod Milburn Houston 10 Feb 1973
most 7 Anatoliy Mikhailov 14.4 (USSR) 1958 to 13.6 1960

4 × 200 metres relay *1:22.32* Italy Turin 11 Feb 1984

4 × 400 metres relay *3:05.9* USSR Vienna 14 Mar 1971
3:02.95 (oversized track) Southern Methodist Univ. Flagstaff, Ariz. (352y) 2 Mar 1985

High jump *2.39* Dietmar Mögenburg (GFR) Köln 24 Feb 1985
most 11 John Thomas (USA) 2.10 1959 to 2.21 1961
7 Dwight Stones (USA) 2.26 1975 to 2.30 1976

Pole vault *5.89* Billy Olson (USA) Albuquerque 25 Jan 1986
most 12 Charles Hoff (Nor) 3.985 to 4.17 1926
10 Billy Olson (USA) 5.71 1982 to 5.89 1986
8 Bob Seagren (USA) 5.19 1966 to 5.33 1969
7 Steve Smith (USA) 5.46 1973 to 5.61 1975 (five as pro)
5 Cornelius Warmerdam (USA) 4.42 1939 to 4.79 1943
5 Dan Ripley (USA) 5.51 1975 to 5.63 1979

Long jump *8.79* Carl Lewis (USA) New York 27 Jan 1984
most 3 Igor Ter-Ovanesyan (USSR) 8.18 1963 to 8.23 1966
3 Ralph Boston (USA) 7.87 to 8.08 1961
3 Carl Lewis 8.49 1981 to 8.79 1984

Triple jump *17.50* Charlie Simpkins (USA) Los Angeles 17 Jan 1986
most 4 Viktor Saneyev (USSR) 16.95 1970 to 17.16 1976
4 Oleg Fyedoseyev (USSR) 15.80 1959 to 16.30 1962

Shot *22.15* Ulf Timmermann (GDR) Senftenberg 16 Feb 1985
most 8 Parry O'Brien (USA) 18.08 1954 to 19.24 1961
6 George Woods (USA) 21.27 1973 to 22.02 1974
4 Randy Matson (USA) 20.02 1965 to 21.08 1967
4 Neal Steinhauer (USA) 20.29 to 20.67 1967

Discus *66.20* Wolfgang Schmidt (GDR) East Berlin 9 Jan 1980

35 lb weight *23.94* Tore Johnsen (Nor) Air Academy, Col. 25 Feb 1984
most 6 Harold Connolly (USA) 19.40 1956 to 22.20 1963
5 Robert Backus (USA) 18.81 1953 to 19.59 1956

3000 metres walk *10:54.6* Carlo Mattioli (Ita) Milan 6 Feb 1980

5000 metres walk *18:59.2* Carlo Mattioli (Ita) Milan 19 Feb 1980

10 000 metres walk *38:31.4* Werner Heyer (GDR) East Berlin 12 Jan 1980
most 3 Yevgeniy Yevsyukov (USSR) 41:25.6 1977 to 40:18.4 1979

WOMEN'S RECORDS

50 yards *5.74* Evelyn Ashford (USA) San Diego 18 Feb 1983
5.5 (hand-timing) Iris Davis (USA) Toronto 2 Feb 1973, Alice Annum (Gha) Pittsburgh 5 Jan 1975

50 metres *6.11* Marita Koch (GDR) Grenoble 2 Feb 1980
6.0 (hand timing) by four women
most 5 Renate Stecher (GDR) three hand 6.0 1971, 6.25 1972, 6.19 1974

60 yards *6.54* Evelyn Ashford (USA) New York 26 Feb 1982
most (hand timing) 3 Wyomia Tyus (USA) 6.6 1966 to 6.5 1974

60 metres *7.04* Marita Koch (GDR) Senftenberg 16 Feb 1985
most 3 Marlies Göhr (GDR) 7.12 1978 to 7.10 1980
3 Marita Koch 7.10 1981 to 7.04 1985
6.9 (hand timing) Alice Annum (Gha) Mainz 17 Jun 1975 and Marlies Göhr Cottbus 10 Feb 1979

100 yards *10.25* Marita Koch (GDR) Senftenberg 16 Feb 1985
most 3 Doris Selmigkeit (GDR) 10.78 to 10.69 1973
3 Marita Koch 10.47 1978 to 10.25 1985

100 metres *11.15* Marita Koch (GDR) East Berlin 12 Jan 1980

200 metres *22.39* Marita Koch (GDR) Budapest 5 Mar 1983
most 3 Rita Wilden (GFR) 23.7 1972 to 23.4 1975

300 yards *32.63* Merlene Ottey (Jam) Cedar Falls, Iowa 13 Mar 1982
most 8 Merlene Ottey 34.13 1980 to 32.63 1982

300 metres *35.83* Merlene Ottey (Jam) Pocatello, Idaho 14 Mar 1981
most 3 Merlene Ottey 37.13 1980 to 35.83 1981

400 metres *49.59* Jarmila Kratochvilova (Cs) Milan 7 Mar 1982
most 3 Marita Koch (GDR) 51.80 1977 to 51.14 1977

500 yards *1:02.3* Valerie Brisco-Hooks (USA) San Diego 15 Feb 1985

500 metres *1:09.38* Cathy Rattray (Jam) Gainesville, Fl. 11 Feb 1984

600 yards *1:17.38* Delisa Walton (USA) Cedar Falls, Iowa 13 Mar 1982

600 metres *1:26.56* Delisa Walton (USA) Pocatello, Idaho 14 Mar 1981; *1:26.2* (oversized track) Anita Weiss (GDR) East Berlin 12 Jan 1980

800 metres *1:58.4* Olga Vakrusheva (USSR) Moscow 16 Feb 1980; *1:58.33* (oversized track) Jarmila Kratochvilova (Cs) Jablonec 12 Feb 1983

1000 yards *2:23.8* Mary Decker (USA) Inglewood, Cal. 3 Feb 1978

1000 metres *2:34.8* Brigitte Kraus (GFR) Dortmund 19 Feb 1978

1500 metres *4:00.8* Mary Decker (USA) New York 8 Feb 1980; *4:00.2* (oversized track) Mary Decker Houston 16 Feb 1980
most 4 Francie Larrieu (USA) 4:12.2 1974 to 4:09.8 1975

1 mile *4:20.5* Mary Decker (USA) San Diego 19 Feb 1982
4:17.55 (oversized track) Mary Decker Houston 16 Feb 1980
most 4 Francie Larrieu (USA) 4:35.6 1973 to 4:28.5 1975

2000 metres *5:34.52* Mary Decker (USA) Los Angeles 18 Jan 1985

3000 metres *8:42.3* Olga Bandarenko (USSR) Volgagrad 25 Jan 1986

2 miles *9:31.7* Mary Decker (USA) Los Angeles 21 Jan 1982

3 miles *14:53.80* Chris McMiken (NZ) Lincoln 23 Feb 1985

5000 metres *15:34.5* Margaret Groos (USA) Blacksburg, Va 20 Feb 1981

50 yards hurdles *6.20* Johanna Klier (GDR) Toronto 10 Feb 1978

50 metres hurdles (five hurdles at 2ft 9in) *6.73* Cornelia Oshkenat (GDR) E. Berlin 26 Jan 1986
most 3 Annelie Ehrhardt (GDR) 6.85 1972 to 6.74 1973
6.6 (hand timing) Annelie Ehrhardt E.Berlin 13 Feb 1972
most 5 Karin Balzer (GDR) 6.8–6.7 1971 (also 4 7.0–6.9 1967–8 with four hurdles)

60 yards hurdles (five hurdles at 2ft 9in) *7.36* Stephanie Hightower (USA) New York 25 Feb 1983
most 4 Candy Young (USA) 7.50 1979 to 7.37 1982
4 Stephanie Hightower (USA) 7.47 1980 to 7.36 1983
most (hand timing) 5 Karin Balzer (GDR) 7.6 1969 to 7.4 1974

60 metres hurdles (six hurdles at 2ft 9in) *7.75* Bettina Jahn (GDR) Budapest 5 Mar 1983
most 3 Karin Balzer (GDR) hand timed 8.2 1970 to 8.0 1971
3 Grazyna Rabsztyn (Pol) hand timed 7.9 1974 to 7.84 1980

100 metres hurdles *13.12* Annelie Ehrhardt (GDR) East Berlin 14 Jan 1976

4 × 200 metres relay *1:34.05* Italy Turin 11 Feb 1984

4 × 400 metres relay *3:34.38* West Germany Dortmund 30 Jan 1981

High jump *2.03* Tamara Bykova (USSR) Budapest 6 Mar 1983
most 3 Rosemarie Ackermann (GDR) 1.91 1973 to 1.95 1977
3 Tamara Bykova (USSR) 2.00 to 2.03 1983

Long jump *7.29* Heike Drechsler (GDR) E. Berlin 26 Jan 1986
most 6 Tatyana Shchelkanova (USSR) 6.29 1962 to 6.73 1966
4 Heike Drechsler (GDR) 6.88 1983 to 7.29 1986

Triple jump *13.51* Esmeralda Garcia (Bra) Syracuse, NY 9 Mar 1985

Shot *22.50* Helena Fibingerova (Cs) Jablonec 19 Feb 1977
most 8 Nadezhda Chizhova (USSR) 17.86 1967 to 20.40 1974
6 Helena Fibingerova 20.36 1974 to 22.50 1977
5 Tamara Press (USSR) 17.11 1960 to 17.75 1965

1 mile walk *6:28:46* Giuliana Salce (Ita) Genoa 16 Feb 1985

3000 metres walk *12:31.57* Giuliana Salce (Ita) Florence 6 Feb 1985
most 4 Margareta Simu (Swe) 14:54.0 1974 to 13:46.1 1978

5000 metres walk *21:44.52* Giuliana Salce (Ita) Turin 20 Feb 1985

Olympic Games

The first Olympic Games of the modern era were staged in Athens, Greece from 6–15 Apr 1896. The driving force behind their revival was Pierre de Fredi, Baron de Coubertin, who was born in Paris in 1863. He believed in the Greek athletic ideal of perfection of mind and body, and his energies were devoted to achieving his dream of reintroducing the Olympic Games, which had been staged for more than a thousand years before their prohibition in AD 393.

In 1889 de Coubertin was commissioned by the French government to form a universal sports association and he visted other European nations to gather information. He made public his views on 25 Nov 1892 at the Sorbonne in Paris. These led to the formation of the International Olympic Committee in 1894 and thence to the staging of the Olympic Games, which were opened in Athens on Easter Monday 1896.

The International Olympic Committee meets at the first Games, in 1896. Pierre de Coubertin is seated on the left.

The airship *Hindenburg* over the Olympic stadium, Berlin 1936.

Just 59 athletes from ten nations contested the athletics events in Athens. The 1900 and 1904 Games were also small-scale affairs, with just over 100 athletes at each, but from 1908 the Games grew rapidly in importance to true world championships. Women's events were first included in 1928, and the number of contestants in athletics passed 1000 for the first time at the 1960 Games.

VENUES

1896	Athens	1948	London
1900	Paris	1952	Helsinki
1904	St Louis	1956	Melbourne
1906	Athens*	1960	Rome
1908	London	1964	Tokyo
1912	Stockholm	1968	Mexico City
1920	Antwerp	1972	Munich
1924	Paris	1976	Montreal
1928	Amsterdam	1980	Moscow
1932	Los Angeles	1984	Los Angeles
1936	Berlin	1988	Seoul

*Intercalated Games held as the tenth anniversary celebration of the 1896 Games. Results from these 1906 Games have been included in the records in this book.

The most Olympic records set is eight by Shirley Strickland/de la Hunty (Aus): five at 80mh, three at 4×100mR 1952–56. The most in individual events is seven by Wolfgang Nordwig (GDR) in the pole vault: four in 1968 and three in 1972, as he and others took the record from 5.20m to 5.50m. Al Oerter (USA) uniquely set Olympic records at four Games, 1956 to 1968, in the discus.

MOST GOLD MEDALS—ALL EVENTS

MEN
10 Raymond Ewry (USA) StHJ & StLJ 1900–04–06–08, StTJ 1900–04*
 9 Paavo Nurmi (Fin) 1500m & 5000m 1924, 10 000m 1920–28, 3000 mSt 1924, C-C 1920–24, C-C team 1920–24

OLYMPIC GAMES RECORDS prior to 1988   *Performance made in qualifying round.

MEN

	hr:min:sec		
100m	9.95	Jim Hines (USA)	1968
200m	19.80	Carl Lewis (USA)	1984
400m	43.86	Lee Evans (USA)	1968
800m	1:43.00	Joaquim Cruz (Bra)	1984
1500m	3:32.53	Sebastian Coe (UK)	1984
5000m	13:05.59	Said Aouita (Mor)	1984
10 000m	27:38.35	Lasse Viren (Fin)	1972
Marathon	2:09:21	Carlos Lopes (Por)	1984
3000m steeple	8:08.02	Anders Gärderud (Swe)	1976
110mh	13.20	Roger Kingdom (USA)	1984
400mh	47.64	Edwin Moses (USA)	1976
4×100mR	37.83	USA	1984
4×400mR	2:56.16	USA	1968
20kmW	1:23.13	Enesto Canto (Mex)	1984
50kmW	3:47.26	Raul Gonzales (Mex)	1984
	metres		
High jump	2.36	Gerd Wessig (GDR)	1980
Pole vault	5.78	Wladyslaw Kozakiewicz (Pol)	1980
Long jump	8.90	Bob Beamon (USA)	1968
Triple jump	17.39	Viktor Saneyev (USSR)	1968
Shot	21.35	Vladimir Kiselyev (USSR)	1980
Discus	68.28	Mac Wilkins (USA)	*1976
Hammer	81.80	Yuriy Sedykh (USSR)	1980
Javelin	94.58	Miklos Nemeth (Hun)	1976
Decathlon	8847 pts	Daley Thompson (UK)	1984

WOMEN

	hr:min:sec		
100m	10.97	Evelyn Ashford (USA)	1984
200m	21.81	Valerie Brisco-Hooks (USA)	1984
400m	48.83	Valerie Brisco-Hooks (USA)	1984
800m	1:53.43	Nadezhda Olizarenko (USSR)	1980
1500m	3:56.56	Tatyana Kazankina (USSR)	1980
3000m	8:35.96	Maricica Puica (Rom)	1984
Marathon	2:24.52	Joan Benoit (USA)	1984
100mh	12.56	Vera Komissova (USSR)	1980
400mh	54.61	Nawal El Moutawakil (Mor)	1984
4×100mR	41.60	GDR	1980
4×400mR	3:18.29	USA	1984
	metres		
High jump	2.02	Ulrike Meyfarth (GFR)	1984
Long jump	7.06	Tatyana Kolpakova (USSR)	1980
Shot	22.41	Ilona Slupianek (GDR)	1980
Discus	69.96	Evelin Jahl (GDR)	1980
Javelin	69.56	Tessa Sanderson (UK)	1984
Heptathlon	6387 pts	Glynis Nunn (Aus)	1984

5 Martin Sheridan (USA) DT 1904–06–08, SP 1906, DT (Greek style) 1908

5 Ville Ritola (Fin) 10 000m, 3000mSt, C-C team & 3000m team 1924, 5000m 1928

4 Alvin Kraenzlein (USA) 60m, 110mh, 200mh, LJ 1900

4 Archie Hahn (USA) 60m & 200m 1904, 100m 1904–06

4 James Lightbody (USA) 800m & 2500mSt 1904, 1500m 1904–06

4 Myer Prinstein (USA) LJ 1904–06, TJ 1900–04

4 Erik Lemming (Swe) JT 1906–08–12, JT (freestyle) 1908

4 Mel Sheppard (USA) 800m, 1500m & Medley R 1908; 4×400mR 1912

4 Hannes Kolehmainen (Fin) 5000m, 10 000m & C-C 1912, Mar 1920

4 Jesse Owens (USA) 100m, 200m, LJ & 4×100mR 1936

4 Emil Zatopek (Cs) 5000m 1952, 10 000m 1948–52, Mar 1952

4 Harrison Dillard (USA) 100m 1948, 110mh 1952, 4×100mR 1948–52

4 Al Oerter (USA) DT 1956–60–64–68

4 Lasse Viren (Fin) 5000m & 10 000m 1972–76

4 Carl Lewis (USA) 100m, 200m, LJ & 4×100mR 1984

3 Harry Hillman (USA) 400m, 200mh, 400mh 1904

3 John Flanagan (Ire) HT 1900–04–08

3 Ralph Rose (USA) SP 1904–08, SP (2–hand) 1912

3 Ugo Frigerio (Ita) 3kmW 1920, 10kmW 1920–24

3 Clarence Houser (USA) SP 1924, DT 1924–28

3 Frank Wykoff (USA) 4×100mR 1928–32–36

3 Mal Whitfield (USA) 800m 1948–52, 4×400mR 1948

3 Bobby Morrow (USA) 100m, 200m, 4×100mR 1956

3 Glenn Davis (USA) 400mh, 1956–60, 4×400mR 1960

3 Peter Snell (NZ) 800m 1960–64, 1500m 1964

3 Viktor Saneyev (USSR) TJ 1968–72–76

*St = standing events

WOMEN

4 Fanny Blankers-Koen (Hol) 100m, 200m, 80mh & 4×100mR 1948

4 Betty Cuthbert (Aus) 100m, 200m, 4×100mR 1956, 400m 1964

4 Bärbel Wöckel (GDR) 200m & 4×100mR 1976–80

3 Shirley de la Hunty (Aus) 80mh 1952–56, 4×100mR 1956

3 Wilma Rudolph (USA) 100m, 200m, 4×100mR 1960

3 Tamara Press (USSR) SP 1960–64, DT 1964

3 Wyomia Tyus (USA) 100m 1964–68, 4×100mR 1968

3 Irena Szewinska (Pol) 200m 1968, 400m 1976, 4×100mR 1964

3 Renate Stecher (GDR) 100m & 200m 1972, 4×100mR 1976

3 Tatyana Kazankina (USA) 800m 1976, 1500m 1976–80

3 Valerie Brisco-Hooks (USA) 200m, 400m, 4×400mR 1984

Most medals–all events
(G—gold, S—silver, B—bronze)

MEN

12 Paavo Nurmi (Fin) 9G as above; 3S 5000m 1920–28, 3000mSt 1928
10 Raymond Ewry (USA) 10G as above
9 Martin Sheridan (USA) 5G as above; 3S StHJ, StLJ & Stone 1906; 1B StLJ 1908
8 Ville Ritola (Fin) 5G as above; 3S 5000m & C-C 1924, 10 000m 1928
6 Robert Garrett (USA) 2G SP & DT 1896; 1S LJ 1896; 3B HJ 1896, SP & StTJ 1900
6 James Lightbody (USA) 4G as above; 2S 800m 1906, C-C team 1904
6 Erik Lemming (Swe) 4G as above; 2B SP & Pen 1906
6 Ralph Rose (USA) 3G as above; 2S SP 1912, DT 1904; 1B HT 1904
5 Irving Baxter (USA) 2G HJ & PV 1900; 3S StHJ, StLJ, StTJ 1900
5 Walter Tewksbury (USA) 2G 200m & 400mh 1900; 2S 60m & 100m 1900; 1B 200mh 1900
5 Myer Prinstein (USA) 4G as above; 1S LJ 1900
5 Mel Sheppard (USA) 4G as above; 1S 800m 1912
5 Hannes Kolehmainen (Fin) 4G as above; 1S C-C team 1912
5 Phil Edwards (Can) 5B 800m 1932–36, 1500m 1932, 4×400mR 1928–32
5 Mal Whitfield (USA) 3G as above; 1S 4×400m 1952; 1B 400m 1948
5 Emil Zatopek (Cs) 4G as above; 1S 5000m 1948
5 Valeriy Borzov (USSR) 2G 100m & 200m 1972; 1S 4×100mR 1972; 2B 100m & 4×100mR 1976

WOMEN

7 Shirley de la Hunty (Aus) 3G as above; 1S 4×100mR 1948; 3B 100m 1948–52, 80mh 1948
7 Irena Szewinska (Pol) 3G as above; 2S 200m & LJ 1964; 2B 100m 1968, 200m 1972
6 Renate Stecher (GDR) 3G as above; 2S 100m 1976, 4×100mR 1972; 1B 200m 1976

The most medals without a gold is five by Phil Edwards.

The most medals at one games:
(five medals or four golds)

MEN

5G	Paavo Nurmi (Fin) 1924
4G 2S	Ville Ritola (Fin) 1924
4G	Alvin Kraenzlein (USA) 1900
4G	Jesse Owens (USA) 1936
4G	Carl Lewis (USA) 1984
2G 3S	Irving Baxter (USA) 1900
2G 3S	Martin Sheridan (USA) 1906
2G 2S 1B	Walter Tewksbury (USA) 1900

WOMEN

4G	Fanny Blankers-Koen (Hol) 1948

Combination winners

Gold medals won at both track and field events MEN Alvin Kraenzlein, Jesse Owens and Carl Lewis (see above) and by two WOMEN Mildred Didrikson (USA) 80mh and JT 1932, and Heide Rosendahl (GFR) LJ & 4×100mR 1972. Didrikson also won the silver medal for HJ in 1932.

The most games contested

MEN

5 Paul Martin (Swi) 1920–36, John Ljunggren (Swe) 1948–64, Janusz Sidlo (Pol) 1952–68, Abdon Pamich (Ita) 1956–72, Igor Ter-Ovanesyan (USSR) 1956–72, Alex Oakley (Can) 1956–68 and 1976, Vladimir Golubnichiy (USSR) 1960–76, Urs von Wartburg (Swi) 1960–76

WOMEN

6 Lia Manoliu (Bul) 1952–72, DT successively 6th, 9th, 3rd, 3rd, 1st, 9th
5 Olga Fikotova/Connolly (Cs/USA) 1956–72, Willye White (USA) 1956–72, Irena Szewinska (Pol) 1964–80

The most finals (or first eight) at the same event

MEN

5 Vladimir Golubnichiy (USSR) 20kmW 1960–76: 1st, 3rd, 1st, 2nd, 7th
4 Matt McGrath (USA) HT 1908–24: 2nd, 1st, 5th, 2nd
4 Al Oerter (USA) DT 1956–68: 1st, 1st, 1st, 1st
4 Gyula Zsivotzky (Hun) HT 1960–72: 2nd, 2nd, 1st, 5th
4 Janis Lusis (USSR) JT 1964–76: 3rd, 1st, 2nd, 8th
4 Jay Silvester (USA) DT 1964–76: 4th, 5th, 2nd, 8th
4 Viktor Saneyev (USSR) TJ 1968–80: 1st, 1st, 1st, 2nd
4 Pietro Mennea (Ita) 200m 1972–82: 3rd, 4th, 1st, 7th

WOMEN

4 Galina Zybina (USSR) SP 1952–64: 1st, 2nd, 7th, 3rd
4 Lia Manoliu (Rom) DT (see above)
4 Sara Simeoni (Ita) HJ 1972–84: 6th, 2nd, 1st, 2nd

The greatest span of years of competition

24 years by Frantisek Janda-Suk (Cs) 1900–24: DT 2nd 1900, 17th 1912, 29th 1924
20 years by Alex Oakley and Lia Manoliu (see above) and by Dorothy Odam/Tyler (UK) 1936–56

The greatest span between winning medals is 12 years: by double gold medallist Ulrike Meyfarth (GFR) who by winning in 1972 and 1984 is both the oldest and youngest women's high jump champion; Albin Stenroos (Fin), third 10 000m and second C-C team 1912 and first Mar 1924; Matt McGrath (USA), first HT 1912, second HT 1924; Ville Porhola (Fin), first SP 1920 and second HT 1932; Dorothy Odam/Tyler (UK) second HJ 1936 and 1948; and Yelena Gorchakova (USSR) third JT 1952 and 1964.

Oldests (y—years, d—days)

MEN

Winner   42y 23d Pat McDonald (USA) 56lb Wt 1920
Medallist   48y 115d Tebbs Lloyd Johnson (UK) 3rd 50kmW 1948
Competitor   49y 74d John Deni (USA) 15th 50kmW 1952

WOMEN

Winner   36y 176d Lia Manoliu (Rom) DT 1968
Medallist   37y 348d Dana Zatopkova (Cs) 2nd JT 1960
Competitor   46y 282d Joyce Smith (UK) 11th Mar 1984

Youngests

MEN

Winner   17y 263d Bob Mathias (USA) Dec 1948
Medallist   17y 206d Pal Simon (Hun) 3rd Medley relay 1908 (born 1891, but exact date unknown, 17y 206d is oldest possible)
Individual medal   17y 263d Bob Mathias (as above)

WOMEN

Winner   15y 123d Barbara Pearl Jones (USA) 4×100mR 1952
Individual winner   16y 123d Ulrike Meyfarth (GFR) HJ 1972
Medallist   15y 123d Barbara Pearl Jones (as above)
Individual medal   16y 115d Dorothy Odam (UK) 2nd HJ 1936

(left) Tebbs Lloyd Johnson happily completes the 50km walk in third place at Wembley in 1948. At 48 he became the oldest Olympics athletics medallist. (above) Joyce Smith wins for UK v. USSR at 1500m in 1975. Nine years later she became the oldest woman Olympic competitor. (below) Four golds for Lasse Viren. (OPA, ASP, All-Sport)

The most successful athletes at each event

Event	G	S	B	Athlete with medals won (G—gold, S—silver, B—bronze)
MEN				
100m	2	–	–	Archie Hahn (USA) G 1904–06
200m	1	1	–	Andy Stanfield (USA) G 1952, S 1956
400m	1	1	–	Wyndham Halswelle (UK) G 1908, S 1906
800m	2	–	–	Douglas Lowe (UK) G 1924–28
	2	–	–	Mal Whitfield (USA) G 1948–52
	2	–	–	Peter Snell (NZ) G 1960–64
1500m	2	–	–	James Lightbody (USA) G 1904–06
	2	–	–	Sebastian Coe (UK) G 1980–84
5000m	2	–	–	Lasse Viren (Fin) G 1972–76

Event	G	S	B	Athlete
10 000m	2	–	–	Paavo Nurmi (Fin) G 1920–28
	2	–	–	Emil Zatopek (Cs) G 1948–52
	2	–	–	Lasse Viren (Fin) G 1972–76 (5th 1980)
Marathon	2	–	–	Abebe Bikila (Eth) G 1960–64
	2	–	–	Waldemar Cierpinski (GDR) G 1976–80
3000m steeple	2	–	–	Volmari Iso-Hollo (Fin) G 1932–36
110mh	2	–	–	Lee Calhoun (USA) G 1956–60
400mh	2	–	–	Glenn Davis (USA) G 1956–60
	2	–	–	Ed Moses (USA) G 1976–84
High jump	1	1	–	Valeriy Brumel (USSR) G 1964, S 1960
	1	1	–	Con Leahy (Ire) G 1906, S 1908 (tie)
	1	1	–	Jacek Wszola (Poland) G 1976, S 1980
Pole vault	2	–	1	Bob Richards (USA) G 1952–56, B 1948
Long jump	1	1	1	Ralph Boston (USA) G 1960, S 1964, B 1968
Triple jump	3	1	–	Viktor Saneyev (USSR) G 1968–72–76, S 1982
	2	–	–	Myer Prinstein (USA) G 1900–04
	2	–	–	Adhemar Ferreira da Silva (Bra) G 1952–56
	2	–	–	Jozef Schmidt (Pol) G 1960–64 (7th 1968)
Shot	2	1	–	Ralph Rose (USA) G 1904–08, S 1912
	2	1	–	Parry O'Brien (USA) G 1952–56, S 1960 (4th 1964)
Discus	4	–	–	Al Oerter (USA) G 1956–60–64–68
	3	–	–	Martin Sheridan (USA) G 1904–06–08
	1	1	1	Ludvik Danek (Cs) G 1972, S 1964, B 1968 (9th 1976)
Hammer	3	–	–	John Flanagan (USA) G 1900–04–08
	2	–	–	Pat O'Callaghan (Ire) G 1928–32
	2	–	–	Yuriy Sedykh (USSR) G 1976–80
	1	2	–	Matt McGrath (USA) G 1912, S 1908–24
	1	2	–	Gyula Zsivotzky (Hun) G 1968, S 1960–64 (5th 1972)
Javelin	3	–	–	Erik Lemming (Swe) G 1906–08–12
	2	–	–	Jonni Myyrä (Fin) G 1920–24
	1	1	1	Janis Lusis (USSR) G 1968, S 1972, B 1964 (8th 1976)
Decathlon	2	–	–	Bob Mathias (USA) G 1948–52
	2	–	–	Daley Thompson (UK) G 1980–84 (18th 1976)
10kmW	2	–	–	Ugo Frigerio (Ita) G 1920–24
	2	–	–	John Mikaelsson (Swe) G 1948–52
20kmW	2	–	1	Vladimir Golubnichiy (USSR) G 1960–68, B 1964
50kmW	1	1	1	John Ljunggren (Swe) G 1948, S 1960, B 1956 (9th 1952)
WOMEN				
100m	2	–	–	Wyomia Tyus (USA) G 1964–68
200m	2	–	–	Bärbel Wöckel (GDR) G 1976–80
	1	1	1	Irena Szewinska (Pol) G 1968, S 1964, B 1972
400m	–	1	1	Christina Lathan (GDR) S 1976, B 1980
800m	1	–	–	eight winners (no double medallists)
1500m	2	–	–	Tatyana Kazankina (USSR) G 1976–80
3000m	1	–	–	Maricica Puica (Rom) G 1984 (first held)
Marathon	1	–	–	Joan Benoit (USA) G 1984 (first held)
100mh*	2	–	1	Shirley de la Hunty (Aus) G 1952–56, B 1948
400mh	1	–	–	Nawal el Moutawakil (Mor) G 1984 (first held)
High jump	2	–	–	Iolanda Balas (Rom) G 1960–64 (5th 1956)
	2	–	–	Ulrike Meyfarth (GFR) G 1972–84
	1	2	–	Sara Simeoni (Ita) G 1980, S 1976–84
Long jump	1	1	–	Elzbieta Krzesinska (Pol) G 1956, S 1960
Shot	2	–	–	Tamara Press (USSR) G 1960–64
	1	1	1	Galina Zybina (USSR) G 1952, S 1956, B 1964
	1	1	1	Nadezhda Chizhova (USSR) G 1972, S 1976, B 1968
Discus	2	–	1	Nina Ponomaryeva (USSR) G 1952–60, B 1956
	2	–	–	Evelin Jahl (GDR) G 1976–80
	1	–	2	Lia Manoliu (Rom) G 1968, B 1960–64
Javelin	2	–	–	Ruth Fuchs (GDR) G 1972–76 (8th 1980)
Pen/Hep†	–	–	2	Burglinde Pollak (GDR) B 1972–76 (only double medallist)

*Held at 80m hurdles 1932–68
†Pentathlon 1964–76, Heptathlon 1980–84

The above table contains all double gold medallists and all athletes who have won three or more medals at one individual event.

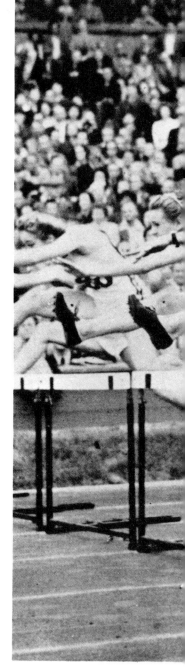

OLYMPIC FIRSTS

Champion: James Connolly (USA) TJ 13.71m on 6 Apr 1896
Women's champion: Halina Konopacka (Pol) DT 39.62m on 31 Jul 1928

(above right) Fanny Blankers-Koen (nearest camera) on her way to victory at 80m hurdles in 1948, when she won four gold medals. Next to her is silver medallist Maureen Gardner (UK). (right): Champions all (from left): Joaquim Cruz, 800m 1984; Elizabeth Robinson (USA – 879), from Fanny Rosenfeld (Can – 677) 100m 1928; Ville Ritola, five golds 1924–8. (All-Sport, Mark Shearman, Central Press, Central Press)

Medal table by nation—including 1906 Games

NATION	MEN			WOMEN			TOTAL
	G	S	B	G	S	B	Medals
USA	234	177	147	26	19	10	613
USSR	29	31	36	25	18	28	167
United Kingdom	40	51	39	4	18	11	162
Finland	46	33	28	–	2	–	109
F. R. Germany*	10	23	32	11	13	11	100
GDR	11	16	11	22	20	17	97
Sweden	17	24	40	–	–	3	84
Australia	6	9	11	10	7	10	53
France	7	19	16	3	1	2	48
Italy	12	6	18	3	4	2	45
Canada	9	9	14	2	5	6	45
Poland	9	7	4	6	8	7	41
Hungary	6	13	16	3	1	2	41
Greece	3	8	12	–	–	–	23
Romania	–	–	1	8	7	6	22
Czechoslovakia	5	6	3	3	2	2	21
Jamaica	4	8	4	–	–	3	19
New Zealand	7	1	7	1	–	1	17
Kenya	6	6	4	–	–	–	16
Japan	4	4	6	–	1	–	15
South Africa	4	4	4	1	1	1	15
Netherlands	–	1	5	5	2	1	14
Norway	3	2	7	–	1	–	13
Cuba	2	5	1	1	1	2	12
Ethiopia	5	1	4	–	–	–	10
Bulgaria	–	–	1	1	5	3	10
Belgium	2	5	2	–	–	–	9
Brazil	3	1	4	–	–	–	8
Switzerland	–	6	1	–	–	–	7
Ireland	4	1	–	–	–	–	5
Mexico	3	2	–	–	–	–	5
Argentina	2	2	–	–	1	–	5
Trinidad & Tobago	1	1	3	–	–	–	5
Austria	–	–	–	1	1	3	5
Tunisia	1	2	1	–	–	–	4
Portugal	1	1	1	–	–	1	4
Morocco	1	1	–	1	–	–	3
Denmark	–	1	1	–	–	1	3
India	–	2	–	–	–	–	2
Tanzania	–	2	–	–	–	–	2
Yugoslavia	–	2	–	–	–	–	2
Estonia	–	1	1	–	–	–	2
Latvia	–	1	1	–	–	–	2
Spain	–	1	1	–	–	–	2
Chile	–	1	–	–	1	–	2
Taiwan	–	1	–	–	–	1	2
Panama	–	–	2	–	–	–	2
Philippines	–	–	2	–	–	–	2

One men's medal: GOLD—Luxembourg, Uganda; SILVER—Haiti, Iceland, Ivory Coast, Sri Lanka; BRONZE—China, Nigeria, Turkey, Venezuela

*Germany 1896–1952, since then the Federal Republic of Germany. Medals won by the combined German teams of 1956, 1960 and 1964 have been allocated to GFR or GDR according to the athlete's origin.

World Championships

The first World Championships in Athletics were staged in the Olympic Stadium, Helsinki, Finland on 7–14 Aug 1983. The athletics events at the Olympic Games have also had world championship status, but these were the first such championships for athletics alone, and were an oustanding success. In an era of boycotts at the Olympic Games, the competition in Helsinki was unaffected by such political considerations, and 1572 competitors took part from a record 157 nations. There was a total attendance at morning and afternoon sessions of 422,402.

Winner of the most medals was Marita Koch (GDR) with golds at the women's 200m, 4×100mR and 4×400mR and silver at 100m. Joining her as winner of three gold medals was Carl Lewis (USA) at 100m, LJ and 4×100mR. In the latter event the USA team's time of 37.86 by Emmit King, Willie Gault, Calvin Smith and Lewis was one of two world records set at the Championships. The other was 47.99 for 400m by Jarmila Kratochvilova (Cs), who also won the 800m on the previous day, just 36 minutes after her 400m semi-final.

Jarmila Kratochvilova powered her way to double victory at the inaugural world championships. She also ran a great 47.75 anchor leg in the 4×400m relay to take Czechoslovakia to the silver medals. (ASP)

Carl Lewis, triple gold in 1983 in preparation for going one better the next year. With the US sprint relay team he set his first world record. (ASP)

MEDAL WINNERS—LEADING NATIONS

NATION	MEN			WOMEN			TOTAL
	G	S	B	G	S	B	Medals
USA	6	8	4	2	1	3	24
USSR	4	2	5	2	4	6	23
GDR	2	3	2	8	4	3	22
Czechoslovakia	1	1	2	3	2	–	9
F. R. Germany	2	3	1	–	2	–	8
United Kingdom	2	–	2	–	2	1	7
Poland	2	2	–	–	–	–	4
Italy	1	1	1	–	–	–	3
Jamaica	1	–	–	–	1	1	3
Finland	–	1	1	1	–	–	3
Bulgaria	–	–	1	–	–	2	3

MEDALLISTS FOR ALL EVENTS

MEN

100 metres (w = −0.3)
1. Carl Lewis (USA) 10.07
2. Calvin Smith (USA) 10.21
3. Emmit King (USA) 10.24

200 metres (w = +1.1)
1. Calvin Smith (USA) 20.14
2. Elliott Quow (USA) 20.41
3. Pietro Mennea (Ita) 20.51

400 metres
1. Bert Cameron (Jam) 45.05
2. Michael Franks (USA) 45.22
3. Sunder Nix (USA) 45.24

800 metres
1. Willi Wülbeck (GFR) 1:43.65
2. Rob Druppers (Hol) 1:44.20
3. Joaquim Cruz (Bra) 1:44.27

1500 metres
1. Steve Cram (UK) 3:41.59
2. Steve Scott (USA) 3:41.87
3. Said Aouita (Mor) 3:42.02

5000 metres
1. Eamonn Coghlan (Ire) 13:28.53
2. Werner Schildhauer (GDR) 13:30.20
3. Martti Vainio (Fin) 13:30.34

10 000 metres
1. Alberto Cova (Ita) 28:01.04
2. Werner Schildhauer (GDR) 28:01.18
3. Hansjörg Kunze (GDR) 28:01.26

Marathon
1. Rob de Castella (Aus) 2:10:03
2. Kebede Balcha (Eth) 2:10:27
3. Waldemar Cierpinski (GDR) 2:10:37

3000 metres steeplechase
1. Patriz Ilg (GFR) 8:15.06
2. Boguslaw Maminski (Pol) 8:17.03
3. Colin Reitz (UK) 8:17.75

110 metres hurdles (w = +1.3)
1. Greg Foster (USA) 13.42
2. Arto Bryggare (Fin) 13.46
3. Willie Gault (USA) 13.48

400 metres hurdles
1. Edwin Moses (USA) 47.50
2. Harald Schmid (GFR) 48.61
3. Aleksandr Kharlov (USSR) 49.03

High jump
1. Gennadiy Avdeyenko (USSR) 2.32
2. Tyke Peacock (USA) 2.32
3. Zhu Jianhua (Chi) 2.29

Pole vault
1. Sergey Bubka (USSR) 5.70
2. Konstantin Volkov (USSR) 5.60
3. Atanas Tarev (Bul) 5.60

Long jump
1. Carl Lewis (USA) 8.55
2. Jason Grimes (USA) 8.29
3. Mike Conley (USA) 8.12

Triple Jump
1. Zdzislaw Hoffmann (Pol) 17.42
2. Willie Banks (USA) 17.18
3. Ajayi Agbebaku (Nig) 17.18

Shot
1. Edward Sarul (Pol) 21.39
2. Ulf Timmermann (GDR) 21.16
3. Remigius Machura (Cs) 20.98

Discus
1. Imrich Bugar (Cs) 67.72
2. Luis Delis (Cs) 67.36
3. Gejza Valent (Cs) 66.08

Hammer
1. Sergey Litvinov (USSR) 82.68
2. Yuriy Sedykh (USSR) 80.94
3. Zdzislaw Kwasny (Pol) 79.42

Javelin
1. Detlef Michel (GDR) 89.48
2. Tom Petranoff (USA) 85.60
3. Dainis Kula (USSR) 85.58

Decathlon (1964/1984 tables)
1. Daley Thompson (UK) 8666/8714
2. Jürgen Hingsen (GFR) 8561/8599
3. Siegfried Wentz (GFR) 8478/8513

4 × 100 metres relay
1. USA 37.86
2. Italy 38.37
3. USSR 38.41

4 × 400 metres relay
1. USSR 3:00.79
2. GFR 3:01.83
3. UK 3:03.53

20 000 metres walk
1. Ernesto Canto (Mex) 1:20:49
2. Jozef Pribilinec (Cs) 1:20:59
3. Yevgeniy Yevsyukov (USSR) 1:21:08

50 000 metres walk
1. Ronald Weigel (GDR) 3:43:08
2. José Marin (Spa) 3:46:42
3. Sergey Yung (USSR) 3:49:03

WOMEN
100 metres (w = −0.5)
1. Marlies Göhr (GDR) 10.97
2. Marita Koch (GDR) 11.02
3. Diane Williams (USA) 11.06

200 metres (w = +1.5)
1. Marita Koch (GDR) 22.13
2. Merlene Ottey (Jam) 22.19
3. Kathy Cook (UK) 22.37

400 metres
1. Jarmila Kratochvilova (Cs) 47.99
2. Tatana Kocembova (Cs) 48.59
3. Maria Pinigina (USSR) 49.19

800 metres
1. Jarmila Kratochvilova (Cs) 1:54.68
2. Lyubov Gurina (USSR) 1:56.11
3. Yekaterina Podkopayeva (USSR) 1:57.58

1500 metres
1. Mary Decker (USA) 4:00.90
2. Zamira Zaitseva (USSR) 4:01.19
3. Yekaterina Podkopayeva (USSR) 4:02.25

3000 metres
1. Mary Decker (USA) 8:34.62
2. Brigitte Kraus (GFR) 8:35.11
3. Tatyana Kazankina (USSR) 8:35.13

Marathon
1. Grete Waitz (Nor) 2:28:09
2. Marianne Dickerson (USA) 2:31:09
3. Raisa Smekhnova (USSR) 2:31:13

100 metres hurdles (w = +2.4)
1. Bettina Jahn (GDR) 12.35
2. Kerstin Knabe (GDR) 12.42
3. Ginka Zagorcheva (Bul) 12.62

400 metres hurdles
1. Yekaterina Fesenko (USSR) 54.14
2. Anna Ambraziene (USSR) 54.15
3. Ellen Fiedler (GDR) 54.55

High jump
1. Tamara Bykova (USSR) 2.01
2. Ulrike Meyfarth (GFR) 1.99
3. Louise Ritter (USA) 1.95

Long jump
1. Heike Daute (GDR) 7.27w
2. Anisoara Cusmir (Rom) 7.15w
3. Carol Lewis (USA) 7.04w

Shot
1. Helena Fibingerova (Cs) 21.05
2. Helma Knorscheidt (GDR) 20.70
3. Ilona Slupianek (GDR) 20.56

Discus
1. Martina Opitz (GDR) 68.94
2. Galina Murashova (USSR) 67.44
3. Maria Vergova (Bul) 66.44

Javelin
1. Tiina Lillak (Fin) 70.82
2. Fatima Whitbread (UK) 69.14
3. Anna Verouli (Gre) 65.72

Heptathlon (1971/1984 tables)
1. Ramona Neubert (GDR) 6714/6770
2. Sabine Paetz (GDR) 6662/6713
3. Anke Vater (GDR) 6532/6524

4 × 100 metres relay
1. GDR 41.76
2. UK 42.71
3. Jamaica 42.73

4 × 400 metres relay
1. GDR 3:19.73
2. Czechoslovakia 3:20.32
3. USSR 3:21.16

The championships bests are as for the winner's performances above except for:
MEN

1500m	3:35.77	Steve Cram (UK) (semi-final)
10 000m	27:45.54	Fernando Mamede (Por) (heat)
110mh	13.22	Greg Foster (USA) (semi-final)
Javelin	90.40	Detlef Michel (GDR) (qualifying)

The oldest world champion was Helena Fibingerova SP at 34yr 30d. The youngest world champion was Heike Daute LJ 18yr 241d.

WORLD CHAMPIONSHIPS PRIOR TO 1983

Events not included on the Olympic programme had separate world championships—one in 1976 and two in 1980.
Winners were:

1976 MEN 50kmW: Venyamin Soldatenko (USSR) 3:54:40

1980 WOMEN 3000m: Birgit Friedmann (GFR) 8:48.1; 400mh: Bärbel Broschat (GDR) 54.55

(far left) Javelin throwing is Finland's national sport, so Tiina Lillak's glorious last round victory was ecstatically received at Helsinki, all the more for being the first success for a Finnish woman at the event. (Mark Shearman)

(below) Eamonn Coghlan goes for gold in the 5000 metres. Dmitriy Dmitriyev (817) came fourth as Martti Vainio (third) and Werner Schildhauer (second – 377) passed him. (ASP)

The IAAF World Cup

The idea of having a competition between teams representing the continents and top athletics nations was conceived in 1975 and the first World Cup was staged in Düsseldorf (GFR) on 2–4 Sep 1977. The combination of national and continental teams was admitted by the then President of the IAAF, Adriaan Paulen, to be a somewhat artificial formula but with each event thus a straight final, magnificent athletics ensued. The aggregate attendance was over 135 000 and, with television fees, a profit of over 1.2 million Deutschmarks was reported. Undoubtedly the fourfold aims of the IAAF were achieved. These were to provide a great athletics meeting, to offer additional world-class competition for the sport's élite, to stimulate the continental areas not only in the World Cup competition itself but also by the staging of trial meetings to determine the teams, and not least to provide additional revenue for the development of athletics throughout the world.

The second World Cup was contested in the Montreal Olympic Stadium, Canada on 24–26 Aug 1979. On this occasion, however, a loss of some 50 000 Canadian dollars was made as the total three-day attendance was only just over 54 000.

The World Cup returned to Europe when staged in the Olympic Stadium, Rome, Italy on 4–6 Sep 1981 in front of a combined attendance of 185 000.

With the advent of the World Championships in 1983, the World Cup was not held that year, so is now a quadrennial affair. In 1985 it was staged on 4–6 Oct in Canberra, Australia.

The competing teams represent each of the five continents, with national teams from the USA and the top two men's and women's teams from the European Cup. Host nation Italy competed as a ninth team in 1981.

At the first World Cup in 1977, Irena Szewinska (l) beat Bärbel Eckert (later Wöckel) (r) at 200m, and completed a double with victory over Marita Koch at 400m. (All-Sport)

TEAM POSITIONS

TEAM	MEN				WOMEN			
	1977	1979	1981	1985	1977	1979	1981	1985
Africa	6	6	7	5	7	7	9	8
Americas	5	5	5	6	5	5	5	4
Asia	8	8	9	8	8	8	8	7
Europe	4	2	1	4	1	3	2	3
GDR	1	3	2	3	2	1	1	1
GFR	3	–	–	–	–	–	–	–
Italy	–	–	6	–	–	–	6	–
Oceania	7	7	8	7	6	6	7	6
USA	2	1	3	1	4	4	4	5
USSR	–	4	4	2	3	2	3	2

BEST PERFORMANCES

Three world records have been set in World Cup competition:
MEN 4×100mR USA (Bill Collins, Steve Riddick, Cliff Wiley and Steve Williams) 38.03 1977
WOMEN 400m Martita Koch (GDR) 47.60 1985; 4×100mR GDR (Silke Gladisch, Sabine Rieger, Ingrid Auerswald, Marlies Göhr) 41.37 1985

MEN

	min:sec		
100m	10.00	Ben Johnson (Can)	1985
200m	20.17	Clancy Edwards (USA)	1977
400m	44.47	Mike Franks (USA)	1985
800m	1:44.04	Alberto Juantorena (Cub)	1977
1500m	3:34.45	Steve Ovett (UK)	1977
5000m	13:13.82	Miruts Yifter (Eth)	1977
10 000m	27:38.43	Werner Schildhauer (GDR)	1981
3000m steeple	8:19.89	Boguslaw Maminski (Pol)	1981
110mh	13.32	Greg Foster (USA)	1981
400mh	47.31	Edwin Moses (USA)	1981
4×100mR	38.03	USA	1977
4×400mR	2:59.12	USA	1981
	metres		
High jump	2.31	Patrik Sjöberg (Swe)	1985
Pole vault	5.85	Sergey Bubka (USSR)	1985
Long jump	8.52	Larry Myricks (USA)	1979
Triple jump	17.58	Willie Banks (USA)	1985
Shot	22.00	Ulf Timmermann (GDR)	1985
Discus	69.08	Gennadiy Kolnootchenko (USSR)	1985
Hammer	82.12	Juri Tamm (USSR)	1985
Javelin	96.96	Uwe Hohn (GDR)	1985

WOMEN

	min:sec		
100m	11.02	Evelyn Ashford (USA)	1981
200m	21.83	Evelyn Ashford (USA)	1979
400m	47.60	Marita Koch (GDR)	1985
800m	1:57.48	Lyudmila Veselkova (USSR)	1981
1500m	4:03.33	Tamara Sorokina (USSR)	1981
3000m	8:36.32	Svyetlana Ulmasova (USSR)	1979
10 000m	32:07.50	Aurora Cunha (Por)	1985
100mh	12.67	Grazyna Rabsztyn (Pol)	1979
400mh	54.45	Sabine Busch (GDR)	1985
4×100mR	41.37	GDR	1985
4×400mR	3:19.50	GDR	1985
	metres		
High jump	2.00	Stefka Kostadinova (Bul)	1985
Long jump	7.27	Heike Drechsler (GDR)	1985
Shot	20.98	Ilona Slupianek (GDR)	1979
Discus	69.78	Martina Opitz (GDR)	1985
Javelin	70.08	Antoaneta Todorova (Bul)	1981

(above) Miruts Yifter's finishing kick brought him two World Cup doubles. (All-Sport)
(below) A hat-trick of wins for Udo Beyer. (ASP)

MOST INDIVIDUAL EVENT WINS

MEN
4 Miruts Yifter (Afr/Eth) 5000m & 10 000m 1977–79
3 Ed Moses (USA) 400mh 1977–79–81
3 Joao Carlos de Oliveira (Ame/Bra) TJ 1977–79–81
3 Udo Beyer (GDR) SP 1977–79–81
2 Alberto Juantorena (Ame/Cub) 400m & 800m 1977
2 Mike Tully (USA) PV 1977–79
2 Wolfgang Schmidt (GDR) DT 1977–79
2 Steve Ovett (Eur/UK) 1500m 1977–81

WOMEN
4 Evelyn Ashford (USA) 100m & 200m 1981–83
3* Ilona Slupianek (GDR) SP 1977*–79–81

3 Marita Koch (GDR) 400m 1979–85, 200m 1985
2 Irena Szewinska (Eur/Pol) 200m & 400m 1977
2 Grazyna Rabsztyn (Eur/Pol) 100mh 1977–79
2 Evelin Jahl (GDR) DT 1979–81
2 Ruth Fuchs (GDR) JT 1977–79
2 Marlies Göhr (GDR) 100m 1977–85
*Subsequently disqualified for failing the drugs test at the preceding European Cup Final in 1977.

Totka Petrova (Eur/Bul) won at 800m in 1977 and at 1500m in 1979, but was disqualified for infringing the doping regulations on the latter occasion.

World Cross-Country Championships

The International Cross-Country Championships were first held at Hamilton Park Racecourse, Glasgow on 28 Mar 1903. A race over 8 miles (12.87km) was contested by the four countries from the British Isles, so it was international in name only. The race was held annually, with France first entering in 1907, Belgium in 1923 and thereafter other Western European nations also participated occasionally as the event steadily gained in international prestige.

The first non-European nation to enter a team was Tunisia in 1958, the first Oceanic team was New Zealand in 1965 and the USA competed for the first time in 1966. A junior race was first added in 1961, although there had been an international race for juniors between England, France and Belgium in 1940, and the first women's race was at Barry, Wales in 1967. There were two women's races in 1970.

From 1973 (when the races were held at the Hippodrome de Waregem, Belgium), the event has had official world championship status, for then the IAAF took control of the event from the International Cross-Country Union.

The distances raced now are: men—12km, women—5km, junior men—8km.

Teams are: men—maximum of nine runners, six to score; women and junior men—maximum of six runners, four to score.

COMPETING TEAMS—progressive totals of nations whose team scored:

MEN: 1903—4, 1907—5, 1924—6, 1929—10, 1963—11, 1965—15, 1973—18, 1975—23, 1981—27, 1984—28, 1985—33
WOMEN: 1967—4, 1968—5, 1969—7, 1971—10, 1973—12, 1977—17, 1983—19, 1985—23
JUNIOR MEN: 1961—6, 1962—8, 1965—9, 1971—10, 1972—12, 1974—13, 1976—15, 1978—16, 1980—17, 1981—19, 1985—22

New records were set for the numbers of competitors in 1985, with a total of 563 finishers: 293 men, 139 junior men and 131 women.

WINNING TEAMS

MEN

England	1903–14, 1920–1, 1924–5, 1930–8, 1951, 1953–5, 1958–60, 1962, 1964–72, 1976, 1979–80
France	1922–3, 1926–9, 1939, 1946–7, 1949–50, 1952, 1956, 1978
Belgium	1948, 1957, 1961, 1963, 1973–4, 1977
Ethiopia	1981–5 (every time they have competed!)
New Zealand	1975

WOMEN

USA	1968–9, 1975, 1979, 1983–5
England	1967, 1970–74
USSR	1976–7, 1980–2
Romania	1978

JUNIOR MEN

England	1961–2, 1964–71, 1978
USA	1974–7, 1981
Ethiopia	1982–5
Spain	1973, 1979
Belgium	1965
Italy	1972
USSR	1980

Two men with great records in the International Cross-Country: Gaston Roelants leads Mariano Haro. (ASP)

Alain Mimoun won a French record four Olympic medals, topped by his 1956 marathon victory. He was even more successful over the country. Here he leads at Glasgow in 1952. (H. W. Neale)

Summary of all placings in the first three

Country	MEN 1st	MEN 2nd	MEN 3rd	WOMEN 1st	WOMEN 2nd	WOMEN 3rd	JUNIOR MEN 1st	JUNIOR MEN 2nd	JUNIOR MEN 3rd	First Year Competed
Belgium	7	7	16	–	–	–	1	4	–	1923
Canada	–	–	–	–	–	1	–	1	2	1969
England	45	15	7	6	3	3	11	4	4	1903
Ethiopia	5	–	–	–	–	–	4	–	–	1981
Finland	–	–	–	–	1	1	–	–	–	1971
France	14	24	10	–	–	–	–	–	–	1907
Ireland	–	9	5	–	1	1	–	2	1	1903
Italy	–	–	–	–	3	1	1	2	3	1929
Kenya	–	1	2	–	–	–	–	1	–	1981
Morocco	–	1	1	–	–	–	–	2	4	1959
New Zealand	1	1	2	–	3	2	–	–	–	1965
Portugal	–	–	1	–	–	–	–	–	–	1955
Romania	–	–	–	1	–	1	–	–	–	1978
Scotland	–	7	17	–	–	3	2	5	6	1903
Spain	–	1	3	–	–	–	2	5	6	1929
Tunisia	–	–	–	–	–	–	–	1	–	1958
USA	–	3	1	7	6	4	5	1	1	1966
USSR	–	1	3	5	3	–	1	–	1	1973
Wales	–	1	2	–	–	–	–	–	–	1903
Yugoslavia	–	–	1	–	–	–	–	–	–	1953

World cross-country champions 1973–85

Year	MEN	WOMEN	JUNIOR MEN
1973	Pekka Paivarinta (Fin)	Paola Cacchi (Ita)	Jim Brown (Sco)
1974	Eric De Beck (Bel)	Paola Cacchi (Ita)	Richard Kimball (USA)
1975	Ian Stewart (Sco)	Julie Brown (USA)	Robert Thomas (USA)
1976	Carlos Lopes (Por)	Carmen Valero (Spa)	Eric Hulst (USA)
1977	Leon Schots (Bel)	Carmen Valero (Spa)	Thom Hunt (USA)
1978	John Treacy (Ire)	Grete Waitz (Nor)	Mick Morton (Eng)
1979	John Treacy (Ire)	Grete Waitz (Nor)	Eddy de Paauw (Bel)
1980	Craig Virgin (USA)	Grete Waitz (Nor)	Jorge Garcia (Spa)
1981	Craig Virgin (USA)	Grete Waitz (Nor)	Mohammed Chouri (Tun)
1982	Mohamed Kedir (Eth)	Maricica Puica (Rom)	Zurubachev Gelaw (Eth)
1983	Bekele Debele (Eth)	Grete Waitz (Nor)	Fesseha Abede (Eth)
1984	Carlos Lopes (Por)	Maricica Puica (Rom)	Pedro Casacuberta (Spa)
1985	Carlos Lopes (Por)	Zola Budd (Eng)	Kimeli Kipkemboi (Ken)

Most successful individuals

MEN

Most wins: 4 Jack Holden (Eng) 1933–5, 1939; 4 Alain Mimoun (Fra) 1949, 1952, 1954, 1956; 4 Gaston Roelants (Bel) 1962, 1967, 1969, 1972; 3 Jean Bouin (Fra) 1911–3; 3 Carlos Lopes (Por) 1976, 1984–5

Most placings in first three (1st, 2nd, 3rd): 7 Gaston Roelants (4, 3, 0), 6 Jack Holden (4, 2, 0), 6 Alain Mimoun (4, 2, 0), 6 Frank Sando (Eng) (2, 3, 1), 5 Carlos Lopes (Por) (3, 1, 1), Mariano Haro (Spa) (0, 4, 1)

Most placings in first ten (years): 10 Jack Holden (1930–46); 9 Frank Sando (1952–60), Gaston Roelants (1960–75); 8 Mariano Haro (1963–75); 7 Alain Mimoun (1949–59), Marcel Van de Wattyne (Bel) (1946–62), Noel Tijou (Fra) (1967–74)

Most appearances: 20 Marcel Van de Wattyne (1946–65), 14 Danny Phillips (War) (1922–37), Jim Alder (Sco) (1962–76), Noel Tijou (1963–77), Mariano Haro (1963–77)

WOMEN

Most wins: 5 Doris Brown (USA) 1967–71, 5 Grete Waitz (Nor) 1978–81, 1984

Most placings in first three (1st, 2nd, 3rd): 7 Grete Waitz (5, 0, 2), 5 Doris Brown (5, 0, 0), 4 Rita Ridley (Eng) (0, 2, 2)

Most placings in first ten (years): 7 Grete Waitz (1978–84), 6 Rita Ridley (1967–74), Joyce Smith (Eng) (1967–78)

Most appearances: 16 Jean Lochhead (Wal) (1967–84), 14 Margaret Coomber (Sco) (1967–80)

Athletes to have won junior and senior race: Mike Tagg (Eng) Jnr 1966, Snr 1970; Dave Bedford (Eng) Jnr 1969, Snr 1971

Greatest winning margins:
MEN: 56 sec Jack Holden (Eng) 1934
WOMEN: 40 sec Grete Waitz (Nor) 1980
JUNIOR MEN: 25 sec Ian McCafferty (Sco) 1964

Doris Brown dominated the early days of the women's international. She (21) beats Bernie Boxem (Hol) at San Sebastian in 1971.

IAAF World Race Walking Cup

This competition is held biennially for the Lugano Trophy (men) and the Eschborn Cup (women). Lugano, Switzerland was the first venue for this competition, which was then for men's European teams; the first team from the rest of the world to take part was the USA in 1967. From 1977 the event has been officially recognized by the IAAF with the above name.

The finalists are nations from each continent, with additional European nations qualifying for the final from three qualifying matches.

VENUES

1961 Lugano; 1963 Varese, Italy; 1965 Pescara, Italy; 1967 Bad Saarow, GDR; 1970 Eschborn, GFR; 1973 Lugano; 1975 Le Grand Quevilly, France; 1977 Milton Keynes, England; 1979 Eschborn; 1981 Valencia, Spain; 1983 Bergen, Norway; 1985 Douglas, Isle of Man

Most finals:
7 Gerhard Weidner (GFR) 50km (1965–77) (best 2nd 1975)
6 Roger Mills (UK) 20km (1973–83) (best 8th 1973)

THE ESCHBORN CUP

In 1975 a women's race over 5km was held in conjunction with the Lugano Trophy races. This event was maintained and when held at Eschborn in 1979 a cup was introduced for the team competition. The distance was increased to 10 km from 1983.

The leading teams from 1979 have been:

	1979	1981	1983	1985
Australia	4	3	3	4
Canada	–	6	–	3
China	–	–	1	1
Italy	8	–	5	6
Norway	3	5	6	–
Sweden	2	2	4	5
United Kingdom	1	4	7	12
USA	5	7	8	8
USSR	–	1	2	2

One final appearance: 1985 8th Spain, 9th Finland, 10th Czechoslovakia, 11th Denmark

Individual winners have been:
50km 1975 Margareta Simu (Swe) 23:40.6, 1977 Siw Gustavsson (Swe) 23:19, 1979 Marion Fawkes (UK) 22:51, 1981 Siw Gustavsson 22:56.9
10km 1983 Xu Yongju (Chn) 45:13.4, 1985 Yan Hong (Chn) 46:22

THE LUGANO TROPHY

Contested by men's national teams walking over 20km and 50km. All final placings:

	1961	1963	1965	1967	1970	1973	1975	1977	1979	1981	1983	1985
Australia	–	–	–	–	–	–	–	–	9	13	11	9
Canada	–	–	–	–	–	9	–	–	–	12	14	11
China	–	–	–	–	–	–	–	–	–	15	12	13
Czechoslovakia	–	5	–	–	–	–	–	9	5	5	4	5
France	–	–	7	–	–	–	8	7	–	10	7	–
F. R. Germany	–	6	6	4	3	4	3	6	8	–	10	–
GDR	–	–	1	1	1	1	2	2	3	4	–	1
Hungary	4	2	3	7	8	–	6	10	7	–	–	–
Italy	3	4	5	8	5	3	5	3	4	1	2	3
Mexico	–	–	–	–	–	–	–	1	1	3	3	–
Poland	–	–	–	–	–	7	–	5	6	6	8	6
Spain	–	–	–	–	–	–	–	–	11	11	6	4
Sweden	2	3	4	5	7	8	7	8	10	9	–	12
United Kingdom	1	1	2	3	4	6	4	11	12	8	5	7
USA	–	–	–	6	6	5	9	12	13	7	9	8
USSR	–	–	–	2	2	2	1	4	2	2	1	2

Two final appearances: Norway 14th 1981, 13th 1983.
One final appearance: Colombia 10th 1985, New Zealand 14th 1979, Algeria 14th 1985, Kenya 15th 1985.

Best performances:
20km 1:19:30 Josef Pribilinec (Cs) 1983
       1:18:49 (short course) Daniel Bautista (Mex) 1979
50km 3:43:36 Martin Bermudez (Mex) 1979

Best individual records:

1st	2nd	3rd	
3	–	1	Christoph Höhne (GDR) 50km 1st 1965–67–70, 3rd 1973
3	–	–	Raul Gonzales (Mex) 50km 1st 1977–81–83, 4th 1979
2	–	–	Ken Matthews (UK) 20km 1st 1961–63
2	–	–	Hans-Georg Reimann (GDR) 20km 1st 1970–73, 11th 1975
2	–	–	Daniel Bautista (Mex) 20km 1st 1977–79
1	1	1	Karl-Heinz Stadtmuller (GDR) 20km 1st 1975, 2nd 1973, 3rd 1977

In the 1982 European 20km walk José Marin (92) won and Maurizio Damilano (551) was disqualified. They were first and second respectively in the 1985 World Race Walking Cup 20km. (Mark Shearman)

Other World Championships and IAAF Events

1977 Göteborg, 1979 Hannover, 1981 Christchurch, 1983 Puerto Rico.

Veterans compete in five-year age bands, from the minimum ages of 40 (men) and 35 (women).

Olympic silver medallist at 3000m in 1984, Wendy Sly won the first Women's World Road Race Championship. (ASP)

IAAF WORLD CUP MARATHON

This event was first staged at Hiroshima, Japan on 13–14 Apr 1985. With three team members to score, 41 men's teams and 17 women's teams completed the course. The men's race was of exceptionally high standard, with the first three running times in the world's fastest six of all time.

Team result:
MEN 1. Djibouti, 2. Japan, 3. Ethiopia, 4. Italy, 5. GDR, 6. GFR
WOMEN 1. Italy, 2. USSR, 3. GDR, 4. France, 5. Japan, 6. UK
Individual result:
MEN 1. Ahmed Salah (Dji) 2:08:09, 2. Takeyuki Nakayama (Jap) 2:08:15, 3. Djama Robleh (Dji) 2:08:26
WOMEN 1. Katrin Dörre (GDR) 2:33:30, 2. Zoya Ivanova (USSR) 2:34:17, 3. Karolina Szabo (Hun) 2:34:57

IAAF WOMEN'S WORLD ROAD RACE CHAMPIONSHIP

This annual event was first held at 10km at San Diego, Cal. on 4 Dec 1983. The 1984 venue was Madrid and in 1985 was Gateshead, when the distance was increased to 15km.

Team medallists:
1983 1. USA, 2. Canada, 3. Ireland
1984 1. UK, 2. USA, 3. Portugal
1985 1. UK, 2. USSR, 3. USA
Individual medallists:
1983 1. Wendy Sly (UK) 32:23, 2. Betty Springs (USA) 32:23, 3. Lesley Welch (USA) 32:41
1984 1. Aurora Cunha (Por) 33:04, 2. Rosa Mota (Por) 33:18, 3. Carole Bradford (UK) 33:25
1985 1. Aurora Cunha (Por) 49:17, 2. Judy St. Hilaire (USA) 49:25, 3. Carole Bradford (UK) 49:59

WORLD JUNIOR CHAMPIONSHIPS

The inaugural championships will be held at Athens on 16–20 Jul 1986.

WORLD VETERANS CHAMPIONSHIPS

The first major veterans championships were the US Masters in 1968, although the Veterans AC had been formed in London back in 1931. In recent years veterans athletics has flourished, the World Veterans Championships in Rome in 1985 attracting over 4000 athletes from 50 countries. This event was the sixth such championships—the first, then entitled World Masters, was held in Toronto in 1975. The other venues have been:

World Student Games

The 'Universiade' or World Student Games, organized by the Fedération Internationale du Sport Universitaire (FISU), is well established as one of the world's most important meetings, although they have been somewhat under-regarded in the UK and perhaps in the USA.

The first 'International Universities' Games were held in Warsaw in 1924, organized by the Confédération Internationale des Étudiants (CIE). From 1951 to 1962 rival Games were staged by FISU and the UIE. The latter, Communist inspired, were known as the World Youth Games from 1954 and these had the higher standards. From 1963, however, the Games merged and are now held biennially.

Sofia 1977 – Alejandro Casanas set a world record for the 110m hurdles at the World Student Games. (Keystone Press)

VENUES (from 1951–62: U—UIE, F—FISU)

1924 Warsaw, 1927 Rome, 1928 Paris, 1930 Darmstadt, 1933 Turin, 1935 Budapest, 1937 Paris, 1939 Monaco, 1947 Paris, 1949 Budapest, 1951 Berlin (U) & Luxembourg (F), 1953 Bucharest (U) & Dortmund (F), 1954 Budapest (U), 1955 Warsaw (U) & San Sebastian (F), 1957 Moscow (U) & Paris (F), 1959 Vienna (U) & Turin (F), 1961 Sofia (F), 1962 Helsinki (U), 1963 Porto Alegre, 1965 Budapest, 1967 Tokyo, 1970 Turin, 1973 Moscow, 1975 Rome (unofficial), 1977 Sofia, 1979 Mexico City, 1981 Bucharest, 1983 Edmonton, 1985 Kobe.

CHAMPIONSHIP BEST PERFORMANCES prior to 1987

MEN .... hr:min:sec

100m	10.08	Silvio Leonard (Cub)	1977
	9.97w	Andres Simon (Cub).. (heat)	1985
200m	19.72	Pietro Mennea (Ita)	1979
400m	44.98	Harald Schmid (GFR)	1979
800m	1:43.44	Alberto Juantorena (Cub)	1977
1500m	3:38.43	Said Aouita (Mor)	1981
5000m	13:41.25	Mikhail Zhelobovskiy (USSR)	1973
10 000m	28:48.90	Dane Korica (Yug)	1973
Marathon	2:17:10	Osvaldo Faustini (Ita)	1983
3000m steeple	8:21.26	John Gregorek (USA)	1981
110mh	13.21	Alejandro Casanas (Cub)	1977
400mh	48.44	Harry Schulting (Hol)	1979
4×100mR	38.42	Italy	1979
4×400mR	3:00.98	USA	1979
20kmW	1:24:03	Guillaume LeBlanc (Can)	1983
	metres		
High jump	2.41	Igor Paklin (USSR)	1985
Pole vault	5.75	Konstantin Volkov (USSR)	1981
	5.75	Rodion Gataullin (USSR)	1985
Long jump	8.21	Yussuf Alli (Nig)	1983
	8.23w	Laszlo Szalma (Hun)	1981
Triple jump	17.86	Charlie Simpkins (USA)	1985
Shot	21.13	Remigius Machura (Cs)*	1985
	20.85	Alessandro Andrei (Ita)	1985
Discus	69.46	Luis Delis (Cub)	1983
Hammer	77.74	Klaus Ploghaus (GFR)	1981
Javelin	89.52	Dainis Kula (USSR)	1981
Decathlon	8194 pts	Josef Zeilbauer (Aut)	1979

*Later found to have had a positive drugs test at the preceding European Cup Final (although he passed in Kobe).

WOMEN min:sec

100m	11.00	Marlies Göhr (GDR)	1979
200m	21.91	Marita Koch (GDR)	1979
400m	50.35	Maria Pinigina (USSR)	1979
800m	1:57.81	Doina Melinte (Rom)	1981
1500m	4:05.35	Gabriella Dorio (Ita)	1981
3000m	8:53.78	Breda Pergar (Yug)	1981
10 000m	32:58.45	Marina Rodchenkova (USSR)	1985
100mh	12.62	Lucyna Langer (Pol)	1979
400mh	54.97	Yekaterina Fesenko (USSR)	1983
4×100mR	42.82	USA	1983
4×400mR	3:24.97	USSR	1983
5km walk	22:21.10	Aleksandra Grigoryeva (USSR)	1985
	metres		
High jump	2.01	Silvia Costa (Cub)	1985
Long jump	7.04	Irina Valyukevich (USSR)	1985
	7.06w	Anisoara Cusmir (Rom)	1983
Shot	20.82	Nadyezhda Chizhova (USSR)	1973
Discus	67.48	Florenta Craciunescu (Rom)	1981
Javelin	71.82	Ivonne Leal (Cub)	1985
Heptathlon	6616 pts	Malgorzata Nowak (Pol)	1985

17 world records have been set in these meetings from 1933: 3:49.2 at 1500m by Luigi Beccali (Ita) and 14.4 at 110mh by John Morriss (USA), to 1985: 2.41m high jump by Igor Paklin.

MOST GOLD MEDALS—INDIVIDUAL EVENTS

With the confused state of this meeting in the 1950s and early 1960s it was possible to gain many more medals at that time than from 1963, with the present stricter rules on participation. The most titles:

MEN

5 Janusz Sidlo (Pol) JT 1951–54–55–57–59
5 Igor Ter-Ovanesyan (USSR) LJ 1959–61–62–63–65

WOMEN

10 Aleksandra Chudina (USSR) HJ 1949–51–53, 80mh 1951, LJ & Pen 1951–53, JT 1953–55
8 Iolanda Balas (Rom) HJ UIE 1954–55–57–59–62, FISU 1957–59–61
8 Tamara Press (USSR) SP 19–9–61–62–63–65, DT 1959–61–63

The highest totals in pre-war or post-1963 days:

MEN

4 Pietro Mennea (Ita) 200m 1973–75–79, 100m 1975 (and 4×100mR 1979)

WOMEN

5 Gisela Mauermeyer (Ger) HJ & DT 1935–37, SP 1937

MOST WINS AT ONE GAMES: all women

4 Aleksandra Chudina (USSR) 1951 and 1953 (UIE) as above
3 Trebisonda Valla (Ita) 100m, 80mh, HJ 1933 (and 4×100 mR)
3 Ingeborg Braumüller (Ger) 100m, HJ, LJ 1930
3 Stanislawa Walasiewicz (Pol) 100m, 400m, LJ 1935
Claudia Testoni (Ita) won five medals in 1933: gold LJ & 4×100 mR, silver 80 mh & HJ, bronze 100 m.

ATHLETES TO HAVE WON THE SAME EVENT TWICE SINCE 1963

MEN

100m	Chidi Imo (Nig) 1983–85
200m	Pietro Mennea (Ita) 1973–75–79 (only 3-time winner)
	Edvin Ozolin (USSR) 1963–65
800m	Ryszard Ostrowski (Pol) 1983–85
1500m	Bodo Tummler (GFR) 1965–67
5000m	Keisuke Sawaki (Jap) 1965–67 (& 10 000m 1967)
110mh	Eddy Ottoz (Ita) 1965–67
	Andrey Prokofyev (USSR) 1979–83
400mh	Roberto Frinolli (Ita) 1963–65
High jump	Igor Paklin (USSR) 1983–85
Pole vault	Wladyslaw Kozakiewicz (Pol) 1977–79
	Konstantin Volkov (USSR) 1981–83
Long jump	Igor Ter-Ovanesyan (USSR) 1963–65
	Valeriy Podluzhniy (USSR) 1973–77
Shot	Mike Carter (USA) 1981–83
Discus	Luis Delis (Cub) 1983–85
Hammer	Klaus Ploghaus (GFR) 1979–81
Javelin	Dainis Kula (USSR) 1981–83
Decathlon	Josef Zeilbauer (Aut) 1977–79

WOMEN

400m	Maria Pinigina (USSR) 1979–83
800m	Gabriella Dorio (Ita) 1981–83
100mh	Grazyna Rabsztyn (Pol) 1975–77
High jump	Sara Simeoni (Ita) 1977–81
Shot	Nadyezhda Chizhova (USSR) 1970–73 (& 2nd 1965)
	Natalya Lisovskaya (USSR) 1983–85
Discus	Florenta Craciunescu (Rom) 1981–83 (& 3rd 1979)
	Maria Vergova (Bul) 1975–77
Heptathlon	Malgorzata Nowak (Pol) 1981–85

Commonwealth Games

The Commonwealth Games are multi-sport competitions, held every four years, and contested by athletes representing the nations of the British Commonwealth. They were first staged as the British Empire Games at Hamilton, Canada, opening on 16 Aug 1930. The eleven nations participating were Australia, Bermuda, British Guiana, Canada, England, Ireland, Newfoundland, New Zealand, Scotland, South Africa and Wales. Six sports were included, but there were women's events only in swimming. Women first competed in athletics in 1934.

The idea of staging such an event was first put forward by a Yorkshireman, Rev. J. Astley Cooper in the Magazine *Greater Britain* in 1891. The first Inter-Empire Sports meeting was held at Crystal Palace, London in 1911, forming part of the celebrations for the coronation of King George V. Four sports were contested—athletics (five events), boxing, swimming and wrestling.

The Games became the British Empire and Commonwealth Games in 1954, and simply the British Commonwealth Games in 1970, in which year the Games went metric, rather than the yards and miles imperial distances raced hitherto.

GAMES BEST PERFORMANCES prior to 1986

MEN

Event	hr:min:sec	Athlete	Year
100m	10.02w	Allan Wells (Sco) (and 10.20*)	1982
200m	20.12w	Allan Wells (Sco)	1978
	20.43	Allan Wells and Mike McFarlane (Eng)	1982
400m	45.01	Charles Asati (Ken)	1970
800m	1:43.95	John Kipkurgat (Ken)	1974
1500m	3:32.16	Filbert Bayi (Tan)	1974
5000m	13:14.4	Ben Jipcho (Ken)	1974
10 000m	27:46.4	Richard Tayler (NZ)	1974
Marathon	2:09:12	Ian Thompson (Eng)	1974
3000m steeple	8:20.8	Ben Jipcho (Ken)	1974
110mh	13.37	Mark McKoy (Can)	1982
400mh	48.83	Alan Pascoe (Eng)	1974
4×100mR	39.15	Nigeria	1982
4×400mR	3:02.8	Trinidad & Tobago	1966
30kmW	2:10:16	Steve Barry (Wal)	1982
	metres		
High jump	2.31	Milt Ottey (Can) and Stephen Wray (Bah)	1982
Pole vault	5.20	Raymond Boyd (Aus), Jeff Gutteridge (Eng), Graham Eggleton (Sco)	1982
Long jump	8.13	Gary Honey (Aus)	1982
Triple jump	17.81w	Keith Connor (Eng)	1982
	16.76*	Keith Connor	1978
Shot	20.74	Geoff Capes (Eng)	1978
Discus	64.04	Brad Cooper (Bah)	1982
Hammer	75.08	Robert Weir (Eng)	1982
Javelin	89.48	Michael O'Rourke (NZ)	1982
Decathlon	8469w pts	Daley Thompson (Eng)	1978

WOMEN

Event	min:sec	Athlete	Year
100m	10.92w	Angella Taylor (Can) (and 11.00*)	1982
200m	22.19w	Merlene Ottey (Jam)	1982
	22.50	Raelene Boyle (Aus)	1974
400m	51.02	Marilyn Neufville (Jam)	1970
800m	2:01.1	Charlene Rendina (Aus)	1974
1500m	4:06.34	Mary Stewart (Eng)	1978
3000m	8:45.53	Anne Audain (NZ)	1982
100mh	12.78w	Shirley Strong (Eng)	1982
	13.07*	Lorna Boothe (Eng)	1982
400mh	55.89	Debbie Flintoff (Aus)	1982
4×100mR	43.15	England	1982
4×400mR	3:27.19	England	1978
	metres		
High jump	1.93	Katrina Gibbs (Aus)	1978
Long jump	6.91w	Shonel Ferguson (Bah)	1982
	6.73	Sheila Sherwood (Eng)	1970
Shot	17.92	Judith Oakes (Eng)	1982
Discus	62.98	Margaret Ritchie (Sco)	1982
Javelin	64.46	Suzanne Howland (Aus)	1982
Heptathlon	6254 pts	Glynis Nunn (Aus)	1982

w = wind assisted (wind over 2.0 m/s). The best 'legal' mark is also shown.
*Performance made in heat or qualifying round.

VENUES

1930 Hamilton, Canada.	1962 Perth, Australia.
1934 London, England.	1966 Kingston, Jamaica.
1938 Sydney, Australia.	1970 Edinburgh, Scotland.
1950 Auckland, New Zealand.	1974 Christchurch, New Zealand.
1954 Vancouver, Canada.	1978 Edmonton, Canada.
1958 Cardiff, Wales.	1982 Brisbane, Australia.
	1986 Edinburgh, Scotland.

MOST GOLD MEDALS—ALL EVENTS

MEN
6 Don Quarrie (Jam) 100m 1970–74–78, 200m 1970–74, 4×100mR 1970
4 Harry Hart (SAf) SP & DT 1930–34
4 Charles Asati (Ken) 400m & 4×400mR 1970–74
4 Allan Wells (Sco) 100m 1982, 200m 1978–82, 4×100 mR 1978
3 Lord Burghley (Eng) 120yh, 440yh, 4×440yR 1930
3 Arthur Sweeney (Eng) 100y, 220y, 4×110yR 1934
3 John Loaring (Can) 440yh, 4×110yR, 4×440yR 1938
3 John Treloar (Aus) 100y, 220y, 4×110yR 1950
3 Keith Gardner (Jam) 120yh 1954–58, 100y 1958
3 Howard Payne (Eng) HT 1962–66–70
3 Kip Keino (Ken) 1M 1966, 1500m 1970, 3M 1966

WOMEN
7 Marjorie Jackson (Aus) 100y 1950–54, 220y 1950–54, 4×110yR 1954, 440yR & 660yR 1950
7 Raelene Boyle (Aus) 100m 1970–74, 200m 1970–74, 400m 1982, 4×100mR 1970–74
6 Pam Kilborn/Ryan (Aus) 80mh 1962–66–70, LJ 1962, 4×100mR 1966–70
5 Decima Norman (Aus) 100y, 220y, LJ, 440yR, 660yR 1938
5 Valerie Sloper/Young (NZ) SP 1962–66–70, DT 1962–66
4 Yvette Williams (NZ) LJ 1950–54, SP and DT 1954
3 Eileen Hiscock (Eng) 100y, 220y, 440yR 1934
3 Shirley Strickland (Aus) 80 mh, 440yR, 660yR 1950
3 Diane Burge (Aus) 100y, 220y, 4×110yR 1966
3 Jennifer Lamy (Aus) 4×100mR 1966–70–74
3 Mary Peters (NI) Pen 1970–74, SP 1970
3 Sonia Lannaman (Eng) 100m 1978, 4×100mR 1978–82

MOST MEDALS—ALL EVENTS
(*G*—gold, *S*—silver, *B*—bronze)

MEN
6 Don Quarrie 6G as above
6 Harry Hart 4G as above; 1S JT 1934; 1B JT 1930
6 Allan Wells 4G as above; 1S 100m 1978; 1B 4×100mR 1982
5 Keith Gardner 3G as above; 1S 220y 1958; 1B 4×440yR 1958
5 Les Mills (NZ) 1G DT 1966; 3S DT 1958–70, SP 1966; 1B SP 1970
5 Ed Roberts (Tri) 1G 4×440yR 1966; 3S 220y/200m 1966–70, 4×400mR 1970; 1B 100y 1966

WOMEN
9 Raelene Boyle 7G as above; 2S 100m 1978, 4×400mR 1982
8 Denise Robertson/Boyd (Aus) 2G 200m 1978, 4×100mR 1974; 3S 200m 1974, 4×400mR 1978–82; 3B 100m 1974–78, 4×100mR 1978
7 Marjorie Jackson 7G as above
7 Valerie Young 5G as above; 1S SP 1974; 1B DT 1958
6 Pam Ryan 6G as above
5 Decima Norman 5G as above
5 Shirley Strickland 3G as above; 2S 100y, 220y 1950
5 Yvette Williams 4G as above; 1S JT 1950
5 Sonia Lannaman 3G as above; 2S 200m 1978, 4×100mR 1974

Four silver medals, but no gold were won by one man: Ron Clarke (Aus) 3M 1962, 3M and 6M 1966, 10 000m 1970, and one woman: Ann Wilson (Eng) HJ, LJ, Pen 1970 and Pen 1974.

(above) Yvette Williams might well have won more than four Commonwealth gold medals if there had been a full women's programme in the early 1950s. (below) Don Quarrie wins the 1970 100m. Behind him is third-placed Hasely Crawford, who like Quarrie went on to Olympic gold. (Keystone Press)

Allan Wells and Mike Mcfarlane (top) tie at 200m 1982. (All-Sport)

THE MOST MEDALS AT ONE GAMES:

MEN
4 Keith Gardner 1958 2*G*, 1*S*, 1*B*

WOMEN
5 Decima Norman 1938 5*G*
5 Shirley Strickland 1950 3*G*, 2*S*
4 Eileen Hiscock (Eng) 1934 3*G* as above, 1*S* 660yR
4 Marjorie Jackson 1950 4*G*
4 Denise Boyd 1978 1*G*, 1*S*, 2*B*
4 Angella Taylor (Can) 1982 2*G* 100m, 4×400mR; 1*S* 4×100mR; 1*B* 200m

The above tables contain many cases of sprinters winning two or more events at one Games. Doubles at other events:

MEN

880y/1M	Herb Elliott (Aus) 1958, Peter Snell (NZ) 1962
1M/3M	Kip Keino (Ken) 1966
3M/6M	Cecil Matthews (NZ) 1938
5000m/ 3000m St	Ben Jipcho (Ken) 1974, Henry Rono (Ken) 1978
6M/Mar	Dave Power (Aus) 1958
LJ/TJ	Ken Wilmshurst (Eng) 1954

WOMEN

LJ/SP/DT	Yvette Williams (NZ) 1950
880y/JT	Gladys Lunn (Eng) 1934

THE MOST GAMES CONTESTED

MEN
6 Robin Tait (NZ) 1962–82, successively 4–3–6–1–4–8 DT
5 Howard Payne at hammer, for Rhodesia in 1958 (fourth) and then for England, three golds 1962–66–70 and silver in 1974
5 Dave Norris (NZ) 1958–74, successively 3–6–5–11–6 TJ and 8–2–7–5 LJ at the first four Games.

WOMEN
5 Mary Peters (NI) 1958–74, successively 8–4–2–1–4 SP, first Pen 1970–74, fifth 100mh 1970.

THE GREATEST SPAN OF COMPETITION: 20 years by the New Zealand javelin thrower Stanley Lay, who won his event in 1930, was third in 1938 and placed sixth in 1950. The greatest span of medal winning is 16 years by high jumper Dorothy Tyler (née Odam) from 1928 to 1954 and by Valerie Sloper/Young from 1958 to 1974.

OLDESTS (y—years, d—days)

MEN

Winner	42y	335d	Jack Holden (Eng) Mar 1950
Medallist	42y	335d	Jack Holden
Field medallist	41y	356d	Mohammed Nawaz (Pak) 3rd JT 1966
Track medallist	38y	53d	Thomas Lavery (SAf) 3rd 120yh 1950

WOMEN

Winner	37y	60d	Rosemary Payne (Sco) DT 1970
Medallist	40y	252d	Rosemary Payne (Sco) 2nd DT 1974

YOUNGESTS

MEN

Winner	16y	263d	Sam Richardson (Can) LJ 1934
Medallist	16y	260d	Sam Richardson (Can) 2nd TJ 1934

WOMEN

Winner	17y	137d	Debbie Brill (Can) HJ 1970
Medallist	c.15y		Sabine Chebichi (Ken) 3rd 800m 1974

Commonwealth Shorts

Husbands and wives to win gold medals: John and Sheila Sherwood (Eng) at 400mh and LJ respectively in 1970; Howard (Eng) and Rosemary (Sco) Payne HT and DT respectively on the same day in 1970.

Brother and sister gold medallists: Yvette Williams (NZ) won four gold medals, 1950–54, and her younger brother Roy won the decathlon in 1966. Ian Stewart (Sco) won the 1970 5000m, and his sister Mary (Eng) won the 1500m in 1978.

The first black champion was Phil Edwards who won the 1934 880y, representing British Guiana.

Daley Thompson of England is the only athlete to have won World, Olympic and Commonwealth titles. He first won the Commonwealth decathlon in 1978, going on to Olympic titles in 1980 and 1984, another Commonwealth gold in 1982 and the World title in 1983. He also won the 1982 European decathlon.

The biggest margin of victory in any Commonwealth Games timed event was 4min 32sec by which Harold Webster of Canada beat Sydney Luyt of South Africa in the 1934 marathon.

Commonwealth Shorts

The first world records to be set at the Games were at 100y (10.8) and 220y (24.3) by Marjorie Jackson in 1950. The first by a man was 49.72 for 400yh by Gert Potgieter (SAf) in 1958.

The first tie in a track event at any major championships came at 200m in 1982 when Allan Wells and Mike McFarlane were both awarded the gold medal at 200m in 20.43.

(right) Tessa Sanderson placed fifth as a 17-year-old in 1974, and won the Commonwealth gold for javelin in 1978, but had to miss the 1982 Games through injury. (All-Sport)

(bottom right) 17-year-old Marilyn Neufville won the 1970 400m title in a world record 51.02, shortly after switching her allegiance to her native Jamaica. She had won the European Indoor title representing Britain. (Keystone)

THE MOST SUCCESSFUL ATHLETES AT EACH EVENT

Event	G	S	B	Athlete with medals won (G—gold, S—silver, B—bronze)
MEN				
100y/m	3	–	–	Don Quarrie (Jam) G 1970–74–78
	–	3	–	Tom Robinson (Bah) S 1958–62–66
220y/200m	2	–	–	Don Quarrie (Jam) G 1970–74
440y/400m	2	–	–	Charles Asati (Ken) G 1970–74
880y/800m	1	1	–	Mike Boit (Ken) G 1978, S 1974 (3rd 1500m 1982)
1M/1500m	2	–	–	Kip Keino (Ken) G 1966–70
3M/5000m	2	–	–	Murray Halberg (NZ) G 1958–62
6M/10 000m	1	1	–	Dave Power (Aus) G 1958, B 1962
3000m steeple	1	1	–	Ben Jipcho (Ken) G 1974, S 1970
Mar	1	1	–	Dave Power (Aus) G 1958, S 1962
	1	1	–	Jim Alder (Sco) G 1966, S 1970
120y/110mh	2	–	–	Keith Gardner (Jam) G 1954–58
	2	–	–	David Hemery (Eng) G 1966–70
	1	–	2	Ghulam Raziq (Pak) G 1962, B 1958–66
440y/400mh	2	–	–	Ken Roche (Aus) G 1962–66
High jump	2	1	–	Lawrie Peckham (Aus) G 1966–70, S 1974 (6th 1962)
	2	–	–	Edwin Thacker (SAf) G 1934–38
Pole vault	1	2	–	Mike Bull (NI) G 1970, S 1966–74
	2	–	–	Geoff Elliott (Eng) G 1954–58
	2	–	–	Trevor Bickle (Aus) G 1962–66
Long jump	2	–	–	Lynn Davies (Wal) G 1966–70 (4th 1962)
Triple jump	2	–	–	Jack Metcalfe (Aus) G 1934–38
	2	–	–	Ian Tomlinson (Aus) G 1958–62
	2	–	–	Keith Connor (Eng) G 1978–82
Shot	2	–	1	Dave Steen (Can) G 1966, B 1962–70
	2	–	–	Geoff Capes (Eng) G 1974–78 (4th 1970)
	2	–	–	Harry Hart (SAf) G 1930–34
Discus	2	–	–	Harry Hart (SAf) G 1930–34
	2	–	–	Stephanus du Plessis (SAf) G 1954–58
	1	2	–	Les Mills (NZ) G 1966, S 1958–70 (5th 1962)
Hammer	3	1	–	Howard Payne (Eng) G 1962–66–70, S 1974 (4th 1958)
	2	–	–	Malcolm Nokes (Eng) G 1930–34
	1	1	1	Muhammad Iqbal (Pak) G 1954, S 1958, B 1966
Javelin	1	1	–	Stanley Lay (NZ) G 1930, B 1938 (6th 1950)
	1	1	–	David Travis (Eng) G 1970, S 1974 (6th 1966)
	1	1	–	Colin Smith (Eng) G 1958, S 1962
	1	1	–	Mike O'Rourke (NZ) G 1982, S 1978
Decathlon	2	–	–	Daley Thompson (Eng) G 1978–82
Road walk	1	–	–	all winners, no double medallists
4×100mR	2	–	–	John Brown (Can) G 1930–38
	2	–	–	Peter Radford (Eng) G 1958–62

4×400mR	2	–	–	Charles Asati and Julius Sang (Ken) *G* 1970–74
	2	–	–	William Koskei (Ken) *G* 1974–78

WOMEN

100y/m	2	1	–	Raelene Boyle (Aus) *G* 1970–74, *S* 1978
	2	–	–	Marjorie Jackson (Aus) *G* 1950–54
220y/200m	2	–	–	Marjorie Jackson (Aus) *G* 1950–54
	2	–	–	Raelene Boyle (Aus) *G* 1970–74
440y/400m	–	2	–	Verona Elder (Eng) *S* 1974–78
880y/800m	1	–	–	all winners, no double medallist
1500m	–	–	2	Thelma Wright (NZ) *B* 1970–74
3000m	1	–	–	Paula Fudge (Eng) *G* 1978, Anne Audain (NZ) *G* 1982
80/100mh	3	–	–	Pam Ryan (Aus) *G* 1962–66–70
High jump	2	1	–	Debbie Brill (Can) *G* 1970–82, *S* 1978
	2	–	1	Dorothy Tyler (Eng) *G* 1938–50, *B* 1954
	2	–	1	Michelle Brown (Aus) *G* 1958–66, *B* 1962
Long jump	2	–	–	Yvette Williams (NZ) *G* 1950–54
Shot	3	1	–	Valerie Young (NZ) *G* 1962–66–70, *S* 1974
	–	1	2	Jean Roberts (Aus) *S* 1962, *B* 1970–74
Discus	2	–	1	Valerie Young (NZ) *G* 1962–66, *B* 1958
	–	–	3	Carol Martin (Can) *B* 1966–70–74
Javelin	2	1	–	Petra Rivers (Aus) *G* 1970–74, *S* 1982
Pen/Hep	2	–	–	Mary Peters (NI) *G* 1970–74
4×100mR	3	–	–	Jennifer Lamy (Aus) *G* 1966–70–74
	2	1	–	Sonia Lannaman (Eng) *G* 1978–82, *S* 1974
	2	–	–	Marjorie Jackson (Aus) *G* 1950–54
	2	–	–	Joyce Bennett (Aus) *G* 1962–66
	2	–	–	Pam Ryan (Aus) *G* 1966–70
	2	–	–	Raelene Boyle (Aus) *G* 1970–74
	2	–	–	Beverley Callender (Eng) *G* 1978–82
	2	–	–	Kathy Cook (Eng) *G* 1978–82
4×400mR	2	–	–	Ruth Kennedy and Verona Elder (Eng) *G* 1974–78

The above table contains all double gold medallists and all athletes who have won three or more medals at one event.

One of the most dramatic moments at the 1970 Games was the fall by favourite Kerry O'Brien (Aus) when he fell headlong into the water jump when leading with a lap to go. (All-Sport)

MEDAL TABLE BY NATION

NATION	MEN			WOMEN			Total
	G	S	B	G	S	B	Medals
England	74	61	56	33	43	34	301
Australia	45	52	41	49	36	25	248
Canada	32	40	43	13	17	34	179
New Zealand	18	15	23	10	11	11	88
South Africa	16	13	14	4	2	2	51
Kenya	21	9	17	–	1	1	49
Scotland	11	10	18	3	2	3	47
Jamaica	14	7	8	2	2	3	36
Nigeria	3	8	4	1	1	2	19
Ghana	4	4	5	–	2	2	17
Wales	5	4	4	1	1	1	16
Trinidad & Tobago	3	7	3	–	–	–	13
Northern Ireland	2	4	–	4	2	–	12
Pakistan	2	3	6	–	–	–	11
Bahamas	2	6	1	1	–	–	10
Uganda	–	4	3	–	1	1	9
Tanzania	3	3	2	–	–	–	8
India	1	2	2	–	–	–	5
Fiji	1	2	1	–	–	–	4
Guyana	1	2	–	–	–	1	4
Zimbabwe	–	1	2	–	–	1	4
Zambia	–	–	–	1	1	1	3
Bermuda	–	1	1	–	–	–	2
Barbados	–	–	2	–	–	–	2
Sri Lanka	1	–	–	–	–	–	1
The Gambia	–	–	1	–	–	–	1
Swaziland	–	–	1	–	–	–	1

African Games and Championships

Three great Kenyan distance runners of the late sixties and early seventies: (l–r) Naftali Temu, Kip Keino and Ben Jipcho. (Keystone)

The first African Games, at ten sports, were contested in Brazzaville, Congo on 18–25 Jul 1965. Subsequent Games were staged at Lagos, Nigeria in 1973 and at Algiers in 1978. Games scheduled for Kenya in 1982 were cancelled. African Championships, for athletics only, were first held at Dakar, Senegal in 1979, and have subsequently been held at Cairo, Egypt in 1982, Rabat, Morocco in 1984 and Cairo in 1985. In this survey Games and Championships results have been combined.

CHAMPIONSHIPS AND GAMES BEST PERFORMANCES prior to 1986

MEN

	hr:min:sec		
100m	10.19w	Théophile Nkounkou (Congo)	*1979
	10.22	Chidi Imo (Nig)	1985
	10.0	Peter Okodogbe (Nig)	*1979
200m	20.66	Innocent Egbunike (Nig)	1984
400m	45.22	Innocent Egbunike (Nig)	1985
800m	1:45.17	Sammy Koskei (Ken)	1984
1500m	3:36.21	Filbert Bayi (Tan)	1978
5000m	13:41.94	Abderrazak Bounour (Alg)	1984
10 000m	27:58.9	Henry Rono (Ken)	1978
Marathon	2:21:05	Juma Ikangaa (Tan)	1982
3000m steeple	8:15.82	Henry Rono (Ken)	1978
110mh	13.76w	Godwin Obasogie (Nig)	1979
	13.89	Fatwell Kimaiyo (Ken)	1978
400mh	48.29	Amadou Dia Ba (Sen)	1985
4×100R	39.24	Ghana	1978
4×400mR	3:01.86	Nigeria	1985
20kmW	1:30:01.1	Abdelwahab Ferguène (Alg)	1984
	metres		
High jump	2.20	Moussa Fall (Sen)	1982
Pole vault	5.00	Lakhdar Rahal (Alg)	1979
Long jump	8.00w	Joshua Owusu (Nig)	1973
	7.95	Paul Emordi (Nig)	1985
Triple jump	17.19	Joseph Taiwo (Nig)	1984
Shot	20.44	Nagui Assad (Egy)	1982
Discus	63.56	Christian Okoye (Nig)	1985
Hammer	70.56	Hakim Toumi (Alg)	1985
Javelin	80.04	Ahmed Mahour Balcha (Alg)	1985
Decathlon	7338 pts	Mohamed Ben Saad (Alg) (1964 Tables)	1978

WOMEN

	min:sec		
100m	11.47	Hannah Afriyie (Gha)	*1978
200m	23.01	Hannah Afriyie (Gha)	1978
400m	53.33	Grace Bakari (Gha)	1979
	53.33	Kehinde Vaughan (Nig)	1985
800m	2:03.70	Selina Chepchirchir (Ken)	1985
1500m	4:16.4	Sakina Boutamine (Alg)	1978
3000m	9:18.53	Helen Kimaiyo (Ken)	1985
10 000m	35:09.58	Hassania Darani (Mor)	1985
100mh	13.42	Maria Usifo (Nig)	1984
400mh	56.00	Nawal el Moutawakil (Mor)	1985
4×100mR	44.63	Nigeria	1978
4×400mR	3:35.55	Ghana	1978
	metres		
High jump	1.77	Modupe Oshikoya (Nig)	1978
Long jump	6.32	Modupe Oshikoya (Nig)	1978
Shot	15.51	Odette Mistoul (Gabon)	1984
Discus	52.70	Zoubida Laayouni (Mor)	1984
Javelin	54.00	Agnès Chuinté (Cam)	1985
Heptathlon	5334 pts	Chérifa Meskaoui (Mor)	1984

*Performance set in heats.

Most gold medals—individual events

MEN

4 Nagui Assad (Egy) SP 1973–78–79–82
4 Amadou Dia Ba (Sen) 400mh 1982–84–85, 400m 1982
3 Namakoro Niare (Mali) DT 1965–73–78
3 Miruts Yifter (Eth) 5000m 1979, 10 000m 1973–79
3 El Kasheef Hassan (Sud) 200m 1978, 400m 1978–79
3 Wodajo Bulti (Eth) 5000m 1982-85, 10 000m 1985
3 Paul Emordi (Nig) LJ 1984–85, TJ 1985

WOMEN

5 Modupe Oshikoya (Nig) 100mh 1973, HJ 1973–78, LJ 1973–78
5 Nawal el Moutawakil (Mor) 100mh 1982, 400mh 1982–84–85, 200m 1984
4 Justina Chepchirchir (Ken) 800m 1984, 1500m 1982–84, 3000m 1982
4 Zoubida Laayouni (Mor) DT 1979–82–84–85
3 Alice Annum (Gha) LJ 1965, 100m & 200m 1973
3 Hannah Afriyie (Gha) 100m 1978, 200m 1978–79
3 Sakina Boutamine (Alg) 1500m 1978–79, 3000m 1979
3 Bella Bellgam (Nig) Pen 1978–79, LJ 1979
3 Odette Mistoul (Gabon) SP 1979–82–84
3 Agnès Chuinté (Cam) JT 1979–82–85
3 Chérifa Meskaoui (Mor) Hep 1982–84–85

Three gold medals at one Games were won by Modupe Oshikoya in 1973. Alice Annum also won three in 1973, including the 4×100m relay.

Most medals—all individual events
(G—gold, S—silver, B—bronze)

MEN

5 Namakoro Niare (Mali) 3G as above; 2S SP 1973–78
5 Nagui Assad (Egy) 4G as above; 1S DT 1973
5 Amadou Dia Ba (Sen) 4G as above; 1B HJ 1978
4 Miruts Yifter (Eth) 3 G as above; 1S 5000m 1973
4 Yohannes Mohammed (Eth) 1G 5000m 1978; 1S 5000m 1979; 2B 3000mSt 1973–79
4 Phillip Sang (Ken) 2G 110mh 1982–84; 2S 110mh 1978–79
4 El Kasheef Hassan (Sud) 3G as above; 1B 400m 1984
4 Omar Khalifa (Sud) 1G 1500m 1985, 2S 800m 1979, 1500m 1984, 1B 800m 1984
4 Wodajo Bulti (Eth) 3G as above; 1B 1500m 1982
4 Mohamed Naguib (Egy) 2G DT 1982–84, 2S DT 1979–85

WOMEN

6 Nawal el Moutawakil (Mor) 5G as above; 1S 100m 1982
6 Chérifa Meskaoui (Mor) 3G as above; 3B 100mh 1982–84, DT 1984
5 Modupe Oshikoya (Nig) 5G as above
5 Bella Bellgam (Nig) 3G as above; 2B 100mh & LJ 1978
5 Agnès Chuinté (Cam) 3G as above; 2S JT 1978, SP 1985
4 Hannah Afriyie (Gha) 3G as above; 1S 100m 1979
4 Sakina Boutamine (Alg) 3G as above; 1S 800m 1978
4 Justina Chepchirchir (Ken) 4G as above
4 Ruth Kyalisima (Uga) 3S 100mh 1978–82, 400mh 1982; 1B 400mh 1979
4 Zoubida Laayouni (Mor) 4G as above
4 Odette Mistoul (Gabon) 3G as above, 1B SP 1985

Medal table by nation

NATION	MEN			WOMEN			TOTAL
	G	S	B	G	S	B	Medals
Kenya	35	31	28	19	20	17	150
Nigeria	24	26	13	24	22	12	121
Algeria	16	12	19	3	6	7	63
Ghana	6	3	5	15	14	11	54
Senegal	13	14	13	4	3	4	51
Morocco	3	2	11	15	8	12	51
Uganda	3	8	10	6	9	10	46
Egypt	10	16	14	–	1	1	42
Ivory Coast	12	7	7	2	4	9	41
Ethiopia	12	12	9	–	1	1	35
Tunisia	4	8	5	2	4	–	23
Tanzania	4	2	2	1	2	2	13
Sudan	4	2	4	–	–	–	10
Cameroun	–	–	2	3	3	2	10
Congo	–	3	3	–	–	1	7
Chad	1	1	4	–	–	–	6
Mali	3	2	–	–	–	–	5
Djibouti	2	2	1	–	–	–	5
Gabon	–	–	1	2	–	2	5
Somalia	1	1	–	–	–	–	2
Swaziland	1	–	1	–	–	–	2
The Gambia	–	1	–	–	–	1	2

One medal: **MEN**—B: Madagascar, Rwanda.
WOMEN—B: Togo, Upper Volta, Zimbabwe.

The most successful woman athlete at African championships – Modupe Oshikoya (right) competing in the 1974 Commonwealth Games, at which she won the long jump, was runner-up to Mary Peters in the pentathlon and was third in the 100m hurdles, when Gaye Dell (Aus – left) was second behind Judy Vernon (Eng). (Mark Shearman)

Asian Games

VENUES

1951 New Delhi, 1954 Manila, 1958 Tokyo, 1962 Djakarta, 1966 Bangkok, 1970 Bangkok, 1974 Teheran, 1978 Bangkok, 1982 New Delhi, 1986 Seoul

The first Asian Games were held at New Delhi, India on 8–11 Mar 1951, when ten nations took part. These multi-sport Games have since 1954 been held at four-yearly intervals, and a record 29 nations competed in 1982.

ASIAN GAMES BEST PERFORMANCES prior to 1986

MEN

	hr:min:sec		
100m	10.42	Anat Ratanapol (Tha)	1974
200m	20.89	Chang Jae Keun (Kor)	1982
400m	46.21	Wickrames Wimaladase (Sri)	1974
800m	1:46.81	Charles Boromeo (Ind)	1982
1500m	3:43.49	Faleh Naji Jarallah (Iraq)	1982
5000m	13:53.74	Masanari Shintaku (Jap)	1982
10 000m	29:37.56	Zhang Guo wei (Chn)	1982
Marathon	2:15:29.7	Minetaku Sakamoto (Jap)	1978
3000m steeple	8:40.7	Masanari Shintaku (Jap)	1978
110mh	14.09	Yoshifumi Fujimori (Jap)	1982
400mh	50.60	Takashi Nagao (Jap)	1982
4×100mR	39.82	China	1982
4×400mR	3:06.75	Japan	1982
20kmW	1:29:29	Chand Ram (Ind)	1982
	metres		
High jump	2.33	Zhu Jian hua (Chn)	1982
Pole vault	5.30	Tomomi Takahashi (Jap)	1982
Long jump	8.07	T. C. Yohanan (Ind)	1974
Triple jump	16.80	Zou Zhen xian (Chn)	1982
Shot	18.53	Bahadur Singh (Ind)	1982
Discus	58.50	Li Wei nan (Chn)	1982
Hammer	71.14	Shigenobu Morofushi (Jap)	1982
Javelin	79.24	Shen Mao Mao (Chn)	1978
Decathlon	7417 pts	Wang Kang qiang (Chn)	1982

WOMEN

100m	11.76	Lydia de Vega (Phi)	1982
	11.6	Chi Cheng (Tai)	1970
200m	23.79	Esther Rot (Isr)	1974
	23.7	Chi Cheng (Tai)	1970
400m	54.11	Junko Yoshida (Jap)	*1982
800m	2:05.69	Chang Jong Ae (NKo)	1982
1500m	4:18.40	Chang Jong Ae (NKo)	1982
3000m	9:24.7	Kim Ok Sun (NKo)	1978
100mh	13.31	Esther Rot (Isr)	1974
400mh	58.47	M. D. Valsamma (Ind)	1982
4×100mR	45.13	Japan	1982
4×400mR	3:37.44	Japan	1982
	metres		
High jump	1.89	Zheng Da zhen (Chn)	1982
Long jump	6.41	Liao Wen feng (Chn)	1982
Shot	17.77	Li Mei su (Chn)	1982
Discus	57.24	Li Xiao hui (Chn)	1982
Javelin	60.52	Emi Matsui (Jap)	1982
Heptathlon	5462 pts	Ye Pei su (Chn)	1982

*Performance set in heats.

MOST GOLD MEDALS—INDIVIDUAL EVENTS

MEN

4 Shigenobu Murofushi (Jap) HT 1970–74–78–82
3 Milkha Singh (Ind) 200m 1958, 400m 1958–62 (& 4×400mR 1962)
3 Mubarak Shah (Pak) 3000mSt 1958–62, 5000m 1962
3 Manikavasagam Jegathesan (Mal) 100m 1966, 200m 1962–66 (& 4×100mR 1966)
3 Anat Ratanapol (Tha) 100m 1974, 200m 1970–74 (& 4×100mR 1970–74)

WOMEN

5 Toyoko Yoshino (Jap) SP & DT 1951–54, JT 1951
5 Esther Rot (Isr) 100mh 1970–74, Pen 1970, 100m & 200m 1974

3 Khana Sheziffi (Isr) 800m 1966–70, 1500m 1970
3 Kim Ok Sun (NKo) 1500m 1978, 3000m 1978–82

Three individual event gold medals at one Games were won by Toyoko Yoshino in 1951 and by Esther Rot in 1974.

MOST MEDALS—ALL INDIVIDUAL EVENTS
(*G*—gold, *S*—silver, *B*—bronze)

MEN

5 Yang Chuan-kwang (Tai) 2*G* Dec 1954–58; 2*S* 110mh & LJ 1958; 1*B* 400mh 1958
5 Anat Ratanapol (Tha) 3*G* as above; 1*S* 200m 1970; 1*B* 200m 1978
4 Mubarak Shah (Pak) 3*G* as above; 1*S* 10 000m 1958

4 Manikavasagam Jegathesan (Mal) 3*G* as above; 1*S* 100m 1962
4 Praveen Kumar (Ind) 2*G* DT 1966–70; 1*S* DT 1974; 1*B* HT 1966
4 Joginder Singh (Ind) 2*G* SP 1966–70; 2*B* 1962–74
4 Shigenobu Morofushi (Jap) 4*G* as above

WOMEN
5 Toyoko Yoshino (Jap) 5*G* as above
5 Esther Rot (Isr) 5 *G* as above
5 Kim Ok Sun (NKo) 3*G* as above; 1*B* 1500m 1978

MEDAL TABLE BY NATION—men and women

NATION	G	S	B
Japan	139	146	83
India	50	51	50
China	29	30	31
Pakistan	13	13	10
Israel*	11	3	5
Philippines	9	9	25
South Korea	9	8	18
Thailand	9	4	6
Malaysia	8	7	14
Taiwan	6	9	16
Iran	6	8	7
North Korea	5	3	6
Sri Lanka	5	3	3
Iraq	4	2	4
Singapore	2	7	9
Indonesia	2	1	13
Burma	1	3	4
Kuwait	–	1	2

One medal: MEN—*S*: Mongolia; *B*: Bahrain, Hong Kong, Qatar.

*Israel were not permitted to compete in 1978 and 1982.

Asian Track & Field Championships

The first Asian Championships, as opposed to the multi-sport Games, were held at Marakina, near Manila, Phillippines in 1973. They are now entitled Asian Track & Field meetings, rather than Championships, due to the exclusion of Israel.

VENUES
1973 Marakina, 1975 Seoul, 1979 Tokyo, 1981 Tokyo, 1983 Kuwait, 1985 Djakarta

The most individual gold medals is four by Anat Ratanapol (Tha) 100m and 200m 1973–75. Athletes to have won their event three times are:
MEN Suchart Chairsuvaparb (Tha) 100m 1979–81–83, Mohamed Zinkhawi (Kuwait) SP 1979–81–83, Liu Yuhuang (Chn) LJ 1981–83–85, Li Weinan (Chn) DT 1981–83–85.
WOMEN Li Xiaohui (Chn) DT 1979–81–85. Lee Chiu-hsia won at 800m, 1500m and 3000m in 1975, but this was surpassed by P. T. Usha (Ind) in 1985, when she won at 100m, 200m, 400m and 400mh, a fifth gold at 4×400mR and a bronze at 4×100mR. She also won at 400m in 1983.

European Championships

VENUES

1934	Turin	Stadio Communale (men)
1938	Paris	Stade Olympique de Colombes (men)
	Vienna	Prater Stadium (women)
1946	Oslo	Bislett Idrettsplass
1950	Brussels	Stade du Heysel
1954	Berne	Neufeld Stadion
1958	Stockholm	Olympiska Stadion
1962	Belgrade	Stadion JNA
1966	Budapest	Nepstadion
1969	Athens	Stadion George Karaiskakis
1971	Helsinki	Olympiastadion
1974	Rome	Stadio Olimpico
1978	Prague	Stadion Evzen Rosicky
1982	Athens	Stadion Kalogreza
1986	Stuttgart	Neckarstadion

The first European Championships were staged at the Stadio Communale, Turin on 7–9 Sep 1934. They were for men only and neither the Soviet Union nor Great Britain took part. The decision to hold them was taken at a meeting of the newly formed European Committee of the IAAF, held on 3 Nov 1932 in Budapest, the hometown of their leading advocate Szilard Stankovits, President of the Hungarian Athletics Federation. Great Britain contested the second Championships held in 1938.

The first women's European championships were held separately in 1938, but men's and women's events were included from 1946, when the Soviet Union made its debut. The Championships are organized by the European Athletic Association and are held at four-yearly intervals, although there was a break in that pattern when the Championships were held in 1969 and 1971.

MOST GOLD MEDALS—ALL EVENTS

MEN
4 Janis Lusis (USSR) JT 1962–66–69–71
4 Valeriy Borzov (USSR) 100m 1969–71–74, 200m 1971
4 Harald Schmid (GFR) 400mh 1978–82, 4×400mR 1978–82
3 Adolfo Consolini (Ita) DT 1946–50–54
3 Emil Zatopek (Cs) 5000m 1950, 10 000m 1950–54
3 Heinz Fütterer (GFR) 100m 1954, 200m 1954, 4×100mR 1958
3 Vasiliy Kuznyetsov (USSR) Dec 1954–58–62
3 Manfred Germar (GFR) 200m 1958, 4×100mR 1958–62
3 Igor Ter-Ovanesyan (USSR) LJ 1958–62–69
3 Wolfgang Nordwig (GDR) PV 1966–69–71
3 Pietro Mennea (Ita) 100m 1978, 200m 1974–78

WOMEN

5 Fanny Blankers-Koen (Hol) 100m & 200m 1950, 80mh 1946–50, 4×100mR 1946
5 Irena Szewinska (Pol) 100m 1974, 200m 1966–74, LJ & 4×100mR 1966
4 Maria Itkina (USSR) 200m 1954, 400m 1958–62, 4×100mR 1954
4 Nadezhda Chizhova (USSR) 1966–69–71–74
4 Renate Stecher (GDR) 100m & 200m 1971, 4×100mR 1969–74
4 Marita Koch (GDR) 400m 1978–82, 4×400mR 1978–82
3 Maria Itkina (USSR) 200m 1954, 400m 1958–62
3 Galina Bystrova (USSR) 80mh 1958, Pen 1958–62
3 Tamara Press (USSR) DT 1958–62, SP 1962
3 Karin Balzer (GDR) 80mh 1966, 100mh 1969–71
3 Petra Vogt (GDR) 100m, 200m & 4×100mR 1969
3 Marlies Göhr (GDR) 100m 1978–82, 4×100mR 1982
3 Bärbel Wöckel (GDR) 200m 1982, 4×100mR 1974–82

Pietro Mennea sets the European championship best for 200m at Prague in 1978 to complete the sprint double of 100m and 200m. (All-Sport)

CHAMPIONSHIP BEST PERFORMANCES prior to 1986

MEN
	hr:min:sec		
100m	10.19	Pietro Mennea (Ita)*	1978
200m	20.16	Pietro Mennea (Ita)	1978
400m	44.72	Hartmut Weber (GFR)	1982
800m	1:43.84	Olaf Beyer (GDR)	1978
1500m	3:35.59	Steve Ovett (UK)	1978
5000m	13:17.21	Brendan Foster (UK)	1974
10 000m	27:30.99	Martti Vainio (Fin)	1978
Marathon	2:11:57.5	Leonid Moseyev (USSR)	1978
3000m steeple	8:15.04	Bronislaw Malinowski (Pol)	1974
110mh	13.40	Guy Drut (Fra)	1974
400mh	47.48	Harald Schmid (GFR)	1982
4×100mR	38.58	Poland	1978
4×400mR	3:00.51	F. R. Germany	1982
20kmW	1:23:11.5	Roland Wieser (GDR)	1978
50kmW	3:53:29.9	Jorge Llopart (Spa)	1978
	metres		
High jump	2.30	Vladimir Yashchenko (USSR)	1978
	2.30	Dietmar Mögenburg (GFR)	1982
Pole vault	5.60	Aleksandr Krupskiy (USSR)	1982
	5.60	Vladimir Polyakov (USSR) (2nd)	1982
	5.60	Atanas Tarev (Bul) (3rd)	1982
Long jump	8.41w	Lutz Dombrowski (GDR) (and 8.30)	1982
Triple jump	17.34w	Viktor Saneyev (USSR)	1969
	17.29	Keith Connor (UK)	1982
Shot	21.50	Udo Beyer (GDR)	1982
Discus	67.20	Wolfgang Schmidt (GDR)*	1978
Hammer	81.66	Yuriy Sedykh (USSR)	1982
Javelin	91.52	Janis Lusis (USSR)	1969
Decathlon	8774 pts	Daley Thompson (UK)	1982

WOMEN
	hr:min:sec		
100m	11.01	Marlies Göhr (GDR)	1982
200m	22.04	Bärbel Wöckel (GDR)	1982
400m	48.15	Marita Koch (GDR)	1982
800m	1:55.41	Olga Mineyeva (USSR)	1982
1500m	3:57.80	Olga Dvirna (USSR)	1982
3000m	8:30.28	Svyetlana Ulmasova (USSR)	1982
10 000m and 10km Walk to be included for the first time in 1986			
Marathon	2:36:04	Rosa Mota (Por)	1982
100mh	12.45	Lucyna Kalek (Pol)	1982
400mh	54.58	Ann-Louise Skoglund (Swe)	1982
4×100mR	42.19	GDR	1982
4×400mR	3:19.05	GDR	1982
	metres		
High jump	2.02	Ulrike Meyfarth (GFR)	1982
Long jump	7.09	Vilma Bardauskiene (USSR)*	1978
Shot	21.59	Ilona Slupianek (GDR)	1982
Discus	69.00	Faina Melnik (USSR)	1974
Javelin	70.02	Anna Verouli (Gre)	1982
Heptathlon	6664 pts	Ramona Neubert (GDR)	1982

*Performance made in heat or qualifying round.

In all, 29 world records have been set at the Championships, 6 men's and 23 women's.

MOST MEDALS—ALL EVENTS
(*G*—gold, *S*—silver, *B*—bronze)

MEN
6 Pietro Mennea (Ita) 3*G* as above; 2*S* 100m & 4×100mR 1974; 1*B* 4×100mR 1971
5 Igor Ter-Ovanesyan (USSR) 3*G* as above; 2*S* LJ 1966–71
5 Valeriy Borzov (USSR) 4*G* as above; 1*S* 4×100mR 1969
5 Jean-Claude Nallet (Fra) 2*G* 400mh 1971, 4×400mR 1969; 2*S* 400m 1969, 400mh 1974; 1*B* 200m 1966

WOMEN
10 Irena Szewinska (Pol) 5*G* as above, 1*S* 100m 1966, 4*B* 200m 1971, 400m 1978, 4×100mR 1974, 4×400mR 1978
8 Fanny Blankers-Koen (Hol) 5*G* as above, 1*S* 4×100mR 1950, 2*B* 100m & 200m 1938
8 Renate Stecher (GDR) 4*G* as above, 4*S* 100m 1974, 200m 1969–74, 4×100mR 1971
6 Yevgeniya Sechenova (USSR) 2*G* 100m & 200m 1946; 2*S* 100m & 200m 1950, 2*B* 4×100mR 1946–50
5 Maria Itkina (USSR) 4*G* as above, 1*B* 200m 1958
5 Karin Balzer (GDR) 3*G* as above, 2*S* 80mh 1962, 4×100mR 1971
5 Marlies Göhr (GDR) 3*G* as above, 1*S* 200m 1978, 1*B* 4×100mR 1978

Ter-Ovanesyan's five is the most medals at one event. The most medals without a gold is four by discus thrower Lothar Milde (GDR) second 1971, third 1962–66–69.

THE MOST MEDALS AT ONE CHAMPIONSHIPS
(four medals or three golds)

WOMEN
3*G* 1*S* Fanny Blankers-Koen (Hol) 1950 (see above)
3*G* 1*S* Irena Kirszenstein (Pol) 1966 (see above)
2*G* 2*S* Stanislawa Walasiewicz (Pol) 1938 first 100m & 200m, second LJ & 4×100mR
3*G* Petra Vogt (GDR) 1969 first 100m, 200m, 4×100mR

OTHER DOUBLE INDIVIDUAL EVENT WINNERS

MEN
100m/200m: Christian Berger (Hol) 1934, Martinus Osendarp (Hol) 1938, Heinz Fütterer (GFR) 1954, Valeriy Borzov (USSR) 1971, Pietro Mennea (Ita) 1978
5000m/10 000m: Emil Zatopek (Cs) 1950, Zdzislaw Krzyszkowiak (Pol) 1958, Juha Väätäinen (Fin) 1971

WOMEN
100m/200m: Yevgeniya Sechenova (USSR) 1946, Renate Stecher (GDR) 1971, Irena Szewinska (Pol) 1974
80mh/Pen: Galina Bystrova (USSR) 1958
Shot/discus: Tamara Press (USSR) 1962

THE MOST CHAMPIONSHIPS CONTESTED
6 Abdon Pamich (Ita) 50kmW 1954 7th, 1958 2nd, 1962 1st, 1966 1st, 1969 dnf (and 6th at 20kmW), 1971 8th
6 Ludvik Danek (Cs) DT 1962 9th, 1966 5th, 1969 4th, 1971 1st, 1974 2nd, 1978 15th

THE GREATEST SPAN OF YEARS OF COMPETITORS
20 years Adolfo Consolini DT 1938 5th, 1946, 1950 and 1954 1st, 1958 6th

GDR sprinters to the fore as Petra Vogt (l) beats Renate Meissner (later Stecher) at 200m in the 1969 Championships. Val Peat (UK – r) was third. (Keystone)

O<small>LDESTS</small> (y—years, d—days)

MEN

Winner	43y 163d	Jack Holden (UK) marathon 1950
Medallist	46y 235d	Väinö Muinonen (Fin) marathon 2nd 1946
Competitor	49y 23d	Edgar Brunn (Nor) 50km walk 9th 1954

WOMEN

Winner	35y 334d	Dana Zatopkova (Cs) javelin 1958
Medallist	35y 334d	Dana Zatopkova (Cs) as above

Y<small>OUNGESTS</small>

MEN

Winner	18y 260d	François St Gilles (Fra) 4×100mR 1969
Individual winner	19y 80d	David Jenkins (UK) 400m 1971
Medallist	18y 73d	Alan Paterson (UK) HJ 2nd 1946

WOMEN

Winner	16y 75d	June Foulds (UK) 4×100mR 1950
Individual winner	17y 346d	Vera Nikolic (Yug) 800m 1966
Medallist	16y 73d	June Foulds (UK) 100m 3rd 1950

T<small>HE MOST SUCCESSFUL ATHLETES AT EACH EVENT</small>

Event	G	S	B	Athlete with medals won (G—gold, S—silver, B—bronze)
MEN				
100m	3	–	–	Valeriy Borzov (USSR) G 1969–71–74 (8th 1978)
200m	2	–	–	Pietro Mennea (Ita) G 1974–78
400m	1	1	–	David Jenkins (UK) G 1971, S 1974.
800m	2	–	1	Manfred Matuschewski (GDR) G 1962–66, B 1969
1500m	1	1	–	Michel Jazy (Fra) G 1962, S 1966
5000m	1	–	1	Emil Zatopek (Cs) G 1950, B 1954
10 000m	2	1	–	Jürgen Haase (GDR) G 1966–69, S 1971
	2	–	–	Ilmari Salminen (Fin) G 1934–38
	2	–	–	Emil Zatopek (Cs) G 1950–54
Marathon	1	–	2	Karel Lismont (Bel) G 1971, B 1978–82
3000m steeple	2	–	–	Bronislaw Malinowski (Pol) G 1974–78
110mh	2	–	–	Eddy Ottoz (Ita) G 1966–69
	2	–	–	Thomas Munkelt (GDR) G 1978–82 (4th 1974)
400mh	2	–	–	Harald Schmid (GFR) G 1978–82
	1	2	–	Yuriy Lituyev (USSR) G 1958, S 1950–54
High jump	1	1	–	Kalevi Kotkas (Fin) G 1934, S 1938
	1	1	–	Alan Paterson (UK) G 1950, S 1946
	1	1	–	Kestutis Sapka (USSR) G 1971, S 1974
Pole vault	3	–	–	Wolfgang Nordwig (GDR) G 1966–69–71
	2	–	–	Eeles Landström (Fin) G 1954–58
Long jump	3	2	–	Igor Ter-Ovanesyan (USSR) G 1958–62–69, S 1966–71
	2	–	–	Wilhelm Leichum (Ger) G 1934–38
Triple jump	2	2	–	Viktor Saneyev (USSR) G 1969–74, S 1971–78
	2	–	–	Leonid Shcherbakov (USSR) G 1950–54
	2	–	–	Jozef Schmidt (Pol) G 1958–62 (5th 1966)
Shot	2	–	–	Vilmos Varju (Hun) G 1962–66 (4th 1971, 7th 1958–69)
	2	–	–	Gunnar Huseby (Ice) G 1946–50
	2	–	–	Hartmut Briesenick (GDR) G 1971–74
	2	–	–	Udo Beyer (GDR) G 1978–82
Discus	3	–	–	Adolfo Consolini (Ita) G 1946–50–54 (5th 1938, 6th 1958)
	–	1	3	Lothar Milde (GDR) S 1971, B 1962–66–69
	–	3	–	Giuseppe Tosi (Ita) S 1946–50–54
Hammer	2	–	–	Yuriy Sedykh (USSR) G 1978–82
	1	1	1	Gyula Zsivotzky (Hun) G 1962, S 1966, B 1958 (4th 1969)
	–	1	2	Reinhard Theimer (GDR) S 1971, B 1969–74
Javelin	4	–	–	Janis Lusis (USSR) G 1962–66–69–71 (6th 1974)
	2	–	1	Janusz Sidlo (Pol) G 1954–58, B 1969 (7th 1962–66)
	2	–	–	Matti Järvinen (Fin) G 1934–38
Decathlon	3	–	–	Vasiliy Kuznyetsov (USSR) G 1954–58–62
20kmW	1	1	1	Vladimir Golubnichiy (USSR) G 1974, S 1966, B 1962
50kmW	2	1	–	Abdon Pamich (Ita) G 1962–66, S 1958 (7th 1954, 8th 1971)
	2	1	–	Christoph Höhne (GDR) G 1969–74, S 1971
	1	1	1	Venyamin Soldatenko (USSR) G 1971, S 1978, B 1969
	–	1	2	Peter Selzer (GDR) S 1969, B 1971–74
WOMEN				
100m	2	–	–	Marlies Göhr (GDR) G 1978–82
200m	2	–	1	Irena Szewinska (Pol) G 1966–74, B 1971
	1	2	–	Renate Stecher (GDR) G 1971, S 1969–74
400m	2	–	–	Maria Itkina (USSR) G 1958–62
	2	–	–	Marita Koch (GDR) G 1978–82
800m	2	–	1	Vera Nikolic (Yug) G 1966–71, B 1969
1500m	1	1	–	Gunhild Hoffmeister (GDR) G 1974, S 1971
3000m	2	–	–	Svyetlana Ulmasova (USSR) G 1978–82
Marathon	1	–	–	Rosa Mota (Por) G 1982, when event first held

continued

100mh*	3	1	—	Karin Balzer (GDR) *G* 1966–69–71, *S* 1962
	2	—	—	Fanny Blankers-Koen (Hol) *G* 1946–50
400mh	1	—	—	Tatyana Zelentsova (USSR) *G* 1978, year first held
	1	—	—	Ann-Louise Skoglund (Swe) *G* 1982
High jump	2	1	—	Iolanda Balas (Rom) *G* 1958–62, *S* 1954
	1	—	2	Sara Simeoni (Ita) *G* 1978, *B* 1974–82
Long jump	—	1	1	Elzbieta Krzesinska (Pol) *S* 1962, *B* 1954
Shot	4	—	—	Nadezhda Chizhova (USSR) *G* 1966–69–71–74
	2	—	—	Ilona Slupianek (GDR) *G* 1978–82
	—	2	1	Helena Fibingerova (Cs) *S* 1978–82, *B* 1974 (10th 1969)
	—	2	1	Margitta Gummel (GDR) *S* 1966–69, *B* 1971
	—	1	2	Margitta Lange (GDR) *S* 1971, *B* 1966–69 (6th 1974)
Discus	2	—	—	Nina Dumbadze (USSR) *G* 1946–50
	2	—	—	Tamara Press (USSR) *G* 1958–62
	2	—	—	Faina Melnik (USSR) *G* 1971–74 (5th 1978)
Javelin	2	—	1	Ruth Fuchs (GDR) *G* 1974–78, *B* 1971
	2	—	—	Dana Zatopkova (Cs) *G* 1954–58 (5th 1950)
Pen/Hep†	2	—	—	Galina Bystrova (USSR) *G* 1958–62
	—	3	—	Burglinde Pollak (GDR) *S* 1971–74–78 (8th 1969)

*Held at 80m hurdles 1938–66.
†Pentathlon 1950–78, Heptathlon 1982. Nadyezhda Tkachenko (USSR) won in 1974 and 1978, but lost the latter title due to a positive drugs test.

The above table contains all double gold medallists and all athletes who have won three or more
medals at one event.

MEDAL TABLE BY NATION

NATION	MEN			WOMEN			TOTAL
	G	S	B	G	S	B	Medals
USSR	54	58	50	48	30	34	274
GDR	34	29	26	33	31	21	174
United Kingdom	38	26	31	8	16	16	135
F. R. Germany	24	20	30	7	18	17	116
Poland	17	21	16	14	5	16	89
Finland	25	21	30	2	1	3	82
France	21	24	14	3	5	8	75
Sweden	19	27	27	1	1	—	75
Italy	18	20	12	2	1	8	61
Czechoslovakia	9	9	21	5	7	6	57
Germany*	14	7	7	5	6	4	43
Hungary	9	8	15	4	4	2	42
Netherlands	7	4	4	7	7	5	34
Romania	—	4	1	3	10	1	19
Norway	2	7	5	—	—	4	18
Belgium	2	7	5	—	—	—	14
Switzerland	2	4	5	—	2	—	13
Yugoslavia	2	4	—	2	1	2	11
Bulgaria	2	1	1	2	4	1	11
Denmark	2	3	2	—	1	1	9
Spain	2	2	2	—	—	—	6
Iceland	3	1	1	—	—	—	5
Greece	—	1	2	1	—	1	5
Austria	—	—	—	2	1	1	4
Estonia	2	—	1	—	—	—	3
Ireland	—	2	1	—	—	—	3
Lithuania	1	—	—	—	—	—	1
Portugal	—	—	—	1	—	—	1
Turkey	—	—	1	—	—	—	1

*Germany—1934 and 1938 Championships. After the war the Federal Republic of Germany took part from 1954 and the German Democratic Republic from 1958.

Note that the above tables are after adjustments made for the disqualification for positive drugs tests in 1978 of Yevgeniy Mironov (USSR)—second SP, and Nadyezhda Tkachenko (USSR)—first Pen.

European Indoor Championships

European Indoor Games were held for the first time on 27 Mar 1966 at the Westfallenhalle in Dortmund. From 1970 they received IAAF sanction as the official European Indoor Championships.

VENUES—with circumference of track

1966 Dortmund (GFR)—Westfallenhalle (160m)
1967 Prague (Cs)—Palac Lodowy (150m)
1968 Madrid (Spa)—Palacio de los deportes (178m)
1969 Belgrade (Yug)—Sportovni hala (150m)
1970 Vienna (Aut)—Stadthalle (200m)
1971 Sofia (Bul)—Festivalna (200m)
1972 Grenoble (Fra)—Palais des Sports (180m)
1973 Rotterdam (Hol)—Aloy (180m)
1974 Göteborg (Swe)—Scandinavium (196m)
1975 Katowice (Pol)—Rondo (160m)
1976 Munich (GFR)—Olympiahalle (179m)
1977 San Sebastian (Spa)—Anoeta (200m)
1978 Milan (Ita)—Palasport (200m)
1979 Vienna (Aut)—Hallestadion (200m)
1980 Sindelfingen (GFR)—Sporthalle (200m)
1981 Grenoble (Fra)—Palais des Sports (180m)
1982 Milan (Ita)—Palasport (200m)
1983 Budapest (Hun)—(200m)
1984 Göteborg (Swe)—Scandinavium (196m)
1985 Athens (Gre)—Palais des Sports (200m)
1986 Madrid (Spa)—(166m)

MOST GOLD MEDALS—ALL EVENTS

MEN
7 Valeriy Borzov (USSR) 60m 1970–71–74–75–76–77; 50m 1972
6 Viktor Saneyev (USSR) TJ 1970–71–72–75–76–77

WOMEN
8 Helena Fibingerova (Cs) SP 1973–74–77–78–80–83 –84–85
5 Karin Balzer (GDR) 50mh 1967–68–69; 60mh 1970–71
5 Nadezhda Chizhova (USSR) SP 1967–68–70–71–72
5 Marlies Göhr (GDR) 1977–78–79–82–83

MOST MEDALS—ALL EVENTS
(*G*—gold, *S*—silver, *B*—bronze)

MEN
10 Thomas Wessinghage (GFR) 4*G* 1500m 1975–80–81–83; 5*S* 1500m 1974–76–78–79, 3000m 1985; 1*B* 1500m 1984
8 Valeriy Borzov (USSR) 7*G* as above, 1*S* 50m 1969
7 Viktor Saneyev (USSR) 6*G* as above, 1*S* 1968
6 Wolfgang Nordwig (GDR) 4*G* PV 1968–69–71–72, 2*B* 1967–70
6 Geoff Capes (UK) SP 2*G* 1974–76, 3*S* 1975–77–79, 1*B* 1978

WOMEN
11 Helena Fibingerova (Cs) 8*G* as above, 3*S* 1975–81–82
7 Nadezhda Chizhova (USSR) 5*G* as above, 1*S* 1974, 1*B* 1966
7 Grazyna Rabsztyn (Pol) 3*G* 60mh 1974–75–76, 3*S* 60mh 1978–79–80, 1*B* 50mh 1972
7 Meta Antenen (Swi) 1*G* LJ 1974; 2*S* 50mh 1969, LJ 1972; 4*B* 60 mh 1972–4, LJ 1969–75
6 Marlies Göhr (GDR) 5*G* as above, 1*S* 60m 1985
6 Brigitte Kraus (GFR) 3*G* 1500m 1976–83, 3000m 1984; 1*S* 1500m 1982; 2*B* 1500m 1978–85
6 Sylviane Telliez (Fra) 1*G* 50m 1968, 3*S* 60m 1969–70–71, 2*B* 50m 1972, 60m 1973

CHAMPIONSHIP BEST PERFORMANCES prior to 1986

MEN	min:sec		
60m	6.57	Marian Woronin (Pol)	1979
200m	20.77	Stefano Tilli (Ita)	1985
400m	45.56	Todd Bennett (UK)	1985
800m	1:46.54	Sebastian Coe (UK)	1977
1500m	3:37.54	Thomas Wessinghage (GFR)	1980
3000m	7:44.43	Markkus Ryffel (Swi)	1979
60mh	7.48	Thomas Munkelt (GDR)	1983
	metres		
High jump	2.35	Vladimir Yashchenko (USSR)	1978
	2.35	Patrik Sjöberg (Swe)	1985
Pole vault	5.85	Thierry Vigneron (Fra)	1985
Long jump	8.23	Igor Ter-Ovanesyan (USSR)	1966
Triple jump	17.33	Grigoriy Yemets (USSR)	1984
Shot	21.74	Remigius Machura (Cs)	1985
WOMEN	min:sec		
60m	7.09	Marlies Göhr (GDR)	1983
200m	22.39	Marita Koch (GDR)	1983
400m	49.59	Jarmila Kratochvilova (Cs)	1982
800m	1:59.52	Milena Matejkovicova (Cs)	1984
1500m	4:02.54	Doina Melinte (Rom)	1985
3000m	8:53.77	Agnese Possamai (Ita)	1982
60mh	7.75	Bettina Jahn (GDR)	1983
	metres		
High jump	2.03	Tamara Bykova (USSR)	1983
Long jump	7.02	Galina Chistyakova (USSR)	1985
Shot	21.46	Helena Fibingerova (Cs)	1977

THE MOST SUCCESSFUL ATHLETES AT EACH EVENT

Event	G	S	B	Athlete with medals won (G—gold, S—silver, B—bronze)
MEN				
50m/60m	7	1	–	Valeriy Borzov (USSR) G 1970–71–72–74–75–76–77, S 1969
	4	–	1	Marian Woronin (Pol) G 1979–80–81–82, B 1977
200m	2	–	1	Aleksandr Yevgenyev (USSR) G 1983–84, B 1985
400m	2	1	–	Andrzej Badenski (Pol) G 1968–71, S 1970
800m	3	–	1	Noel Carroll (Ire) G 1966–67–68, B 1969
1500m	4	4	1	Thomas Wessinghage (GFR) G 1975–80–81–83, S 1974–76–78–79, B 1984
	4	–	–	Henryk Szordykowski (Pol) 1500m 1970–71–73–74
	3	–	–	John Whetton (UK) G 1966–67–68
3000m	2	1	1	Markkus Ryffel (Swi) G 1978–79, S 1984, B 1977
50m/60mh	4	–	1	Thomas Munkelt (GDR) G 1973–77–78–79–83
	3	–	–	Eddy Ottoz (Ita) G 1966–67–68
High jump	3	1	–	Istvan Major (Hun) G 1971–72–73, S 1974
	3	1	–	Dietmar Mögenburg (GFR) G 1980–82–84, S 1981
Pole vault	4	–	2	Wolfgang Nordwig (GDR) G 1968–69–71–72, B 1967–70
	1	3	1	Antti Kalliomaki (Fin) G 1975, S 1974–76–77, B 1972
Long jump	3	2	–	Hans Baumgartner (GFR) G 1971–73–77, S 1972–74
Triple jump	6	1	–	Viktor Saneyev (USSR) G 1970–71–72–75–76–77, S 1968
	1	3	1	Carol Corbu (Rom) G 1973, S 1971–72–76, B 1969
Shot	3	1	–	Hartmut Briesenick (GDR) G 1970–71–72, S 1969
	3	–	–	Reijo Stahlberg (Fin) G 1978–79–81
	2	3	1	Geoff Capes (UK) G 1974–76, S 1975–77–79, B 1978
	–	3	2	Wladyslaw Komar (Pol) S 1968–72–78, B 1967–77
WOMEN				
50m/60m	6	1	–	Marlies Göhr (GDR) G 1977–78–79–82–83, S 1985
	4	–	–	Renate Stecher (GDR) G 1970–71–72–74
	1	3	2	Sylviane Telliez (Fra) G 1968, S 1969–70–71, B 1972–73
200 m	2	–	–	Marita Koch (GDR) G 1983–85 (also won 400m 1977)
400m	3	1	1	Verona Elder (UK) G 1973–75–79, S 1977, B 1981
	3	1	–	Jarmila Kratochvilova (Cs) G 1981–82–83, S 1979 (won 200m 1984)
800m	2	1	–	Nikolina Shtereva (Bul) G 1976–79, S 1981
1500m	2	1	2	Brigitte Kraus (GFR) G 1976–83, S 1982, B 1978–85
3000m	2	1	–	Agnese Possamai (Ita) G 1982–85, S 1983 (won 1500m 1981)
50m/60mh	5	–	–	Karin Balzer (GDR) G 1967–68–69–70–71
	3	3	1	Grazyna Rabsztyn (Pol) G 1974(=)–75–76, S 1978–79–80, B 1972
High jump	4	–	–	Sara Simeoni (Ita) G 1977–78–80–81
	3	–	2	Rita Kirst (GDR) G 1968–69–72, B 1970–74
	3	–	–	Rosemarie Ackermann (GDR) G 1974–75–76
Long jump	2	3	1	Jarmila Nygrynova (Cs) G 1977–78, S 1973–76–79, B 1972
Shot	8	3	–	Helena Fibingerova (Cs) G 1973–74–77–78–80–83–84–85, S 1975–81–82
	5	1	1	Nadezhda Chizhova (USSR) G 1967–68–70–71–72, S 1974, B 1966

The above table contains all athletes who have won three golds or five medals at one event.

The only athletes to have won medals at three different events have been:
Mary Rand (UK) S LJ, B 60mh & HJ—all in 1966
Rita Bottiglieri (Ita) S 400m 1978, B 60m & 60mh 1977

VALERIY BORZOV

Borzov not only set a record for the most European Indoor gold medals by a man, but achieved an amazing consistency in so doing. His indoor career started with a silver medal at 50m to Zenon Nowosz (Pol) in 1969 and he won at that shorter distance in 1972 with 5.75. At 60m his winning times were as follows: 1970—6.6, 1971—6.6, 1974—6.58, 1975—6.59, 1976–6.58, 1977—6.59. He did not run in 1973. He ran at 50m (5.75 sec) in 1972.

<u>MEDAL TABLE BY NATION</u>

NATION	**MEN**			**WOMEN**			TOTAL
	G	S	B	G	S	B	Medals
USSR	58	47	54	19	39	31	248
GDR	20	29	18	44	35	20	166
F. R. Germany	30	34	20	17	20	22	143
Poland	21	18	18	12	10	18	97
Czechoslovakia	8	11	15	18	12	9	73
United Kingdom	16	12	7	10	7	14	66
Bulgaria	3	5	4	11	12	13	48
France	11	8	15	2	7	5	48
Romania	2	4	9	10	11	10	46
Hungary	10	12	9	4	4	2	41
Italy	9	5	10	8	3	4	39
Spain	5	8	11	–	–	–	24
Switzerland	5	4	5	1	2	5	22
Finland	7	7	7	–	–	–	21
Belgium	8	7	3	–	1	–	19
Yugoslavia	5	1	7	1	2	2	18
Sweden	1	4	5	2	4	1	17
Ireland	4	3	1	–	–	2	10
Netherlands	–	1	1	1	2	2	7
Austria	–	–	–	2	1	3	6
Greece	–	2	2	–	–	–	4
Norway	–	1	–	2	–	–	3
Iceland	1	–	–	–	–	–	1

Individual championship events only.

European Junior Championships

European competitions for Juniors were first held unofficially in 1964 at Warsaw. Games recognized as official by the European AA were staged in 1966 and 1968 as 'European Junior Games' and since 1970 competitions have been the European Championships for Juniors. Junior men must not reach 20 and junior women 19 during the year of competition.

The GDR have by far the best record of any nation, their greatest domination coming in 1981 when from the 38 events their athletes won 22 gold, 13 silver and 7 bronze medals.

<u>MOST GOLD MEDALS—ALL EVENTS</u>

MEN
4 Thomas Schröder (GDR) 100m 1979; 100m, 200m, 4×100mR 1981
3 Valeriy Borzov (USSR) 100m, 200m, 4×100mR 1968
3 Valeriy Podluzhniy (USSR) LJ, TJ, 4×100mR 1970
3 Klaus-Dieter Kurrat (GDR) 100m, 200m, 4×100mR 1973

WOMEN
3 Irena Kirszenstein (Pol) 200m, LJ, 4×100mR 1964
3 Lyudmila Zharkova (USSR) 100m, 200m, 4×100mR 1968
3 Bärbel Eckert (GDR) 200m, 100mh, 4×100mR 1973
3 Petra Koppetsch (GDR) 100m, 200m, 4×100mR 1975
3 Christine Brehmer (GDR) 400m, 4×100mR, 4×400mR 1975
3 Bärbel Lockhoff (GDR) 100m, 200m, 4×100mR 1977
3 Kerstin Walther (GDR) 100m, 200m, 4×100mR 1979
3 Katrin Böhme (GDR) 100m, 100mh, 4×100mR 1981
3 Kerstin Behrendt (GDR) 100m, 200m, 4×100mR 1985

<u>VENUES</u>

1966 Odessa, USSR	1977 Donyetsk, USSR
1968 Leipzig, GDR	1979 Bydgoszcz, Poland
1970 Paris, France	1981 Utrecht, Netherlands
1973 Duisberg, GFR	1983 Schwechat, Austria
1975 Athens, Greece	1985 Cottbus, GDR

Ade Mafe set a UK junior record for 200m of 20.54 to win the 1985 European Junior title and won a second gold at 4 × 400m. (Michael King, All-Sport)

Steve Ovett (191) wins the 1973 800m title from Willie Wülbeck (586) and Erwin Gohlke (GDR). Ten years later Wülbeck became world champion. (ASP)

Many future World, Olympic and European champions have experienced their first international success at these most competitive events.

<u>ATHLETES WHO HAVE WON EUROPEAN JUNIOR (J) AND SENIOR (S) INDIVIDUAL EVENT TITLES</u>

MEN

100m	Valeriy Borzov (USSR) J 1968, S 1969, 1971
200m	Valeriy Borzov (USSR) J 1968, S 1971
100m–400m	Franz-Peter Hofmeister (GFR) J 100m/200m 1970, S 400m 1978
400m	Hartmut Weber (GFR) J 1979, S 1982
800m–1500m	Steve Ovett (UK) J 800m 1973, S 1500m 1978
1500m	Klaus-Peter Justus (GDR) J 1970, S 1974
1500m–10 000m	Jürgen Haase (GDR) J 1500m & 3000m 1964, S 10 000m 1966 & 1979
3000m–1500m	Steve Cram (UK) J 3000m 1979, S 1500m 1982
2000m–3000m steeple	Bronislaw Malinowski (Pol) J 2000mSt 1970, S 3000mSt 1974 & 1978
High jump	Dietmar Mögenburg (GFR) J 1979, S 1982
Long jump	Max Klauss (GDR) J 1968, S 1971
	Valeriy Podluzhniy (USSR) J 1970, S 1974
Shot	Hartmut Briesenick (GDR) J 1968, S 1971 & 1974
	Udo Beyer (GDR) J 1973, S 1978 & 1982
Hammer	Yuriy Sedykh (USSR) J 1973, S 1978 & 1982
Javelin	Uwe Hohn (GDR) J 1981, S 1982
Decathlon	Daley Thompson (UK) J 1977, S 1982

WOMEN

200m	Irena Kirszenstein/Szewinska (Pol) J 1964, S 1966 & 1974
	Bärbel Eckert/Wöckel (GDR) J 1973, S 1982
800m	Vera Nikolic (Yug) J 1966, S 1966 & 1971
Long jump	Irena Kirszenstein (Pol) J 1964, S 1966
Shot	Nadezhda Chizhova (USSR) J 1964, S 1966–69–71–74
	Ilona Schonknecht/Slupianek (GDR) J 1973, S 1978 & 1982
Discus	Evelin Schlaak/Jahl J 1973, S 1978

<u>GOLD MEDALS AT TWO CHAMPIONSHIPS</u>

Ari Paunonen (Fin) 1500m 1975 & 1977
Thomas Schröder (GDR) as above.
Jens Carlowitz (GDR) 4×400mR 1981 & 1983
Nikolay Matyushenko (USSR) 2000m steeple 1983 & 1985

<u>OTHERS TO WIN TWO INDIVIDUAL EVENTS</u>

MEN

Jürgen Haase (GDR) 1500m, 3000m 1964
Geja Fejer (Hun) SP, DT 1966
Mikhail Bariban (USSR) LJ, TJ 1968
Franz-Peter Hofmeister (GFR) 100m, 200m 1970
Werner Bastians (GFR) 100m, 200m 1975
Maik Dreissigacker (GDR) 1500m, 3000m 1983
Volker Mai (GDR) LJ, TJ 1985

WOMEN

Meta Antenen (Swi) 80mh, Pen 1966
Kristine Nitzsche (GDR) HJ, Pen 1977
Heide Krieger (GDR) SP, DT 1983

<u>MOST MEDALS—ALL EVENTS</u>
(G—gold, S—silver, B—bronze)

5 Thomas Schröder (GDR) 4G as above; 1S 200m 1979
4 Jens Carlowitz (GDR) 2G as above; 2S 400m 1981 & 1983

<u>CHAMPIONSHIP BEST PERFORMANCES</u> prior to 1987

MEN	min:sec		
100m	10.14w	Thomas Schröder (GDR)	1981
	10.31	Jürgen Evers (GFR)	1983
200m	20.37	Jürgen Evers (GFR)	1983
400m	45.36	Roger Black (UK)	1985
800m	1:46.17	Jozsef Bereczky (Hun)	1981
1500m	3:39.0	Graham Williamson (UK)	1979
3000m	7:57.18	Rainer Wachenbrunner (GDR)	1981
5000m	13:44.4	Steve Binns (UK)	1979
2000m steeple	5:27.5	Gaetano Erba (Ita)	1979
110mh	13.46	Jonathan Ridgeon (UK)	1985
400mh	49.71	Ruslan Mishchenko (USSR)	1983
4×100mR	39.25	F. R. Germany	1983
4×400mR	3:04.58	GDR	1981
10kmW	39:56.23	Ralf Kowalsky (GDR)	1981
	metres		
High jump	2.30	Vladimir Yashchenko (USSR)	1977
Pole vault	5.55	Rodion Gataulin (USSR)	1983

Long jump	7.99	Volker Mai (GDR)	1985
Triple jump	16.93	Volker Mai (GDR)	1985
Shot	19.65	Udo Beyer (GDR)	1973
Discus	60.02	Attila Horvath (Hun)	1985
Hammer	74.28	Sergey Dorozhon (USSR)	1983
Javelin	86.56	Uwe Hohn (GDR)	1981
Decathlon	7906 pts	Mikhail Romanyuk (USSR)	1981
WOMEN	min:sec		
100m	11.21	Kerstin Behrendt (GDR)	1985
200m	22.85	Bärbel Eckert (GDR)	1983
400m	51.25	Christine Brehmer (GDR)	1975
800m	2:00.25	Katrin Wühn (GDR)	1983
1500m	4:07.5	Inger Knutsson (Swe)	1973
3000m	8:58.30	Lyudmila Sudak (USSR)	1981
100mh	13.10	Monique Ewanje-Epée (Fra)	1985
400mh	56.01	Radostina Shtereva (Bul)	1983
4×100mR	43.77	GDR	1981
4×400mR	3:30.39	GDR	1981
5000mW	22:56.84	Maria Cruz Diaz (Spa) (tie)	1985
	22:56.84	Reyes Sobrino (Spa) (tie)	1985
	metres		
High jump	1.94	Yelena Topchina (USSR)	1983
	1.94	Natalya Golodnova (USSR)	1985
Long jump	7.02	Heike Daute (GDR)	1981
Shot	18.76	Bethina Libera (GDR)	1985
Discus	60.30	Irina Meszynski (GDR)	1979
Javelin	64.12	Antoaneta Todorova (Bul)	1981
Heptathlon	6465 pts	Sybille Thiele (GDR)	1983

European Cup

The European Cup is contested biennially by European nations, with each team entering one athlete per event and one team in each relay. The Cup is dedicated to the memory of Dr Bruno Zauli, the former President of the European Committee of the IAAF, who died suddenly in 1963 soon after the decision had been made to start this competition.

PLACINGS IN THE FINAL (OR 'A' FINAL)

MEN	1965	1967	1970	1973	1975	1977	1979	1981	1983	1985
GDR	4	2	1	2	1	1	1	1	1	2
USSR	1	1	2	1	2	3	2	2	2	1
F. R. Germany	2	3	3	3	5	2	3	4	3	3
United Kingdom	6	–	–	4	4	4	5	3	4	4
Poland	3	4	4	–	3	5	4	6	5	5
France	5	5	5	6	7	6	7	7	7	8
Italy	–	–	7	–	8	8	6	5	6	6
Finland	–	–	–	5	6	7	–	–	–	–
Hungary	–	6	–	–	–	–	–	–	8	–
Sweden	–	–	6	–	–	–	–	–	–	–
Czechoslovakia	–	–	–	–	–	–	–	–	–	7
Yugoslavia	–	–	–	–	–	–	8	8	–	–

'B' Final winners: 1977 France, 1979 Yugoslavia, 1981 France, 1983 Czechoslovakia, 1985 Spain

WOMEN	1965	1967	1970	1973	1975	1977	1979	1981	1983	1985
GDR	2	2	1	1	1	1	1	1	1	2
USSR	1	1	3	2	2	2	2	2	2	1
F. R. Germany	4	3	2	4	3	3*	6	3	5	6
United Kingdom	–	5	5	5	7	4*	4	4	4	3
Poland	3	4	4	–	4	5	7	6	7	5
Bulgaria	–	–	–	3	6	7	3	5	6	4
Romania	–	–	–	6	5	6	5	–	–	–
Hungary	5	6	6	–	–	–	–	7	8	–
Czechoslovakia	–	–	–	–	–	–	–	–	3	7
Italy	–	–	–	–	–	–	8	–	–	8
Netherlands	6	–	–	–	–	–	–	–	–	–
France	–	–	–	–	–	8	–	–	–	–
Finland	–	–	–	–	–	8	–	–	–	–
Yugoslavia	–	–	–	–	–	–	–	8	–	–

*Finished level on points, and originally 3rd UK, 4th GFR, but after the shot winner Ilona Slupianek was disqualified, Eva Wilms (GFR) moved up to first place and that reversed the countback decision between the nations.

From 1965 until 1981 the competition was staged with a qualifying round, semi-finals and final, but from 1983 the nations have been arranged into groups according to strength, with eight men's and eight women's teams in 'A' and 'B' groups, with additional nations in C1 and C2 groups. There is one up and one down promotion and relegation between A and B, and two up and two down between B and C.

<u>Venues of cup finals have been:</u>

1965 Stuttgart (men) Kassel (women), 1967 Kiev, 1970 Stockholm (men) Budapest (women), 1973 Edinburgh, 1975 Nice, 1977 Helsinki, 1979 Turin, 1981 Zagreb, 1983 London, 1985 Moscow

<u>Eleven world records have been set in european cup finals, all by women</u>

1965 Irina Press (USSR) 80mh 10.4, Tamara Press (USSR) SP 18.59; 1973 Faina Melnik (USSR) DT 69.48, Ruth Fuchs (GDR) JT 66.10; 1977 Karin Rossley (GDR) 400mh 55.63, Rosemarie Ackermann (GDR) HJ 1.97; 1979 Marita Koch (GDR) 400m 48.60, GDR 4×100mR 42.09; 1981 Antoaneta Todorova (Bul) JT 71.88; 1983 Ulrike Meyfarth (USSR) and Tamara Bykova (USSR) HJ 2.03m.

<u>Greatest winning margins:</u>

Men, final	12 pts GDR 1977
Men, any round	42 pts GDR 1979 semi-final at Geneva
Women, final	22 pts GDR 1983
Women, any round	28 pts UK 1981 semi-final at Edinburgh

<u>Most individual event wins in finals</u>

MEN
4 Harald Schmid (GFR) 400m 1979, 400mh 1979–83–85
3 Harald Norpoth (GFR) 5000m 1965–67–70
3 Wolfgang Nordwig (GDR) PV 1965–67–70
3 Jean-Claude Nallet (Fra) 200m and 400m 1967, 400mh 1970

<u>European cup best performances</u>

(F achieved in final, SF in semi-final)

MEN — min:sec

Event	Mark	Athlete	
100m	10.12	Eugen Ray (GDR)	F 1977
200m	20.15	Pietro Mennea (Ita)	SF 1977
400m	44.96	Thomas Schönlebe (GDR)	F 1985
800m	1:45.70	Dieter Fromm (GDR)	SF 1973
1500m	3:33.63	José Abascal (Spa)	F (B) 1983
5000m	13.25.2	Emiel Puttemans (Bel)	SF 1973
10 000m	27:32.85	Fernando Mamede (Por)	F (C) 1983
3000m steeple	8:13.32	Mariano Scartezzini (Ita)	F 1981
110 mh	13.37	Thomas Munkelt (GDR)	F 1977
400 mh	47.85	Harald Schmid (GFR)	F 1979
	47.85	Harald Schmid (GFR)	F 1985
4×100mR	38.28	USSR	F 1985
4×400mR	3:00.33	F. R. Germany	F 1985

metres

Event	Mark	Athlete	
High jump	2.32	Dietmar Mögenburg (GFR)	F 1979
	2.32	Franck Verzy (Fra)	F 1983
Pole vault	5.80	Sergey Bubka (USSR)	F 1985
Long jump	8.31	Lutz Dombrowski (GDR)	F 1979
Triple jump	17.77	Khristo Markov (Bul)	F (B) 1985
Shot	22.05	Sergey Smirnov (USSR)	F 1985
Discus	68.64	Wolfgang Schmidt (GDR)	SF 1981
Hammer	82.90	Juri Tamm (USSR)	F 1985
Javelin	92.88	Uwe Hohn (GDR)	F 1985

WOMEN — min:sec

Event	Mark	Athlete	
100m	10.93w	Sonia Lannaman (UK)	SF 1977
	10.95	Marlies Göhr (GDR)	F 1985
200m	22.02	Marita Koch (GDR)	F 1985
400m	48.60	Marita Koch (GDR)	F 1979
	48.60	Olga Vladykina (USSR)	F 1985
800m	1:55.91	Jarmila Kratochvilova (Cs)	F 1985
1500m	3:58.40	Ravilya Agletdinova (USSR)	F 1985
3000m	8:35.32	Zola Budd (UK)	F 1985
10 000m	31:47.38	Olga Bondarenko (USSR)	F 1985
100mh	12.76w	Grazyna Rabsztyn (Pol)	SF 1977
	12.77	Tatyana Anisimova (USSR)	F 1979
	12.77	Ginka Zagorcheva (USSR)	F 1985
400mh	54.13	Sabine Busch (GDR)	F 1985
4×100mR	41.65	GDR	F 1985
4×400mR	3:18.58	USSR	F 1985

metres

Event	Mark	Athlete	
High jump	2.06	Stefka Kostadinova (Bul)	F 1985
Long jump	7.28	Galina Chistyakova (USSR)	F 1985
Shot	21.42	Marianne Adam (GDR)	SF 1975
Discus	70.24	Galina Savinkova (USSR)	F 1985
Javelin	73.20	Petra Felke (GDR)	F 1985

3 Viktor Saneyev (USSR) TJ 1967–73–75
3 Guy Drut (Fra) 110mh 1970–73–75
3 Brendan Foster (UK) 5000m 1973–75, 10 000m 1979
3 Wolfgang Schmidt (GDR) DT 1975–77–79
3 Karl-Hans Riehm (GFR) HT 1975–77–79
3 Udo Beyer (GDR) SP 1977–79–81
3 Thomas Munkelt (GDR) 110mh 1977–79–83
3 Allan Wells (UK) 100m 1981, 200m 1979–83
3 Frank Emmelmann (GDR) 100m 1983, 200m 1981–85

WOMEN
5 Renate Stecher (GDR) 100m 1973–75, 200m
  1970–73–75
5 Marlies Göhr (GDR) 100m 1977–79–81–83–85
4 Irena Szewinska (Pol) 100m 1967, 200m 1967–77,
  400 m 1975
4 Ruth Fuchs (GDR) JT 1970–73–75–77
4 Marita Koch (GDR) 200m 1985, 400m 1977–79–81
3 Nadezhda Chizhova (USSR) SP 1967–70–73
3 Faina Melnik (USSR) DT 1973–75–77
3 Rosemarie Ackermann (GDR) HJ 1975–77–79
3 Jarmila Kratochvilova (Cs) 200m 1983, 800m 1983–85

Most wins in finals including relays

MEN
7 Harald Schmid (GFR) 4 as above, 4×400mR
  1977–79–85
4 Thomas Munkelt (GDR) 3 as above, 4×100mR 1975

WOMEN
10 Marlies Göhr (GDR) 5 as above, 4×100mR
   1977–79–81–83–85
 9 Marita Koch (GDR) 4 as above, 4×100mR 1983–85,
   4×400mR 1977–79–81
 7 Renate Stecher (GDR) 5 as above, 4×100mR 1973–75
 5 Irena Szewinska (Pol) 4 as above, 4×100mR 1965

The most wins in one final is three
(two individual and one relay) by:

MEN Eugen Ray (GDR) 100m, 200m, 4×100mR 1977;
Harald Schmid (GFR) 400m, 400mh, 4×400mR 1979
WOMEN Renate Stecher (GDR) 100m, 200m, 4×100mR
1973 and 1975; Jarmila Kratochvilova (Cs) 200m, 800m,
4×400mR 1983

Highest points scorers in finals

Eight points have been scored for 1st, seven for
2nd, down to 1 for 8th. The 6- or 7-team finals
from 1965 for 1973 have been rescored. Relay
points have been divided by four.

MEN
52	Harald Schmid (GFR) (1977–85)
48.75	Pietro Mennea (Ita) (1975–83)
46	Allan Wells (UK) (1977–83)
42.25	Marian Woronin (Pol) (1977–85)
41.5	Jean-Claude Nallet (Fra) (1967–75)
41	Thomas Wessinghage (GFR) (1975–85)
40.75	Frank Emmelmann (GDR) (1981–5)
37	Thomas Munkelt (GDR) (1973–83)
36	Karl-Hans Riehm (GFR) (1975–83)
34	Harald Norpoth (GFR) (1965–73)
32	Alberto Cova (Ita) (1981–5)
31.5	Valeriy Borzov (USSR) (1975–7)
31.25	David Jenkins (UK) (1973–81)
31	Viktor Saneyev (USSR) (1967–75)
31	Willi Wülbeck (GFR) (1975–83)
31	Olaf Beyer (GDR) (1977–85)
30	Janis Lusis (USSR) (1965–73)
30	Udo Beyer (GDR) (1977–85)

WOMEN
77.5	Irena Szewinska (Pol) (1968–79)
57	Marlies Göhr (GDR) (1977–85)
52.75	Renate Stecher (GDR) (1970–5)
49	Marita Koch (GDR) (1977–85)
45	Ruth Fuchs (GDR) (1967–79)
41.5	Kathy Cook (UK) (1979–85)
34.75	Annegret Richter (GFR) (1973–7)
34	Ulrike Bruns (GDR) (1975–85)
32	Ingrid Mickler (GFR) (1965–70)
30.5	Jarmila Kratochvilova (Cs) (1983–85)

The most individual points scored in a final is 21
by Irena Szewinska in 1975: 1st 400m, 2nd 200m,
6th 100m, and she also ran on the 4th-placed
4×100m relay team.

Szewinska and Wessinghage competed in a record
six European Cup Finals.

The almost skeletal Harald Norpoth was a master tactician at
European Cup races. He won three successive European Cup Final
5000m races. The next two were won by Brendan Foster, who here
(2) is beaten by Norpoth in a UK *v*. GFR fixture at Crystal Palace.
(ASP)

European Combined Events Cup

This competition has been held biennially since 1973. As with the European Cup nations are now divided into A, B, C1 and C2 groups.

PLACINGS OF NATIONS IN THE FIRST SIX

MEN   Decathlon

	1973	1975	1977	1979	1981	1983	1985
USSR	2	1	1	3	4	3	1
F. R. Germany	5	5	2	2	1	1	dnf
GDR	3	4	3	1	2	2	2
Poland	1	2	6	5	3	5	3
France	4	(7)	4	6	–	–	–
Sweden	6	3	5	–	–	–	–
Switzerland	(7)	–	–	–	6	4	4
Bulgaria	(9)	–	–	–	5	6	5
Finland	–	6	–	4	–	–	–
United Kingdom	–	–	–	–	dnf	–	–

WOMEN   Pentathlon 1973–79, Heptathlon since 1981

	1973	1975	1977	1979	1981	1983	1985
GDR	1	1	1	1	1	1	1
USSR	2	2	1	2	3	2	2
F. R. Germany	4	3	2	3	2	4	3
Bulgaria	3	–	6	–	4	3	5
Hungary	5	5	(7)	5	5	6	–
United Kingdom	–	–	4	6	6	5	4
France	6	6	3	–	–	–	–
Netherlands	–	–	5	4	–	–	6
Austria	(7)	4	–	–	–	–	–

INDIVIDUAL RECORDS

Athletes to have won two finals: Burglinde Pollak (GDR) won the women's pentathlon in 1973 and 1975, Ramona Neubert (GDR) won the women's heptathlon in 1981 and 1983.
Most finals: 7 Guido Kratschmer (GFR)—decathlon each year from 1975 to 1985, with a best placing of second in 1979.
Cup records: Decathlon, 8551 Uwe Freimuth (GDR) 1983; Heptathlon, 6772 Ramona Neubert (GDR) 1983 (scored on 1984 tables)

European Marathon Cup

This event has been held biennially since 1981. Men's and women's races have been held each year, but the latter did not incorporate a team competition until 1985. As yet the competition has not succeeded in attracting many of Europe's top marathoners.

Men's team medallists:
1981 1. Italy, 2. USSR, 3. Poland
1983 1. GDR, 2. Italy, 3. Spain
1985 1. GDR, 2. France, 3. Italy

Women's team medallists:
1985 1. GDR, 2. Italy, 3. USSR

Individual winners:
MEN 1981 Massimo Magnani (Ita) 2:13:29, 1983 Waldemar Cierpinski (GDR) 2:12:26, 1985 Michael Heilmann (GDR) 2:11:28.
WOMEN 1981 Zoya Ivanova (USSR) 2:38:58, 1983 Nadyezhda Gumerova (USSR) 2:38:36, 1985 Katrin Dörre (GDR) 2:30:11.

European Clubs' Trophy

MEN

This competition, open to the top club in each European nation, was first staged at Liège, Belgium in 1975. Twelve teams took part that year, but the number was increased to 16 in 1984.

Winning teams:
1975 TV Wattenscheid (GFR)
1976 Athletica Rieti (Ita)
1977 TV Wattenscheid (GFR)
1978 TV Wattenscheid (GFR)
1979 Fiat Iveco (Ita)
1980 Fiat Iveco (Ita)
1981 Dukla Praha (Cs)
1982 Fiamme Oro (Ita)
1983 Fiamme Oro (Ita)
1984 Pro Patria Pierrel Milano (Ita)
1985 Pro Patria Freedent Milano (Ita)

The most successful nations based on their clubs' first three placings:

	1st	2nd	3rd	4th
Italy	7	3	–	–
F. R. Germany	3	3	1	–
Czechoslovakia	1	–	–	–
France	–	3	4	1
Yugoslavia	–	1	1	4
Spain	–	1	1	3
United Kingdom	–	–	4	1
Poland	–	–	–	1
Portugal	–	–	–	1

WOMEN

The women's European Clubs' competition was first held at Naples in 1981. It was won each year from 1981 to 1985 by Bayer Leverkusen (GFR).

The most successful nations based on their clubs' first three placings:

	1st	2nd	3rd	4th
F. R. Germany	5	–	–	–
Italy	–	3	1	1
United Kingdom	–	2	2	–
France	–	–	1	3
Yugoslavia	–	1	–	–
Netherlands	–	–	–	1

The UK's best placed club has been Stretford AC, second in 1981 and second equal in 1982 in the women's competition.

Pan-American Games

1975 Mexico City, Mexico   1983 Caracas, Venezuela
1979 San Juan, Puerto Rico   1987 Indianapolis, USA

The Pan-American Games are multi-sport competitions open to athletes from North, Central and South American nations. They have been held every four years from 1951. The USA has dominated the track and field events, winning by far the highest total of medals. In recent years, however, their less than full strength teams have been strongly challenged by Cuba, whose athletes have won seven, six and eleven medals respectively in the last three Games.

MOST GOLD MEDALS — ALL EVENTS

MEN
4 Osvaldo Suarez (Arg) 5000m 1955–63, 10 000m 1955–59
4 Joao Carlos de Oliveira (Bra) LJ and TJ 1975–79
3 Adhemar Ferreira da Silva (Bra) TJ 1951–55–59
3 Al Hall (USA) HT 1959–63–71
3 Silvio Leonard (Cub) 100m 1975–79, 200m 1979
and the four men to win three golds at one Games:
3 Mal Whitfield (USA) 400m, 800m, 4×400mR 1951
3 Rod Richard (USA) 100m, 200m, 4×100mR 1955
3 Ray Norton (USA) 100m, 200m, 4×100mR 1959
3 Don Quarrie (Jam) 100m, 200m, 4×100mR 1971

WOMEN
3 Isabelle Daniels (USA) 60m 1959, 4×100mR 1955–59
3 Nancy McCredie (Can) SP 1963–67, DT 1963
3 Carmen Romero (Cub) DT 1971–75–79
3 Chandra Cheeseborough (USA) 100m 1975, 4×100mR 1975–79

VENUES

1951 Buenos Aires, Argentina   1963 Sao Paulo, Brazil
1955 Mexico City, Mexico   1967 Winnipeg, Canada
1959 Chicago, USA   1971 Cali, Colombia

CHAMPIONSHIP BEST PERFORMANCES prior to 1987

MEN

	hr:min:sec		
100m	10.06	Leandro Penalver (Cub)	1983
200m	19.86	Don Quarrie (Jam)	1971
400m	44.45	Ronnie Ray (USA)	1975
800m	1:46.3	James Robinson (USA)	1979
	1:46.31	Agberto Guimaraes (Bra)	1983
1500m	3:40.5	Don Paige (USA)	1979
5000m	13:47.4	Van Nelson (USA)	1967
10 000m	28:50.8	Frank Shorter (USA)	1971
Marathon	2:12:42	Jorge Gonzalez (PR)	1983
3000m steeple	8:38.2	Chris McCubbins (USA)	1967
110mh	13.20	Renaldo Nehemiah (USA)	1979
400mh	49.11	Ralph Mann (USA)	1971
4×100mR	38.31	USA	1975
4×400mR	3:00.47	USA	1983
20kmW	1:28:12	Ernesto Canto (Mex)	1983
50kmW	4:00:45	Raul Gonzales (Mex)	1983
	metres		
High jump	2.29	Francisco Centelles (Cub)	1983
Pole vault	5.45	Mike Tully (USA)	1983
Long jump	8.29	Ralph Boston (USA)	1967
Triple jump	17.89	Joao Carlos de Oliveira (Bra)	1975
Shot	20.22	Dave Laut (USA)	1979
Discus	67.32	Luis Delis (Cub)	1983
Hammer	69.64	Scott Neilson (Can)	1979
Javelin	84.16	Duncan Atwood (USA)	1979
Decathlon	8024 pts	Bruce Jenner (USA)	1975

WOMEN

	min:sec		
100m	11.05	Evelyn Ashford (USA) (in SF)	1979
200m	22.24w	Evelyn Ashford (USA) (& 22.45 SF)	1979
400m	51.49	Charmaine Crooks (Can)	1983
800m	2:01.2	Essie Kelley (USA)	1979
	2:01.2	Julie Brown (USA) (2nd)	1979
1500m	4:05.7	Mary Decker (USA)	1979
3000m	8:53.6	Jan Merrill (USA)	1979
100mh	12.90w	Deby La Plante (USA)	1979
	13.16	Benita Fitzgerald (USA)	1983
400mh	56.03	Judi Brown (USA)	1983
4×100mR	42.90	USA	1975
4×400mR	3:29.4	USA	1979
	metres		
High jump	1.93	Louise Ritter (USA)	1979
Long jump	6.70	Kathy McMillan (USA)	1983
Shot	19.34	Maria Sarria (Cub)	1983
Discus	60.58	Carmen Romero (Cub)	1979
Javelin	63.76	Maria Colon (Cub)	1983
Heptathlon	6017 pts	Conceicao Geremias (Bra)	1983

3 Maria Sarria (Cub) SP 1975–79–83
and the one woman to win three golds at one Games:
3 Lucinda Williams (USA) 100m, 200m, 4×100mR 1959

MOST MEDALS — ALL EVENTS

(*G* — gold,
S — silver, *B* — bronze)

MEN

6 Osvaldo Suarez (Arg) 4*G* as above; 2*S* 5000m 1959,
  10 000m 1963
5 Silvio Leonard (Cub) 3*G* as above; 2*S* 4×100mR
  1979–83
5 Alejandro Casanas (Cub) 1*G* 110mh 1975; 4*S* 110mh
  1979–83, 4×100mR 1975–79
5 Mike Agostini (Tri) 2*S* 100m 1955–59; 3*B* 200m 1955–59,
  4×100mR 1959

WOMEN

6 Miguelina Cobian (Cub) 1*G* 4×100mR 1967; 4*S* 100m
  1963–67, 200m 1963, 4×100mR 1963; 1*B* 200m 1967
5 Isabelle Daniels (USA) 3*G* as above; 2*S* 100m 1955,
  200m 1959
5 Abigail Hoffmann (Can) 2*G* 800m 1963–71; 1*S* 800m
  1975; 2*B* 800m 1967, 1500m 1975 (she uniquely won
  medals at four Games)

PAN-AMERICAN JUNIOR CHAMPIONSHIPS

First held in 1980, they are now staged every four
years. The first athlete to win three gold medals
was Joe DeLoach (USA) at 100m, 200m and
4×100m relay in 1984.

MEDAL TABLE BY NATION

NATION	MEN			WOMAN			TOTAL
	G	S	B	G	S	B	Medals
USA	137	96	54	59	45	27	418
Cuba	19	25	29	16	23	16	128
Canada	9	15	26	15	17	28	110
Brazil	9	10	18	2	5	9	53
Argentina	10	10	10	3	4	4	41
Mexico	10	14	15	1	–	1	41
Jamaica	4	7	11	1	2	7	32
Chile	3	5	6	5	5	4	28
Venezuela	1	8	6	–	1	1	17
Colombia	2	3	7	–	–	1	13
Trinidad & Tobago	–	4	7	–	1	1	13
Puerto Rico	1	3	7	–	–	–	11
Peru	–	2	3	2	–	–	7
Guatemala	1	1	3	–	–	–	5
Bahamas	–	3	1	–	–	–	4
Panama	–	–	–	–	1	3	4

MEDALS WON BY OTHER NATIONS:

3 Barbados, Guyana, Uruguay; 1 Antigua, Ecuador,
Netherlands Antilles.

The British West Indies competed in 1959, winning a gold
and a bronze in the men's relays—their individual event
medals have been reallocated amongst their constituent
countries.

The table excludes three athletes disqualified for
drug abuse in 1983. These were two Cuban
women, Maria-Christina Betancourt (DT) and
Rosa Fernandez (SP), and Juan Nunez of the
Dominican Republic, second in the men's 100m,
his country's first Pan-Am placer.

South American Championships

The first official South American Championships
were held at Montevideo, Uruguay in 1919. Since
then they have been held regularly, every two or
three years. The 35th Championships were held
in Santiago, Chile in 1985. Santiago has staged
the most Championships, seven, as well as three
unofficial ones (of which there were eight
between 1918 and 1957). Women's events were
held for the first time in Lima, Peru in 1939.

MOST GOLD MEDALS — ALL INDIVIDUAL EVENTS

MEN

11 Manuel Plaza (Chl) 4 C-C, 3 5000m & 10 000m, 1 Mar
  (1924–33)
11 Osvaldo Suarez (Arg) 5 10 000m, 4 5000m, 2 Mar
  (1956–67)
9 Valerio Vallania (Arg) 4 HJ, 3 110mh, 1 LJ & Dec
  (1924–29)
8 José Bento de Assis (Bra) 4 100m, 3 200m, 1 LJ
  (1937–45)
7 Vicente Salinas (Chl) 4 400m, 2 200m, 1 400mh
  (1929–35)
7 Ramon Sandoval (Chl) 4 800m, 1500m (1954–61)

WOMEN

8 Silvina das Gracas Pereira (Bra) 3 100m & 200m, 2 LJ
  (1967–75) (& 2 relay)
8 Wanda dos Santos (Bra) 6 80mh, 2 LJ (1949–61)
8 Alejandro Ramos (Chl) 4 800m & 1500m (1977–5)
7 Noemi Simonetto (Arg) 3 LJ, 2 100m & 80mh (1943–7)
7 Ingeborg Mello de Preiss (Arg) 4 SP, 3 DT (1945–52)
7 Conceicao Geremias (Bra) 3 Pen, 2 400mh, 1 100m &
  LJ (1975–83)

Others to have won one event four or more times:

MEN

6 Ricardo Heber (Arg) JT (1947–61)
5 Luis Brunetto (Arg) TJ (1924–31), José Carlos Jacques
  (Bra) (1963–71)
4 Federico Kleger (Arg) HT (1926–33), Leopoldo Ledesma
  (Arg) 1500m (1926–31), Juan Dyrzka (Arg) 400mh
  (1961–71), Hector Thomas (Ven) Dec (1963–71), Nelson
  Prudencio (Bra) TJ (1965–71), José Vallejo (Arg) HT

CHAMPIONSHIP BEST PERFORMANCES prior to 1987

MEN	hr:min:sec		
100m	10.39	Arnaldo de Oliveira (Bra)	1985
	10.1	Altevir Araujo (Bra)	1979
	10.1	Katsuiko Nakaia (Bra) (heat)	1981
200m	20.2	Paulo Roberto Correa (Bra)	1981
400m	46.06	Hector Daley (Pan)	1985
800m	1:46.90	Luis Migueles (Arg)	1985
1500m	3:42.16	Adauto Domingues (Bra)	1985
5000m	13:53.69	Omar Aguilar (Chl)	1985
10 000m	28:39.90	Omar Aguilar (Chl)	1985
Marathon	2:15:50	Juan Plagman (Chl)	1983
3000m steeple	8:44.6	Emilio Ulloa (Chl)	1983
110mh	13.87	Paulo Chiamulera (Bra)	1985
400mh	49.71	Paulo Chiamulera (Bra)	1985
4×100mR	39.6	Brazil	1981
4×400mR	3:07.96	Brazil	1985
	metres		
High jump	2.15	Milton Ruitano (Bra)	1985
Pole vault	4.90	Fernando Hoces (Chl)	1981
	4.90	Oscar Veit (Arg)	1985
Long jump	7.95	Joao Carlos de Oliveira (Bra)	1977
Triple jump	17.05	Joao Carlos de Oliveira (Bra)	1981
Shot	20.14	Gert Weil (Chl)	1985
Discus	54.00	Dagoberto Gonzalez (Col)	1967
Hammer	64.66	Daniel Raul Gomez (Arg)	1977
Javelin	75.10	Juan Francisco Garmendia (Arg)	1985
Decathlon	7454 pts	Tito Steiner (Arg)	1975
WOMEN	min:sec		
100m	11.73	Beatriz Allocco (Arg)	1977
	11.2	Carmela Bolivar (Per)	1981
200m	23.4	Silvana das Gracas (Bra)	1975
400m	53.25	Norfalia Carabali (Col)	1985
800m	2:03.54	Alejandro Ramos (Chl)	1985
1500m	4:20.16	Alejandro Ramos (Chl)	1985
3000m	9:29.67	Monica Regonesi (Chl)	1985
100mh	13.2	Beatriz Capotosto (Arg)	1983
400mh	59.45	Maria do Carmo Fialho (Bra)	1985
4×100mR	45.3	Brazil	1981
4×400mR	3:39.77	Brazil	1985
	metres		
High jump	1.88	Ana Maria Marcon (Bra)	1985
Long jump	6.26	Conceicao Geremias (Bra)	1983
Shot	15.01	Maria Reis Fernandes (Bra)	1983
Discus	51.56	Odete Valentina Domingos (Bra)	1975
Javelin	52.08	Monica Medeiros (Bra)	1985
Heptathlon	5701 pts	Conceicao Geremias (Bra)	1983

(1967–79), Joao Carlos de Oliveira (Bra) TJ (1974–81), Gert Weil (Chl) SP (1979–85)

WOMEN
4 Ilse Barends (Chl) (1939–47), Maria Cipriano Conceicao (Bra) HJ (1963–9), Rosa Molina (Chl) SP (1967–74)

SOUTH AMERICAN RECORDS

The most set at one event:

MEN
10 Erico Barney (Arg) PV 4.21m 1963 to 4.87m 1981
 9 Roberto Abugattas (Per) HJ 2.06m 1962 to 2.16m 1970
   (2 ties)
 9 José Vallejos (Arg) HT 59.21m 1964 to 66.04m 1974

WOMEN
 8 Ingeborg Mello de Preiss (Arg) DT 36.80m 1943 to
   42.10m 1949

The most over all events is 15 by Silvana das Gracas Pereira (Bra) 7 200m, 5 LJ, 3 100m at women's events (1969–75)

Other International Games and Championships

Balkan Games

The first official Balkan Games were contested in 1930 by Greece, Yugoslavia, Bulgaria and Romania, after experimental Games had been held the previous year. Turkey competed from the following year and Albania have also occasionally competed.

MOST TITLES WON AT ONE EVENT

MEN
10 Christos Mantikas (Gre) 110mh 1930–7, 1939–40
9 Stanko Lorger (Yug) 110mh 1953–61
8 Christos Mantikas (Gre) 400mh 1930–1, 1933–8
8 Nikolaos Syllas (Gre) DT 1932, 1934–40
8 Christos Papanikolaou (Gre) PV 1965–6, 1968–72, 1977

WOMEN
10 Ivanka Khristova (Bul) SP 1963, 1966–73, 1975
9 Iolanda Balas (Rom) HJ 1957–65
8 Ana Salagean (Rom) SP 1957–62, 1964–5
8 Viorica Viscopoleanu (Rom) LJ 1963–5, 1967–70, 1973

MOST TITLES AT ALL STANDARD INDIVIDUAL EVENTS

MEN
21 Christos Mantikas (Gre) 10 110mh, 8 400mh, 2 400m, 1 200m (1930–40)
14 Nikolaos Syllas (Gre) 8 DT, 6 DT (Greek style) (1932–40)

WOMEN
10 Ivanka Khristova (Bul) 10 SP (1963–75)

Central American & Caribbean Games

These Games have been held every four years, except 1942, since 1926 when they were first staged in Mexico City. The 15th Games will be held in Santiago, Dominican Republic in 1986.

MOST GOLD MEDALS — INDIVIDUAL EVENTS

MEN
5 Alberto Juantorena (Cub) 400m 1974–78, 800m 1978—82 (& 4×400mR 1974—82)
4 Rafael Fortun (Cub) 100m 1946–50–54, 200m 1946 (& 4×100mR 1950)
4 Silvio Leonard (Cub) 100m & 200m 1974–78 (& 4×100mR 1974)
4 Alvaro Mejia (Col) 1500m 1962–66, 5000m & 10 000m 1966
3 Arthur Wint (Jam) 800m 1938–46, 400m 1946 (& 4×400mR 1946)
3 Teodoro Flores (Gua) HJ 1959–62–66
3 Rolando Cruz (PR) PV 1959–62–66
3 José Cobo (Cub) 3000m steeple 1974–78–82
3 Alejandro Casanas (Cub) 110mh 1974–78–82 (4×100mR 1982)
3 Luis Delis (Cub) SP 1978–82, SP 1982

WOMEN
4 Miguelina Cobian (Cub) 100m 1962–66–70, 200m 1970 (& 4×100mR 1970)
4 Hilda Ramirez (Cub) JT 1962–66, SP 1966–78
3 Manuela Elejalde (Cub) 100mh 1970–74, Pen 1970
3 Aurelia Penton (Cub) 400m 1974–78, 800m 1978 (& 4×400mR 1978)
3 Carmen Romero (Cub) DT 1970–74–78

FOUR MEDALS AT ONE EVENT
(*G* — gold,
S — silver, *B* — bronze)

MEN Teodoro Flores HJ 3*G* as above, *S* 1974

WOMEN Carmen Romero DT 3*G* as above, *S* 1982, *B* 1966
Maria Betancourt (Cub) DT *G* 1978, *S* 1970–74–78

MOST MEDALS

MEN
10 George Rhoden (Jam) 4*G* 4×400mR 1946–54, 800m 1950, 4×100mR 1954; 4*S* 400m 1950–54, 4×100mR 1950, 800m 1954; 2*B* 400m 1946, 4×400mR 1950
8 Herb McKenley (Jam) 3*G* 4×400mR 1946, 200m & 400m 1950; 4*S* 100m & 400m 1946, 100m & 4×100mR 1950; 1*B* 200m 1946

WOMEN
8 Miguelina Cobian 5*G* as above; 3*S* 200m 1966, 4×100mR 1962–66

In addition to these Games, Central American & Caribbean Championships are held bienially and Caribbean Junior Championships, the Carita Games, have been held annually since 1972.

South East Asia Games

The SEAP (South East Asia Peninsular) Games were first held at Bangkok in 1959, and apart from 1963 have been held biennially since. 'Peninsular' was dropped from the title from 1977, when the Games were extended to include Philippines, Indonesia etc.

MEDAL TABLE BY NATIONS — Men and Women

NATION	G	S	B
Burma	140	116	70
Malaysia	125	127	118
Thailand	95	68	88
Singapore	41	74	68
Philippines*	21	27	32
Indonesia*	11	22	45
Cambodia	11	8	13
Vietnam	–	–	3
Brunei*	–	–	1

* Competed only since 1977.

MOST GOLD MEDALS — individual events:

MEN
12 Jimmy Crampton (Bur) 800m 1969–73–75–77, 1500m 1969–71–73–75–77–79, 5000m 1969–71

9 Nashatar Singh Sidhu (Mal) JT 1965–67–69–71–73–75,
SP 1965–67–69
7 Anat Ratanapol (Tha) 100m 1971–73–75, 200m
1971–73–75–77
6 Thant Zin (Bur) LJ 1973–75–77–79–81, TJ 1979

WOMEN
15 Jennifer Tin Lay (Bur)
SP 1967–69–71–73–75–77–79–81–83,
DT 1973–75–77–79–81–83,
6 Than Than (Bur) 200m 1975–77, 400m 1977–79,
400mh 1979–81

South Pacific Games

These Games were first held in Suva, Fiji in 1963.
They are now held every four years.

Alain Lazare of New Caledonia has been the
major star. He won the marathon in 1975, and
then twice won five distance running gold-medals,
with the 1500m, 5000m, 10 000m, marathon and
3000m steeplechase in both 1979 and 1983.

Eight gold medals have been won by Arnjolt Beer
(New Caledonia) 1966–83 and seven by Usaia
Sotutu (Fiji) 1969–75.

Women's World Games

These were organized by the first women's international governing body, the Fédération Sportive
Féminine Internationale (FSFI), at four-yearly
intervals from 1922 to 1934. Thereafter women's
events were included in the European Championships, and had by then been incorporated in the
Olympic Games.

Venues: 1922 Paris, 1926 Göteborg, 1930 Prague,
1934 London
Most wins: 4 Stanislawa Walasiewicz (Pol) 60m,
100m, 200m in 1930, 60m 1934
Most medals: 8 Kinue Hitomi (Jap) 1926: 1st
LJ & standing LJ, 2nd DT, 3rd 100y; 1930: 1st
LJ, 2nd Pen, 3rd 60m & JT

Arab Games and Championships

The first Pan-Arab Games were held at Alexandria, Egypt in 1953 and the first Arab Athletics
Championships were held at Damascus, Syria in
1977, with women's events included for the first
time in 1981. Games and Championships are now
held quadrennially and biennially respectively.

Maccabiah Games

These quadrennial Games, for athletes of the
Jewish faith, were first held in Tel Aviv in 1932.
Most wins: 11 Esther Rot (Isr), eight women's
individual and three relay 1969–77.

Mediterranean Games

These Games were first held in Alexandria, Egypt
in 1951, and have been held every four years since
then for those nations bordering the Mediterranean Sea.

Pietro Mennea (Ita) uniquely won gold medals at
four Games — 200m 1971, 100m and 200m 1975,
100m 1979, 200m 1983.

Pacific Conference Games

These Games, for nations bordering the Pacific
Ocean, have been held at the following venues:
1969 Tokyo, 1973 Toronto, 1977 Canberra, 1981
Christchurch, 1985 Berkeley. From 1987 the
Games are to be held biennially with China
joining Australia, Canada, Japan, New Zealand
and the USA as competing nations.

IAAF Golden Events

From 1979 a number of events were designated
as IAAF Golden Events, those in 1981–2 being
sponsored by Citizen Watches. The term arose
from the Golden Mile, which was conceived as
part of a professional venture, the Dubai International Track and Field Championships
announced in 1977. That never materialized but
the Golden Mile was staged as part of the Eight
Nations meeting in Tokyo on 25 Sep 1978.

'GOLDEN' WINNERS (AT VARIOUS VENUES)

Sprints	1979 James Sanford (USA) 100m 10.15 & 200m 20.39; 1981 Allan Wells (UK) 100m 10.15w & 200m 20.15w
1 mile	1978 Steve Ovett (UK) 3:55.5; 1979 Seb Coe (UK) 3:48.95; 1980 Steve Ovett 3:52.84; 1981 Seb Coe 3:47.33
5000m	1981 Barry Smith (UK) 13:21.14
10 000m	1979 Mike McLeod (UK) 27:39.76
Marathon	1982 Rodolfo Gomez (Mex) 2:11:49
Pole vault	1980 Serge Ferreira (Fra) 5.70m
Javelin	1979 Arto Härkönen (Fin) 90.18m

Ekiden Road Relay

Held annually in Japan since 1983 by six-women
national teams over the marathon distance.
Ekiden was the name given to the old Japanese
transportation system for government documents
and officials by relay of horses or men. The
women run legs of 5km, 10km, 5km, 10km,
7.195km, 5km.

Race record: 2:18:27 USSR team of Irina
Bondarchuk, Raisa Smekhnova, Yelena Tsukhlo,
Zoya Ivanova, Tatyana Sokolova, Olga Bonda-
renko in 1985.

IAAF/Mobil Grand Prix

In 1983 and 1984 various major invitational meetings around the world had been given the status of IAAF Permit meetings. In 1985 a start was made to bring such meetings together to provide a coherent competitive structure. Fifteen of them were included in the IAAF/Mobil Grand Prix, leading to a grand final in Rome on 7 Sep 1985.

In the first year half the standard events for men and women were included with the other half scheduled for 1986. Athletes scored points on a 9, 7, 6, 5, 4, 3, 2, 1 basis, with an extra six points for breaking a world record or three for tying one. The top eight athletes in each event, based on scoring from their best five meetings, qualified to compete in the Grand Prix Final, at which double points were given. In 1985 the top six individuals in each event earned prizes to be paid into their trust funds, administered by their national federations, of $10,000, $7000, $4000, $3000, $2000 and $1000. In addition the top four men and top four women over all events received bonuses of $25,000, $15,000, $10,000 and $5000.

Doug Padilla had a magnificent season in 1985, both indoors and out, winning eight major races at 3000m and eleven at 5000m, an astonishing record, and deservedly won the overall men's Grand Prix. (All-Sport)

IAAF/Mobil grand prix winners 1985

MEN points
200m	Calvin Smith (USA)	59
400m	Mike Franks (USA)	60
1500m	Steve Scott (USA)	46
5000m	Doug Padilla (USA)	63
110mh	Mike McKoy (Can)	52
Pole vault	Sergey Bubka (USSR)	59
Long jump	Mike Conley (USA)	49
Discus	Imrich Bugar (Cs)	52
Javelin	Tom Petranoff (USA)	55

Overall   1. Padilla 63, 2. Franks 60, 3. Bubka 59, 4. Smith 59

WOMEN points
100m	Alice Brown (USA)	46
800m	Jarmila Kratochvilova (Cs)	59
3000m	Mary Slaney (USA)	69
400mh	Judi Brown-King (USA)	63
High jump	Stefka Kostadinova (Bul)	63
Shot	Helena Fibingerova (Cs)	30

Overall   1. Slaney 69, 2. Kostadinova 63, 3. Brown-King 63, 4. Kratochvilova 59

THE GRAND PRIX MEETINGS

The following meetings were those that were included in the Grand Prix in 1985. The schedule of meetings may vary from year to year, and other important ones that may come into the Grand Prix in future years are listed at the end of this section.

World records set at each meeting are given; (w) denotes women's event.

Bruce Jenner Classic

Held at the San Jose City College Stadium, California, USA.

The meeting is named after the US decathlete who won the Olympic title in 1976, when he set his third world decathlon record with a score of 8617 points. The Jenner Classic was held annually in mid-April from 1979 to 1982, succeeding the San Jose Invitational meeting. From 1983 the meeting has moved to the last weekend in May.

World record set:
1979 110mh Renaldo Nehemiah (USA) 13.16

Prefontaine Classic

Held at Hayward Field, Eugene, Oregon, USA. The meeting is named after the great distance runner, who was tragically killed in a car accident on 30 May 1975 at the age of 24. Steve Prefontaine had placed fourth at 5000m in the 1972 Olympics and held US records at each distance from 2000m to 10 000m. He was undoubtedly the most popular US athlete, and there was a growing industry in 'Go Pre' sloganed T-shirts. The meeting was first held on 7 Jun 1975. Since then it has usually been held close to the anniversary of Prefontaine's death, although in 1984 it was held in late July. Eugene has become a great centre for distance runners, and fittingly these events have usually been particularly strong.

World records set:
1975 220y Don Quarrie (Jam) and Steve Williams (USA) 19.9 (hand timed) (Quarrie also 200m in 19.8).
1982 5000m (W) Mary Decker (USA) 15:08.26

Znamenskiy Memorial
Held at various venues in the USSR, most commonly Moscow (in the Lenin Stadium).

This meeting has been held annually from 1958, following an earlier meeting in 1949. Its title commemorates Serafim and Georgiy Znamenskiy, the Soviet distance running stars. Between them they attained eleven USSR titles: Serafim at 1500m in 1934, 5000m in 1934, 1936–8 and 1940, 10 000m in 1934, 1936 and 1938; Georgiy at 5000m and 10 000m in 1939. At these three distances they also set 18 Soviet records, with Serafim leading the way with bests at 5000m of 14:37.0 and 10 000m of 30:44.8 and Georgiy at 1500m with 3:57.9. The meeting has been predominantly a Soviet rather than an international meeting.

World records set: all (W)
1960 800m Lyudmila Lisenko (USSR) 2:04.3.
1962 400m Shin Keum Dan (NKo) 53.0.
1963 JT Elvira Ozolina (USSR) 59.78.
1964 LJ Tatyana Shchelkanova (USSR) 6.70.
1976 DT Faina Melnik (USSR) 70.50.
1980 1500m Tatyana Kazankina (USSR) 3:55.0.
1983 400mh Anna Ambraziene (USSR) 54.02.

Rosicky Memorial
Held in Prague, Czechoslovakia.

First held in 1947 in memory of Evzen Rosicky, the middle distance runner killed in the war. He had won Czechoslovak 800m titles each year from 1933 to 1937. His best 800m time was 1:54.6 in 1935. The stadium, originally opened in 1932 and used for the European Championships in 1978, was renamed the Evzen Rosicky Stadium in 1975.

World records set:
1965 100m(W) Eva Klobukowska (Pol) and Irena Kirszenstein (Pol) 11.1. (Klobukowska's record was later disallowed as she failed the femininity test.)

DN Galen
Held in Stockholm, Sweden at the Olympic Stadium, venue for more world records than any other stadium.

First held (as the Stockholm Games) in 1966. DN stands for *Dagens Nyheter*, which is a leading Stockholm daily newspaper.

World records set:
1966 5000m Ron Clarke (Aus) 13:16.0.
1975 3000mSt Anders Gärderud (Swe) 8:09.70.
1977 5000m Dick Quax (NZ) 13:12.86.
1981 DT Ben Plucknett (USA) 72.34 (not ratified due to earlier drugs disqualification).
1984 10 000m Fernando Mamede (Por) 27:13.81.

World Games
Held at Helsinki, Finland; the 'Maailmankisat' has been staged since 1961, originally biennially, in the Olympic Stadium, which was opened in 1938.

World records set:
1967 800m(W) Judy Pollock (Aus) 2:01.0.
1973 3000mSt Ben Jipcho (Ken) 8:13.91.
1977 10 000m Samson Kimobwa (Ken) 27:30.47.
1982 JT(W) Tiina Lillak (Fin) 72.40.

Nikaia
Held annually since 1976 at the Parc des Sports de l'Ouest, Nice, France.

The first world record set at the meeting came in the epic 1500m race in 1985 when Steve Cram (UK) beat Said Aouita (Mor) 3:29.67 to 3:29.71.

Peugeot-Talbot Games
Held annually since 1980 at Crystal Palace, London, UK.

World records set:
1984 PV Sergey Bubka (USSR) 5.90.
1984 2000m(W) Zola Budd 5:33.15 (not then an official distance)

Bislett Games
Held annually in the famous Bislett stadium, Oslo, Norway.

The stadium was opened in 1922 and used for the 1946 European Championships. The track has become famed for its quality races; the thrillingly intimate atmosphere and the balmy Scandinavian evening weather has made it a 'Mecca' for distance runners, including Coe, Ovett and Cram, who have all set records there. To 1985 45 world records had been set on the track including many of the most famous in history, from such pre-war performances as Jack Torrance (USA) 17.40m shot in 1934 and Forrest Towns (USA) 13.7 for 100mh in 1936, to Roger Moens (Bel) 1:45.7 800m in 1955, the first 90m javelin throw by Terje Pedersen (Nor) 91.72m in 1964, Ron Clarke (Aus) 27:39.89 10 000m in 1965, and to these at the Bislett Games (see also Oslo Games):

1976	2000m	John Walker (NZ) 4:51.4. (4:51.52 auto)
1978	3000m	Henry Rono (Ken) 7:32.1.
1979	800m	Sebastian Coe (UK) 1:42.33.
1980	1000m	Sebastian Coe (UK) 2:13.40.
1980	1 mile	Steve Ovett (UK) 3:48.8.
1984	5000m(W)	Ingrid Kristiansen (Nor) 14:58.89.
1985	10 000m(W)	Ingrid Kristiansen (Nor) 30:59.42.
1985	5000m	Said Aouita (Mor) 13:00.40.
1985	1 mile	Steve Cram (UK) 3:46.32.

IAC Meeting
Held annually since 1968 at Crystal Palace, London, except for 1975 when it was held at Meadowbank, Edinburgh. Organized by the International Athletes Club, and, until 1984, sponsored by the British bottlers of Coca-Cola.

World records set:
1968	2 miles	Ron Clarke (Aus) 8:19.6
1968	4×200mR(W)	UK (Maureen Tranter, Della James, Janet Simpson, Val Peat) 1:33.8
1970	4×880yR	Kenya (Naftali Bon, Hezekiah Nyamau, Thomas Saisi, Robert Ouko) 7:11.6
1970	30 000m	Jim Alder (UK) 1hr 31:30.4
1970	4×800mR(W)	UK (Rosemary Stirling, Georgina Craig, Pat Lowe, Sheila Carey) 8:25.0
1978	2 miles	Steve Ovett (UK) 8:13.51 (no longer official record)

Budapest Grand Prix
Held annually in the Nepstadion, Budapest, Hungary since 1978.

This has become a major meeting point for athletes from the Eastern bloc and those from the West. The Nepstadion was opened in 1953 and was the site of the World Student Games in 1965 and the European Championships in 1966.

The first world record set at the meeting was by Steve Cram (UK), 4:51.39 for 2000m in 1985.

Weltklasse in Zürich

First held in 1962, originally as the Züricher International. The Letzigrund stadium in Zürich, Switzerland has hosted, under the organization of the Leichtathletik Club Zürich, the most consistently high-class meeting on the international circuit in recent years. Three world records were set in Zürich at the forerunners of the Weltklasse: 100m in 10.0 by Armin Hary (GFR) in 1960, and 110mh in 13.2 by Martin Lauer (GFR) in 1959 and Willy Davenport (USA) in 1969.

World records set since then:
1973 110mh	Rod Milburn (USA)	13.1
1975 DT(W)	Faina Melnik (USSR)	70.20
1979 1500m	Sebastian Coe (UK)	3:32.03
1980 1500m(W)	Tatyana Kazankina (USSR)	3:52.47
1981 1 mile	Sebastian Coe (UK)	3:48.53
1981 100mh	Renaldo Nehemiah (USA)	12.93
1983 110m	Calvin Smith (USA)	9.97
1984 100m(W)	Evelyn Ashford (USA)	10.76
1985 1 mile(W)	Mary Slaney (USA)	4:16.71

ISTAF (Internationales Stadionfest)

Held in the Olympic Stadium, West Berlin, this is the longest established of all Grand Prix meetings. The ISTAF was first held in 1921 in the 1916 Olympic stadium and was revived in the 1936 Olympic stadium in 1937, when Luz Long set a European long jump record of 7.90m.

World records set:
1937 100mh(W)	Barbara Burke (SAf)	11.6
1939 LJ(W)	Christel Schulz (Ger)	6.12
1970 3000mSt	Kerry O'Brien (Aus)	8:21.98
1975 100m	Steve Williams (USA)	9.9
1975 110mh	Guy Drut (Fra)	13.0
1977 HJ(W)	Rosemarie Ackermann (GDR)	1.97 and 2.00
1978 400mh(W)	Krzystyna Kacperczyk (Pol)	55.44
1985 1500m	Said Aouita (Mor)	3:29.46

Internationales Leichtathletik-Sportfest—Köln

Organized by the club ASV Köln in the Kölner Stadion, Müngersdorf, GFR. The current series has been an annual event since 1976, although international meetings organized by the club date back to 1934.

World records set:
1983 1500m Sydney Maree (USA) 3:31.24.
1983 PV Pierre Quinon (Fra) 5.82.

Ivo van Damme Memorial

Held annually since 1977 in the Heysel Stadium, Brussels, Belgium, in memory of the great Belgian middle distance runner Ivo van Damme. He was killed in a car crash on 29 December 1976 at the age of 22, just a few months after winning Olympic silver medals at both 800m and 1500m.

World records set:
1979 1500m Steve Ovett(UK) 3:32.11.
1981 1 mile Sebastian Coe (UK) 3:47.33

Golden Gala

Held in Rome, Italy in the 1960 Olympic Stadium, which has also hosted the 1974 European Championships and the 1981 World Cup. First staged in 1980; the 1985 event was the IAAF/Mobil Grand Prix Final.

World records set:
1983 PV Thierry Vigneron (Fra) 5.83.
1984 PV Thierry Vigneron 5.91.
1984 PV Sergey Bubka (USSR) 5.94.

Other Major Invitational Meetings

Kusocinski Memorial

Held annually in Poland in June in memory of Janusz Kusocinski, the 1932 Olympic 10 000m champion. He was the first Polish male athlete to win an Olympic title and also the first to set a world record, 8:18.8 for 3000m in 1932. He set 22 Polish records from 1928 to 1939. He was shot by the Gestapo on 21 Jun 1940 for refusing to betray his colleagues, members of the Resistance. The meeting was first held at Zabrze in 1954, but the venue is usually Warsaw.

World records set:
1958 400m(W)	Maria Itkina (USSR)	53.6
1959 DT	Edmund Piatkowski (Pol)	59.91
1961 HJ(W)	Iolanda Balas (Rom)	1.88
1970 100mh(W)	Teresa Sukniwiewicz (Pol)	12.8
1972 100mh(W)	Pam Ryan (Aus)	12.5
1974 400m(W)	Irena Szewinska (Pol)	49.9
1976 400m(W)	Irena Szewinska (Pol)	49.75
1980 100mh(W)	Grazyna Rabsztyn (Pol)	12.36

Olympischer Tag

The major East German international meeting has been held annually since 1963 at various venues. It was added to the Grand Prix in 1986.

World records set:
1970 PV	Wolfgang Nordwig (GDR)	5.45
1974 LJ (W)	Sigrun Siegl (GDR)	6.99
1983 100m (W)	Marlies Göhr (GDR)	10.81
1984 JT	Uwe Hohn (GDR)	104.80
1984 200m (W)	Marita Koch (GDR)	21.71
1984 HJ (W)	Lyudmila Andonova (Bul)	2.07

Pravda Televizia Slovnaft—Bratislava

Held annually since 1957 in the Slovnaft Stadium, Bratislava, Czechoslovakia. It replaced the Rosicky Memorial on the Grand Prix 1986.

World record set:
1984 PV Sergey Bubka (USSR) 5.85

Oslo Games

Held annually in the Bislett Stadium, Oslo since 1975. Usually held a couple of weeks after the Bislett Games.

World records set:
1979 1 mile	Sebastian Coe (UK)	3:48.95
1980 1500m	Steve Ovett (UK)	3:32.09
1981 1000m	Sebastian Coe (UK)	2:12.18
1982 5000m	David Moorcroft (UK)	13:00.41

Internationales Leichtathletik–Abendsportfest Rot-Weiss

Held annually in the Oberwerth Stadium, Koblenz, GFR since 1952, attaining major international importance from 1977. Organized by the local club Rot-Weiss Koblenz.

World records set:
1980 1500m   Steve Ovett (UK) 3:31.36
1981 1 mile   Steve Ovett (UK) 3:48.40
1983 400mh   Edwin Moses (USA) 47.02

Citta di Rieti

Held annually since 1971.

World records set:
1982 1 mile(W) Maricica Puica (Rom) 4:17.44.
1983 1500m   Steve Ovett (UK) 3:30.77

Major International Marathons

Athens

The International Classical Marathon was held over the original Olympic course from Marathon to Athens approximately biennially from 1955 to 1979. There is now a race over the course every October.
Race record: 2:11:08 Bill Adcocks (UK) 1969

Avon

The Avon International Marathon for women was instigated by Kathy Switzer, who had forced her way into the 1967 Boston marathon. From 1978 to 1984 it was staged at various locations around the world, attracting strong fields of the best women runners.
Most wins: 3 Lorraine Moller (NZ) 1980, 1982, 1984
Race record: 2:26:26 Julie Brown (USA) 1983 at Los Angeles

Boston

The Boston marathon is the world's oldest annual race. It was first run by 15 men on 19 Apr 1897 from Metcalf's Mill in Ashland to the Irvington Oval over a distance of 24 miles 1232 yards (39 750m). Since then it has been run every year on or about 19 Apr, Patriot's Day, which honours the famed ride of Paul Revere through Boston. Except for changes at the start and finish the course has remained the same, with the full marathon distance first being run in 1927.
The first field of over 1000 was in 1969 and the record was 7910 plus about 2000 'gate-crashers' in 1979, before qualifying standards brought the numbers down. In recent years the race has not attracted the same quality of top-class runners as of yore, and this forced the promotors to offer prizes from 1986 to restore the race's prestige.
Kathy Switzer (USA) contested the race in 1967, although the race director tried to prevent her, but her pioneering efforts helped force the acceptance of women runners, and they were admitted officially for the first time in 1972. In 1983 Joan Benoit smashed the women's world record.

Most wins:
MEN   7 Clarence De Mar (USA) 1911,
            1922–4, 1927–8, 1930; 4 Gérard Côté
            (Can) 1940, 1943–4, 1948; 4 Bill
            Rodgers (USA) 1975, 1978–80
WOMEN   2 Miki Gorman (USA) 1974, 1977; Joan
            Benoit (USA) 1979, 1983

Race records:
MEN   2:08:51 Alberto Salazar (USA) 1982
WOMEN   2:22:43 Joan Benoit (USA) 1983
John A. Kelley won twice, 1935 and 1945, was second seven times, in the top ten 18 times, and ran the race 54 times from 1928 to 1985.

Chicago

First held in 1977 as the Mayor Daley Marathon, world-class fields have been attracted annually since 1983. Record prize-money succeeded in luring away many top runners from New York which is held annually in close proximity. By setting a world best time in 1984 Steve Jones enriched his trust fund by some $97,500. In 1985 the total race fund was reported as $270,000, including $35,000 for men's and women's winners and $50,000 if a world record were to be set. By then, however, the prize funds for New York and, for 1986, Boston, which had not previously paid runners, had topped even that figure. As it happened, both men's and women's winners in 1985 narrowly missed the world's best: Steve Jones by just one second, and Joan Benoit by 15 seconds. Jones ran the first half in an amazing 1:01:43.

Winners from 1983:

MEN   1983 Joseph Nzau (Ken) 2:09:45, 1984
            Steve Jones (UK) 2:08:05, 1985 Steve
            Jones (UK) 2:07:13.
WOMEN   1983 Rosa Mota (Por) 2:31:12, 1984 Rosa
            Mota (Por) 2:26:01, 1985 Joan Benoit
            (USA) 2:21:21.

Fukuoka

The Asahi marathon was first run in 1947 at Kumamoto. It was first held at Fukuoka in 1951, and the race has been held there every year since 1964, in early December. Over the past 20 years it has consistently attracted world-class fields. Derek Clayton (Aus) set a world record of 2:09:37 in 1967.

Most wins: 4 Frank Shorter (USA) 1971–4
              4 Toshihiko Seko 1978–80, 1983
Race record: 2:08:18 Rob de Castella (Aus) 1981

Kosice

Held annually in Czechoslovakia since 1924, with the exception of 1938 to 1944. The race is now named the International Peace Marathon. Women took part for the first time in 1980, which was the 50th running of the race and the 750th anniversary of the founding of the town of Kosice.

Most wins:
MEN   4 Jozsef Galambos (Hun) 1927–8, 1932–3
            3 Pavel Kantorek (Cs) 1958, 1962, 1964
WOMEN   2 Christa Vahlensieck (GFR) 1981, 1984

Race records:
MEN   2:13:35 Chun Son Goe (NKo) 1978
WOMEN   2:34:41 Raisa Sadreydinova (USSR) 1983

London

The first London marathon was run on 29 Mar 1981. Organized and inspired by the 1956 Olympic steeplechase gold medallist, Chris Brasher, it caught the public's imagination in an astonishing way, and was a great success. 7055 runners started and 6418 finished the course in that first year. Those totals were left far behind in the ensuing years as the organizers strived to cater for the maximum numbers possible in this hugely oversubscribed event, which has quickly become established as one of the major annual sporting occasions. In 1985 15 841 runners finished of some 17 500 starters. The standards at the top have been most impressive, with a world record number of 93 men under 2:20 in 1983 while the Norwegians Grete Waitz and Ingrid Kristiansen have set women's world records in the race, but just as importantly it is also a race for every man and woman—truly a folk festival of running.

Winners:

MEN	1981 Dick Beardsley (US) & Inge Simonsen (Nor) 2:11:48, 1982 Hugh Jones (UK) 2:09:24, 1983 Mike Gratton (UK) 2:09:43, 1984 Charlie Spedding (UK) 2:09:57, 1985 Steve Jones (UK) 2:08:16
WOMEN	1981 Joyce Smith (UK) 2:29:57, 1982 Joyce Smith 2:29:43, 1983 Grete Waitz (Nor) 2:25:29, 1984 Ingrid Kristiansen (Nor) 2:24:26, 1985 Ingrid Kristiansen 2:21:06

Montreal

The first Montreal marathons were staged in 1979 in conjunction with the World Cup, held in the city that year. There were two races, for elite runners and a mass event attracting over 8500 runners. These races have been combined since 1982. Kebede Balcha (Eth) is the only double winner and has now won four times: 1979, 1981, 1983, 1985. He set the race record of 2:10:03 in 1983. The women's race record is 2:30:58 by Patti Catalano (USA) in 1980.

New York

Fred Lebow has organized the New York marathon annually from 1970. The race was run in Central Park each year until 1976, when to celebrate the US Bicentennial the course was changed to a route through all five boroughs of the city. In the earlier years the fields were small, but that changed in 1976, when, at the start of the marathon boom, the race attracted 2090 starters, seven times more than the previous year. There followed world record fields of 4823 in 1977 and 9875 in 1978, 11 503 in 1979 increasing to further records of 14 012 in 1980, 14 496 in 1981 and 15 881 in 1985. By then the New York Marathon was truly established and it has attracted many of the world's greatest runners.

In 1984 the course was re-measured and that used from 1981 to 1983 was found to be 170y (155m) short of the full marathon distance, equivalent to about 30 sec at top men's pace. That sadly meant that the world best time set by Alberto Salazar in 1981 of 2:08:13 was invalidated.

Winners since 1976:

MEN	Bill Rodgers (USA) 1976 2:10:10, 1977 2:11:29, 1978 2:12:12, 1979 2:11:42; Alberto Salazar (USA) 1980 2:09:41, 1981 2:08:13, 1982 2:09:29; Rod Dixon (NZ) 1983 2:08:59; Orlando Pizzolato (Ita) 1984 2:14:53, 1985 2:11:34.
WOMEN	Miki Gorman (USA) 1976 2:39:11, 1977 2:43:10; Grete Waitz (Nor) 1978 2:32:30, 1979 2:27:33, 1980 2:25:41; Allison Roe (NZ) 1981 2:25:29; Grete Waitz 1982 2:27:14, 1983 2:27:00, 1984 2:29:30, 1985 2:28:34.

Polytechnic Harriers

Second only to Boston as a long-running series, the Poly marathon has sadly declined in importance in recent years. The race was first run in 1909 from Windsor to Stamford Bridge for a silver trophy presented by the *Sporting Life* to encourage British marathoners, who had fared badly in the previous year's Olympic marathon. The destination changed to the White City Stadium from 1932–7, before reverting to Chiswick, the home of the organizing club, the Polytechnic Harriers. From 1973 traffic conditions forced the organizers to hold the race around Windsor Great Park, rather than running to London. Eight world men's marathon records were set in the race, including three by Jim Peters (UK).

Most wins:	8 Sam Ferris (UK) 1925–9, 1931–3; 4 Jim Peters 1951–4
Race record:	2:12:00 Morio Shigematsu (Jap) 1965

A women's race was first held in 1978. Gillian Adams won twice, 1978 and 1980, and the race record was set at 2:36:12 by Kath Binns (UK) in 1982.

Rotterdam

Since its inception in 1981 Rotterdam has not attempted to match the numbers of the world's largest races, but has aimed to attract élite fields. It has certainly succeeded in producing races of the highest quality, including the clash between Alberto Salazar (USA) and Rob de Castella (Aus) in 1983, when the Australian won, but by only two seconds from Carlos Lopes (Por), with Salazar fifth.

Carlos Lopes set a world record in 1985.

Winners:

MEN	1981 John Graham (UK) 2:09:28, 1982 Rodolfo Gomez (Mex) 2:11:57, 1983 Rob de Castella 2:08:37, 1984 Gidamis Shahanga (Tan) 2:11:12, 1985 Carlos Lopes 2:07:12.
WOMEN	1983 Rosa Mota (Por) 2:32:27, 1984 Carla Beurskens (Hol) 2:34:56, 1985 Wilma Rusman (Hol) 2:35:32.

Australian Darren Clark (1) beat Derek Redmond (42) in 1985 to complete a hat-trick of English AAA titles before his 20th birthday. No. 47 is Alan Slack. (All-Sport)

Australia

The first properly organized club was Sydney Harriers (later AAC) in 1872. The Australian Athletic Union was formed in 1897, ten years after the first state governing body, that of New South Wales. The latter was also the first state to hold championships, starting with just one event, at 1000 yards, in 1888. The Australian Women's Athletic Union was founded in 1932, three years after Queensland and Victoria had been the first states to have women's governing bodies.

NATIONAL CHAMPIONSHIPS

Australasian Championships were held from 1893 to 1927, before becoming simply Australian Championships. Until 1937 they were held irregularly, approximately every two years. Men's championships were revived in 1947, since when they have been annual.

Australian women's championships were first staged in 1930, then in 1932–3, 1935–7, 1940, bienially 1948–62 and annually since then.

From 1966 (men) and 1967 (women) championships have been at metric distances. In the tables that follow imperial distances have been combined with their metric equivalents.

Most titles won at each event
(Includes all who won 7 or more titles)

MEN

Event	Titles	Athlete
100m/100y	7	Hec Hogan 1952–8
200m/220y	5	Peter Norman 1966–70
400m/440y	5	Kevan Gosper 1956–60
800m/880y	5	Ralph Doubell 1965–7, 1969–70
1500m/1M	5	Mike Hillardt 1980, 1982–5
5000m/3M	5	Ron Clarke 1965–9
10 000m/6M	4	Dave Power 1958–60, 1962
	4	Dave Fitzsimons 1976–9
Marathon	4	Derek Clayton 1967–8, 1971, 1973
	4	John Farrington 1969–70, 1974–5
3000m steeple	7	Kerry O'Brien 1966–7, 1969–73
	7	Peter Larkins 1976–81, 1983
110mh	5	Ray Weinberg 1948, 1950–3
400mh	7	Geoffrey Goodacre 1948–51, 1955–7
	7	Gary Knoke 1965–7, 1970–3
High jump	10	Lawrie Peckham 1965–7, 1969–75
	7	Charles Porter 1955–61
Pole vault	12	Ray Boyd 1970, 1972–6, 1978–83
Long jump	6	Gary Honey 1979, 1981–5

Triple jump	6	Ian Tomlinson 1957–9, 1962, 1964–5
	6	Phil May 1966–9, 1971, 1973
Shot	7	Peter Hanlin 1952–8
	7	Warwick Selvey 1960–64, 1966–7
Discus	11	Warwick Selvey 1960, 1962–7, 1970–3
Hammer	12	Richard Leffler 1959–67, 1969–70, 1973
	7	Gus Puopolo 1974–9, 1981
Javelin	9	Nick Birks 1958–61, 1963–6, 1974
Decathlon	9	Peter Hadfield 1976–7, 1979–85
3kmW	7	Don Keane 1950–4, 1957–8
	7	Ross Hayward 1966, 1971–6
10kmW*	7	Ted Allsopp 1948, 1950, 1952–3, 1955, 1957, 1959
20kmW	3	Willi Sawall 1976, 1978, 1980
50kmW	4	Bob Gardiner 1964, 1966, 1968, 1971

WOMEN

100m/100y	6	Raelene Boyle 1970–3, 1976–7
200m/220y	6	Raelene Boyle 1970–3, 1976–7
	6	Denise Boyd 1974–5, 1978–80, 1983
400m/440y	4	Judy Pollock 1965–7, 1972
800m/880y	5	Charlene Rendina 1973–6, 1979
1500m	4	Jenny Orr 1971–4
3000m	2	Phyllis Lazarakis 1977–8
	2	Donna Gould 1984–5
80mh	7	Pam Kilborn 1963–9
100mh	5	Pam Gillies 1972, 1977, 1979–82
400mh	4	Debbie Flintoff 1982–5
High jump	6	Christine Stanton 1976–7, 1980–1, 1983, 1985
Long jump	4	Erica Hooker 1973–6
	4	Lynette Jacenko 1972, 1977–9
Shot	9	Gael Martin 1976–81, 1983–5
	8	Jean Roberts 1963–70
Discus	7	Gael Martin 1977–81, 1983–4
Javelin	7	Petra Rivers 1970–1, 1974, 1981–4
Pen/Hep	5	Helen Frith 1959, 1962, 1964–6
	5	Erica Hooker 1973–7
	5	Glynis Nunn 1978, 1980–2, 1984
5kmW	6	Sue Cook 1977–8, 1980–1, 1984–5

*Discontinued event.

MOST NATIONAL CHAMPIONSHIP TITLES—at all standard individual events:

MEN
18 Warwick Selvey (1960–73) 11 DT, 7 SP

WOMEN
16 Pam Kilborn/Ryan (1963–72) 7 80mh; 3 LJ, Pen; 1 100y, 100mh, 200mh
16 Gael Martin (1976–85) 9 SP, 7 DT
14 Raelene Boyle (1970–82) 6 100m, 200m; 2 400m
13 Jean Roberts (1963–70) 8 SP, 5 DT

Firsts

Olympic champion: Edwin Flack 800m and 1500m 1896
Olympic medallist (woman): Shirley Strickland third 100m and 80mh 1948
Olympic champion (woman): Marjorie Jackson 100m and 200m 1952

Czechoslovakia

The oldest club, AC Praha, was formed in 1890 and the AAU of Bohemia was founded in 1897. Bohemian athletes competed in the Olympic Games of 1900, 1908 and 1912, prior to Czechoslovakia being established as an independent nation in 1918.

NATIONAL CHAMPIONSHIPS

First held for men in 1907 in the 'Czech Crown Territories'. Czechoslovak national championships were first held in 1919 for men and 1923 for women.

Most Titles Won at Each Event
(Includes all who won 7 or more titles)

MEN

100m	6	Miroslav Horcic 1941, 1945, 1948–50, 1952
200m	7	Vilem Mandlik 1956, 1958, 1960–2, 1964–5
400m	8	Josef Trousil 1956–7, 1960–2, 1964–6
800m	10	Jozef Plachy 1968–77
1500m	5	by four men
5000m	8	Jozef Koscak 1927–34
	8	Emil Zatopek 1945–8, 1950, 1952–4
10 000m	6	Jozef Koscak 1925, 1929–32, 1934
Marathon	7	Pavel Kantorek 1956, 1958–9, 1961–2, 1964, 1967
3000m steeple	6	Bohumir Zhanal 1957–8, 1961–4
110mh	12	Otakar Jandera 1923–34
400mh	6	Miroslav Kodejs 1970, 1973–4, 1978–9, 1981
High jump	6	Jiri Lansky 1954, 1958–60, 1963–4
Pole vault	8	Rudolf Tomasek 1961–7, 1971
Long jump	10	Jan Leitner 1975–82, 1984–5
	9	Jiri Hofmann 1928–36
Triple jump	7	Jiri Vycichlo 1968, 1971, 1973–4, 1976–8
Shot	12	Jiri Skobla 1951–4, 1956–8, 1960–2, 1964, 1966
	11	Frantisek Douda 1928–37, 1939
	8	Jaroslav Brabec 1971–3, 1975–6, 1979, 1981–2
Discus	13	Ludvik Danek 1963–9, 1971–6
	9	Jaroslav Knotek 1936–7, 1941–4, 1946–8
	8	Imrich Bugar 1978–85
Hammer	13	Jaroslav Knotek 1935–7, 1939–44, 1946–8, 1950
	10	Josef Prusa 1925–34
Javelin	9	Milos Vojtek 1958–9, 1961–2, 1966, 1968–71
Decathlon	4	by four men
20kmW	10	Alexandr Bilek 1962–4, 1966–72
50kmW	11	Josef Dolezal 1946–7, 1949–56, 1960

WOMEN

100m	6	Eva Gleskova 1964, 1966–9, 1972
200m	7	Libuse Strejckova 1953–9
	7	Eva Gleskova 1962–4, 1966, 1968–9, 1972
400m	4	Bedriska Kulhava 1955–7, 1959
	4	Anna Chmelkova 1964, 1966, 1968–9
	4	Jarmila Kratochvilova 1976, 1982–4
800m	11	Bedriska Kulhava 1951–61
1500m	5	Bozena Sudicka 1973–5, 1977, 1979
3000m	4	Bozena Sudicka 1974–5, 1977, 1979
100mh	8	Monika Schönauerova 1972–9
400mh	3	Anna Filickova 1982–4

High jump	12	Olga Davidova 1949–60
Long jump	8	Eva Suranova 1965–9, 1972, 1974–5
Shot	15	Helena Fibingerova 1970–9, 1981–5
	7	Jaroslava Kritkova 1945–50, 1952
Discus	8	Libuse Dudova 1934–5, 1939–44
	8	Jirina Nemcova 1960–7
Javelin	13	Dana Zatopkova 1946–52, 1954–6, 1958–60
	7	Elena Burgarova 1977, 1980–5
Pen/Hep	8	Marcela Koblasova 1976–81, 1983–4

MOST TITLES—at all standard individual events:

MEN
26 Jaroslav Knotek (1935–50) 13 HT, 9 DT, 4 SP
25 Josef Dolezal (1946–60) 11 50kmW, 8 25kmW, 4 10kmW, 2 20kmW
18 Otakar Jandera (1922–34) 12 110mh, 4 TJ, 1 HJ & LJ

WOMEN
27 Olga Davidova (1949–60) 12 HJ, 7 Pen, 3 200m, 2 100m & 80mh, 1 LJ
18 Anna Janecka (1938–42) 5 Pen, 4 LJ, 3 80mh, 2 SP & JT, 1 100m & HJ (also 4 triathlon)
15 Stefania Pekarova (1933–7) 4 SP & JT, 3 LJ, 2 200m, 1 100m & Pen (also 2 triathlon)
15 Bedriska Kulhava (1950–61) 11 800m, 4 400m
15 Helena Fibingerova (1970–85) 15 SP

CZECHOSLOVAK RECORDS

The most set at one event:

MEN
20 Jiri Skobla SP 16.20m 1951 to 18.52m 1963 (3 ties)
15 Rudolf Tomasek PV 4.50m 1960 to 5.00m 1966 (1 tie)
13 Frantisek Douda SP 14.04m 1928 to 16.20m 1932
12 Milan Cecman 110mh 14.2 1962 to 13.9 1967 (9 ties)

WOMEN
25 Helena Fibingerova SP 16.32m 1970 to 22.32m 1977 (2 ties)
19 Eva Gleskova 100m 11.9 1962 to 11.0 1971 (11 ties)
18 Miroslava Trkalova 80mh 11.7 1954 to 11.0 1958 (12 ties)
17 Dana Zatopkova JT 38.07m 1948 to 56.67m 1958
13 Jaroslava Kritkova SP 11.07m 1945 to 13.75m 1952

Most at all standard events:

MEN
42 Emil Zatopek (1944–54) 10 5000m, 9 3000m, 7 10 000m, 5 2000m, 2 each at 20km, 25km, 10M, 15M, 1 Hr; 1 at 30km (also 3 at 6M)

WOMEN
26 Eva Gleskova (1926–72) 19 100m, 7 200m (also 8 60m, 4 100y, 14 4×100mR for grand total of 52)
24 Jarmila Kratochvilova (1978–83) 10 200m, 9 400m, 3 100m, 2 800m (also 7 each at 4×100mR, 4×400mR)

Firsts

Olympic champion: Emil Zatopek 10000m 1948
Olympic champion (woman): Dana Zatopkova JT 1952
Olympic medallist: Frantisek Janda-Suk (Bohemia) second DT 1900
European champion: Emil Zatopek 5000m & 10 000m 1950
International match: (women) 21 May 1922 at Paris, v France; (men) 5–6 Aug 1922 at Prague, v Poland & Yugoslavia
World best: Frantisek Janda-Suk (Bohemia) DT 39.42m 1901
Women's world best: Marie Mejzlikova I 50m 6.6 1920
IAAF world record: Frantisek Douda SP 16.04m 1931

Jiri Skobla won 68 successive shot competitions 1952–5, including the 1954 European title. (Keystone)

Jarmila Kratochvilova set her first national record at the age of 27, and world records at 400m and 800m at 32. (ASP)

Finland

Athletics has long been the major sport of Finland, whose athletes have achieved greater success per capita than any other nation, at least until the rise of the GDR. Finland's golden age was the 1912–36 era, when they were runners-up to the USA in the medal tables at each Olympic Games. Particularly strong traditions were built up in javelin throwing and distance running. This success is, however, at men's athletics, Finnish women achieving rather less until recently.

Greg Foster (l) won the 110mh gold and Arto Bryggare (r) the silver at the 1983 World Championships. The Finn has been one of the few Europeans to vie with the top US hurdlers. (ASP)

NATIONAL CHAMPIONSHIPS

First held at Tampere in 1907, when the country was still a part of the Russian Empire (independence achieved 1917). They were not held in the war year of 1941. Women's championships were held from 1913 to 1923, and from 1945.

Most Titles Won at Each Event
(Includes all who won 7 or more titles)
MEN

100m	5	Nils Kronqvist 1939–40, 1942–3, 1945
	5	Antti Rajamäki 1973–5, 1977–8
200m	8	Ossi Karttunen 1966–70, 1973–4, 1977
400m	7	Bertel Storskrubb 1936, 1942–7
800m	6	Olavi Salonen 1958–63
1500m	6	Olavi Salonen 1959–63, 1965
5000m	4	Albin Stenroos 1912–3, 1915–6
	4	Paavo Nurmi 1920–1, 1926–7
	4	Viljo Heino 1943–6
	4	Martti Vainio 1978, 1980–2*
10 000m	6	Martti Vainio 1977–8, 1980–3*
Marathon	4	Mikko Hietanen 1945–8
	4	Håkan Spik 1976–8, 1983
3000m steeple	7	Tapio Kantanen 1972–7, 1980
110mh	10	Bengt Sjöstedt 1927–31, 1933–7
	9	Arto Bryggare 1977–85
	7	Erik Wilen 1921–6, 1932
	7	Väinö Suvivuo 1939, 1945, 1948–50, 1952–3
400mh	12	Erik Wilen 1918–20, 1923–8, 1930–2
	8	Bertel Storskrubb 1937, 1940, 1942–47
High jump	6	Nils Nicklen 1940, 1943, 1945–6, 1949, 1951
	6	Eero Salminen 1953, 1955, 1957–60
Pole vault	8	Eeles Landström 1953–60
	8	Antti Kalliomäki 1971–5, 1977–8, 1982
Long jump	10	Jorma Valkama 1951–9, 1961
Triple jump	9	Vilho Tuulos 1919–25, 1927–8
	7	Onni Rajasaari 1933–9
	7	Pentti Kuukasjärvi 1971–2, 1974–8
Shot	11	Elmer Niklander 1909–10, 1912–8, 1920, 1924
	9	Reijo Stahlberg 1973–4, 1976–82
	7	Sulo Bärlund 1935–8, 1940, 1946, 1948
Discus	11	Elmer Niklander 1909–18, 1920 (double or single-handed)
	7	Pentti Repo 1959–60, 1962–6
	7	Pentti Kahma 1970–1, 1973–6, 1978
Hammer	7	Erik Eriksson 1919, 1921–4, 1927–8
Javelin	8	Matti Järvinen 1929–31, 1933–5, 1940, 1942
Decathlon	6	Hannes Sonck 1939–40, 1942–4, 1948

20kmW	12	Reima Salonen 1973–83, 1985
	8	Pentti Kallionpää 1955–61, 1963
50kmW	10	Paavo Saira 1954, 1956, 1958–60, 1962–4, 1969, 1971
	9	Reima Salonen 1974–5, 1977–9, 1981–2, 1984–5

*Vainio stripped of 5000m and 10 000m titles won in 1984 following his suspension for drug usage at the subsequent Olympic Games.

WOMEN

100m	9	Mona-Lisa Pursiainen 1967–70, 1973–7
	7	Olga Virtanen 1916–7, 1919–23
200m	6	Aulikki Jaakkola 1955–60
400m	8	Eeva Haimi 1962–9
800m	6	Eila Mikola 1956–60, 1965
1500m	5	Sinikka Tyynelä 1971–3, 1977–8
3000m	3	Sinikka Tyynelä 1974, 1977–8
10 000m	2	Tuija Toivonen 1984–5
Marathon	3	Sinikka Keskitalo 1983–5
80mh/100mh	12	Sirkka Norrlund 1961–72
400mh	6	Tuija Helander 1977, 1980, 1982–5
High jump	6	Susanne Sundqvist 1973–8
Long jump	8	Maire Osterdahl 1949–56
Shot	8	Meeri Saari 1948–55
Discus	8	Marjatta Kuuluvainen 1963–70
Javelin	5	Raija Mustonen 1961, 1963, 1965–7
Pen/Hep	5	Anne Kyllönen 1979–83
5kmW	9	Sirkka Oikarinen 1976–82, 1984–5

MOST TITLES—at all standard individual events:

MEN
29 Erik Wilen (1918–32) 12 400mh, 7 110mh, 6 400m, 2 800m, 1 100m, 1 200m. Vilen won a further 21 relay titles, for a grand total of 50.
27 Elmer Niklander (1909–24) 11 SP double-handed (and 7 single), 11 DT double (and 5 single), 5 HT. Total 44 titles including other discontinued events.
24 Bertel Storskrubb (1936–47) 8 400mh, 7 400m, 7 200mh, 2 200m

WOMEN
23 Sirkka Norrlund (1961–72) 12 80mh/100mh, 4 200mh, 3 200m, 3 Pen, 1 100m
14 Mona-Lisa Pursiainen (1967–77) 9 100m, 4 200m, 1 400m (24 including relays)

FINNISH RECORDS

The most set at one event:
MEN
15 Matti Yrjölä SP 16.61m 1958 to 20.49m 1973
13 Eeles Landström PV 4.32m 19&4 to 4.57m 1958
11 Pentti Kahma DT 59.80m 1969 to 66.82m 1975
11 Arto Bryggare 110mh 14.06 1976 to 13.35 1984

WOMEN
12 Inkeri Lehtonen DT 42.60m 1955 to 48.75m 1963
11 Tiina Lillak JT 59.16m 1980 to 74.76m 1983

Most at all standard events:
MEN
20 Paavo Nurmi (1920–30) 5 3000m; 4 1500m; 2 at 1M,
2000m, 5000m & 10000m; 1 800m, 1Hr, 20km. 33
including discontinued events and also two relay records
1920–33.
28 Hannes Kolehmainen (1910–22) 5 3000m, 5000m &
10 000m; 3 1500m; 2 1M, 2000m, 1Hr, 25km; 1
20 km & 30 km. 4 more at discontinued imperial events.

WOMEN
20 Mona-Lisa Pursiainen (1966–73) 10 200m, 9 100m,
3 400m. Also 19 relay records.

Firsts

Olympic champion: Werner Järvinen DT (Greek style) 1906
Olympic medal (woman): Kaisa Parviainen second JT 1948
International match: 24 Sep 1922 at Paris, v France

France

The first French running club was formed in Paris
in 1875, although Englishmen had held a meeting
at Boulogne in September 1866. The famous
Racing Club was formed in 1882, adding 'de
France' in 1885.

NATIONAL CHAMPIONSHIPS

The first championships were held at five running
events at Croix-Catelan on 29 Apr 1888. Field
events were first included in 1892, and the first
women's events were held in 1918. The championships were not held in the war years of
1915–6 and 1940.

Most titles won at each event
(Includes all who won 7 or more titles)

MEN
100m	5	René Valmy 1939, 1941–3, 1945
200m	6	André Mourlon 1922–6, 1929
400m	6	Gaston Fery 1919–24
800m	9	Marcel Hansenne 1939, 1941–5, 1947–8, 1950
1500m	7	Jacques Keyser (Hol) 1907–10, 1913–4, 1917
5000m	8	Alain Mimoun 1947, 1949, 1951–6
10 000m	12	Alain Mimoun 1947, 1949–59
Marathon	6	Alain Mimoun 1958–60, 1964–6
3000m steeple	8	Guy Texereau 1960, 1962–8
110mh	11	Gabriel Sempe 1923–31, 1933, 1935
	8	Guy Drut 1970–6, 1980
400mh	6	Prudent Joye 1936–9, 1941, 1943
High jump	6	Géo André 1907–9, 1911, 1914, 1919
	6	Georges Damitio 1947–9, 1951–3
Pole vault	11	Pierre Ramadier 1928–32, 1934, 1936–9, 1942
	8	Victor Sillon 1947–51, 1954, 1956, 1958
Long jump	6	Robert Paul 1931–6
Triple jump	11	Eric Battista 1955–60, 1962–6
Shot	8	Pierre Colnard 1960–1, 1963, 1965–7, 1969–70
	8	Raoul Paoli 1912, 1919–20, 1922–6
	7	André Tison 1905, 1907–8, 1910–1, 1913–4
	7	Edouard Dehour 1927–8, 1931–2, 1934–5, 1941
Discus	11	Pierre Alard 1956, 1959–65, 1967–9
	9	André Tison 1907–14, 1920
	8	Jules Noel 1928–30, 1932, 1934, 1936, 1938–9
	8	Frédéric Piette 1973–4, 1976–81
Hammer	15	Guy Husson 1954–68
	8	Robert Saint Pe 1926, 1928, 1931–6
Javelin	10	Michel Macquet 1953, 1955–61, 1964–5
Decathlon	8	Yves Le Roy 1971–5, 1977–9
20kmW	13	Gérard Lélièvre 1972–84
50kmW	10	Gérard Lélièvre 1973–7, 1979–83
Cross-country	7	Noel Tijou 1967, 1969–71, 1973, 1975, 1977

WOMEN
100m	8	Sylviane Telliez 1968–75
200m	6	Marguerite Gaspard 1934–9
	6	Sylviane Telliez 1967, 1969–73
400m	3	Maryvonne Dupereur 1959, 1963–4
	3	Monique Noirot 1965–7
800m	6	Nicole Goullieux 1952–3, 1957–9, 1962
	6	Maryvonne Dupereur 1960, 1963–4, 1967–9
1500m	3	Véronique Renties 1978–80
3000m	4	Joëlle Debrouwer 1975, 1978, 1980–1
Marathon	2	Chantal Langlacé 1982, 1984
	2	Sylviane Levesque 1983, 1985
80mh/100mh	6	Denise Guenard 1954–5, 1960–2, 1965
400mh	4	Dominique Le Disses 1980–1, 1983–4
High jump	5	Simone Peirone 1951–2, 1954–6
	5	Marie-Christine Debourse 1971, 1974–7
Long jump	7	Odette Ducas 1962, 1968–73
Shot	11	Léone Bertimon 1973–80, 1982–4
	8	Lucienne Velu 1928, 1930–5, 1937
Discus	14	Lucienne Velu 1925–30, 1932–7, 1939, 1942
	8	Marthe Bretelle 1957, 1960–6
Javelin	10	Evelyne Pinard 1947–53, 1955–7
	7	Yolande Behr 1932–8
Pen/Hep	9	Denise Guenard 1953–4, 1961, 1963–8
	7	Florence Picaut 1974, 1978–83
5kmW	5	Suzanne Griesbach 1981–5
10kmW	3	Suzanne Griesbach 1982–4
Cross-country	8	Joëlle Debrouwer 1975–9, 1981, 1983–4

MOST TITLES—at all individual events (excluding walks):
MEN
32 Alain Mimoun (1947–59) 12 10 000m, 8 5000m, 6 C-C,
6 Mar
21 Géo Andre (1908–22) 6 HJ, 6 standing HJ, 5 400mh, 4
110mh
16 André Tisson (1905–20) 9 DT, 7 SP

WOMEN
33 Lucienne Velu (1925–42) 14 DT, 8 SP, 4 80m, 4 200m,
3 60m
20 Denise Guenard (1953–68) 9 Pen, 6 80mh, 2 HJ, 2 LJ,
1 DT

FRENCH RECORDS

The most set at one event outdoors:

MEN
22 Guy Husson HT 54.00m 1950 to 69.40m 1967

Nicole Duclos (l) & Colette Besson (r), first and second for France in the 1969 European 400m. (Central Press)

17 Pierre Colnard SP 16.61m 1961 to 19.77m 1970
14 Michel Macquet JT 64.60m 1954 to 83.36m 1961
13 Marcel Duriez 110mh 14.2 1960 to 13.7 1968 (12 ties)

WOMEN
13 Catherine Capdevielle 100m 12.0 1955 to 11.4 1960 (9 ties)

Most at all standard events:

MEN
42 Michel Jazy (1957–66) 9 1500m, 7 1M, 7 2000m, 6 800m, 6 5000m, 4 1000m, 3 3000m. Also 2 at 4×1500mR and at former recognized events: 2 at 2M, 1 each at 880y, 3M, 6M, making a grand total of 49!

WOMEN
19 Micheline Ostermeyer (1944–50) 10 SP, 4 DT, 3 Pen, 1 80mh, 1 HJ

Firsts
Olympic medallist: Alexandre Tuffère second TJ 1896
Olympic champion: Michel Théato Mar 1900
International match: 1 Sep 1912 at Brussels, v Belgium
World record: Fernand Gonder PV 3.74m 1905

Federal Republic of Germany

Amateur athletics in Germany dates from at least 1862 when English residents in Bonn staged a meeting. The first major event was in Hamburg-Horn on a horse racing track on 6 Jun 1880. In this section details are included of pre-war Germany as well as the post-war Federal Republic. See also GDR.

NATIONAL CHAMPIONSHIPS

The first championships were at 100y and 1 mile in Berlin on 23 Aug 1891, both won by Englishmen: Alec Hyman in 10.6 and J. Swait in 4:34.6 respectively. The Deutsche Sportbehörde für Leichtathletik was formed in 1898, and held its first championships in Hamburg on 4 Sep 1898. With the exception of 1914, championships were held annually until 1943. After the war they were restarted in the Federal Republic in 1946.

Most titles won at each event
(Includes all who won 6 or more titles)
MEN

Event	Titles	Name, Years
100m	6	Richard Rau 1909–12, 1919–20
200m	6	Manfred Germar 1956–9, 1961–2
400m	5	Karl-Friedrich Haas 1952–6
800m	10	Willi Wülbeck 1974–83
	6	Otto Peltzer 1923–5, 1931–2, 1934
	6	Rudolf Harbig 1936–41
	6	Paul Schmidt 1956–8, 1960–2
1500m	7	Bodo Tummler 1965–9, 1971–2
	7	Thomas Wessinghage 1975, 1977–82
5000m	8	Harald Norpoth 1966–73
	7	Max Syring 1932, 1934–5, 1937–8, 1942–3
10 000m	6	Max Syring 1932–4, 1936, 1939, 1941
Marathon	5	Ralf Salzmann 1980–4
3000m steeple	5	Michael Karst 1974–7, 1979
	5	Patriz Ilg 1978, 1980–2, 1985
110mh	7	Hans Zepernick 1941–3, 1946–7, 1949–50
400mh	8	Harald Schmid 1977–8, 1980–5
	7	Helmut Janz 1957–63
High jump	6	Theo Püll 1956–61
	6	Dietmar Mögenburg 1980–5
Pole vault	9	Günther Löhre 1975–80, 1982–4
	6	Klaus Lehnertz 1959–61, 1966–8
Long jump	6	Luz Long 1933–4, 1936–9
Triple	8	Michael Sauer 1963–5, 1967–71
Shot	9	Ralf Reichenbach 1972–5, 1977–81
	7	Hans Wöllke 1934–8, 1941–2
	6	Heinfried Birlenbach 1966–71
Discus	6	Hein-Direck Neu 1966–9, 1974, 1976
Hammer	10	Karl-Hans Riehm 1973, 1975–81, 1983–4
	8	Karl Storch 1941–3, 1948, 1950, 1952, 1954–5
	8	Uwe Beyer 1964–71
Javelin	6	Hermann Salomon 1960, 1962–4, 1967–8
	6	Klaus Wolfermann 1969–74
Decathlon	6	Guido Kratschmer 1975–80
20kmW	4	Alfons Schwarz 1978, 1981–2, 1984

50kmW .... 9 Karl Hähnel 1922, 1926–30, 1932,
1934–5

WOMEN
100m ....6 Käthe Krauss 1933–8
200m ....5 Annegret Richter 1974, 1976,
1978–80
400m ....5 Rita Wilden 1972–6
800m ....5 Antje Gleichfeld 1961, 1963–6
5 Margrit Klinger 1980–2, 1984–5
1500m ....7 Brigitte Kraus 1976, 1978–9, 1981,
1983–5
3000m ....6 Brigitte Kraus 1976–7, 1979, 1983–5
10 000m ....3 Charlotte Teske 1983–5
Marathon..............5 Christa Vahlensieck 1975–8, 1980
80mh ....8 Maria Domagalla/Sander 1943, 1946,
1948–9, 1951–4
100mh ....6 Sylvia Kempin 1975–8, 1980–1
400mh ....4 Silvia Hollman 1976, 1978–80
High jump.............7 Ulrike Meyfarth 1973, 1975, 1979–83
Long jump ....5 Helga Hoffmann 1961–4, 1966
5 Heide Rosendahl 1968–72
Shot......................8 Marlene Fuchs/Klein 1962, 1964–5,
1967–8, 1970–2
8 Eva Wilms 1974–81
7 Gisela Mauermayer 1934 , 1937–42
6 Marianne Werner 1953–4, 1956–9
Discus ....10 Liesel Westermann 1966–70, 1972–6
9 Gisela Mauermayer 1934–42
8 Kriemhild Hausmann/Limberg
1958–65
8 Ingra Manecke 1977–84
Javelin..................7 Anneliese Gerhards 1961–6, 1971
7 Ameli Koloska 1967–70, 1972–4
6 Ingrid Thyssen 1979–84
Pen/Hep ....5 Heide Rosendahl 1966, 1968, 1970–2

MOST TITLES—at all standard individual events:

MEN
14 Otto Peltzer (1922–34) 6 800m, 5 1500m, 2 400mh,
1 200m
13 Max Syring (1932–43) 7 5000m, 6 10 000m
12 Richard Rau (1909–20) 6 100m, 5 200m, 1 110mh
11 Manfred Germar (1956–62) 6 200m, 5 100m
11 Martin Lauer (1956–60) 5 110mh, 4 200mh, 2 Dec
11 Harald Norpoth (1962–73) 8 5000m, 3 1500m

WOMEN
19 Gisela Mauermayer (1933–42) 9 DT, 7 SP, 3 Pen
16 Maria Sander (1943–54) 8 80mh, 4 100m, 4 Pen
14 Brigitte Kraus (1976–85) 7 1500m, 6 3000m, 1 800m
11 Liesel Westermann (1966–76) 10 DT, 1 SP
11 Heide Rosendahl (1966–72) 5 LJ, 5 Pen, 1 100mh

Top West German runners: 1983 world 800m champion Willi Wülbeck
(l) and Harald Schmid (r), winner of four European gold medals.
Both had long runs of success in their national championships. (ASP,
All-Sport)

INDOOR CHAMPIONSHIPS

These, in a nation with marvellous indoor facilities, have been held annually at a variety of venues since the first at Frankfurt in 1954.

Most individual titles:

MEN
12 Michael Sauer TJ 1963–72, 1979; LJ 1968
8 Günther Löhre PV 1975–80, 1982–3
7 Hermann Lingnau SP 1955–61
7 Heinfried Birlenbach SP 1965–71

WOMEN
13 Brigitte Kraus 1500m 1974, 1976–80, 1982–5; 800m
1973, 1975–6
9 Annegret Richter 50/60m 1970–5, 1977, 1979; 200m
1977, 1979
8 Ilia Hans HJ 1957–8, 1961–6
8 Marlene Fuchs SP 1964–71
8 Heide Rosendahl LJ 1966–72, 50mh 1971
7 Eva Wilms SP 1974–80
6 Erike Fisch LJ 1954–5; 50/60mh 1958, 1961–2, 1964
6 Ulrike Meyfarth HJ 1975–6, 1979–81, 1984
6 Heide-Elke Gaugel 60m 1981–3; 200m 1980, 1982–3

In all GFR championships, indoors and out, individual and team—Brigitte Kraus has a record 39 titles (with a further 16 at junior level). The men's record is 35 by Harold Norpoth.

GERMAN RECORDS

The most set at one event outdoors:

MEN
15 Hubert Houben 100m 10.5 1922 to 10.4 1927 (all ties)
15 Klaus Lehnertz PV 4.40m 1959 to 4.55m 1962 (9 ties)
13 Martin Lauer 110mh 14.3 1956 to 13.2 1959 (9 ties)
12 Uwe Beyer HT 64.48m 1964 to 74.90m 1971
12 Klaus Wolfermann JT 83.54m 1969 to 94.08m 1973

WOMEN
19 Eva Wilms SP 17.53m 1975 to 21.43m 1977 (1 tie)
16 Ulrike Meyfarth HJ 1.84m 1972 to 2.03m 1983 (5 ties)
15 Liesel Westermann DT 57.04m 1966 to 64.96m 1972
12 Marianne Werner SP 14.75 m 1954 to 15.84m 1958
12 Marlene Klein/Fuchs SP 15.90m 1964 to 17.34m 1968

Most at all standard events:

MEN
18 Richard Rau (1909–14) 9 200m, 6 100m, 3 110mh (11
ties)
17 Robert Pasemann (1909–13) 9 PV, 5 HJ, 3 LJ
17 Hubert Houben (1922–7) 15 100m, 2 200m (16 ties)
16 Martin Lauer (1956–9) 13 110mh, 2 Dec, 1 400mh

WOMEN
22 Eva Wilms (1975–7) 19 SP, 3 Pen
19 Heide Rosendahl (1968–72) 1 100mh, 6 Pen, 5 LJ, 2
200m
16 Ingrid Becker/Mickler (1960–71) 100m, 4 LJ, 3 HJ, 2
Pen
16 Ulrike Meyfarth (1972–83) 16 HJ

The widest range is that by Hanns Braun—100m 10.8, 200m 22.4, 400m 48.3, 800m 1:53.1, 1500m 4:14.6, 110mh 16.2 in 1907–12.

Firsts

Olympic medallist: Fritz Hofmann second 100m 1896
Olympic champion (woman): Lina Radtke 800m 1928
Olympic champion: Hans Woellke SP 1936
International match: 4 Sep 1921 at Basle, v Switzerland

German Democratic Republic

The GDR has maintained an astonishing level of sporting prowess over the past decade or so. From a nation of less than 17 million people they have produced a stream of top-class athletes with 33 Olympic and 67 European gold medals since 1962. They have been undefeated internationally since 1970 except by the USSR. The GDR constitution promulgated on 9 Apr 1968 guarantees the right of GDR citizens to take part in sport and encourages participation by its citizens. The policy has been an outstanding success.

<u>NATIONAL CHAMPIONSHIPS</u>

The first official GDR championships were held at Halberstadt on 22–23 Jul 1950, but these had been preceded by Eastern Zone championships in 1948 and 1949.

Most titles won at each event
(Includes all who won 6 or more titles)

MEN

100m	4	Heinz Erbstösser 1962, 1964–5, 1968
200m	5	Heinz Erbstösser 1962–6
400m	3	Wolfgang Müller 1969–70, 1972
	3	Thomas Schönlebe 1983–5
800m	9	Manfred Matuschewski 1959–66, 1969
1500m	5	Klaus-Peter Justus 1970, 1972–5
5000m	4	Siegfried Herrmann 1956, 1964–6
	4	Jörg Peter 1976–8, 1980
10 000m	6	Jürgen Haase 1965–6, 1968, 1970, 1972–3

While pole vault standards soar, Wolfgang Nordwig's ninth GDR record of 5.50m in 1972 stood for 12 years. (All-Sport)

Marathon	4	Hans-Joachim Truppel 1970, 1973, 1975, 1979
3000m steeple	4	Hermann Buhl 1958–9, 1961–2
	4	Dieter Herrmann 1967–9, 1971
	4	Ralf Pönitzsch 1976–7, 1979, 1981
110mh	9	Thomas Munkelt 1975–80, 1982–4
400mh	5	Hans Dittner 1953–6, 1958
High jump	7	Rolf Beilschmidt 1974–9, 1981
Pole vault	8	Manfred Preussger 1955–8, 1960, 1962–4
	8	Wolfgang Nordwig 1965–72
Long jump	7	Klaus Beer 1961–2, 1964, 1967–70
Triple jump	5	Jörg Drehmel 1969–72, 1974
Shot	9	Udo Beyer 1977–85
Discus	6	Wolfgang Schmidt 1975–80
Hammer	6	Roland Steuk 1978–83
Javelin	8	Manfred Stolle 1965, 1967–73
Decathlon	5	Wolfgang Utech 1959–61, 1963–4
20kmW	5	Hans-Joachim Pathus 1959–61, 1963, 1965
50kmW	7	Christoph Höhne 1963–5, 1968–71

WOMEN

100m	9	Marlies Göhr 1977–85
	6	Gisela Birkemeyer 1955–60
200m	5	Gisela Birkemeyer 1955–7, 1959–60
400m	5	Marita Koch 1977–8, 1980–1, 1984
800m	6	Gunhild Hoffmeister 1970–4, 1976
1500m	8	Gunhild Hoffmeister 1968–74, 1976
3000m	3	Ulrike Bruns 1976, 1981, 1984
	3	Gabriele Lehmann 1977–8, 1983
80mh	9	Gisela Birkemeyer 1953–61
80mh/100 mh	7	Karin Balzer 1962–3, 1966–8, 1969, 1971
400mh	3	Ellen Fiedler 1981–3
High jump	7	Rita Kirst 1967–72, 1975
	6	Rosemarie Ackermann 1973–4, 1976–7, 1979–80
Long jump	6	Hildrun Claus 1957–62
Shot	7	Ilona Slupianek 1977, 1979–84
	6	Renate Garisch/Boy 1961–5, 1967
Discus	6	Evelin Jahl 1976–81
Javelin	11	Ruth Fuchs 1967, 1970–3, 1975–80
Pen/Hep	5	Gisela Berkemeyer 1953–7
	5	Burglinde Pollak 1969–70, 1973–4, 1979

MOST TITLES—at all standard individual events:

MEN
10 Ernst Schmidt (1950–4) 5 SP, 4 DT, 1 Dec
10 Manfred Matuschewski (1959–69) 9 800m, 1 1500m (and 6 relay titles)

WOMEN
25 Gisela Birkemeyer (1953–61) 9 80mh, 6 100m, 5 200 m, 5 Pen (also 14 relay titles for a grand total of 39)
14 Gunhild Hoffmeister (1968–76) 8 1500m, 6 800m
12 Marlies Göhr (1977–85) 9 100m, 3 200m
11 Karin Balzer (1962–71) 5 80mh, 2 100mh, 2 Pen, 1 200m, 1 LJ
11 Ruth Fuchs (1967–80) 11 JT

<u>GDR RECORDS</u>

The most set at one event outdoors:
MEN
18 Manfred Preussger PV 4.25m 1955 to 5.15m 1964
17 Horst Niebisch HT 54.34m 1955 to 62.77m 1959
15 Lothar Milde DT 55.66m to 64.16m 1969
12 Ernst Schmidt SP 13.35m 1949 to 15.85m 1952
12 Günter Lein HJ 1.92m 1955 to 2.04m 1957 (2 ties)
12 Siegfried Herrmann 1500m 3:57.0 1952 to 3:41.8 1956

WOMEN
20 Johanna Lüttge SP 13.77m 1955 to 16.70m 1960
15+ Gisela Birkemeyer 80mh 11.4 1953 to 10.5 1960
13 Ursula Donath 800m 2:19.4 1951 to 2:05.73 1960
12 Margitta Gummel SP 17.68m 1967 to 20.22m 1972
12 Renate Stecher 100m 11.3 1970 to 10.8 1973 (8 ties)

Gunhild Hoffmeister (132) leads Wenche Sørum (Nor) in the heats of the 1972 Olympic 1500m, at which she took the silver medal. The 1974 European 1500m champion, she became a member of the GDR parliament. (Ed Lacey/ASP)

Most at all standard events:

MEN
28 Siegfried Herrmann (1952–65) 12 1500m, 5 3000m, 4 800m, 3 1000m, 3 5000m, 1 2000m
22 Ernst Schmidt (1949–54) 12 SP, 8 DT, 2 Dec

WOMEN
21 Renate Stecher (1970–3) 12 100m, 9 200m (12 ties)
20+ Gisela Birkemeyer (1953–60) 15+ 80mh, 3 Pen, 2 100m (47 all events including relays)
20 Johanna Lüttge (1955–60) 20 SP
17 Ursula Donath (1951–60) 13 800m, 4 400m

Firsts

Olympic medallist (woman): Christa Stubnick second 100m & 200m 1956
Olympic champion (woman): Karin Balzer 80mh 1964
European champion: Manfred Matuschewski 800m 1962
International match: 6–7 Oct 1951 against Poland at Warsaw

Italy

The current national federation, Federazione di Atletica Leggera (FIDAL), was founded in 1926.

<u>NATIONAL CHAMPIONSHIPS</u>

First held for men at Milan in 1906 and for women at Bologna in 1927. They were not held in the war year of 1944.

Most titles won at each event
(Includes all who won 7 or more titles)

MEN

Event	Titles	Champion
100m	7	Orazio Mariani 1933, 1936–9, 1942–3
200m	11	Pietro Mennea 1971–4, 1976–80, 1983–4
	8	Livio Berruti 1957–62, 1965, 1968
400m	5	Ettore Tavernari 1928–9, 1932, 1934–5
	5	Mario Lanzi 1937, 1940–3
	5	Mario Fraschini 1958, 1960–3
	5	Sergio Bello 1965–9
800m	8	Mario Lanzi 1934–6, 1938–9, 1942–3, 1946
1500m	8	Luigi Beccali 1928–31, 1934–6, 1938
5000m	6	Giuseppe Beviacqua 1938–43
	6	Antonio Ambu 1958, 1961–2, 1964–5, 1967
10 000m	7	Giuseppe Beviacqua 1936–7, 1942–3, 1946–8
	7	Antonio Ambu 1958, 1962, 1964–8
Marathon	7	Antonio Ambu 1962, 1964–9
3000m steeple	5	Nello Bartolini 1926–7, 1931–2, 1934
	5	Giuseppe Lippi 1933, 1935–6, 1940, 1948
110mh	6	Albano Albanese 1945, 1948–52
	6	Giuseppe Buttari 1972, 1974–6, 1978–9
400mh	11	Luigi Facelli 1924–31, 1935–6, 1938
	8	Armando Filiput 1942, 1946, 1949–54
High jump	8	Alfredo Campagner 1940–3, 1945–7, 1951
Pole vault	10	Danilo Innocenti 1927–8, 1930–7
	10	Renato Dionisi 1964–71, 1977–8
Long jump	8	Arturo Maffei 1930, 1932, 1935–40
	7	Attilio Bravi 1952, 1954–5, 1957–60
Triple jump	5	Giuseppe Gentile 1965–6, 1968, 1970–1
Shot	15	Angiolo Profeti 1938–42, 1945–54
	13	Silvano Meconi 1955–65, 1967–8
Discus	15	Adolfo Consolini 1939, 1941–2, 1945, 1949–50, 1952–60
	10	Silvano Simeon 1966–7, 1969–74, 1977, 1979
Hammer	14	Teseo Taddia 1939, 1941–3, 1945, 1947–51, 1953–6
	10	Giampaulo Urlando 1967, 1975–83
Javelin	8	Amos Matteucci 1942, 1945–6, 1948–52
	7	Renzo Cramerotti 1970–3, 1975–7
Decathlon	8	Lorenzo Vecchiutti 1946–51, 1953–4
	8	Franco Sar 1958–65
10kmW	14	Abdon Pamich 1956–69
	10	Giuseppe Dordoni 1946–55
20kmW	12	Abdon Pamich 1958–69
50kmW	14	Abdon Pamich 1955–68
	7	Vittorio Visini 1970–5, 1981

WOMEN

Event	Titles	Champion
100m	9	Giuseppina Leone 1952–60
	7	Donata Govoni 1961–3, 1965–7, 1969
200m	9	Giuseppina Leone 1952–60

High hurdler Eddy Ottoz in his habitual dark glasses. He was European champion in 1966 and Olympic bronze medallist in 1968. (ASP)

400m	10	Erika Rossi 1976–85
	7	Donata Govoni 1966, 1968–9, 1971, 1973–5
800m	7	Leandra Bulzacchi 1930–1, 1934–8
	7	Gabriella Dorio 1974–6, 1980–3
1500m	10	Gabriella Dorio 1973, 1976–84
3000m	4	Margherita Gargano 1973, 1976, 1979–80
	4	Agnese Possamai 1982–5
Marathon	2	Alba Milana 1982–3
80mh	7	Letizia Bertoni 1958–64
100mh	7	Ileana Ongar 1972–8
400m	9	Giuseppina Cirulli 1977–85
High jump	14	Sara Simeoni 1970–80, 1982–3, 1985
	8	Osvalda Giardi 1954, 1956–8, 1960, 1962, 1964, 1966
Long jump	7	Claudia Testoni 1931–5, 1937–8
	7	Magali Vettorazzo 1961–4, 1966–7, 1969
Shot	12	Amelia Piccinini 1941–3, 1946–54
	10	Bruna Bertolina 1928–37
	8	Cinzia Petrucci 1973–8, 1980–1
Discus	9	Edera Cordiale 1943, 1946–53
	9	Elivia Ricci 1958–66
	7	Renata Scaglia 1973–6, 1978, 1981, 1984
Javelin	12	Ada Turci 1943, 1946–55, 1958
	9	Giuliana Amici 1970–8
Pen/Hep	7	Magali Vettorazzo 1962–3, 1965–7, 1969–70
5kmW	3	Giuliana Salce 1982–4

MOST TITLES—at all standard individual events:

MEN
40 Abdon Pamich (1955–69) 14 10kmW, 14 50kmW, 12 20 kmW
20 Antonio Ambu (1958–68) 7 10 000m, 7 Mar, 6 5000m
16 Luigi Facelli (1924–38) 11 400mh, 2 400m, 2 110mh, 1 TJ
16 Angiolo Profeti (1938–54) 15 SP, 1 DT
16 Pietro Mennea (1971–84) 11 200m, 3 100m, 2 400m
15 Adolfo Consolini (1939–60) 15 DT

WOMEN
19 Claudia Testoni (1932–40) 7 LJ, 5 80mh, 3 100m, 2 200m, 1 60m, 1 80m
19 Donata Govoni (1961–75) 7 100m, 7 400m, 5 200m
18 Giuseppina Leone (1952–60) 9 100m, 9 200m
18 Maggali Vettorazo (1961–70) 7 LJ, 7 Pen, 3 80mh, 1 100mh
17 Gabriella Dorio (1973–84) 10 1500m, 7 800m
16 Amelia Piccinini (1937–54) 12 SP, 4 Pen
15 Sara Simeoni (1970–85) 14 HJ, 1 Pen

The most set at one event:

MEN
19 Eddy Ottoz 110mh 13.9 1964 to 13.4 (13.46 auto) 1968 (15 ties)
18 Renato Dionisi PV 4.50m 1964 to 5.45m 1972 (1 tie)
15 Alessandro Andrei SP 20.35m 1982 to 21.95m 1985
13 Silvano Meconi SP 15.82m 1955 to 18.82m 1960

WOMEN
21 Sara Simeoni HJ 1.71m to 2.01m 1978
14 Ileana Ongar 100mh 13.8 1971 to 13.1 1976 (9 ties)
12 Amelia Piccinini SP 12.10m 1940 to 13.39m 1949
12 Giuseppina Leone 200m 24.9 1952 to 23.7 1960 (3 ties)

Most at all standard events:

MEN
23 Eddy Ottoz (1964–8) 19 110mh, 4 200mh

WOMEN
21 Sara Simeoni (1970–8) 21 HJ
19 Claudia Testoni (1933–9) 7 LJ, 5 80mh, 4 200m, 3 100m
19 Giuseppina Leone (1952–60) 12 200m, 7 100m (6 ties)
19 Rita Bottiglieri (1974–80) 6 200m; 3 400m, 400mh, Pen; 2 100m, 100mh

Firsts

Olympic medallist: Emilio Lunghi second 1500m 1908
Olympic champion: Ugo Frigerio 10kmW & 3kmW 1920
Olympic champion (woman): Trebisonda Valla 80mh 1936
International match: 30 May 1925 at Prague, v Czechoslovakia

Poland

The Polish athletics federation, Polski Zwiazek Lekkiej Atletyki (PZLA), was founded in Cracow on 11 Oct 1919, one month before Poland achieved independence.

First held for men at Lvov in 1920 and for women in Warsaw in 1922. They were not held in the war years 1940–4.

Most titles won at each event
(Includes all who won 7 or more)

MEN

100m	7	Marian Woronin 1978–83, 1985
200m	6	Marian Foik 1955, 1958–9, 1961, 1963–4
400m	7	Klemens Biniakowski 1928, 1930–5
800m	5	Stefan Kostrzewski 1925–9
1500m	5	Kazimierz Kucharski 1933–7
	5	Witold Baran 1962–4, 1966–7
5000m	5	Jozef Noji 1935–9
	5	Zdzislaw Krzyszkowiak 1955–9
10 000m	6	Stanislaw Ozog 1954, 1956–7, 1959, 1961–2
Marathon	4	Zdzislaw Bogusz 1966, 1968–70
3000m steeple	6	Jerzy Chromik 1952, 1954, 1956, 1960–2
110mh	6	Romuald Giegiel 1978, 1981–5
400mh	8	Antoni Maszewski 1930–3, 1935–8
	7	Stefan Kostrzewski 1924–9, 1934
High jump	10	Jacek Wszola 1974–80, 1982, 1984–5
Pole vault	8	Stefan Adamczyk 1923–5, 1927–31
	7	Wladyslaw Kozakiewicz 1973, 1976–9, 1981, 1984
Long jump	5	Edward Adamczyk 1946–7, 1949–51
	5	Andrzej Stalmach 1963–4, 1966–8
Triple jump	10	Jozef Schmidt 1958, 1960, 1962–3, 1965–7, 1969–71
Shot	14	Wladyslaw Komar 1963–4, 1966–73, 1975–8, 1977–8
	7	Zygmunt Heljasz 1928–34
Discus	13	Edmund Piatkowski 1955, 1957–66, 1968–9
Hammer	7	Tadeusz Rut 1955–8, 1961, 1964–5
Javelin	14	Janusz Sidlo 1951–61, 1963, 1966, 1969
	7	Wladyslaw Nikiciuk 1962, 1964, 1967–8, 1970–1, 1973
Decathlon	4	by three men

WOMEN

100m	7	Irena Szewinska 1966–8, 1972–4, 1979
200m	10	Barbara Sobotta 1953–5, 1957–63
	8	Irena Szewinska 1966, 1968, 1971–5, 1979
400m	4	Krystyna Kacpercyk 1971, 1973–4, 1977
800m	7	Danuta Wierzbowska 1964–7, 1970, 1972–3
	6	Jolanta Januchta 1974, 1977–80, 1983
1500m	3	Bronislawa Ludwichowska 1973, 1975–6
	3	Zofia Kolakowska 1968–9, 1972
3000m	3	Celina Sokolowska 1977–9
100mh	6	Grazyna Rabszytn 1973, 1975–6, 1978–80
400mh	4	Genowefa Blaszak 1976, 1981, 1983, 1985

Wladyslaw Komar had a chequered career, the athletic highpoint of which was the 1972 Olympic title. Before concentrating on the shot he had set a national decathlon record. (**Mark Shearman**)

High jump	8	Jaroslava Bieda 1957, 1959–62, 1964–6
Long jump	7	Elzbieta Krzesinska 1952–4, 1957, 1959, 1962–3
Shot	11	Ludwika Chewinska 1970–6, 1980–3
Discus	10	Jadwiga Wajsowna 1932–7, 1945–8
	7	Halina Konopacka 1924–8, 1930–1
	7	Kazimiera Rykowska 1959, 1961–6
Javelin	10	Daniela Jaworska 1964, 1966–71, 1973–4, 1976
Pen/Hep	5	Malgorzata Nowak 1980–4

MOST TITLES—at all standard individual events:

MEN
24 Antoni Cejzik (1924–30) 5 HT & Pen, 4 Dec, 2 each at 110mh, HJ, TJ, SP, DT
17 Witold Gerutto (1936–48) 5SP, 4DT & JT, 3HJ, 1 Dec
16 Stefan Kostrzewski (1923–34) 7 400mh, 5 800m, 1 each at 400m, 5000m, 3km St, 110mh (also a further 11 in relays)

WOMEN
20 Irena Szewinska (1965–79) 8 200m, 7 100m, 4 LJ, 1 400m
19 Jadwiga Wajsowna (1932–48) 10 DT, 6SP 3HJ
18 Halina Konopacka (1924–31) 7 DT, 5 SP, 4 Pen, 1 HJ & JT
16 Stanislawa Walasiewicz (1934–47) 4 100m, 200m; 3 Pen; 2 LJ, 80mh; 1 JT

The most set at one event:

MEN
18 Tadeusz Rut HT 56.04m 1954 to 67.04 1964
17 Alfred Sosgornik SP 16.46m 1956 to 18.58m 1961
16 Wladyslaw Komar SP 18.60m 1963 to 21.19m 1974
14 Stefan Kostrzewski 400mh 60.6 1924 to 54.2 1929
13 Edmund Piatkowski DT 50.93m 1955 to 61.12m 1967

WOMEN
18 Stanislawa Walasiewicz 100m 12.8 1929 to 11.6 1937 (11 ties)
15 Jaroslava Bieda HJ 1.60m 1958 to 1.75m 1958 (3 ties)
13 Elzbieta Wagner 80mh 12.2 1953 to 11.1 1956 (5 ties)
12 Irena Szewinska 100m 11.1 1965 to 10.9 1974
11 Jadwiga Wajsowna DT 39.76m 1932 to 46.55m 1936

Most at all standard events:

MEN
25 Stefan Kostrzewski (1924–9) 14 400mh, 5 800m, 2 110mh & 400m, 1 1500m & 2000m

22 Janusz Kusocinski (1928–39) 11 5000m, 3 3000m &
10 000m, 2 1000m & 1500m, 1 2000m
22 Jerzy Chromik (1953–8) 5 3000m & 3000mSt, 4 5000m,
3 1500m and 2000m, 2 10 000m
20 Bronislaw Malinowski (1971–6) 10 3000mSt, 5 5000m,
3 3000m, 2 10 000m

WOMEN
40 Stanislawa Walasiewicz (1929–37) 18 100m, 10 200m,
5 LJ, 3 800m, 2 400m, 2 Pen
31 Irena Szewinska (1964–74) 12 100m, 8 200m, 6 LJ,
4 400m, 1 Pen

Firsts

Olympic champion (woman): Halina Konopacka DT 1928
Olympic champion: Janusz Kusocinski 10 000m 1932
International match: 5–6 Aug 1922 at Prague, v
Czechoslovakia and Yugoslavia. First women's 9 Oct 1927
at Cracow v Austria

Sweden

The national federation, Svenska Idrottsför-
bundet, was founded on 30 Oct 1895, and the
name changed to Svenska Fri-Idrottsförbundet in
1949. In the immediate post-war years of the late
1940s Sweden was the most powerful athletics
nation in Europe. No doubt this pre-eminence
owed something to the fact that Sweden had not
been directly involved in the war or its aftermath,
but there was at the time a fine tradition for
athletics, particularly fostered by the great middle
distance runners led by Gunder Hägg and Arne
Andersson.

While in many nations dual international matches
have gone out of fashion, that between Sweden
and Finland remains of intense importance,
attended by large crowds. In recent years Finland
have dominated, particularly in the men's match,
but a sign of a possible resurgence in Swedish
athletics came with victory in both men's and
women's matches in 1985. This fixture was first
contested in 1925 and the matches show 31–14 for
Finland's men, but 25–10 for Sweden's women.

NATIONAL CHAMPIONSHIPS

First held for men in 1896 and for women in 1927.

Most titles won at each event
(Includes all who won 7 or more titles)

MEN
100m ....11 Lennart Strandberg 1934–8, 1940–3,
1945, 1947
8 Knut Lindberg 1904–9, 1911–2
200m ....12 Lennart Strandberg 1934–45
400m ....6 Nils Engdahl 1919–20, 1922–4, 1927
800m ....4 Sven Lundgren 1919–21, 1923
1500m ....5 Dan Waern 1956–61
5000m ....5 Bertil Albertsson 1947, 1949, 1951–3
10 000m ....8 Jean-Gunnar Lindgren 1928–31,
1933–6
Marathon............10 Gustav Kinn 1917, 1919–22, 1924–6,
1928–9
10 Henry Palmé 1934–42, 1944
3000m steeple ......7 Bengt Persson 1963–9

110mh ....14 Hakan Lidman 1934–45, 1947–8
10 Bo Forssander 1960–1, 1963–4,
1967–72
400mh ....7 Sten Pettersson 1923, 1925–30
7 Kell Areskoug 1931, 1933, 1935–9
High jump.............8 Stig Pettersson 1956–62, 1964
Pole vault .... 11 Ragnar Lundberg 1948–58
10 Kjell Isaksson 1968–71, 1973–5,
1977–9
Long jump............8 Olle Hallberg 1925–30, 1932, 1934
7 Åke Stenqvist 1935–8, 1940–2
7 Lars-Olof Höök 1963–9
Triple jump .... 7 Roger Norman 1952–8
7 Birger Nyberg 1964–5, 1968–9,
1971–2, 1977
Shot.....................8 Gunnar Bergh 1935–42
8 Erik Uddebom 1955–7, 1959–61,
1963–4
Discus ....11 Rickard Bruch 1967, 1969–70,
1972–8, 1983
7 Gunnar Bergh 1937–41, 1943–4
Hammer ....15 Birger Asplund 1954–68
10 Bo Ericson 1941–5, 1947–51
7 Carl-Johan Lind 1918–24
7 Sune Blomqvist 1969–73, 1975–6
Javelin ....10 Erik Lemming 1899, 1902–5, 1907–9,
1911–2
8 Lennart Atterwall 1934–5, 1937–41,
1946
Decathlon.............8 Lennart Hedmark 1967–8, 1970–1,
1973–6

WOMEN
100m ....8 Ann-Britt Leyman 1941–4, 1946–9
7 Linda Haglund 1974–9, 1981
200m ....7 Ann-Britt Leyman 1942–7, 1949
400m ....6 Karin Lundgren 1966, 1968–72
800m ....7 Anna Larsson 1943–9
1500m ....3 Inger Knutsson 1972–3, 1975
3000m ....2 by two women
80mh ....10 Maud Nörklitt 1931–4, 1936–9,
1941–2
100mh ....6 Gun Olsson 1969–74
400mh ....2 by two women
High jump.............6 Susanne Lorentzon 1979, 1981–5
Long jump............5 Ulla-Britt Althin 1942–6
5 Gunilla Cederström 1961–4, 1968
Shot...................14 Eivor Olson 1943–56
8 Gun-Britt Flink 1961–5, 1967–8, 1970
7 Ingrid Wehomen 1973–5, 1977–80
Discus ....7 Birgit Nyhed 1935, 1937–41, 1944
7 Barbro Schönberg 1952, 1954–6,
1958–9, 1961
Javelin ....15 Ingrid Almqvist 1947, 1949–52,
1954–8, 1960–4
7 Asa Westman 1970–1, 1973, 1975–8
Pen/Hep ....9 Kristine Tännander 1974–5, 1978–9,
1980–3, 1985

MOST TITLES—at all standard individual events:
MEN
25 Erik Lemming (1899–1917) 10 JT, 6 SP, 5 HT, 3 DT,
1 PV
23 Lennart Strandberg (1934–45) 12 200m, 11 100m (also
16 relay titles, 13 at 4×100m & 3 at 4×400m, for a
record grand total of 39)
19 Sten Pettersson (1923–33) 7 400mh, 6 110mh, 3 200 m,
2 100m, 1 400m
15 Ragnar Lundberg (1948–58) 11 PV, 4 110mh
WOMEN
18 Ruth Svedberg (1927–49) 6 DT, 6 Pen, 3 JT, 2 SP, 1 LJ
(& 5 at slingball for 23 in all)
17 Karin Lundgren (1965–72) 6 200m, 6 400m, 5 100m
17 Ulla-Britt Wieslander (1959–67) 6 100m, 6 200m,
5 80mh
16 Eivor Olson (1943–56) 14 SP, 2 JT
Majken Aberg won 16 titles at the old Swedish event of
slingball, successively 1937–52 and also one DT.

WALKING

Walking in Sweden is governed by a separate federation.

Most national titles:

MEN
15 John Mikaelsson 8 15km, 5 10km, 2 3km
11 John Ljunggren 8 25km, 2 50km, 1 20km
11 Hans Tenggren 5 5km, 2 each 10km, 20km, 50km
11 Stefan Ingvarsson 4 20km, 3 10km, 2 5km & 50km

WOMEN
20 Mary Nilsson 10 5km, 10 10km

SWEDISH RECORDS

The most set at one event:

MEN
17 Birger Asplund HT 57.19m 1955 to 66.37m 1964
15 Rickard Bruch DT 60.58m 1968 to 71.26m 1984
13 Kjell Isaksson PV 5.05m 1968 to 5.55m 1972
11 Ragnar Lundberg PV 4.21m 1947 to 4.46m 1956
11 Erik Uddebom SP 16.68m 1956 to 17.67m 1962
11 Lennart Hedmark Dec 6973 1966 to 8188 1973 (1964 Tables scores)

WOMEN
16 Ingrid Almqvist JT 39.24m 1947 to 52.32m 1964

Most at all standard events:

MEN
20 Rickard Bruch (1968–84) 15 DT, 5 SP
18 Erik Lemming (1900–12) 8 JT, 6 HT, 4 DT
18 Dan Waern (1956–60) 6 1000m, 4 1500m, 3 800m & 1M, 1 2000m & 3000m

Firsts

Olympic champion: Erik Lemming JT 1906
European Champion: Harald Andersson DT 1934
International match: 13 Jul 1913 at Brussels, v Belgium

UK

AAA CHAMPIONSHIPS

The first AAA Championships were held at Lillie Bridge, London on 3 Jul 1880. They have been held annually with the exception of the war years, 1915–8 and 1940–5, ever since, and have always been not only the national championships of England and Wales, but also open to all-comers. Indeed for many years they were the world's premier meeting.

The AAA (Amateur Athletic Association) was founded on 24 Apr 1880 to resolve the chaos threatened in the sport by the rivalry between the Amateur Athletic Club (AAC), who had staged the world's first national championships at Beaufort House, Welham Green, London on 23 Mar 1866, and the London Athletic Club.

AAA Venues
Lillie Bridge 1880, 1883; Birmingham 1881, 1884, 1890; Stoke-on-Trent 1882; Southport 1885; Stamford Bridge 1886, 1889, 1892, 1895, 1898, 1900, 1902, 1905–6, 1909–14, 1919–31; Stourbridge 1887; Crewe 1888; Manchester 1891, 1897, 1907; Northampton 1893, 1896, 1903; Huddersfield 1894, 1901; Wolverhampton 1899; Rochdale 1904; White City 1908, 1932–9, 1946–70; Crystal Palace 1971–date

AAA Championship best performances prior to 1986 (Competitors UK unless indicated)

MEN	hr:min:sec		
100m	10.16w	Vassilios Papageorgopoulos (Gre)	1972
	10.16w	Steve Williams (USA)	1974
200m	20.35	Don Quarrie (Jam)	1976
400m	45.05	Darren Clark (Aus)	1983
800m	1:45.12	Andy Carter	1973
1500m	3:36.14	Steve Cram	1982
5000m	13:17.21	David Bedford	1972
10 000m	27:30.3	Brendan Foster	1978
Marathon	2:08:16	Steve Jones	1985
3000m steeple	8:23.12	Domingo Ramon (Spa)	1984
110mh	13.60	Mark Holtom	1982
400mh	48.58	Edwin Moses (USA)	1979
3kmW	11:36.04	David Smith (Aus)	1983
10kmW	40:54.7	Steve Barry	1983
	metres		
High jump	2.30	Francisco Centelles (Cub)	1984
	2.30	Javier Sotomayor (Cub)	1984
Pole vault	5.59	Brian Hooper	1980
Long jump	8.38	Larry Myricks (USA)	1981
Triple jump	17.22	Willie Banks (USA)	1985
Shot	21.37	Al Feuerbach (USA)	1974
Discus	65.72	Juan Martinez (Cuba)	1985
Hammer	77.30	David Smith	1985
Javelin	88.32	David Ottley	1985
Decathlon	7564 pts	Colin Boreham (1984 Tables)	1981

The Championships were contested at imperial distances until 1968, so in the tables that follow yards events are combined with equivalent metric distances.

Most titles won at each AAA event
(Includes all who won 6 or more)

100m/100y	7	McDonald Bailey 1946–7, 1949–53
200m/220y	7	McDonald Bailey 1946–7, 1949–53
400m/440y	6	David Jenkins 1971–6
800m/880y	4	Brian Hewson 1953–4, 1958–9
1500m/1 mile	5	Sydney Wooderson 1935–9

5000m/3 miles	3	Bruce Tulloh 1959, 1962–3
	3	Ron Clarke (Aus) 1965–7
	3	Brendan Foster 1973–4, 1976
4 miles*	4	Alfred Shrubb 1901–4
10 000m/6 miles	5	David Bedford 1970–4
10 miles*	5	Ron Hill 1965–9
Marathon	6	Donald McNab Robertson 1932–4, 1936–7,1939
3000m steeple	8	Maurice Herriott 1959, 1961–7
110mh/120 yh	8	Donald Finlay 1932–8, 1949
	6	Berwyn Price 1973–8
400mh/440yh	7	Harry Whittle 1947–53
High jump	6	Howard Baker 1910, 1912–3, 1919–21
Pole vault	7	Thomas Ray 1881–2, 1884–8
Long jump	6	Peter O'Connor (Ire) 1901–6
Triple jump	6	Willem Peters (Hol) 1927–30, 1935, 1937
Shot	13	Denis Horgan (Ire) 1893–9, 1904–5, 1908–10, 1912
	7	Geoff Capes 1972–3, 1975–9
Discus	7	Bill Tancred 1966–70, 1972–3
Hammer	6	Thomas Nicolson 1903–5, 1907, 1909, 1912
Javelin	7	David Travis 1965, 1968, 1970–4
Decathlon	4	Leslie Pinder 1951–4
3000m/2M walk	10	Roger Mills 1969, 1972–4, 1976–9 1981–2
	7	Albert Cooper 1932–8
10 000m/7M walk	5	Roland Hardy 1950–3, 1955
	5	Ken Matthews 1959–61, 1963–4
	5	Brian Adams 1975–9

*Events no longer staged.

Most AAA individual titles
14 McDonald Bailey (1946–53) 7 100y, 7 220y
13 Denis Horgan (Ire) (1893–1912) 13 SP
11 Harry Whittle (1947–53) 7 440yh, 2 LJ, 1 220yh & Dec
11 Roger Mills (1969–82) 10 3km walk, 1 10km walk
10 Ken Matthews (1959–64) 5 each 2M walk & 7M walk
10 Alfred Shrubb (1901–4) 4 each 4M & 10M, 2 1M

In AAC championships Walter Slade won five titles at 1 mile in 1873–7, and Robert Mitchell won 11 (3 each at HJ, PV, LJ and 2 SP) in 1868–71.

WAAA Championships

The WAAA (Women's Amateur Athletic Association) was formed in 1922 and staged championships at Waddon, London in September that year at two events—120y hurdles and 220y. The following year full-scale championships were staged on 18 Aug at the Oxo Sports Ground, Bromley. They have been held annually with the exception of the war years, 1915–8 and 1940–5, ever since, and have been not only the national championships of England and Wales, but also open to all-comers.

WAAA Venues
Waddon 1922; Bromley 1923; Woolwich 1924; Stamford Bridge 1925–6, 1928–32; Reading 1927; White City 1933, 1935–9, 1946, 1949–57, 1960–7; Herne Hill 1934; Tooting Bec 1945; Chiswick 1947–8; Motspur Park 1958–9; Crystal Palace 1968–84; Birmingham 1985

WAAA Championship best performances prior to 1986
(Competitors UK unless indicated)

	hr:min:sec		
100m	11.22	Andrea Lynch	1976
200m	22.77	Kathy Cook	1984
400m	51.05	Michelle Scutt	1982
800m	2:00.5	Vera Nikolic (Yug)	1968
1500m	4:07.27	Christine Benning	1984
3000m	8:50.50	Zola Budd	1985
5000m	15:45.26	Monica Joyce (Ire)	1982

10 000m	33:53.3	Susan Crehan	1985
Marathon	2:28:06	Sarah Rowell	1985
100mh	12.95	Shirley Strong	1983
400mh	56.06	Christine Warden	1979
5kmW	23:03.52	Susan Cook (Aus)	1982
10kmW	48:37.6	Marion Fawkes	1979
	metres		
High jump	1.92	Barbara Simmonds	1982
Long jump	6.79w	Susan Telfer (& 6.71)	1984
Shot	18.01	Judy Oakes	1984
Discus	62.22	Meg Ritchie	1981
Javelin	66.38	Tessa Sanderson	1985
Heptathlon	5850 pts	Judy Simpson (1984 tables). 1983

The championships were contested at imperial distances in various years prior to 1968, so in the tables that follow yards events are combined with equivalent metric distances.

Most WAAA titles won at each event
(Includes all who won 6 or more titles at one event)

60m (1935–50)	4	Betty Lock 1936–9
100m/100y	4	Eileen Hiscock 1930, 1933–5
	4	Winifred Jordan 1937, 1945, 1947–8
	4	Dorothy Hyman 1959–60, 1962–3
	4	Kathy Cook 1978, 1980, 1983–4
200m/220y	6	Sylvia Cheeseman 1946–9, 1951–2
	6	Kathy Cook 1978–80, 1982, 1984–5
400m/440y	6	Valerie Winn (née Ball) 1948–53
800m/880y	5	Edith Trickey 1923–7
	5	Gladys Lunn 1930–2, 1934, 1937
	5	Joy Jordan 1958–62
1500m/1 mile	5	Rita Ridley 1966–8, 1970–1
5000m	2	Monica Joyce (Ire) 1982, 1985
10 000m	1	each (first held 1983)
Marathon	2	Joyce Smith 1979–80
80mh (1929–68)	5	Elsie Green 1931–5
100mh	6	Shirley Strong 1979–84
400mh	3	Christine Warden 1976, 1979, 1981
High jump	8	Dorothy Tyler 1936–9, 1948–9, 1952, 1956
Long jump	6	Ethel Raby 1935–9, 1946
Shot	7	Suzanne Allday 1954, 1956, 1958–62
	6	Bevis Reid/Shergold 1938–9, 1947–9, 1951
	6	Judy Oakes 1979–80, 1982–5
Discus	7	Suzanne Allday 1952–3, 1956, 1958–61
	6	Florence Birchenough 1923–8
Javelin	8	Susan Platt 1959–62, 1966–9
	6	Tessa Sanderson 1975–7, 1979–80, 1985
Pen/Hep	8	Mary Peters 1962–6, 1968, 1970, 1973
Walk	10	Judy Farr 1960, 1962–8 (at 1½M), 1969–70 (at 2500m)

Most individual WAAA titles
14 Suzann Allday (1952–61) 7 SP & DT
13 Nellie Halstead (1930–8) 4 220y/200m and 440y/400m; 2 800m and C-C, 1 100y
11 Mary Peters (1962–73) 8 Pen, 2 SP, 1 100mh
10 Kathy Cook (1978–84) 4 100m, 6 200m
10 Judy Farr (1960–70) walks
10 Mary Bignal/Rand (1959–66) 5 LJ, 2 Pen, 1 each at 80mh, 100mh and HJ

Rosemary Payne in the discus was the highest placed British competitor for 11 successive years, 1964–74. In this period she won five times, was second three times, third twice and fourth once.
The most placings in the top three is 24 by Suzanne Allday, 12 each at shot and discus between 1951 and 1964. She is followed on 17 by Judy Farr, at the various walks distances, and Mary Rand (née Bignal), at six events. Dorothy Tyler (née Odam) placed 14 times over a record span of 22 years in the high jump, 1935–56.

Youngest WAAA senior champion:
Indoors—14 yr 312 days Sonia Lannaman 60m indoors 1971
Outdoors—15yr 72 days Betty Lock 60m 1936
Oldest WAAA champion: 42yr 281 days Joyce Smith marathon 1980.

AAA AND WAAA INDOOR CHAMPIONSHIPS

These were first held at the Empire Pool, Wembley from 1935 to 1939. They were revived at Wembley 1962–4 and since 1965 have been held annually at Cosford except that no women's events were held in 1968.

Most AAA indoor titles:
MEN
8 Mike Bull PV 1967–72, 1974, 1977
7 John Whetton 1500m 1963–7, 1M 1968, 1000y 1964
7 Mike Winch SP 1973, 1979–84
6 Geoff Capes SP 1971–2, 1974–5, 1977–8
6 Brian Hooper PV 1973, 1975–6, 1978–9, 1981
5 Fred Alsop LJ 1962, 1965; TJ 1965, 1967–8
5 Alan Pascoe 60y/mh 1967–70, 1973
5 Aston Moore TJ 1976–7, 1981–2; LJ 1981

WOMEN
9 Verona Elder 400m 1972–3, 1975–7, 1979, 1981–2; 800m 1978
8 Judy Oakes SP 1977–80, 1982, 1984–6
6 Mary Peters SP 1964–6, 1970, 1972; 60mh 1970
6 Mary Stewart 800m 1976; 1500m 1975, 1977, 1979; 3000m 1976–7
5 Ethel Raby LJ 1935–9
5 Rosemary Wright 440y 1967, 400m 1969; 800m 1970–1, 1974
5 Ann Wilson 60mh 1971–2; HJ 1971, 1974; LJ 1970
5 Brenda Bedford SP 1967, 1969, 1971, 1973, 1975
5 Lorna Boothe 60mh 1975, 1977–9, 1983

UK CHAMPIONSHIPS

These championships, for British athletes only, were first staged at Cwmbran in 1977. However, except when doubling as selection trials for major championships, their relegation to an end of May date, too early in the season for many athletes, has meant that they have often failed to establish true championship status.

Fatima Whitbread has moved steadily to the top in world javelin throwing. The 1979 European Junior champion, she won bronze medals at the 1982 Commonwealth and 1984 Olympic Games and silver in the 1983 World Championships. (All Sport)

VENUES

1977 Cwmbran, 1978 Edinburgh, 1979 Birmingham, 1980 London (Crystal Palace) & Edinburgh (3 events), 1981 Antrim, 1982 Cwmbran, 1983 Edinburgh, 1984 Cwmbran, 1985 Antrim

CHAMPIONSHIP BEST PERFORMANCES prior to 1986

MEN	min:sec		
100m	10.08w	Mike McFarlane	1984
	10.15	Allan Wells	1978
200m	20.36	Todd Bennett	1984
400m	45.26	Phil Brown	1985
800m	1:45.49	Peter Elliott	1983
1500m	3:37.5	Steve Ovett	1977
5000m	13:20.6	Nick Rose	1977
10 000m	27:51.30	Ian Stewart	1977
3000m steeple	8:25.98	Dennis Coates	1978
110mh	13.93	Berwyn Price	1978
400mh	50.15	Gary Oakes	1982
10kmW	40:53.60	Phil Vesty	1984
	metres		
High jump	2.22	Mark Naylor	1980
Pole vault	5.40	Brian Hooper	1979
Long jump	7.74	Roy Mitchell	1980
Triple jump	16.80	Aston Moore	1984

Shot	20.04	Geoff Capes	1977
Discus	59.70	Paul Mardle	1984
Hammer	77.04	David Smith	1985
Javelin	85.36	David Ottley	1982
Decathlon	7922w pts	Brad McStravick	1984

WOMEN	min:sec		
100m	11.08w	Heather Oakes	1984
	11.24	Sonia Lannaman	1978
200m	22.62	Kathy Cook	1980
400m	50.63	Michelle Scutt	1982
800m	2:01.36	Shireen Bailey	1983
1500m	4:04.39	Zola Budd	1984
3000m	8:52.88	Paula Fudge	1982
5000m	15:27.56	Angela Tooby	1984
100mh	13.12w	Pat Rollo	1984
	13.15	Shirley Strong	1983
400mh	56.67	Susan Morley	1983
5kmW	23:20.00	Virginia Birch	1985
	metres		
High jump	1.90	Diana Elliott	1984
Long jump	7.00w	Susan Hearnshaw	1984
	6.50	Beverly Kinch	1982
Shot	17.94	Judy Oakes	1984
Discus	62.16	Margaret Ritchie	1980
Javelin	65.62	Fatima Whitbread	1982
Heptathlon	6092 pts	Kim Hagger	1984

Harold Abrahams (r) wins, in 1920, the 100 yards at the 'Varsity match, for years a highpoint of the British season, for Cambridge University. Second was the 1920 Olympic 400m champion, Bevil Rudd (South Africa) for Oxford University. Third was Guy Butler, who shares with Seb Coe the distinction of four Olympic medals, the most by a British athlete.

Most titles

MEN
5 David Ottley JT 1978–82
5 Aston Moore TJ 1977, 1979, 1982–4
4 Keith Stock PV 1978, 1980, 1983–4

WOMEN
6 Heather Oakes 100m 1979–80, 1982, 1984; 200m 1979, 1984
6 Venissa Head SP 1977, 1981, 1983; DT 1981, 1983–4
5 Fatima Whitbread JT 1981–5
4 Sonia Lannaman 100m & 200m 1977–8
4 Margaret Ritchie DT 1977–80
4 Kathy Cook 100m 1983; 200m 1980, 1983, 1985
4 Judy Oakes SP 1978, 1982, 1984–5

UK RECORDS

The most set at one event:

MEN
17 Geoff Elliott PV 4.11m 1952 to 4.30m 1959 (11 ties)
17 Bill Tancred DT 57.26 m 1968 to 64.94m 1974
17 Geoff Capes SP 19.56m 1972 to 21.68m 1980 (2 ties)
16 Brian Hooper PV 5.29m 1976 to 5.59m 1980
15 Arthur Rowe SP 16.94m 1957 to 19.56m 1961
11 Mike Bull PV 4.72m 1966 to 5.25m 1973

WOMEN
12 Rosemary Payne DT 48.06m 1964 to 58.02m 1972
11 Suzanne Allday SP 12.70m 1953 to 15.18m 1964
11 Barbara Lawton HJ 1.76m 1969 to 1.87m 1973

Most at all standard events:

MEN
20 Geoff Elliott (1950–9) 17 PV, 3 Dec
17–15 as above
(Also: 22 Gordon Pirie (1951–6) 5 3000m; 2 2000m, 5000m, 10 000m; and at previously recognized events: 5 3M, 4 6M, 2 2M)

WOMEN
20 Mary Rand (1958–64) 11 LJ, 6 Pen, 2 80mh, 1 100mh (also 1 at 100y)
19 Suzanne Allday (1952–64) 11 SP, 8 DT
15 Diane Leather (1954–8) 8 800m, 5 1M, 2 1500m
15 Dorothy Hyman (1960–63) 9 100m, 6 200m (9 ties)

Firsts
Olympic champion: Charles Bennett 1500m 1900
Olympic champion (woman): Mary Rand LJ 1964
European champion: Don Finlay 110mh and Godfrey Brown 400m 1938
International match: 11 Sep 1921 at Colombes, v France

WALKING CHAMPIONSHIPS

In addition to the track championships staged by the AAA, national road walking championships are organized by the Race Walking Association. Events and most titles won at each distance are:

10 miles (since 1947): 6 Ken Matthews 1959–64
20 km (since 1965): 6 Paul Nihill 1965–6, 1968–9, 1971–2
35 km (20 miles 1908–77, 30km 1978, 35km since 1979): 6 Harold Ross 1908, 1910, 1912–14, 1920; 6 Paul Nihill 1963–5, 1968–9, 1971
50 km (since 1930): 8 Don Thompson 1956–62, 1966;6 Harold Whitlock 1933, 1935–9
100 (since 1979) 1 win each

Most titles overall:
19 Paul Nihill (1963–72) 6 20km & 20M, 4 10M, 3 50km
9 Don Thompson (1956–66) 8 50km, 1 20M
9 Olly Flynn (1974–8) 5 20km, 3 10M, 1 30km
8 Lawrence Allen (1949–58) 5 20M, 3 10M

The English Women's Road Walk Championship has been held annually since 1933, apart from 1940–5.
Most wins: 8 Judy Farr 1962–5, 1968, 1970, 1975–6

ENGLISH NATIONAL CROSS-COUNTRY CHAMPIONSHIP

This is the oldest (first run in 1876) and biggest national championships in the world. In 1985 at Milton Keynes there were a record 1907 starters, of whom 1806 finished, in the senior race. Senior, junior and youth championships are staged annually.

Most senior team titles: 28 Birchfield Harriers; 6 Salford Harriers, Tipton Harriers; 5 Hallamshire Harriers, Sutton Harriers, Gateshead Harriers

Team winners since 1975; Gateshead 1975–7, 1979; Tipton 1978, 1980–2; Aldershot, Farnham & District 1983–5

Most senior individual titles: 4 Percy Stenning 1877–80; Alfred Shrubb 1901–4; 3 Edward Parry 1888–9, 1891; Jack Holden 1938–9, 1946; Frank Aaron 1949–51; Gordon Pirie 1953–5; Basil Heatley 1960–1, 1963

Winners since 1975: 1975 Tony Simmons. 1976 Bernie Ford. 1977 Brendan Foster. 1978 Bernie Ford. 1979 Mike McLeod. 1980 Nick Rose. 1981 Julian Goater. 1982 Dave Clarke. 1983 Tim Hutchings. 1984 Eamonn Martin. 1985 David Lewis.
Most placings in the top ten: 10 Bernie Ford. (1973–83)

Athletes to have won at each age group: (Y—youth, J—junior, S—senior)
Walter Hesketh Y 1948, J 1950–1, S 1952
David Black Y 1971, J 1972, S 1974

ENGLISH WOMEN'S CROSS-COUNTRY CHAMPIONSHIP

First held at Luton in 1927. There are now four age categories: senior, intermediate, junior and girls.

Most senior team titles: 12 Birchfield Harriers; 7 London Olympiades; 6 Ilford

Team winners since 1975: Cambridge Harriers 1975; London Olympiades 1976; Sale Harriers 1977–8, 1981–3; Aldershot, Farnham & District 1979, 1984; Birchfield 1980; Crawley 1985

Most senior individual titles:
6 Lilian Styles 1928–30, 1933–4, 1937
5 Rita Ridley 1969–72, 1974
4 Diane Leather 1953–6; Pam Davies 1965–8
3 Roma Ashby 1958, 1961–2; Joyce Smith 1959–60, 1973

Winners since 1975: 1975 Deidre Nagle (Ire). 1976 Ann Ford. 1977 Glynis Penny. 1978 Mary Stewart. 1979 Kathryn Binns. 1980 Ruth Smeeth. 1981 Wendy Sly. 1982 Paula Fudge. 1983 Christine Benning. 1984 Jane Furniss. 1985 Angela Tooby.

Most placings in the top ten: 15 Joyce Smith (1956–82), 12 Lilian Styles (1927–38), Phyllis Perkins (1951–65)

Winner at three age groups: Mary Stewart junior 1970, intermediate 1971–3, senior 1978

ROAD RUNNING

Most wins in AAA Championships
12–stage road relay, first held 1967: 6 Tipton Harriers 1972, 1974, 1978, 1981, 1984–5; 4 Coventry Godiva 1967–70; Gateshead Harriers 1975–7, 1979

6–stage road relay, first held 1969: 4 City of Stoke-on-Trent 1969–72; 3 Liverpool Harriers 1974–6; Tipton Harriers 1977, 1980, 1983

Individual events have been introduced: 10 miles 1983, 10km 1984, half-marathon 1984. Steve Jones won at 10km in 1984 and half-marathon in 1985.

Avon Women's National 10 Miles
First held in 1981 this race has developed into Britain's biggest women's only race with a record 881 starters in 1983.
The race record is 54:06 by Paula Fudge in 1982.

Great North Run
The largest fields in any British race are about 25,000 each year who contest this half-marathon from Newcastle to South Shields. Running in the North East of England had benefited enormously from the inspiration of the European and Commonwealth champion Brendan Foster, and he played a major role in instigating this race, which was first run in 1981 when huge crowds watched 10,681 runners finish from an entry of around 12,500.

Winners have been:
MEN 1981 Mike McLeod (UK) 63:23, 1982 Mike McLeod 62:44, 1983 Carlos Lopes (Por) 62:44, 1984 Oyvind Dahl (Nor) 64:36, 1985 Steve Kenyon (UK) 62:44
WOMEN 1981 Karen Goldhawk (UK) 77:36, 1982 Margaret Lockley (UK) 77:00, 1983 Julie Barleycorn (UK) 76:39, 1984 Grete Waitz (Nor) 70:27, 1985 Rosa Mota (Por) 69:54

SCOTLAND

Scottish championships were first held at Powderhall, Edinburgh in 1883, following the formation of the Scottish AAA on 26 Feb that year. This annual event has been staged at Meadowbank, Edinburgh since 1970, in which year the stadium was opened for the Commonwealth Games. Women's championships were first held in 1931.

Most individual titles at one event:
MEN
21 Tom Nicolson HT 1902–14, 1919–24, 1926–7
14 Tom Nicolson S 1903–5, 1909–14, 1919–23
13 Crawford Fairbrother HJ 1957–69
11 Andrew Nicolson SP 1924–8, 1930–1, 1933–6
9 John Milne HJ 1897–1900, 1902–3, 1905–7
9 Alexander Smith 56 lb Wt 1925–32, 1934
9 Alexander Smith DT 1925–8, 1930–4
9 Chris Black HT 1971–7, 1981, 1985
8 Thomas Riddell 1M 1925–6, 1930–5
8 Patrick Ogilvie PV 1929–36
8 Fraser Riach JT 1953, 1955, 1957, 1959–60, 1962, 1964–5
8 Graham Everett 1M 1955–61, 1963
8 David Stevenson PV 1962–4, 1966–70
WOMEN
10 Sylvia Brodie JT 1965, 1967–71, 1973–6
8 Diane Royle JT 1977–84

Most individual titles overall:
MEN
42 Tom Nicolson (1902–27) 21 HT, 14 SP, 4 56lb Wt, 3 Scots HT
27 Alexander Smith (1925–34) 9 DT, 9 56lb Wt, 6 HT, 3 Scots HT
WOMEN
18 Alix Stevenson (1958–70) 7 LJ, 6 Pen, 3 80mh, 2 100y

Wyndham Halswelle won four titles, at 100y, 220y, 440y and 880y, in one day on 23 Jun 1906.

Cross-country championships were first held for men in 1886 and for women in 1954. Most individual titles: Nat Muir youth 1975, junior 1976–8, senior 1979–81, 1983–5.

WALES

Welsh championships were first held at two events, 100y and 1 mile in 1893. Women's championships were first held in 1952.

Most individual titles at one event:
MEN 10 Laurie Hall HT 1958–67; 9 Paul Rees SP 1973–4, 1976–82; 8 Ken Jones 220y 1946–9, 1951–4; 8 John Phillips TJ 1970, 1973–9.

WOMEN
12 Venissa Head SP 1974–85; 8 Venissa Head DT 1976, 1979–85

Most individual titles overall:
MEN
20 D.J.P. 'Dippy' Richards (1923–48) 5 at 2M walk; 4 each at 1M, 4M, 10M walk; 3 at 15M walk
16 Ken Jones (1946–54) 8 220y, 7 100y, 1 LJ
16 Paul Rees (1973–82) 9 SP, 7 DT
15 Frank Whitcutt (1926–34) 6 HJ, 5 TJ, 2 each 120yh, LJ
WOMEN
20 Venissa Head (1974–85) 12 SP, 8 DT

Cross-country championships were first held for men in 1886 and for women in 1954. Most individual titles: 8 Steve Jones 1977–80, 1982–5.

BRITISH LEAGUES and CUPS

The British Athletics League (BAL) was formed in 1969, following a pilot league season in 1968. The format has expanded from the original three divisions to five, with eight clubs in Division One, and six clubs in the remainder.

BAL Champions:
Birchfield Harriers 1969, 1983, 1985; Thames Valley Harriers 1970–1; Cardiff AAC 1972–4; Wolverhampton & Bilston 1975–82; Haringey 1984

The BAL introduced a knock-out cup competition for men's clubs in 1973 and for women's in 1974. These competitions are now known as the GRE Gold Cup and GRE Jubilee Cup respectively after the sponsors, Guardian Royal Exchange. There was a record entry in 1985 of 179 men's and 137 women's teams.

Cup winners: **MEN** Wolverhampton & Bilston 1973, 1976–7 1979–80; Cardiff AAC 1974; Edinburgh Southern Harriers 1975; Shaftesbury Harriers 1978, 1985; Haringey 1981–3; Birchfield Harriers 1984.

WOMEN
Mitcham 1974; Edinburgh Southern Harriers 1975; Stretford 1976–81; Hounslow 1982–3; Essex Ladies 1984–5

The British Women's League has comprised four divisions of six clubs since 1975, when it succeeded three years of the Motorway League. Champions of these Leagues:
Edinburgh Southern Harriers 1972–3, 1975; Stretford 1974, 1979, 1981, 1985; Sale Harriers 1976–8, 1983–4; Bristol 1980; Notts 1982

BRITISH INTERNATIONALS

The first full internationals by British teams were against France: men on 11 Sep 1921 and women on 23 Sep 1923, although an unofficial women's match had been held on 30 Oct 1921. All these matches were in Paris.

These British internationals had been preceded by matches between the home counties, starting with an England v Ireland fixture at Lansdowne Road, Dublin on 5 June 1876. A series of fixtures between Ireland and Scotland began in 1895, and triangular matches between England, Ireland and Scotland were held between 1914 and 1938.

Most international appearances for the UK:

MEN	WOMEN
67 Geoff Capes 1969–80	72 Verona Elder 1971–83
66* Mike Bull 1965–77	65 Brenda Bedford 1961–8
62 Brian Hooper 1971–82	51 Rosemary Payne 1963–74
61 Howard Payne 1960–74	46 Tessa Sanderson 1974–85
53 Crawford Fairbrother 1957–69	43 Mary Peters 1961–73
	43 Ann Wilson 1966–78
53 Bill Tancred 1964–76	42 Sonia Lannaman 1971–80
52 Mike Winch 1973–84	41 Barbara Lawton 1966–76
50 Alan Pascoe 1967–78	40 Lorna Boothe 1975–83
50 Berwyn Price 1971–82	39 Mary Rand 1957–67
46 David Travis 1965–78	39 Andrea Lynch 1970–8
42 Alan Lerwill 1967–76	39 Margaret Ritchie 1973–84
41 Lynn Davies 1962–72	39 Wendy Hoyte 1975–84

*And a further three at the then unofficial European Junior Games.

Geoff Capes had a record 35 individual event wins. Mary Rand was an individual winner 30 times: 17 LJ, 5 Pen, 4 80mh, 3 HJ, 1 100mh. David Jenkins won 25 individual (18 400m, 7 200m) and 19 relay races.

USA

The premier club in the early days of athletics in the USA was the New York Athletic Club, founded on 8 Sep 1868. The club staged the first ever indoor track meeting in the USA in New York on 11 Nov 1868.

TAC CHAMPIONSHIPS

The first US Championships were staged by the New York Athletic Club in New York in 1876, 1877 and 1878. Then from 1879 to 1888 championships were organized by the National Association of Amateur Athletes of America. In the latter year the Amateur Athletic Union of America (AAU) was founded and this multi-sport body organized championships therefrom (both NAAA and AAU staged championships in 1888). In 1979 The Athletics Congress of the USA (TAC) replaced the AAU as the national governing body for track and field athletics. The championships venue varies annually.

A tremendous total of 59 men's and 9 women's officially ratified world records have been set in AAU/TAC Championships and many more world bests were set in the first 44 years of the championships before the first IAAF record list. The pace of such record breaking has, however, slowed in recent years, as in the ten years 1976–85 only two records have been set: Bruce Jenner Dec 1976, Ed Moses 400mh 1977.

Jim Ryun was a teenage prodigy, who reached the apex of his brilliant career in 1966 and 1967, when he smashed the world records for 1500m and the mile. (ASP)

CHAMPIONSHIP BEST PERFORMANCES prior to 1986

(Competitors US unless indicated)

MEN

Event	hr:min:sec	Athlete	Venue	Year
100m	10.03	Jim Hines (sf)	Sacramento	1968
200m	19.75	Carl Lewis	Indianapolis	1983
400m	44.70	Cliff Wiley	Sacramento	1981
800m	1:43.9	Rick Wohlhuter	Los Angeles	1974
1500m	3:34.92	Steve Scott	Knoxville	1982
5000m	13:16.42	Doug Padilla	Indianapolis	1985
10 000m	27:39.4	Craig Virgin	Walnut	1979
3000m steeple	8:18.35	Henry Marsh	Indianapolis	1985
110mh	13.15	Greg Foster	Indianapolis	1983
400mh	47.45	Edwin Moses	Los Angeles	1977
5kmW	20:27.8	Ray Sharp	Walnut	1980
20kmW	1:26:54.2	Jim Heiring	Indianapolis	1983

Event	metres	Athlete	Venue	Year
High jump	2.32	Jim Howard	San Jose	1984
Pole vault	5.80	Earl Bell	San Jose	1984
Long jump	8.79	Carl Lewis	Indianapolis	1983
Triple jump	17.97	Willie Banks	Indianapolis	1985
Shot	21.82	Brian Oldfield	Walnut	1980
Discus	71.26	John Powell	San Jose	1984
Hammer	76.58	Giampaulo Urlando (Ita)	Walnut	1980
Javelin	88.32	Bob Roggy	Knoxville	1982
Decathlon	8491 pts	Bruce Jenner	Eugene	1976

WOMEN

Event	min:sec	Athlete	Venue	Year
100m	10.96	Evelyn Ashford	Knoxville	1982
200m	21.88	Evelyn Ashford	Indianapolis	1983
400m	49.83	Valerie Brisco-Hooks	San Jose	1984
800m	1:58.50	Madeline Manning	Sacramento	1981
1500m	4:03.37	Mary Decker	Knoxville	1982
3000m	8:38.36	Mary Decker	Indianapolis	1983
5000m	15:57.50	Suzanne Girard	Indianapolis	1985
10 000m	32:18.29	Francie Larrieu Smith	Indianapolis	1985
100mh	12.85	Rhonda Blanford	Idianapolis	1985
400mh	54.99	Judi Brown	San Jose	1984
5kmW	23:19.1	Sue Brodock	Walnut	1980
10mW	48:38.16	Maryanne Torrellas	Indianapolis	1985

Event	metres	Athlete	Venue	Year
High jump	1.95	Pam Spencer	Sacramento	1981
	1.95	Debbie Brill (Can)	Knoxville	1982
Long jump	6.91	Carol Lewis	Indianapolis	1983
	6.92w	Carol Lewis	Indianapolis	1985
Triple jump	13.17	Wendy Brown	Indianapolis	1985
Shot	19.09	Maren Seidler	Walnut	1979
Discus	67.58	Ria Stalman (Hol)	San Jose	1984
Javelin	66.52	Kate Schmidt	Los Angeles	1976
Heptathlon	6587w pts	Jane Frederick	Indianapolis	1985

(6548 points with allowable wind on long jump)

The championships were contested at imperial distances on many occasions up to 1973, so in the tables that follow yards events are combined with equivalent metric distances.

Most titles won at each event

(Includes all who won 6 or more)

MEN

Event		Athlete
100m/100y	3	by nine men—first Malcolm Ford 1884–6
200m/220y	5	Ralph Metcalfe 1932–6
400m/440y	6	Lon Myers 1879–84
800m/880y	7	James Robinson 1976, 1978–82, 1984
1500m/1 mile	8	Joie Ray 1915, 1917–23
	6	George Orton (Can) 1892–6, 1900
5000m/3 miles	5	Greg Rice 1938–42
10 000m/6 miles	7	Lou Gregory 1929–31, 1933, 1939, 1941, 1943
Marathon	8	John J. Kelley 1956–63
3000m steeple	9	Joe McCluskey 1930–3, 1935, 1938–40, 1943
	7	George Orton 1893–4, 1896–99, 1901
	7	Henry Marsh 1978–9, 1981–5
110mh/120yh	5	Hayes Jones 1958, 1960–1, 1963–4
400mh/440yh	5	Arky Erwin 1941, 1943–6
High jump	7	Dave Albritton 1936–8, 1945–7, 1950
	6	Dwight Stones 1973–4, 1976–8, 1983
Pole vault	9	Bob Richards 1948–52, 1954–7
	8	Cornelius Warmerdam 1937–44
Long jump	6	DeHart Hubbard 1922–7
	6	Ralph Boston 1961–6
	6	Arnie Robinson 1971–2, 1975–8
Triple Jump	8	Daniel Ahearn 1910–1, 1913–8
	6	William Brown 1936–7, 1940–3
Shot	10	George Gray (Can) 1887–94, 1896, 1902
	8	Parry O'Brien 1951–5, 1958–60
	7	Frank Lamprecht 1881–6, 1888 (AAU)
	6	Pat McDonald 1911–2, 1914, 1919–20, 1922

Discus ....6 Fortune Gordien 1947–50, 1953–4
6 Al Oerter 1957, 1959–60, 1962, 1964, 1966
6 Mac Wilkins 1973, 1976–80
Hammer ....9 James Mitchel 1889–96, 1903
9 Hal Connolly 1955–61, 1964–5
8 Patrick Ryan 1913–7, 1919–21
7 John Flanagan 1897–9, 1901–2, 1906–7
7 Matt McGrath 1908, 1910, 1912, 1918, 1922, 1925–6
Javelin ....6 George Bronder 1914–9
6 Bud Held 1949, 1951, 1953–5, 1958
Decathlon.............5 Bill Toomey 1965–9
10kmW .... 11 Henry Laskau 1947–57
20kmW .... 7 Ron Laird 1958, 1963–5, 1967–9
50kmW .... 8 Larry Young 1966–8, 1971, 1974–7
Cross-country ......7 Don Lash 1934–40

WOMEN

100m/100y ....5 Evelyn Ashford 1977, 1979, 1981–3
200m/220y ....11 Stella Walsh 1930–1, 1939–40, 1942–8
400m/440y ....3 Denean Howard 1981–3
800m/880y ....6 Madeline Manning 1967, 1969, 1975–6, 1980–1
1500m/1 mile ....7 Francie Larrieu 1970, 1972–3, 1976–7, 1979–80
3000m ....3 Jan Merrill 1976–8
5000m ....1 each (first held 1983)
10 000m ....1 each (first held 1977)

100mh* ....5 Helen Filkey 1925–9
5 Nancy Phillips 1943, 1946–7, 1951, 1953
400mh ....2 Debbie Esser 1975, 1978
2 Judi Brown-King 1984–5
High jump...........10 Alice Coachman 1939–48
6 Eleanor Montgomery 1963–7, 1969
Long jump ....11 Stella Walsh 1930, 1939–46, 1948, 1951
10 Willye White 1960–2, 1964–6, 1968–70, 1972
Triple jump .... 1 Wendy Brown 1985 (first held)
Shot....................11 Maren Seidler 1967–8, 1972–80
8 Earlene Brown 1956–62, 1964
Discus ....6 Frances Kaszubski 1945, 1947–51
Javelin............... 11 Dorothy Dobson 1939–49
7 Kate Schmidt 1969, 1973–7, 1979
Pen/Hep ....8 Pat Daniels 1961–7, 1970
8 Jane Frederick 1972–3, 1975–6, 1979, 1981, 1983, 1985
5000mW...............6 Susan Brodock 1973, 1975–7, 1979–80
10 000mW............5 Susan Brodock 1975, 1977–80
Cross-country ......2 by four women

*Sprint hurdles held at 60y 1923–28, 80m 1929–64, 1966–8, 100m 1965 and since 1969.

MOST TITLES

At all events, indoors and out, the greatest collection of US titles is 65 by Ron Laird at various walking events from 1958 to 1976. Another walker Henry Laskau held the previous record at 42.

Excluding the walks the greatest number is 40 by Stella Walsh who won women's events between 1930 and 1954 as follows: indoors—6 200m/220y, 1 each 60y, basketball throw; outdoors—33 as below.

James Mitchel won 11 titles at the 56lb weight (contested 1878–1975) in addition to his 9 at hammer.

Other leaders at standard individual outdoor events:

MEN

15 Lon Myers (1879–84) 6 440y, 4 220y, 3 880y, 2 100y
13 George Orton (1892–1901) 7 2MSt, 6 1M
12 Bob Richards (1948–57) 9 PV, 3 Dec

WOMEN

33 Stella Walsh (1930–54) 11 200m/220y, 11 LJ, 5 Pen, 4 100y/m, 2 DT
15 Dorothy Dodson (1939–49) 11 JT, 3 SP 1 DT
13 Alice Coachman (1939–48) 10 HJ, 3 100 m

Babe Didrikson won the widest range of titles: 80mh 1931–2, HJ 1932, LJ 1931, SP 1932, JT 1930 and 1932.

US RECORDS

Most set at one standard event outdoors:

MEN

16 Parry O'Brien SP 18.00m 1953 to 19.30m 1959
12 Hal Connolly HT 59.70m 1955 to 71.26m 1965
11 John Flanagan HT 45.93m 1897 to 56.18m 1909

WOMEN

14 Jane Frederick 8 Pen 1974–9 6 Hep 1981–4
10 Maren Seidler SP 16.72m 1974 to 19.09m 1979

Most at all events:

MEN

16 Parry O'Brien (1953–9) 16 SP

WOMEN

21 Mary Decker (1980–5) 5 1500m, 1M; 3 3000m; 2 800m, 2000m, 5000m; 1 1000m, 10 000m

US INDOOR CHAMPIONSHIPS

Staged annually since 1906, with the exception of 1912. Women's championships were first held in 1927.

Gerry Lindgren had brilliant careers both in high school and at Washington State University. He set one world record: 27:11.6 for 6 miles in 1965. (Mark Shearman)

Most titles at one event:

MEN

10 Henry Dreyer 35lb Wt 1934–5, 1939, 1941–7
10 Henry Laskau 1M Walk 1948–57
 9 Pat McDonald SP 1909–10, 1914–7, 1919–21
 9 Parry O'Brien SP 1953–61
 8 Joseph McCluskey 2000/3000mSt 1932–6, 1938, 1940–1
 8 Harrison Dillard 60yh 1947–53, 1955
 8 Bob Richards PV 1948, 1950–3, 1955–7
 7 Bob Backus 35lb Wt 1954–9, 1961

WOMEN

 8 Sue Brodock 1M Walk 1974–8, 1980, 1982–3
 7 Rena McDonald SP 1927, 1929–34
 7 Maren Seidler SP 1968–9, 1972, 1974, 1977–8, 1980

NCAA CHAMPIONSHIPS

The National Collegiate Athletic Association Championships have been held annually since 1921, except for 1924. They have long been established as the premier competition for athletes attending colleges and universities in the USA. The NCAA women's championships were first held in 1982.

The first twelve meetings were held at Chicago, but now the venue varies annually.

Athletes may now compete for fours years in this competition, but the limit was three years until the 1970s.

Most team wins

MEN

27 University of Southern California (USC) 1926, 1930–1, 1935–43, 1949–55, 1958, 1961, 1963, 1965 (tie), 1967–8, 1976, 1978
 5 University of California at Los Angeles (UCLA) 1956, 1966, 1971–3
 5 Illinois 1921, 1927, 1944, 1946–7
 5 University of Texas at El Paso (UTEP) 1975, 1979–82
 4 Oregon 1962, 1964–5, 1984

WOMEN

 2 UCLA 1982–3; 1 Florida State 1984; Oregon 1985

Most individual victories

8 Jesse Owens (Ohio State) 100y, 220y, 220yh, LJ 1935–6
7 Suleiman Nyambui (UTEP) 10 000m 1979–82, 5000m 1980–2
6 Ralph Metcalfe (Marquette) 100m/100y, 220m/200y 1932–4
6 Gerry Lindgren (Washington State) 5000m/3M, 10 000m/6M 1966–8

4 wins at one event:
5000m/3M Steve Prefontaine (Oregon) 1970–3
10 000m Suleiman Nyambui (UTEP) 1979–82
HT Scott Neilson (Washington) 1976–9

3 wins at one event:

100m/100y	Ralph Metcalfe (Marquette) 1932–4, Mel Patton (USC) 1947–9, Charles Greene (Nebraska) 1965–7
200m/220y	Ralph Metcalfe (Marquette) 1932–4
400m/440y	Hermon Phillips (Butler) 1925–7, George Rhoden (Morgan State) 1949–51, Bert Cameron (UTEP) 1980–1, 1983
800m/880y	Charles Hornbostel (Indiana) 1932–4, John Woodruff (Pittsburgh) 1937–9
1500m/1M	Don Gehrmann (Wisconsin) 1948–50, Ron Delany (Villanova) 1956–8, Dyrol Burleson (Oregon) 1960–2, Marty Liquori (Villanova) 1969–71
2M	Frank Martin (Notre Dame/New York) 1944–6, Jerry Thompson (Texas) 1942, 1947–8 (event now replaced by 5000m)

5000m/3M	Gerry Lindgren (Washington State) 1966–8, Suleiman Nyambui (UTEP) 1980–2
10 000m/6M	Gerry Lindgren (Washington State) 1966–8, John Ngeno (Washington State) 1974–6
3000mSt	James Munyala (UTEP) 1975–7
110mh/120y	Jack Davis (USC) 1951–3
220yh	Fred Wolcott (Rice) 1938–40 (discontinued event)
400mh/ 440yh	Ralph Mann (Brigham Young) 1969–71
High jump	Dave Albritton (Ohio State) 1936–8, Ken Wiesner (Marquette) 1944–6
Pole vault	Tom Warne (Northwestern) 1929–31, Bill Sefton (USC) 1935–7, Dave Roberts (Rice) 1971–3, Earl Bell (Arkansas State) 1975–7
Long jump	Edward Gordon (Iowa) 1929–31
Triple jump	Ron Livers (San Jose State) 1975, 1977–8
Shot	Harlow Rothert (Stanford) 1928–30, Al Blozis (Georgetown) 1940–2, Dallas Long (USC) 1960–2, Karl Salb (Kansas) 1969–71, Mike Carter 1980–1, 1983
Discus	Peter Zagar (Stanford) 1937–9, Fortune Gordien (Minnesota) 1946–8, John van Reenan (Washington State) 1968–70
Javelin	Bud Held (Stanford) 1948–50
Decathlon	Tito Steiner (Brigham Young) 1977, 1979, 1981

No woman has yet won three titles at one event.

NCAA Indoor Championships

Held annually since 1965, women from 1982.

Most team wins:
MEN 7 UTEP 1974–6, 1978, 1980–2.
WOMEN 2 Nebraska 1983–4

Most individual wins:
7 Suleiman Nyambui (UTEP) 1M 1979–82, 2M 1970–80, 1982
4 at one event: Suleiman Nyambui 1M, Mike Carter SP 1980–1, 1983–4

NCAA Cross-country Championships

Held annually since 1938, women from 1981.

Most team wins:
MEN 8 Michigan State 1939, 1948–9, 1952, 1955–6, 1958–9
7 UTEP 1975–6, 1978–81, 1983
WOMEN 2 Virginia 1981–2

3 individual titles:
Gerry Lindgren (Washington State) 1966–7, 1969; Steve Prefontaine (Oregon) 1970–1, 1973; Henry Rono (Washington State) 1976–7, 1979
2 women's titles: Betty Springs (N. Carolina State) 1981, 1983

First

International match (full team): 13–14 Aug **1938**, v Germany at Berlin.

USSR

The first Russian athletics meeting was held in 1867, and the first representation at the Olympic Games by a Russian team was in 1912. Following the revolution of 1917, the current governing body, the Light Athletic Federation of the USSR, was formed.

the first Soviet appearance in an international meeting was at the 1946 European Championships, when 17 medals, including six gold, were won. This was followed by admittance to the IAAF in 1947 and the IOC in 1951, and the first Olympic appearance in 1952.

USSR CHAMPIONSHIPS

The first USSR Championships were held in 1920 for men and 1922 for women. They have been held annually since then with the exception of 1921, 1925–6, 1929–30, 1932–3, 1941–2.

The first World Workers' Spartakiad was held in 1928. These Games were the predecessor of the current Summer People's Games of the USSR—the Spartakiad, the first of which was held in 1956. From 1959 the Spartakiad has been held four-yearly, embracing a large number of sports—32 in 1983. In these years the USSR Championships are incorporated in this event.

CHAMPIONSHIP BEST PERFORMANCE prior to 1986

MEN

Event	hr:min:sec	Athlete	Place	Year
100m	10.0	Vladislav Sapeya	Leningrad	1968
	10.0	Valeriy Borzov	Kiev	1969
	10.0	Valeriy Borzov	Moscow	1972
	10.0	Aleksandr Kornelyuk	Moscow	1973
	10.27	Valeriy Borzov	Kiev	1976
200m	20.2	Valeriy Borzov	Moscow	1971
	20.46	Vladimir Muravyev (sf)	Moscow	1983
400m	45.44	Viktor Markin	Moscow	1983
800m	1:44.93	Viktor Zemlyanskiy	Leningrad	1985
1500m	3:36.09	Igor Lotarev	Leningrad	1985
5000m	13:19.18	Dmitriy Dmitriyev	Kiev	1982
10 000m	27:47.4	Aleksandr Antipov	Moscow	1979
Marathon	2:10:58	Vladimir Kotov	Moscow	1980
3000m steeple	8:22.2	Vladimir Dudin	Kiev	1969
110mh	13.50	Viktor Myasnikov	Kiev	1976
400mh	48.33	Aleksandr Vasilyev	Leiningrad	1985
20kmW (road)	1:21:33	Viktor Mostovik	Leningrad	1985
50kmW (road)	3:37:36	Yevgeniy Ivchenko & Boris Yakovlyev	Moscow (short course)	1980

Event	metres	Athlete	Place	Year
High jump	2.35	Valeriy Sereda	Moscow	1983
Pole vault	5.80	Sergey Bubka	Donyetsk	1984
Long jump	8.32	Sergey Layevskiy	Donyetsk	1984
Triple jump	17.69	Oleg Protsenko	Leningrad	1985
Shot	21.53	Yevgeniy Mironov	Kiev	1976
Discus	68.52	Igor Duginyets	Kiev	1982
Hammer	84.14	Sergey Litvinov	Moscow	1983
Javelin	91.10	Janis Lusis	Leninaken	1968
Decathlon	8698 pts	Grigoriy Degtyaryev	Kiev	1984

WOMEN

Event	hr:min:sec	Athlete	Place	Year
100m	11.19	Lyudmila Kondratyeva	Moscow	1979
200m	22.50	Elvira Barbashina	Leningrad	1985
400m	48.96	Olga Vladykina	Leningrad	1985
800m	1:56.0	Valentina Gerasimova	Kiev	1976
1500m	3:54.23	Olga Dvirna	Kiev	1982
3000m	8:26.78	Svyetlana Ulmasova	Kiev	1982
5000m	15:05.31	Olga Bondarenko	Leningrad	1985
10 000m	31:25.18	Olga Bondarenko	Moscow	1985
Marathon	2:31:11	Zoya Ivanova	Baku	1984
100mh	12.59	Vera Akimova	Leningrad	1985
400mh	54.37	Marina Styepanova	Leningrad	1985
5kmW	22:48.21	Lyudmila Khruscheva	Kiev	1982
10kmW (road)	44:54	Vera Osipova	Leningrad	1985

Event	metres	Athlete	Place	Year
High jump	2.00	Tamara Bykova	Leningrad	1985
Long jump	7.12	Yelena Kokonova	Leningrad	1985
Shot	21.20	Nunu Abashidze	Kiev	1982
Discus	73.28	Galina Savinkova	Donyetsk	1984
Javelin	69.86	Natalya Kolenchukova	Leningrad	1985
Heptathlon	6859 pts	Natalya Shubenkova	Kiev	1984

Most titles won at each event
(Includes all who won 6 or more)
MEN

100m	7	Nikolay Karakulov 1943–9
	7	Valeriy Borzov 1969, 1971–2, 1974–7
	6	Edvin Ozolin 1959–63, 1966
200m	6	Robert Lyulko 1934–9
	6	Nikolay Karakulov 1943–4, 1946–9
	6	Valeriy Borzov 1971–5, 1977
400m	7	Sergey Komarov 1943–7, 1949–50
	6	Ardalion Ignatyev 1952–6, 1959
800m	7	Aleksandr Pugachevskiy 1939–40, 1943–4, 1946–8
1500m	7	Aleksandr Pugachevskiy 1938–40, 1943–4, 1947–8
5000m	5	Serafim Znamenskiy 1934, 1936–8, 1940
	5	Vladimir Kuts 1953–7
	5	Pyotr Bolotnikov 1958–62
10 000m	7	Feodosiy Vanin 1940, 1943–5, 1947–9
	7	Pyotr Bolotnikov 1957–62, 1964
Marathon	4	Viktor Baikov 1961–4
3000m steeple	5	Semyon Rzhishchin 1955–9
110mh	10	Anatoliy Mikhailov 1957–66
	8	Yevgeniy Bulanchik 1948–55
400mh	8	Yuriy Lituyev 1950–5, 1957–8
High jump	5	Edmund Rokhlin 1934–7, 1939
	5	Aleksandr Grigoryev 1975, 1977–9, 1981
Pole vault	12	Nikolay Ozolin 1928, 1934, 1938–40, 1943–4, 1946–50
	7	Gennadiy Bliznyetsov 1963–6, 1968, 1970, 1972
Long jump	12	Igor Ter-Ovanesyan 1957, 1959–60, 1962–9, 1971
	7	Sergey Kuznyetsov 1943–9
	6	Valeriy Podluzhniy 1973–7, 1979
Triple jump	8	Viktor Saneyev 1968–71, 1973–5, 1978
	6	Leonid Shcherbakov 1951–6
Shot	6	Heino Lipp 1946–51
Discus	5	Sergey Lyakhov 1934–5, 1937–8, 1940
	5	Otto Grigalka 1953–6, 1959
	5	Vladimir Lyakhov 1969–72, 1976
Hammer	8	Aleksandr Shekhtyel 1936–7, 1939–40, 1944–7
	6	Mikhail Krivonosov 1952, 1954–8
Javelin	12	Janis Lusis 1962–6, 1968–73, 1976
Decathlon	10	Vasiliy Kuznyetsov 1953–60, 1962–3
	7	Aleksandr Demin 1927–8, 1935–6, 1938–40
20kmW	6	Vladimir Golubnichiy 1960, 1964–5, 1968, 1972, 1974
50kmW	6	Venyamin Soldatenko 1969–72, 1975–6

WOMEN

100m	6	Marina Shamanova 1927–8, 1931, 1934–5, 1943
200m	6	Maria Itkina 1954, 1956–7, 1960–2
400m	5	Maria Itkina 1959–60, 1963–5
800m	5	Yevdokiya Vasilyeva 1937–8, 1943–5
	5	Lyudmila Lysenko 1955–6, 1959, 1961–2
1500m	6	Yevdokiya Vasilyeva 1938, 1943–5, 1949, 1951
	6	Lyudmila Bragina 1968–70, 1972–4
3000m	3	Svyetlana Ulmasova 1978–9, 1982
5000	1	1 each (first held 1985)
10 000m	1	1 each (first held 1982)
80mh/100m	8	Valentina Fokina 1938–9, 1943–8
400mh	2	Tatyana Zelentseva 1976, 1978
	2	Marina Styepanova 1979, 1985
High jump	7	Aleksandra Chudina 1946–7, 1949–51, 1953–4
	6	Galina Ganeker 1939–40, 1943–5, 1948

Igor Ter-Ovanesyan sets a world indoor record for the long jump at 8.18m in New York at the Millrose Games in 1963. (Keystone)

Long jump	7	Aleksandra Chudina 1947–51, 1953–4
	6	Tatyana Shchelkanova 1961–6
Shot	9	Tamara Press 1958–66
	6	Tatyana Sevryukova 1939–40, 1944–47
	6	Nadezhda Chizhova 1967–70, 1972, 1974
	6	Svyetlana Krachevskaya 1973, 1975–8, 1980
Discus	9	Faina Melnik 1970, 1972–7, 1980–1
	8	Nina Dumbadze 1939, 1943–4, 1946–50
	8	Nina Ponomaryeva 1951–6, 1958–9
	7	Tamara Press 1960–6
Javelin	6	Klavdiya Mayuchaya 1938–9, 1943–4, 1946–7
Pen/Hep	9	Aleksandra Chudina 1946–51, 1953–5
	6	Irina Press 1959–61, 1964–6

MOST TITLES—all individual events:

MEN
16 Aleksandr Pugachevskiy (1938–48) 7 800m, 7 1500m, 2 3000mSt
13 Robert Lyulko (1931–40) 6 200m, 5 400m, 1 100m & LJ
13 Nikolay Karakulov (1943–9) 7 100m, 6 200m
13 Valeriy Borzov (1969–77) 7 100m, 6 200m
12 Nikolay Ozolin (1928–50) 12 PV
12 Feodosiy Vanin (1940–50) 7 10 000m, 3 5000m, 2 Mar
12 Heino Lipp (1946–51) 6 SP, 4 DT, 2 Dec
12 Pyotr Bolotnikov (1957–64) 7 10 000m, 5 5000m
12 Igor Ter-Ovanesyan (1959–71) 12 LJ
12 Janis Lusis (1962–76) 12 JT

WOMEN
- 31 Aleksandra Chudina (1945–56) 9 Pen, 7 HJ, 7 LJ, 4 JT, 3 80mh, 1 400m
- 16 Tamara Press (1958–66) 9 SP, 7 DT
- 15 Maria Itkina (1954–65) 6 200m, 5 400m, 4 100m
- 13 Yevdokiya Vasilyeva (1937–51) 6 1500m, 5 800m, 1 1000m & 2000m
- 11 Irina Press (1959–66) 6 Pen, 5 80mh

USSR RECORDS

The most set at one event outdoors:

MEN
- 15 Gennadiy Blizneytsov PV 4.70m 1963 to 5.30m 1968 (1 tie)
- 14 Anatoliy Mikhailov 110mh 14.1 1956 to 13.7 1965 (10 ties)
- 12 Igor Ter-Ovanesyan LJ 7.74m 1956 to 8.35m 1967
- 12 Romuald Klim HT 69.67m 1964 to 74.52m 1969
- 11 Sergey Lyakhov DT 43.37m 1934 to 50.74m 1939
- 11 Aleksandr Shekhtyel HT 49.18m 1935 to 55.81m 1948
- 11 Mikhail Krivonosov HT 59.18m 1952 to 67.32m 1956
- 10 Heino Lipp SP 15.62m 1946 to 16.98m 1951
- 10 Leonid Shcherbakov TJ 15.43m 1949 to 16.46m 1956
- 10 Valeriy Brumel HJ 2.17m 1960 to 2.28m 1963

WOMEN
- 17 Irina Press 80mh 10.6 1960 to 10.3 1965 (13 ties)
- 14 Galina Zybina SP 15.19m 1952 to 16.76m 1956
- 12 Faina Melnik DT 62.90m 1971 to 70.50m 1976
- 11 Nina Dumbadze DT 42.13m 1937 to 57.04m 1952
- 11 Maria Itkina 400m 55.8 1953 to 52.9 1965
- 11 Nadezhda Chizhova SP 18.67m 1968 to 21.45m 1973

Most at all events:

MEN
- 27 Sergey Lyakhov (1928–39) 11 DT, 8 SP, 8 HT
- 22 Serafim Znamenskiy (1933–40) 8 5000m, 6 10 000m, 5 3000m, 2 1500m, 1 2000m
- 18 Aleksandr Pugachevskiy (1938–48) 6 1500m, 5 800m, 5 1000m, 2 2000m
- 16 Ardalion Ignatyev (1952–6) 9 400m, 7 200m
- 14 Nikolay Denisov (1928–35) 6 800m, 6 1500m, 2 1000m
- 14 Anatoliy Mikhailov (1956–65) 14 110mh

WOMEN
- 25 Irina Press (1959–65) 17 80mh, 8 Pen
- 21 Aleksandra Chudina (1946–55) 9 HJ, 6 LJ, 6 Pen
- 20 Maria Itkina (1953–65) 11 400m, 8 200m, 1 100m

Firsts

Olympic champion (woman): Nina Romashkova (later Ponomaryeva) DT 1952
European champion (woman): Tatyana Sevryukova SP and Yevgeniya Sechenova 100m 1946
Prior to USSR competing, golds for the Baltic republics (now in the USSR) were first won in 1934 by Arnold Viiding (Estonia) SP and Janis Dalins (Latvia) 50km walk.
World record (at event then standard) (woman): Yevdokiya Vasilyeva 800m in 2:15.3 1938.
International match: 20 Oct 1934 v Czechoslovakia (men). USSR won eight events to two. The second was not until 23, 25 Aug 1949, also v Czechoslovakia, with men's and women's events.

Other Nations— Short Summaries

AUSTRIA

The national federation, Osterreichischer Leicht-athletik-Verband, was founded in 1900. Herma Bauma, at women's javelin, won Austria's first Olympic gold medal in 1948.

National Championships were first held in 1911 for men and 1918 for women.

Most titles won at one event:

MEN	12	Adolf Gruber Mar 1952–63
	11	Ferdinand Friebe 1500m 1913, 1919–24, 1926–9
	11	Arnulf Pilhatsch HJ 1941–3, 1946–9, 1951–4
	11	Emil Janausch HT 1929–39
	11	Wolfgang Tschirk HJ 1974–84
WOMEN	15	Herma Bauma JT 1931–4, 1936–7, 1941–3, 1946–50, 1952
	14	Eva Janko JT 1966, 1968, 1970, 1972–82
	13	Margit Signoretti DT 1976–77, 1979–80

Most titles at all standard individual events:

MEN	26	Horst Mandl (1962–73) 9 TJ, 6 Dec, 4 LJ, 3 110mh, 2 HJ & Pen
	24	Emil Janausch (1923–39) 11 HT, 7 DT, 6 SP (also at both hands events: 8 DT, 4 SP)
	24	Hans Muchitsch (1954–62) 7 Dec, 6 LJ & 110mh, 5 400mh
	21	Adolf Gruber (1952–63) 12 Mar, 5 10 000m, 2 5000m & 3000mSt (and 8 25km road)
WOMEN	28	Karoline Käfer (1972–85) 9 200m & 400m, 8 100m, 2 800m
	21	Ronny Kohlbach (1927–36) 7 LJ, 6 DT, 4 200m, 3 100m, 18mh
	21	Liese Prokop (1961–76) 7 Pen, 6 SP, 4 HJ, 2 100m, 1 LJ

Records
The most set at one event:

MEN	15	Heinrich Thun HT 53.10m 1957 to 69.77m 1963
WOMEN	14	Herma Bauma JT 36.31m 1931 to 48.63m 1948

Most at all standard events:

MEN	19	Ferdinand Friebe (1913–26) 6 1500m & 2000m, 5 1000m, 1 800m & 3000m
WOMEN	24	Liese Prokop (1963–9) 8 Pen, 7 SP & 100mh, 1 HJ & LJ
	24	Liesl Perkaus (1924–31) 8 SP, 7 DT, 3 100m, 2 300m, 1 60m, 200m, JT & Pen
	23	Maria Sykora (1967–73) 11 400m, 5 800m, 3 400mh, 2 200m, 1 100mh & 200mh

BELGIUM

The original governing body, founded in 1889, is split into federations for the two linguistic groups: the VAL (Vlaamse Atletiek Liga) and the LBFA (Ligue Belge Francophone d'Athlétisme).

National Championships were first held in 1889 for men and 1921 for women.

Most titles won at one event:

MEN	17	Henri Haest HT 1948–64
WOMEN	11	Simone Saenen SP 1953–62, 1965

Most titles at all standard individual events:

MEN 28 Gaston Roelants (1959–72) 13 CC,
9 3000mSt, 4 10 000m, 1 1500m & 5000m
24 Emile Binet (1930–42) 10 LJ, 6 110mh, 4 Dec,
2 200mh & TJ
21 Georges Schroder (1970–85) 13 DT, 11 SP
19 Walter Herssens (1949–60) 8 HJ & TJ, 2 Dec,
1 LJ
18 Pol Braekman (1938–51) 12 110mh,
4 200mh, 1 100m & 200m

WOMEN 21 Simone Saenen (1953–65) 11 SP, 10 DT
15 Hilde De Cort (1955–64) 8 80mh, 4 Pen, 2 SP,
1 100m
15 Lea Alearts (1972–80) 7 100m, 5 200m,
1 400m, 100mh & 400mh

Records
The most set at one event:
MEN 23 Henri Haest HT 34.11m 1947 to 55.33m 1957

WOMEN 18 Simone Saenen DT to 36.81m to 46.29m 1960

Most at all standard events:
MEN 29 Gaston Roelants (1959–72) 11 3000mSt,
7 10 000m, 6 5000m, 2 20km & 1Hr,
1 3000m (and 1 at 4x1500mR)

WOMEN 28 Lea Alearts (1972–8) 8 100mh, 7 400mh,
5 200m, 3 60m & 200mh, 1 400m & 100mh
(and 15 relays)

BULGARIA

Bulgaria has in recent years been a major force,
particularly in women's athletics, but it is a late-
comer, as the first meeting was held as recently as
1924, when the national federation was founded.

National Championships were first held in 1926
for men and 1938 for women.

Most titles won at one event:

MEN 14 Stoyan Slavkov Dec 1951–64
14 Dmitriy Khlebarov PV 1955–9, 1961–6, 1968,
1970–1
11 Todor Artarski DT 1956, 1959–60, 1962–3,
1965, 1967–71.

WOMEN 14 Ionna Arsova JT 1948, 1950–8, 1960–1,
1964–5
13 Ivanka Khristova SP 1961–6, 1968–74
12 Verzhinia Mikhailova DT 1953–8, 1960–5

Most titles at all standard individual events:

MEN 22 Stoyan Slavkov (1951–64) 14 Dec, 5 LJ, 3 HJ
20 Petar Spasor (1946–55) 6 5000m & 10 000m,
5 3kmSt, 3 1500m

WOMEN 20 Snezhana Kerkova (1957–67) 10 80mh,
4 100m & 200m, 2 Pen

Records
The most set at one event:

MEN 19 Dmitriy Khlebarov PV 4.02m 1954 to 4.96m
1965
19 Georgi Kaburov 110mh 15.6 1954 to 14.4
1958 (10 ties)
17 Valcho Stoev SP 17.81m 1971 to 20.72m
1980
16 Atanas Tarev PV 5.07m 1977 to 5.75m 1985
13 Boris Popov HT 45.45m 1948 to 58.90m 1956
13 Emanuil Dyulgerov HT 74.00m 1977 to
80.64m 1984

WOMEN 36 Ivanka Khristova SP 15.42m 1962 to 21.89m
1976
24 Verzhinia Mikhailova DT 38.78m 1953 to
56.70m 1964

23 Ioana Arsova JT 32.72m 1948 to 52.01m 1964
22 Deana Yorgova LJ 5.58m 1959 to 6.77m 1972
19 Snezhana Kerkova 80mh 11.9 1957 to 10.7
1964 (9 ties)

Most at all standard events:

MEN 22 Stoyan Slavkov (1953–9) 11 Dec, 8 HJ, 3 LJ
22 Petar Spasor (1946–57) 6 5000m, & 3kmSt,
5 1500m & 10 000m

WOMEN 36 Ivanka Khristova (1962–76) 36 SP
29 Snezhana Kerkova (1957–64) 19 80mh,
4 100m & Pen, 2 200m
25 Ionna Arsova (1948–64) 23 JT, 1 DT & Pen

DENMARK

The Dansk Athletik Forbund was formed in 1907.
A Danish athlete has yet to win as Olympic title,
the best placing being Henry Petersen's silver
medal at pole vault in 1920.

National Championships were first held in 1894
for men and 1944 for women.

Most titles won at one event:

MEN 11 Thyge Tögersen 10 000m 1953, 1955–64
11 John Hansen JT 1940–7, 1949, 1952, 1955
11 Kaj Andersen DT 1962–72

WOMEN 17 Karen Inge Halkier SP 1956–72; 15 Karen
Inge Halkier DT 1957–60, 1962–8, 1970–3

Most titles at all standard individual events:

MEN 28 Thyge Tögersen (1951–64) 11 10 000m,
8 5000m, 6 20 km, 3 Mar
23 Jesper Törring (1969–80) 9 LJ, 8 HJ, 6 110mh

WOMEN 33 Karen Inge Halkier (1956–72) 17 SP, 15 DT,
1 HJ
30 Nina Hansen (1959–68) 10 Pen, 9 LJ, 8 80mh,
2 100m, 1 200m

Records
The most set at one event:

MEN 12 Jørgen Munk Plum DT 46.41m 1949 to
50.35m 1961
12 Kaj Andersen DT 50.54m 1964 to 59.63m
1971

WOMEN 12 Nina Hansen Pen 1959–69

Most at all standard events:

MEN 21 Jesper Törring (1969–74) 6 110mh & HJ, 5 LJ,
2 200mh & 400m

WOMEN 25 Nina Hansen (1957–69) 12 Pen, 6 LJ & 80mh,
2 200mh, 1 100mh
20 Anneliese Damm Olesen (1968–72) 7 100mh,
6 400m & 800m, 1 1500m

HUNGARY

The national federation was formed in 1897.
National Championships were first held in 1896 at
two events with a full programme instituted in
1903. Women's events were first held in 1932.

Most titles won at one event:

MEN 20 Jozsef Varszegi JT 1932–43, 1945–52
13 Gyula Zsivotzky HT 1958–70
13 Vilmos Varju SP 1958–60, 1963–72
12 Jozsef Daranyi SP 1926–35, 1938–9

Most titles at all standard individual events:

MEN 21 Jeno Szilagyi (1932–50) 11 10 000m,
8 5000m, 2 3000mSt (and 4 C–C).
20 Jozsef Varszegi (1932–52) 20 JT

WOMEN 24 Olga Gyarmati (1941–56) 8 LJ, 7 80mh,
3 100m, 2 200m, HJ & Pen

Records

The most set at one event:

MEN   17 Vilmos Varju SP 16.63m 1958 to 20.45m 1971

WOMEN 21 Judit Bognar SP 14.36m 1957 to 18.23m 1972
         16 Jolan Kleiber DT 50.28m 1960 to 60.68m 1971
         14 Maria Feher SP 12.38m 1948 to 14.35m 1956

Most at all standard events:

MEN   23 Miklos Szabo (1929–37) 7 1500m, 5 3000m, 4 2000m, 3 1000m & 5000m, 1 10 000 m

WOMEN 24 Olga Gyarmati (1948–56) 12 80mh, 4 LJ, 3 100m & 200m, 1 60m & Pen
         24 Judit Bognar (1957–72) 21 SP, 3 DT

IRELAND

Irish athletes played a notable part in the early days of athletics, with their field event men in particular featuring prominently on world bests lists and at the AAA Championships. The Irish AAA was founded in 1885, a year after the Gaelic Athletics Foundation.

Thomas Keily won a total of 53 Irish titles, including 18 at the hammer. He won seven Gaelic AA titles on one day, 10 Sep 1892, and was also the first Irishman to win an Olympic title, the all-around event in 1904.

National Championships—The current governing body, the Bord Luthchleas na h'Eireann was founded in 1967.

Most BLE titles won at one event:

MEN   7 Hugo Duggan LJ 1967, 1970–2, 1974, 1980, 1983

WOMEN 9 Patricia Walsh DT 1978–85
         8 Marita Walton SP 1976–8, 1980–4
         7 Mary Purcell 1500m 1972–6, 1978, 1980

Most BLE titles at all standard individual events:

MEN 11 Eamonn Coghlan (1974–83) 5 800m, 5 1500m, 1 5000m
          Note that Tadgh Twomey at the 56lb weight won 12 titles for height and 10 for distance.

WOMEN 16 Claire Walsh (1968–73) 6 200m, 4 100m & 400m, 1 800m & Pen

NETHERLANDS

The Nederlandsche Athletiek-Bond was formed in 1896 and was followed in 1901 by the founding of the present governing body, the Nederlandsche Athletiek-Unie.

National Championships were first held in 1910 for men and 1921 for women.

Most titles won at one event:

MEN 16 Willem Peters TJ 1924–30, 1934–42
WOMEN 14 Ans Panhorst DT 1937–44, 1946, 1948–9, 1952–4
         13 Fanny Blankers-Koen 100m 1937–40, 1942–4, 1946–9, 1951–2
         12 Fanny Blankers-Koen 200m 1936–40, 1944, 1946–8, 1950–2

Most titles won at all standard individual events:

MEN 20 Evert Kamerbeek (1954–64) 11 Dec, 7 110mh, 2 200mh

WOMEN 58 Fanny Blankers-Koen (1936–55) 13 100m, 12 200m, 11 80mh, 10 HJ, 9 LJ, 2 SP, 1 Pen
         21 Ans Panhorst (1937–54) 14 DT, 7 SP

Records

The most set at one event:

MEN   15 Ruud Wielard HJ 2.11m 1973 to 2.28m 1979

WOMEN 16 Ria Stalman DT 54.14m 1974 to 71.22m 1984
         12 Els van Noorduyn SP 15.52m 1967 to 17.87m 1971
         11 Gerda Kraan 800m 2:16.6 1958 to 2:02.8 1962

Most at all standard event:

MEN   31 Jos Hermans (1971–8) at distance events
         21 Eef Kamerbeek (1954–63) 12 Dec, 7 110mh, 2 110mh

WOMEN 26 Fanny Blankers-Koen (1936–52) 8 200m, 5 LJ, 4 100m & HJ, 2 80mh & Pen, 1 800m (and many others at imperial distances and other events)

NEW ZEALAND

The New Zealand AA was formed in 1887. The first New Zealander to set a world record and to win an Olympic title was Jack Lovelock. He ran a world mile record of 4:07.6 in 1933 and three years later won the Olympic 1500m in another world record of 3:47.8.

National Championships were first held for men in 1888 and for women in 1926.

Most titles won at one event:

MEN 18 Dave Norris TJ 1957–71, 1974–5, 1977
      14 Les Mills SP 1955, 1957–62, 1965–70, 1972
      13 Peter Munro DT 1920–3, 1925–6, 1928–30, 1932–5 (1st NZ 1931)
      12 Peter Munro SP 1920–2, 1925–6, 1928–30, 1932–5 (1st NZ 1923 & 1931)
      11 J. W. McHolm HT 1913–15, 1920–2, 1924–5, 1928–30 (1st NZ 1923)
      11 Mervyn Richards PV 1952–62

WOMEN 18 Valerie Young DT 1957–8, 1961–6, 1972–3, 1975–82
        17 Valerie Young SP 1956–66, 1972–4, 1979–81

Most titles at all standard individual events:

MEN 28 Dave Norris (1957–77) 18 TJ, 8 LJ, 2 220yh
      27 Peter Munro (1920–35) 13 DT, 12 SP, JT (and a further 4 in which he finished as first NZ athlete)
      25 Les Mills (1955–72) 14 SP, 11 DT

WOMEN 37 Valerie Young (1956–82) 18 DT, 17 SP, 2 Pen
        21 Yvette Williams (1947–54) 8 SP, 7 LJ, 4 DT, 1 80mh & JT

NORWAY

The national federation (Norsk Idraetsforbund, since 1928 Norges Fri-idrettsforbund) was formed in 1896. The first Norwegian Olympic champion was Ferdinand Bie at pentathlon in 1912.

National Championships were first held for men in 1897 and for women in 1947

Most titles won at one event:

MEN 12 Bjørn Bang Andersen SP 1961–6, 1968, 1970–4

WOMEN 11 Berit Berthelsen LJ 1962–6, 1968–70, 1972–4

Most titles at all standard individual events:

MEN 20 Martin Stokken (1946–53) 6 10 000m & C-C, 4 5000m & 3000mSt

WOMEN 34 Berit Berthelsen (1962–74) 11 LJ, 8 200m, 5 100m, 4 400m & C-C, 1 80mh & Pen

Records
The most set at one event:

MEN   21 Sverre Strandli HT 50.82m 1949 to 63.88m
              1962
           17 Bjørn Bang Andersen SP 16.34m 1961 to
              19.29m 1972
           12 Kjell Hovik PV 4.32m 1960 to 4.70m 1964
           11 Ernst Larsen 3000mSt 9:14.6 1951 to 8:42.4
              1956
           11 Egil Danielsen JT 70.77m 1953 to 85.71m
              1956
WOMEN 19 Berit Berthelsen LJ 5.79m 1961 to 6.56m 1968
           12 Edel Leveras SP 11.79m 1956 to 13.24m 1961

Most at all standard events:

MEN   19 Auden Boysen (1950–5) 6 800m, 5 1000m,
              5 1500m, 2 400m, 1 1M.
WOMEN 39 Berit Berthelsen (1961–8) 19 LJ, 8 400m,
              4 Pen, 3 100m & 200m, 2 100mh.
           24 Grete Waitz (1971–83) 5 1500m & 3000m,
              4 800m & Mar, 2 1000m, 1M & 5000m.

PORTUGAL
The national federation was founded in 1921. In the past decade their distance runners have achieved great success, but it was not until Carlos Lopes was second in the 1976 Olympic 10 000m and won the 1977 world cross-country title that any Portuguese athlete won a medal in a major championships. Lopes went on to Olympic marathon victory in 1984 and Fernando Mamede became his country's first world record holder, at 10 000m in 1984.

National Championships were first held in 1910 for men and 1937 for women.

Most titles won at one event:

MEN   16 Herculano Mendes HT 1928, 1930–44
           12 Matos Fernandes 400mh 1940–2, 1944–7,
              1949–51, 1954–5
           12 Manuel da Silva DT 1941, 1943–5, 1947–51,
              1953–5
           12 José Pedroso HT 1974–85
WOMEN 18 Adelia Silverio ST 1967–77 1979–85
           17 Adelia Silverio DT 1968–77, 1979–85
           11 Georgette Duarte 80mh 1948–58

Most titles at all standard individual events:

MEN   32 Matos Fernandes (1940–55) 12 400mh,
              8 Dec, 5 110mh & HJ, 1 400m & LJ (and 5
              relay)
           29 Manuel de Silva (1941–58) 12 DT, 9 SP, 8 HT
           25 Herculano Mendes (1928–44) 16 HT, 9 DT
           25 José Carvalho (1972–85)
WOMEN 43 Georgette Duarte (1946–68) 11 80mh, 9 LJ,
              8 100m, 4 200m & Pen, 3 HJ, 2 150m,
              1 60m & DT
           36 Adelia Silverio (1967–85) 18 SP, 17 DT
           25 Lidia Faria (1960–8) 8 DT, 5 SP, 4 80mh &
              Pen, 2 200m, 1 100m & 400m

Records
The most set at one event:

MEN   12 Matos Fernandes 110mh 15.3 1951 to 14.8
              1956 (8 ties)
WOMEN 15 Adelia Silverio SP 11.92m 1969 to 16.20m
              1976
           15 Aurora Cunha 3000m 9:54.0 1976 to 8:46.37
              1984

Most at all standard events:
MEN   24 Matos Fernandes (1942–51) 12 110mh,
              7 Dec, 5 400mh

MEN   24 Fernando Mamede (1970–84) 7 1500m,
              5 800m, 4 10 000m, 2 1000m, 3000m &
              5000m, 1 1M & 2000m.
           23 Carlos Lopes (1971–83) 9 5000m, 8 10 000m,
              2 3000m 1 each at 2M, 15km, 20km, 1Hr
              (also 2 at marathon)
WOMEN 41 Aurora Cunha (1976–85) 15 3000m,
              12 1500m, 6 5000m, 3 2000m, 2 1000m &
              10 000m, 1 800m
           32 Lidia Faria (1962–8) 10 80mh & SP, 7 DT,
              5 Pen
           23 Adelia Silverio (1969–76) 15 SP, 8 DT

ROMANIA
The national federation was founded in 1912 and Romanian athletes first competed in the Olympic Games in 1928. In recent years their men have not made much international impact, but their women, especially middle and long distance runners, have achieved great success.

National Championships were first held in 1921 for men and 1925 for women.

Most titles won at one event:

WOMEN 17 Ana Salagean SP 1954–70.
           16 Iolanda Balas HJ 1951–66
           12 Lia Manoliu DT 1952–6, 1960, 1962–4,
              1968–70

Most titles at all standard individual events:

MEN   50 Cristea Dinu (1935–58) at all events
WOMEN

Records
The most set at one event:
WOMEN 25+ Iolanda Balas HJ 1.51m 1951 to 1.91m 1961
           12 Mihaela Loghin SP 1975 to 21.00m 1984

SOUTH AFRICA
The South African AAU was founded in 1894, and its athletes had a long tradition of success in major events, but due to the country's apartheid policies they were expelled from the IAAF in 1976 and its athletes are no longer eligible for international competition. The first South African Olympic champion was Reggie Walker at 100m in 1908.

National Championships were first held in 1894 for men and 1929 for women.

Most titles won at one event:
MEN   14 Cecil McMaster 3MW 1914, 1920–30, 1932,
              1935
           13 Harry Hart SP 1926–35, 1939–40, 1946
           11 Stephanus du Plessis DT 1951–60, 1967
WOMEN 11 Ronelle Boshoff DT 1964, 1967, 1969,
              1971–2, 1974–9

Most titles at all standard individual events:
MEN   31 Harry Hart (1926–46) 13 SP, 9 DT, 4 PV, 3 JT,
              2 HT
           22 George Hazle (1958–68) 9 3MW, 1 5kmW,
              6 20kmW, 6 50kmW
WOMEN 18 Marjorie Clark (1929–35) 6 HJ, 4 100yh,
              3 100y, 3 220y, 1 LJ & 80mh

Records
The most set at one event:
MEN   19 Adam Barnard HT 62.18m 1970 to 73.86m
              1976
WOMEN 20 Anne McKenzie 800m/880y 2:24.8y 1962 to
              2:06.5 1967

Most at all standard events:
MEN   19 Adam Barnard (1970–6) 19 HT
WOMEN 24 Anne McKenzie (1962–7) 20 800m/880y, 2
              1500m & 1M
          24 Sonja Laxton (1971–80) 10 1500m, 6 3000m,
              5 1M, 2 Mar, 1 1000m

SPAIN

Spanish athletes first competed in the Olympic Games in 1920, when the national federation was formed. Their athletes have come to the fore recently, with Jorge Llopart winning their first medal at a major championships, the 1978 European 50km walk.

National Championships were first held in 1917 for men and 1931 for women.

Most titles won at one event:

MEN   13 Pedro Apellaniz JT 1944–8, 1950–5, 1957–8

Most titles at all standard individual events:

MEN   19 Felix Errauzquin (1932–49) 9 SP, 9 DT, 1 JT

WOMEN 14 Carmen Valero (1972–8) 7 1500m, 4 3000m,
              3 800m

Records
The most set at one event:
MEN   17 Luis Filipe Areta TJ 14.54m 1959 to 16.36m
              1968
          17 Luis Sanchez 100m 10.4 1965 to 10.3 1977
              (all but one ties)
          15 Luis Garriga HJ 1.98m 1963 to 2.13m 1970 (3
              ties)
          15 Ignacio Sola PV 4.25m 1963 to 5.20m 1978

WOMEN 16 M. José Martinez 100mh 14.6 1973 to 13.3
              1980 (7 ties)
          13 Ana Maria Molina SP 12.40m 1969 to 14.13 m
              1974

Most at all standard events:
MEN   22 Luis Sanchez (1965–77) 17 100m, 5 200m (all
              but one ties!)
          21 Luis Filipe Areta (1959–68) 17 TJ, 4 LJ

WOMEN 30 M. José Martinez (1973–80) 16 100mh, 5 LJ,
              4 Pen, 3 200m, 2 400mh
          26 Ana Maria Molina (1967–74) 13 SP, 10 Pen,
              2 80mh, 1 100mh

SWITZERLAND

The governing body is the Schweizerischer Leictathletikverband, founded in 1905 as the Athletischer Ausschuss des Schweizerischen Fussball-Vernandes.

National Championships were first held for men in 1906 and for women in 1934.

Most titles won at one event:
Men   22 Urs Von Wartburg JT 1957–67, 1969–76,
              1978–80
          14 Jean Studer LJ 1934–44, 1947–9
          13 Mathias Mehr DT 1953, 1955–66
WOMEN 14 Lux Stiefel JT 1937–49, 1953
          14 Gretel Bolliger SP 1938–43, 1945–51

          13 Gretel Bolliger DT 1943–9, 1951–2, 1954–6,
              1958

Most titles at all standard individual events:
MEN   26 Urs Von Wartburg (1957–80) 22 JT, 3 Pen, 1
              Dec
          22 Jean Studer (1934–49) 14 LJ, 5 TJ, 3 100m
WOMEN 44 Gretel Bolliger (1938–58) 14 SP, 13 DT, 7
              Pen, 4 LJ, 3 80mh, 2 HJ, 1 60m
          34 Fry Frischknecht (1957–68) 10 SP, 9 JT,
              4 80mh, LJ & DT, 3 Pen.
          29 Meta Antenen (1964–76) 7 LJ & Pen, 5 100m,
              100mh, 3 80mh, 2 HJ
          23 Cornelia Bürki (1975–85) 11 1500m, 8 3000m
              4 800m (and 9 C-C)
          21 Lux Stiefel (1937–53) 14 JT, 6 Pen, 1 SP

Records

The most set at one event:
MEN   16 Edy Hubacher SP 16.26m 1964 to 19.34m
              1970
WOMEN 19 Rita Pfister DT 44.34m 1970 to 60.60 1976
          16 Meta Antenen LJ 5.64m 1964 to 6.73m 1971
Most at all standard events:
MEN   21 Edy Hubacher (1964–70) 16 SP, 5 DT
WOMEN 53 Meta Antenen (1964–71) 16 LJ, 13 80mh,
              9 100mh, 8 Pen, 6 100m, 1 200m
          22 Cornelia Bürki (1976–85) 8 3000m, 7 1500m,
              5 800m, 2 1M

YUGOSLAVIA

The national federation was formed in 1921, although two Serbian athletes had competed in the 1912 Olympic Games, before the founding of the combined nation. The first Yugoslav world record holder was Draga Stamejcic at women's 80mh in 1964.

National Championships were first held in 1920 for men and 1923 for women.

Most titles won at one event:

MEN   20 Srecko Stiglic HT 1966–85
          12 Franjo Mihalic 10 000m 1946–7, 1949–51,
              1953, 1955–60
WOMEN 10 Snezana Hrpevnik HJ 1967–73, 1975,
              1977–8

Most titles at all standard individual events:

MEN   21 Ivo Buratovic (1928–45) 6 110mh & HJ, 4 LJ,
              2 PV & Dec, 1 100m

WOMEN 18 Zrnka Krajnovic (1930–8) 6 LJ, 5 80mh, 3 HJ,
              2 60m, 1 100m & JT

Records
The most set at one event:

MEN   15 Franjo Mihalic 10 000m 32:59.0 1946 to
              29:37.6 1954

WOMEN 13 Natasa Urbancic JT 50.68m 1964 to 62.12m
              1973

Most at all standard events:

MEN   26 Franjo Mihalic (1946–57) 15 10 000m 4
              5000m, 2 20km & 1 Hr, 1 15km, 25km & 10M
          20 Djari Kovac (1959–64) 9 400mh, 3 200m &
              300m, 2 400m & 200m, ! Pen (and 4 relay)

WOMEN 21 Draga Stamejcic (1955–64) 11 Pen, 6 LJ,
              3 80mh, 1 60m (and 3 at 4x100mR)

Women's Cross Reference Index

This is a list of women, included in this book, who have competed significantly under both single and married names. The list is in alphabetical order of married names, as it is by this I have more usually referred to them. However, where an athlete is best known by her maiden name and referred to as that in this book, I have shown this in capitals. Those athletes who have appended their married names, e.g. Valerie Brisco to Brisco-Hooks, are not included in this list.

First name	Single name	Married name
Rosemarie	Witschas	Ackermann
Suzanne	Farmer	Allday
Lyudmila	Zhecheva	Andonova
Karin	Richert	Balzer
Berit	Toien	Berthelsen
Gisela	Köhler	Birkemeyer
Olga	Krentzer	Bondarenko
Renate	Garisch	Boy
Denise	Robertson	Boyd
Michele	Mason	Brown
Ulrike	Klapezynski	Bruns
Diane	Bowering	Burge
Paola	Pigni	Cacchi
Beverley	Goddard	Callender
Diane	LEATHER	Charles
Susan	Morley	Chick
Olga	Fikotova	Connolly
Susan	Orr	Cook
Kathy	Smallwood	Cook
Margaret	MacSherry	Coomber
Pat	Lowe	Cropper
Olga	Modrachova	Davidova
Diana	Elliott	Davies
Shirley	STRICKLAND	De la Hunty
Ursula	Jurewitz	Donath
Heike	Daute	Drechsler
Annelie	Jahns	Ehrhardt
Verona	Bernard	Elder
Diane	Davies	Elliott
Hildegard	Janze	Falck
Ellen	Neumann	Fiedler
Ruth	Gamm	Fuchs
Eva	Lehocka	Gleskova
Marlies	Oelsner	Göhr
Yekaterina	Fesenko	Grun
Margitta	Helmboldt	Gummel
Doris	BROWN	Heritage
Erica	Nixon	Hooker
Johanna	Lüttge	Hübner
Lynette	Tillett	Jacenko
Madeline	MANNING	Jackson
Evelin	Schlaak	Jahl
Bettina	Gärtz	Jahn
Lucyna	Langer	Kalek
Petra	VOGT	Kandarr
Margarita	Ponomaryeva	Khromova
Rita	Schmidt	Kirst
Marlene	Fuchs	Klein
Kerstin	Klaus	Knabe
Svetla	ZLATEVA	Koleva
Svetlana	Dolzhenko	Krachevskaya
Ingrid	Christensen	Kristiansen
Jaroslava	Komarkova	Kritkova
Elzbieta	Dunska	Krzesinska
Bedriska	Mullerova	Kulhava
Christine	Brehmer	Lathan
Gabrielle	Meinel	Lehmann
Judit	BOGNAR	Lendvay
Kriemhild	Hausmann	Limberg
Karin	Wallgren	Lundgren
Elvira	OZOLINA	Lusis
Natalia	Andrei	Marasescu/Betini
Jadwiga	WAJSOWNA	Marcinkiewicz
Gael	Mulhall	Martin
Lyudmila	Zharkova	Maslakova
Jennifer	Wingerson	Meldrum
Ingrid	Becker	Mickler
Katrina	GIBBS	Morrow
Marjorie	JACKSON	Nelson
Ramona	Göhler	Neubert
Nadezhda	Mushta	Olizarenko
Glynis	Saunders	Nunn
Cornelia	Riefstahl	Orchkenat
Nina	Pletnyeva	Otkalenko
Sabine	Möbius	Paetz
Della	James	Pascoe
Ruth	Kennedy	Patten
June	Foulds	Paul
Rosemary	Charters	Payne
Judy	Canty	Peckham
Maria	VERGOVA	Petkova
Judy	Amoore	Pollock
Galina	Vinogradova	Popova
Liesel	Sykora	Prokop
Maricica	Linca	Puica
Mona-Lisa	Strandvall	Pursiainen
Mary	Bignal	Rand (-Twomey)
Annegret	Irrgang	Richter
Rita	Lincoln	Ridley
Nina	Romashkova	Ponomaryeva
Charlene	Neighbour	Rendina
Pam	Kilborn	Ryan
Anna	Coman	(-Roth) Salagean
Riita	Hagman	Salin
Joan	BENOIT	Samuelson
Maria	Domagalla	Sander
Bärbel	LOCKHOFF	Schölzel
Helga	Fischer	Seidler
Ester	Rot	Shokhamurov
Sheila	Parkin	Sherwood
Lyudmila	LYSENKO	Shevtsova (-Gurevich)
Zdenka	Bartonova	Silhava
Judy	Livermore	Simpson
Mary	Decker	Slaney
Ilona	Schoknecht	Slupianek (-Briesenick)
Wendy	Smith	Sly
Raisa	Katyukova	Smekhnova
Joyce	Byatt	Smith
Francie	LARRIEU	Smith
Iolanda	Balas	Söter
Anisoara	Cusmir	Stanciu
Christine	Annison	Stanton
Renate	Meissner	Stecher
Marise	CHAMBERLAIN	Stephen
Jarmila	Nygrynova	Strejckova
Marina	Makeyeva	Styepanova
Irena	Kirszenstein	Szewinska
Dorothy	Odam	Tyler
Christa	Kofferschlager	Vahlensieck
Faina	MELNIK	Veleva
Viorica	Belmega	Viscopoleanu
Grete	Andersen	Waitz
Marianne	Schulze-Entrup	Werner
Rita	Jahn	Wilden
Marlene	Mathews	Willard
Lynn	Kanuka	Williams
Bärbel	Eckert	Wöckel
Thelma	Fynn	Wright
Rosemary	Stirling	Wright
Valerie	Sloper	Young
Mildred	DIDRIKSON	Zaharias
Dana	Ingrova	Zatopkova

Records and Best Performances

MEN	WORLD RECORD	EUROPEAN RECORD	UK RECORD
100m	9.93 Calvin Smith (USA) 1983	10.00 Marian Woronin (Pol) 1984	10.11 Allan Wells 1980
200m	19.72 Pietro Mennea (Ita) 1979	19.72 Pietro Mennea (Ita) 1979	20.21 Allan Wells 1980
400m	43.86 Lee Evans (USA) 1968	44.50 Erwin Skamrahl (FRG) 1983	44.82 Derek Redmond 1985
800m	1:41.73 Sebastian Coe (UK) 1981	1:41.73 Sebastian Coe (UK) 1981	1:41.73 Sebastian Coe 1981
1000m	2:12.18 Sebastian Coe (UK) 1981	2:12.18 Sebastian Coe (UK) 1981	2:12.18 Sebastian Coe 1981
1500m	3:29.46 Said Aouita (Mor) 1985	3:29.67 Steve Cram (UK) 1985	3:29.67 Steve Cram 1985
1 mile	3:46.32 Steve Cram (UK) 1985	3:46.32 Steve Cram (UK) 1985	3:46.32 Steve Cram 1985
2000m	4:51.39 Steve Cram (UK) 1985	4:51.39 Steve Cram (UK) 1985	4:51.39 Steve Cram 1985
3000m	7:32.1 Henry Rono (Ken) 1978	7:32.79 Dave Moorcroft (UK) 1982	7:32.79 Dave Moorcroft 1982
5000m	13:00.40 Said Aouita (Mor) 1985	13:00.41 Dave Moorcroft (UK) 1982	13:00.41 Dave Moorcroft 1982
10 000m	27:13.81 Fernando Mamede (Por) 1984	27:13.81 Fernando Mamede (Por) 1984	27:30.30 Brendan Foster 1978
20km	57:24.19 Jos Hermens (Hol) 1976	57:24.19 Jos Hermens (Hol) 1976	58:39.0 Ron Hill 1968
1 Hour	20944m Jos Hermens (Hol) 1976	20944m Jos Hermens (Hol) 1976	20472m Ron Hill 1968
25km	1:13:55.8 Toshihiko Seko (Jap) 1981	1:14:16.8 Pekka Päivärinta (Fin) 1975	1:15:22.6 Ron Hill 1985
30km	1:29:18.79 Toshihiko Seko (Jap) 1981	1:31:30.4 Jim Alder (UK) 1970	1:31:30.4 Jim Alder 1970
Mar	2:07.12 Carlos Lopes (Por) 1985	2:07:12 Carlos Lopes (Por) 1985	2:07:13 Steve Jones 1985
3000mSt	8:05.4 Henry Rono (Ken) 1978	8:07.62 Joseph Mahmoud (Fra) 1984	8:13.50 Colin Reitz 1985
110mh	12.93 Renaldo Nehemiah (USA) 1981	13.28 Guy Drut (Fra) 1975	13.43 Mark Holtom 1982
400mh	47.02 Edwin Moses (USA) 1983	47.48 Harald Schmid (FRG) 1982	48.12 David Hemery 1968
HJ	2.41 Igor Paklin (USSR) 1985	2.41 Igor Paklin (USSR) 1985	2.26 Geoff Parsons 1984
PV	6.00 Sergey Bubka (USSR) 1985	6.00 Sergey Bubka (USSR) 1985	5.65 Keith Stock 1981
LJ	8.90 Bob Beamon (USA) 1968	8.54 Lutz Dombrowski (GDR) 1980	8.23 Lynn Davies 1968
TJ	17.97 Willie Banks (USA) 1985	17.77 Khristo Markov (Bul) 1985	17.57 Keith Connor 1982
SP	22.62 Ulf Timmermann (GDR) 1985	22.62 Ulf Timmermann (GDR) 1985	21.68 Geoff Capes 1980
DT	71.86 Yuriy Dumchev (USSR) 1983	71.86 Yuriy Dumchev (USSR) 1983	65.16* Richard Slaney 1985
HT	86.34 Yuriy Sedykh (USSR) 1984	86.34 Yuriy Sedykh (USSR) 1984	77.54 Martin Girvan 1984
JT	104.80 Uwe Hohn (GDR) 1984	104.80 Uwe Hohn (GDR) 1984	91.40 Roald Bradstock 1985
Dec	8846 pts Daley Thompson (UK) 1984	8846 pts Daley Thompson (UK) 1984	8846 pts Daley Thompson 1984
4×100m	37.83 United States 1984	38.26 USSR 1980	38.62 National team 1980
4×400m	2:56.16 United States 1968	2:59.13 UK National team 1984	2:59.13 National team 1984
Track walking			
20km	1:18:40.0 Ernesto Canto (Mex) 1984	1:20:36.7 Erling Andersen (Nor) 1984	1:24:22 Ian McCombie 1985
50km	3:41:38.4 Raul Gonzalez (Mex) 1979	3:46:11 Mykola Udovenko (USSR) 1980	4:05:47.3 Chris Maddocks 1984
Road walking – fastest recorded times			
20km	1:19:29.6 Jozef Pribilinec (Cs) 1983	1:19:29.6 Jozef Pribilinec (Cs) 1983	1:22:37 Ian McCombie 1985
50km	3:38:31 Ronald Weigel (GDR) 1984	3:38:31 Ronald Weigel (GDR) 1984	4:02.00 Chris Maddocks 1984

WOMEN

WOMEN	WORLD RECORD	EUROPEAN RECORD	UK RECORD
100m	10.76 Evelyn Ashford (USA) 1984	10.81 Marlies Göhr (1983)	11.10 Kathy Cook 1981
200m	21.71 Marita Koch (GDR) 1979 & 1984	21.71 Marita Koch (GDR) 1979 & 1984	22.10 Kathy Cook 1984
400m	47.60 Marita Koch (GDR) 1985	47.60 Marita Koch (GDR) 1985	49.43 Kathy Cook 1985
800m	1:53.28 Jarmila Kratochvilova (Cs) 1983	1:53.28 Jarmila Kratochvilova (Cs) 1983	1:57.42 Kirsty McDermott 1985
1000m	2:30.6 Tatyana Providokhina (USSR) 1978	2:30.6 Tatyana Providokhina (USSR) 1978	2:33.70 Kirsty McDermott 1985
1500m	3:52.47 Tatyana Kazankina (USSR) 1980	3:52.47 Tatyana Kazankina (USSR) 1980	3:59.96 Zola Budd 1985
1 mile	4:16.71 Mary Slaney (USA) 1985	4:17.33 Maricica Puica (Rom) 1985	4:17.57 Zola Budd 1985
2000m	5:28.72 Tatyana Kazankina (USSR) 1984	5:22.72 Tatyana Kazankina (USSR) 1984	5:33.15 Zola Budd 1984
3000m	8:22.62 Tatyana Kazankina (USSR) 1984	8:22.62 Tatyana Kazankina (USSR) 1984	8:28.83 Zola Budd 1985
5000m	14:48.07 Zola Budd (UK) 1985	14:48.07 Zola Budd (UK) 1985	14:48.07 Zola Budd 1985
10 000m	30:59.42 Ingrid Kristiansen (Nor) 1985	30:59.42 Ingrid Kristiansen (Nor) 1985	32:57.17 Kathryn Binns 1980
Mar	2:21:06 Ingrid Kristiansen (Nor) 1985	2:21:06 Ingrid Kristiansen (Nor) 1985	2:28:04 Veronique Marot 1985
100mh	12.36 Grazyna Rabsztyn (Pol) 1980	12.36 Grazyna Rabsztyn (Pol) 1980	12.87 Shirley Strong 1983
400mh	53.55 Sabine Busch (GDR) 1985	53.55 Sabine Busch (GDR) 1985	56.04 Sue Chick 1983
HJ	2.07 Lyudmila Andonova (Bul) 1984	2.07 Lyudmila Andonova (Bul) 1984	1.95 Diana Davies 1982
LJ	7.44 Heike Drechsler (GDR) 1985	7.44 Heike Drechsler (GDR) 1985	6.90 Beverley Kinch 1983
SP	22.53 Natalya Lisovskaya (USSR) 1984	22.53 Natalya Lisovskaya (USSR) 1984	19.06i Venissa Head 1984
DT	74.56 Zdenka Silhava (Cs) 1984	74.56 Zdenka Silhava (Cs) 1984	67.48 Margaret Ritchie 1981
JT	75.40 Petra Felke (GDR) 1985	75.40 Petra Felke (GDR) 1985	73.58 Tessa Sanderson 1983
Hep	6946 pts Sabine Paetz (GDR) 1984	6946 pts Sabine Paetz (GDR) 1984	6347 pts Judy Simpson 1983
4×100m	41.37 GDR 1985	41.37 GDR 1985	42.43 National team 1980
4×400m	3:15.92 GDR 1984	3:15.92 GDR 1984	3:25.51 National team 1984
Track walking			
5000m	21:36.2 Olga Krishtop (USSR) 1984	21:36.2 Olga Krishtop (USSR) 1984	23.11.2 Carol Tyson 1979
10km	45:39.5 Yan Hong (Chn) 1984	46:14.3 Ann Jansson (Swe) 1985	47:56.3 Virginia Birch 1985
Road walking – fastest recorded times			
10km	44:43 Yan Hong (Chn) 1985	44:51.6 Olga Krishtop (USSR) 1984	48:47.0 Irene Bateman 1981

*unratified i—indoors

COMMONWEALTH RECORD	USA RECORD	WORLD JUNIOR RECORD	MEN
10.00 Ben Johnson (Can) 1985	9.93 Calvin Smith 1983	10.07 Stanley Floyd (USA) 1980	100m
19.86 Don Quarrie (Jam) 1985	19.75 Carl Lewis 1983	20.07 Lorenzo Daniel (USA) 1985	200m
44.58 Bert Cameron (Jam) 1981	43.86 Lee Evans 1968	44.69 Darrell Robinson (USA) 1982	400m
1:41.73 Sebastian Coe (UK) 1981	1:42.60 Johnny Gray 1985	1:44.3 Joaquim Cruz (Bra) 1981	800m
2:12.18 Sebastian Coe (UK) 1981	2:13.9 Rick Wohlhuter 1974	2:18.31 Andreas Busse (GDR) 1977	1000m
3:29.67 Steve Cram (UK) 1985	3:29.77 Sydney Maree 1985	3:34.92 Kipkoech Cheruiyot (Ken) 1983	1500m
3:46.32 Steve Cram (UK) 1985	3:47.69 Steve Scott 1982	3:51.3 Jim Ryun (USA) 1966	1 mile
4:51.39 Steve Cram (UK) 1985	4:54.20 Sydney Maree 1985	5:04.4 Harald Hudak (FRG) 1976	2000m
7:32.1 Henry Rono (Ken) 1978	7:35.64 Doug Padilla 1983	7:43.20 Ari Paunonen (Fin) 1977	3000m
13:00.41 Dave Moorcroft (UK) 1982	13:01.15 Sydney Maree 1985	13:25.33 Charles Cheruiyot (Ken) 1983	5000m
27:22.47 Henry Rono (Ken) 1978	27:25.61 Alberto Salazar 1982	28:32.7 Rudy Chapa (USA) 1976	10 000m
58:37.2 Rob de Castella (Aus) 1982	58:15.0 Bill Rodgers 1977		20km
20516m Rob de Castella (Aus) 1982	20547 Bill Rodgers 1977		1 Hour
1:15:22.6 Ron Hill (UK) 1985	1:14.11.8 Bill Rodgers 1979		25km
1:31:30.4 Jim Alder (UK) 1970	1:31:49 Bill Rodgers 1979		30km
2:07:13 Steve Jones (UK) 1985	2:08:51 Alberto Salazar 1982	2:15:28 Paul Gompers (USA) 1983	Mar
8:05.4 Henry Rono (Ken) 1978	8:09.17 Henry Marsh 1985	8:29.50 Ralf Pönitzsch (GDR) 1976	3000mSt
13.27 Mark McKoy (Can) 1985	12.93 Renaldo Nehemiah 1981	13.23 Renaldo Nehemiah (USA) 1978	110mh
47.82 John Akii-Bua (Uga) 1972	47.02 Edwin Moses 1983	48.02 Danny Harris (USA) 1984	400mh
2.32 Milt Ottey (Can) 1982	2.35 Jim Howard 1985	2.35‡ Dietmar Mögenburg (FRG) 1980	HJ
5.65 Keith Stock (UK) 1981	5.85 Joe Dial 1985	5.65 Rodion Gataullin (USSR) 1984	PV
8.27 Gary Honey (Aus) 1984	8.90 Bob Beamon 1968	8.34 Randy Williams (USA) 1972	LJ
17.57 Keith Connor (UK) 1982	17.97 Willie Banks 1985	17.50 Volker Mai (GDR) 1985	TJ
21.68 Geoff Capes (UK) 1980	22.19 Brian Oldfield 1984	20.65% Mike Carter (USA) 1979	SP
67.32 Rob Gray (Can) 1984	72.34* Ben Plucknett 1981	63.64 Werner Hartmann (FRG) 1978	DT
77.54 Martin Girvan (UK) 1984	77.24 Jud Logan 1985	78.14 Roland Steuk (GDR) 1978	HT
91.40 Roald Bradstock (UK) 1985	99.72 Tom Petranoff 1983	87.90 Ramon Gonzalez (Cub) 1983	JT
8846pts Daley Thompson (UK) 1984	8634 pts Bruce Jenner 1976	8397 pts Torsten Voss (GDR) 1982	Dec
38.39 Jamaica 1968	37.83 National team 1984	39.00 United States 1983 & 1985	4×100mR
2:59.13 United Kingdom 1984	2:56.16 National team 1968	3:02.46 United States 1983	4×400mR
			Track walking
1:24:17 Marcel Jobin (Can) 1980	1:25:29.3 Marco Evoniuk & Jim Heiring 1982	1:22.42 Andrey Perlov (USSR) 1980	20km
4:05:47.3 Chris Maddocks (UK) 1984	4:12:45.0 Dan O'Connor 1983		50km
			Road walking – fastest recorded times
1:19:52 Dave Smith (Aus) 1985	1:25.23 Marco Evoniuk 1984	1:21.39.1 Ralf Kowalsky (GDR) 1981	20km
3:46:34 Willi Sawall (Aus) 1980	3:56:57 Marco Evoniuk 1983		50km

WOMEN

COMMONWEALTH RECORD	USA RECORD	WORLD JUNIOR RECORD	WOMEN
10.92 Merlene Ottey-Page (Jam) 1985	10.76 Evelyn Ashford 1984	11.13 Chandra Cheeseborough (USA) 1976	100m
21.93 Merlene Ottey-Page (Jam) 1985	21.81 Valerie Brisco-Hooks 1984	22.19 Natalya Bochina (USSR) 1980	200m
49.43 Kathy Cook (UK) 1985	48.83 Valerie Brisco-Hooks 1984	49.77 Christina Brehmer (GDR) 1976	400m
1:57.42 Kirsty McDermott (UK) 1985	1:56.90 Mary Slaney 1985	1:59.40 Christine Wachtel (GDR) 1983	800m
2:33.70 Kirsty McDermott (UK) 1985	2:34.8 Mary Slaney 1985	2:35.4 Irina Nikitina (USSR) 1979	1000m
3:59.96 Zola Budd (UK) 1985	3:57.12 Mary Slaney 1983	4:01.81 Zola Budd (SAf) 1984	1500m
4:17.57 Zola Budd (UK) 1985	4:16.71 Mary Slaney 1985	4:30.7 Zola Budd (UK) 1984	1 mile
5:33.15 Zola Budd (UK) 1984	5:34.52i Mary Slaney 1985	5:33.15 Zola Budd (UK) 1984	2000m
8:28.83 Zola Budd (UK) 1985	8:25.83 Mary Slaney 1985	8:37.5 Zola Budd (SAf) 1984	3000m
14:48.07 Zola Budd (UK) 1985	15:06.53 Mary Slaney 1985	15:01.83 Zola Budd (SAf) 1984	5000m
32:17.86 Lisa Martin (Aus) 1985	31:35.3 Mary Slaney 1982		10 000m
2:26:46 Allison Roe (NZ) 1981	2:21.21 Joan Benoit 1985	2:34.24 Cathy Shiro (USA) 1984	Mar
12.87 Shirley Strong (UK) 1983	12.79 Stephanie Hightower 1984	12.95 Candy Young 1979	100mh
54.80 Debbie Flintoff (Aus) 1985	54.38 Judi Brown-King 1985	55.20 Leslie Maxie (USA) 1984	400mh
1.99i Debbie Brill (Can) 1982 (& 1.98)	2.01 Louise Ritter 1983	1.96† Olga Turchak (USSR) 1984	HJ
6.90 Beverley Kinch (UK)	7.24 Jackie Joyner 1985	6.98 Heike Daute/Dreschler (GDR) 1982	LJ
19.74 Gael Martin (Aus) 1984	19.13 Ramona Pagel 1985	19.57 Grit Haupt (GDR) 1984	SP
67.48 Margaret Ritchie (UK) 1981	65.20 Leslie Deniz 1984	65.96 Grit Haupt (GDR) 1984	DT
73.58 Tessa Sanderson (UK) 1983	69.32 Kate Schmidt 1977	71.88 Antoaneta Todorova (Bul) 1981	JT
6387 pts Glynis Nunn (Aus) 1984	6803 pts Jane Frederick 1984	6465 Sybille Thiele (GDR) 1983	Hep
42.43 United Kingdom 1980	41.61 National team 1983	43.73 United States 1983	4×100mR
3:21.21 Canada 1984	3:18.29 National team 1984	3:30.39 GDR 1981	4×400mR
			Track walking
22:04.42 Sue Cook (Aus) 1984	22:51.10 Maryanne Torrellas 1985	21:40.3 Yan Hong (Chn) 1984	5000m
45:47.0 Sue Cook (Aus) 1983	49:06.0 Teresa Vaill 1984	45:39.5 Yan Hong (Chn) 1984	10km
			Road walking – fastest recorded times
45:26.4 Sue Cook (Aus) 1983	47.49 Teresa Vaill 1984	46:38.7 Guan Ping (Chn) 1983	10km

*despite IAAF drugs ban

†HJ: and 1.96 Charmaine Gale (SAf) 1981
‡HJ: 2.35i Vladimir Yashchenko (USSR) 1978
%SP: 21.05i Terry Albritton (USA) 1974

Names Index

This is a selective index. Thousands of athletes appear in this book. While this index is extensive, it does not attempt to include all those who appear in the various tables or indeed every entry for those that are listed. It shows those who are mentioned in the narrative, those who are profiled, and those who feature in the illustrations. Also included are those leaders of such tables as most medals in major championships, and barrier breakers, as the inclusion of such athletes may be helpful to readers. C indicates inclusion in the colour section following page 64 or 80.

Subject Index